Monemvasia

THROUGH THE LENS OF POUL RASMUSSEN

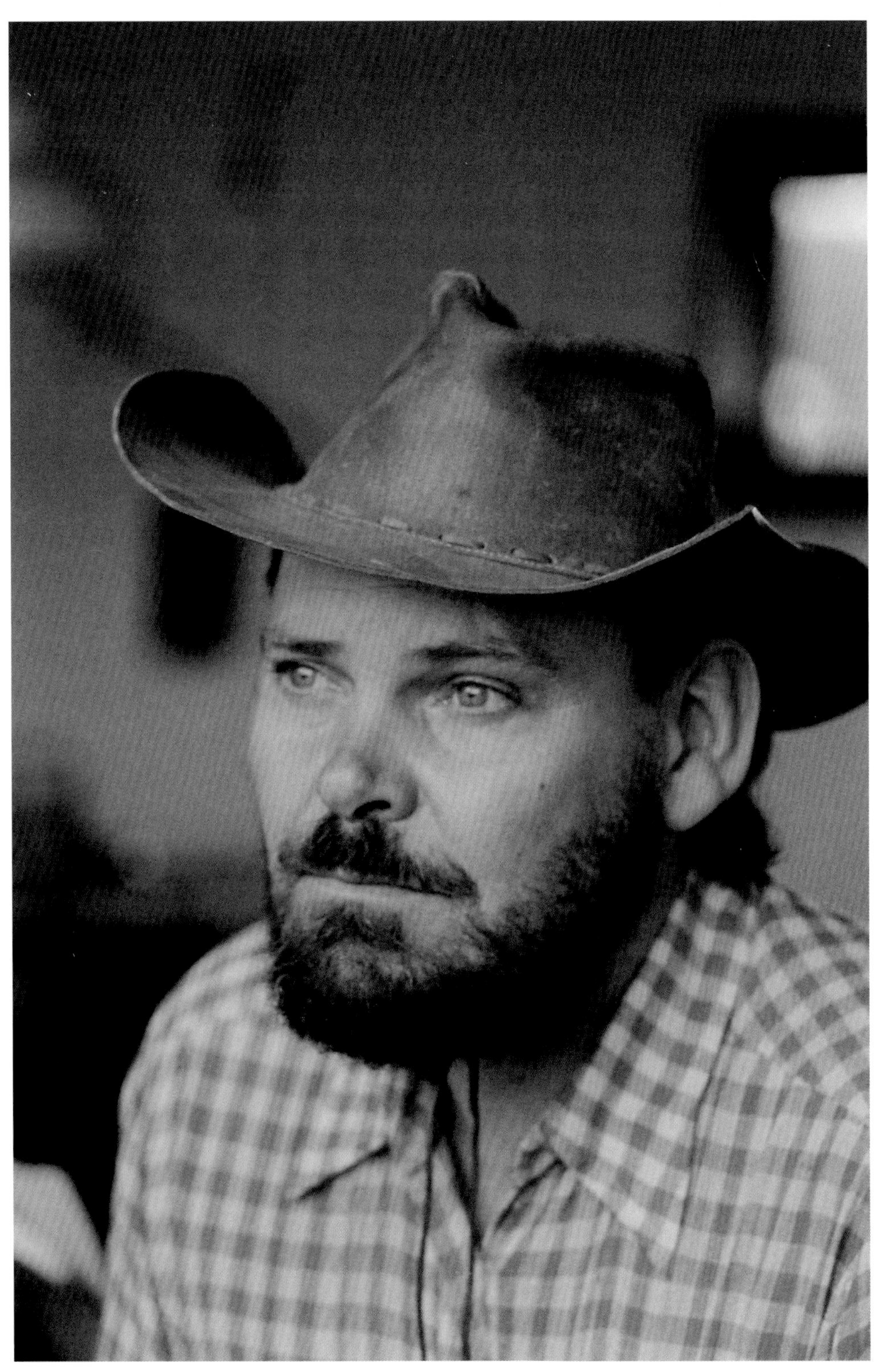

Poul Rasmussen 1929 – 1993

Monemvasia

THROUGH THE LENS OF POUL RASMUSSEN

Μονεμβασιά

ΜΕΣΑ ΑΠΟ ΤΟΝ ΦΑΚΟ ΤΟΥ POUL RASMUSSEN

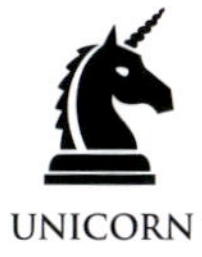

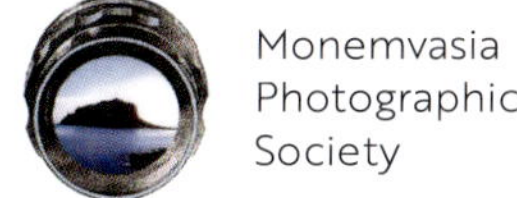

This book is dedicated to Haris A. Kalligas
Αφιερωμένο στην Χάρι Καλλιγά
1941 – 2023

Contents

Prologue

HARIS A. KALLIGAS

The Rock of Monemvasia, with its only entrance, the bordering precipices and the city enclosed by the fortifications, has always charmed visitors. Through the centuries, it constituted a 'kastron', a fortress, which had protected its population, and only in the early fifties of the twentieth century was the walled city gradually drained of its inhabitants. Many settled on the nearby mainland, where a new settlement developed, outside the natural narrow boundaries of the mediaeval city in which all activity had for centuries been confined. Nevertheless, a small nucleus remained within the walls, refusing to desert the ancestral city. The almost empty, although still alive, shell of the 1960s, apart from the magnificent natural landscape, was composed of successive layers of remains from the long centuries of uninterrupted life deposited everywhere.

An extract from *Monemvasia: A Byzantine City State*, by Haris A. Kalligas, 2010

Ο βράχος της Μονεμβασίας με τη μόνη είσοδο, τους περιμετρικούς γκρεμούς και την κλεισμένη στα τείχη πόλη ανέκαθεν μάγευε τους επισκέπτες. Κατά τη διάρκεια των αιώνων υπήρξε ένα "κάστρον", το οποίο προστάτευε τον πληθυσμό του και μόνο κατά τον 20ο αιώνα και από τη δεκαετία του '50 σταδιακά έχασε τους κατοίκου του. Πολλοί εγκαταστάθηκαν στη στεριά, όπου αναπτύχθηκε νέος οικισμός, έξω από τα στενόχωρα τείχη της μεσαιωνικής πόλης, όπου όλες οι δραστηριότητες ήταν επί αιώνες συγκεντρωμένες. Παρ' όλα αυτά ένας μικρός πυρήνας αρνήθηκε να εγκαταλείψει τα πατρογονικά του και παρέμεινε εντός των τειχών. Το σχεδόν άδειο, αν και ακόμη ζωντανό κέλυφος της δεκαετίας του '60, εκτός από το θαυμάσιο φυσικό τοπίο, ήταν συντεθειμένο από διαδοχικά στρώματα υπολειμμάτων των πολλών αιώνων αδιάσπαστης συνέχειας ζωής, που είχαν εναποτεθεί παντού.

Απόσπασμα από το βιβλίο Μονεμβασία: Μια Βυζαντινή Πόλη Κράτος. Χάρις Καλλιγά, 2010

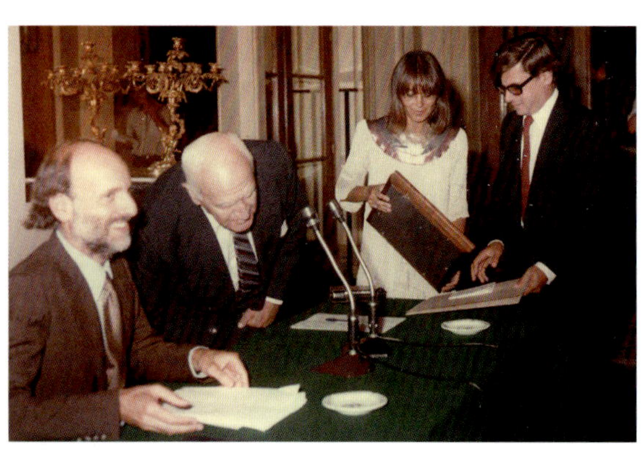

Haris A. Kalligas was an architect and historian, and Director of The Gennadius Library in Athens 1995–2004. In 1980, she and her husband Alexander G.Kalligas were awarded a Europa Nostra Award for their conservation work in the ancient city of Monemvasia.

Η Χάρις Καλλιγά ήταν αρχιτέκτονας και ιστορικός, διευθύντρια της Γενναδίου Βιβλιοθήκης στην Αθήνα 1995–2004. Το 1980, μαζί με τον σύζυγό της Αλέξανδρο Καλλιγά τιμήθηκαν με το Βραβείο Europa Nostra για την δουλειά τους στην αποκατάσταση της πόλης της Μονεμβασίας.

Preface

ANN ELDRIDGE

Altogether they record the impressions of a young man who is discovering an extraordinary place.[1]

What did Monemvasia look like in the recent past; who were the people, how did they live? Young local people, curious visitors and social scientists may well ask. Thanks to these photographs we can unfold their story as they witnessed, and found, their place within a changing world. Each chapter capturing the threads that held the community together.

Poul Rasmussen arrived in 1966 in this isolated area of Southern Greece. He was greeted with interest and hospitality. Since the local inhabitants rarely owned cameras, Poul met the demand for family and ID photographs, thereby gaining rare, intimate access to the local population.

The Second World War and Greece's civil war was over, but it was experiencing high emigration and hardship. However, in the decades from the early 1970s it began to benefit from increased government investment in infrastructure, European funding and a nascent tourist industry. Present day Greece was being born. Rasmussen was uniquely placed to record local lives and the inevitable, often inperceptable, cultural changes taking place. He provided the visual narrative.

The Rock had, since Byzantine times, been the administrative centre of the region. The 1828 census mentions Monemvasia (population: 659) with eighteen settlements totalling a population of 5,335.[2] However, by the late 1960s the Byzantine city had virtually been abandoned. The expanding settlement of Yefira and the mainland absorbed many of the residents of the Castro, providing access to utilities and, importantly, employment.

Nevertheless, the Castro remained at the heart of communal life, with the school and all religious and national events occuring within its walls. The growing restoration of the Byzantine city during the late 1970s became the focal point of economic regeneration, not only of the Castro but the region. Previously isolated villages experienced regeneration with paved roads, telephones and restored, or new homes.

Monemvasia began to attract an artistic, cosmopolitan community. This cultural attraction grew when in 1964, a successful Greek film *Monemvasia* was made. The area became a location for a number of Greek and international films. In 1993, a Greek television series *Anastasia*, set in the Castro, was a boost to romantic local tourism for many years. This exposure to the outside world inevitably had an impact on the social fabric. Poul Rasmussen was not only part of this trend, he was also recording it.

The Rock was always the heart of the region. Visually and emotionally, it was ever present. For many it was their former family home, for others their spiritual home. Generations continue to marry, baptise and hold their funerals in the Church of Elkomenos Christos.

All civic celebrations continue to be held in the main square round the cannon. As the decades progressed, as

1. R.A. McCabe, *Greece: Images of an Enchanted Land 1954–1965*, 2004, p. 22.

2. These included Agia Paraskevi, Aghios Stephanos, Nomia, Kalyves and Foutia.

houses were renovated and tourism increased, the Castro was again the focus of the community.

The photographs in this book will evoke memories for those who recall this period. For those not there, it is a revelation to observe this vanished world through the Rasmussen lens. Places need interpretation. Poul recorded, interpreted and, most crucially, shared in the lives of the local people. His images can be viewed nostalgically; with anxiety at the speed of change; with surprise at the incongruity of the first supermarket and with visitors and newcomers entering this previously closed world. Poul captured these moments, great and small.

Moreover, he revealed the unique sense of place and community in Monemvasia and its local villages. The anchor, as always, the Rock of Monemvasia.

Εισαγωγή

ANN ELDRIDGE

Συνολικά καταγράφουν τις εντυπώσεις ενός νεαρού καθώς ανακαλύπτει ένα ιδιαίτερο μέρος.[1]

Πώς ήταν η Μονεμβασιά στο πρόσφατο παρελθόν; Ποιοι ήταν οι άνθρωποι; Πώς ζούσαν; Τέτοια ερωτήματα μπορούν να θέσουν νεαροί κάτοικοι, περίεργοι επισκέπτες και κοινωνικοί επιστήμονες. Χάρη σε αυτές τις φωτογραφίες οι οποίες μαρτυρούν και βρίσκουν τη θέση τους σε έναν κόσμο που αλλάζει, μπορούμε να ξεδιπλώσουμε την ιστορία. Κάθε κεφάλαιο καταγράφει τα νήματα που έδεναν την κοινότητα.

Ο Poul Rasmussen έφτασε το 1966 σε αυτή την απομονωμένη περιοχή της Νότιας Ελλάδας. Τον υποδέχτηκαν φιλόξενα και με ενδιαφέρον. Δεδομένου ότι σπάνια οι κάτοικοι της περιοχής είχαν φωτογραφικές μηχανές, ο Poul ανταποκρίθηκε στη ζήτηση για φωτογραφίες ταυτότητας και οικογενειακές, αποκτώντας έτσι μια σπάνια οικεία σύνδεση με τον τοπικό πληθυσμό.

Ο Β' παγκόσμιος πόλεμος και ο εμφύλιος πόλεμος στην Ελλάδα είχαν τελειώσει, αλλά η χώρα μαστιζόταν από υψηλή μετανάστευση και κακουχίες. Ωστόσο, μετά την μεταπολίτευση το 1974, άρχισε να επωφελείται από τις αυξανόμενες κρατικές επενδύσεις σε υποδομές, την ευρωπαϊκή χρηματοδότηση και μια αναδυόμενη τουριστική βιομηχανία. Η σημερινή Ελλάδα γεννιόταν. Ο Rasmussen βρέθηκε στην κατάλληλη θέση για να καταγράψει την καθημερινή ζωή του τόπου και τις αναπόφευκτες, συχνά ανεπαίσθητες, πολιτισμικές αλλαγές που συντελούνταν και έτσι μας παρέχει μία οπτική αφήγηση της αλλαγής.

Ο Βράχος ήταν από τα βυζαντινά χρόνια το διοικητικό κέντρο της περιοχής. Η απογραφή του 1828 αναφέρει τη Μονεμβασιά (πληθυσμός: 659), με δεκαοκτώ οικισμούς συνολικού πληθυσμού 5335 κατοίκων.[2] Ωστόσο, στα τέλη της δεκαετίας του 1960 η βυζαντινή πόλη είχε ουσιαστικά εγκαταλειφθεί. Ο επεκτεινόμενος οικισμός της Γέφυρας και της ενδοχώρας απορρόφησε πολλούς

1. R.A. McCabe, Ελλάδα: Τα χρόνια της αθωότητας (1954–1965), 2004, σ. 22

2. Περιλαμβάνουν την Αγία Παρασκευή, τον Άγιο Στέφανο, τα Νόμια, τις Καλύβες και τα Φούτια.

από τους κατοίκους του Κάστρου, παρέχοντας πρόσβαση σε υπηρεσίες και δημιουργώντας θέσεις εργασίας. Ωστόσο, το Κάστρο παρέμεινε στην καρδιά της ζωής της κοινότητας. Το σχολείο λειτουργούσε εντός των τειχών αλλά και όλες οι θρησκευτικές και εθνικές γιορτές τελούνταν εκεί. Η αυξανόμενη αποκατάσταση της βυζαντινής πόλης στα τέλη της δεκαετίας του 1970 έγινε το επίκεντρο της οικονομικής αναγέννησης, όχι μόνο του Κάστρου, αλλά και της περιοχής. Τα απομονωμένα χωριά ξαναζωντάνεψαν με ανακαινισμένα ή νέα σπίτια, τηλέφωνο και ασφαλτοστρωμένους δρόμους.

Η Μονεμβασιά άρχισε να προσελκύει μία καλλιτεχνική και κοσμοπολίτικη κοινότητα. Μετά την επιτυχημένη ελληνική ταινία Μονεμβασιά το 1964, στην περιοχή γυρίστηκαν πολυάριθμες ελληνικές και διεθνείς ταινίες, που την καθιέρωσαν ως πολιτιστικό πόλο έλξης. Το 1993, η ελληνική σειρά Αναστασία, προώθησε το κάστρο ως ρομαντικό προορισμό για πολλά χρόνια. Αυτή η επαφή με τον έξω κόσμο είχε αναπόφευκτα αντίκτυπο στον κοινωνικό ιστό. Ο Poul Rasmussen όχι μόνο ήταν μέρος αυτής της τάσης, αλλά και την κατέγραψε.

Ο Βράχος ήταν πάντα η καρδιά της περιοχής. Οπτικά και συναισθηματικά ήταν πάντα παρόν. Για πολλούς εκεί ήταν το παλιό οικογενειακό τους σπίτι, για άλλους το πνευματικό τους. Γενεές συνεχίζουν να παντρεύονται, να βαφτίζουν και να τελούν τις κηδείες τους στον Ιερό Ναό του Ελκομένου Χριστού.

Όλες οι εθνικές γιορτές συνεχίζουν να γίνονται στην κεντρική πλατεία γύρω από το κανόνι. Καθώς τα σπίτια ανακαινίζονταν και ο τουρισμός αυξανόταν, το Κάστρο έγινε και πάλι το επίκεντρο της κοινότητας.

Οι φωτογραφίες θα ξυπνήσουν μνήμες σε όσους αναπολούν αυτή την περίοδο. Για όσους δεν βρέθηκαν εκεί, είναι μια αποκάλυψη η παρατήρηση αυτού του εξαφανισμένου κόσμου μέσα από τον φακό Rasmussen, που κατέγραψε, ερμήνευσε και, το πιο σημαντικό, μοιράστηκε τις ζωές των κατοίκων της περιοχής. Τις φωτογραφίες μπορούμε να τις δουμε με νοσταλγία. με άγχος για την ταχύτητα της αλλαγής, με έκπληξη για την ασύμβατη καινοτομία του πρώτου σούπερ μάρκετ και των επισκεπτών που εισέρχονται σε αυτόν τον παλαιότερα κλειστό κόσμο. Ο Rasmussen μας αποκάλυψε αυτές τις μεγάλες και μικρές στιγμές. Επιπλέον, αιχμαλώτισε τη μοναδική αίσθηση του τόπου και της κοινότητας της Μονεμβασιάς και των γειτονικών χωριών. Άγκυρα πάντα ήταν ο Βράχος της Μονεμβασιάς.

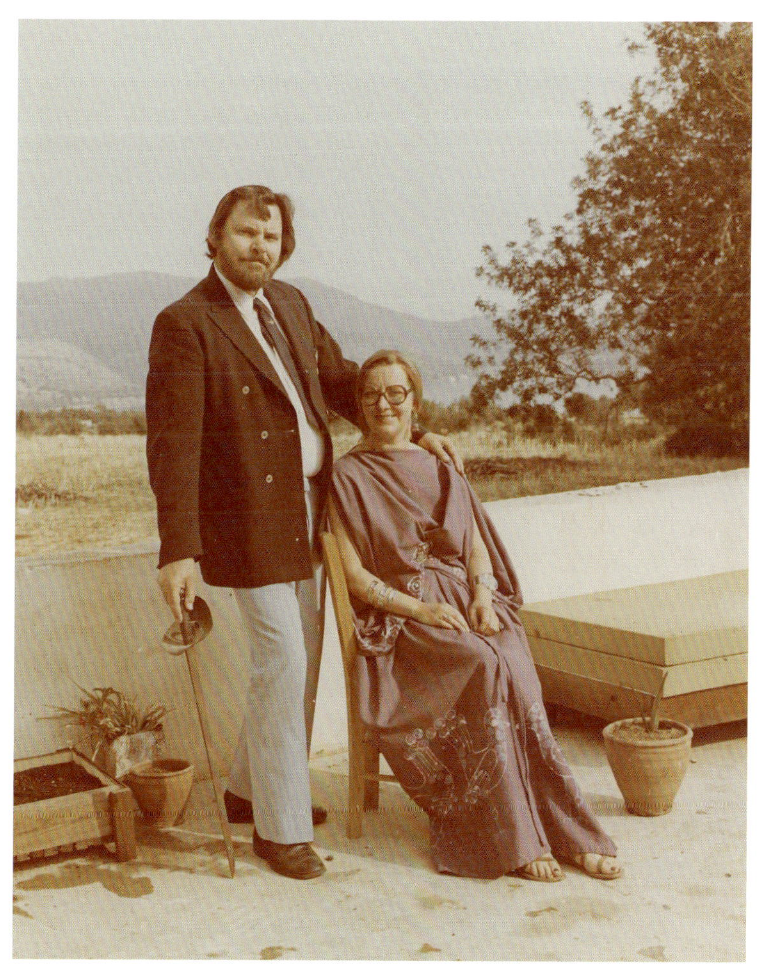

Foreword

LIS RASMUSSEN

My father, Poul Rasmussen, was born in 1929 and grew up close to Copenhagen. His passionate interest in photography was established early on, as well as his longing for adventure. During the Second World War, he joined the navy which gave him an opportunity to explore the world and to learn to fly. In 1966, Poul met a famous Danish journalist and author, Hakon Mielche, and they travelled together to the Peloponnese, a journey that changed his life. Before returning to Denmark he bought a piece of land on Pori beach, where he built his own house and spent most of the next decade.

My father and Thea met in Copenhagen in 1972. In 1978, they moved permanently to Pori. They loved the climate, the life and, most importantly, the people. With this freedom to be artistic and creative, my father became a genius at woodworking, engineering and photography. Thea was a talented weaver, and my father built her the looms on which she created beautiful works, reintroducing the tradition of weaving to the local women.

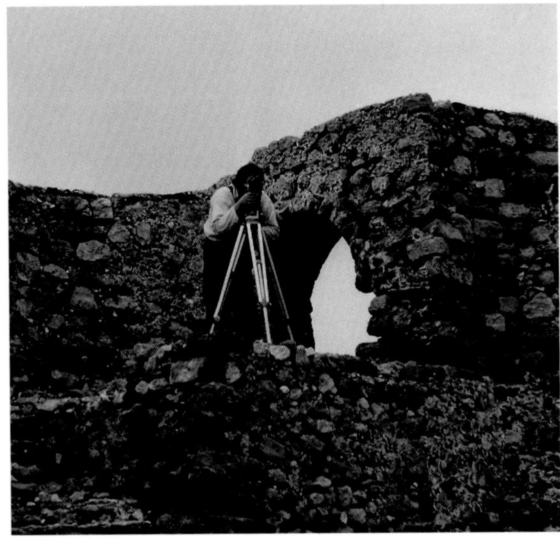

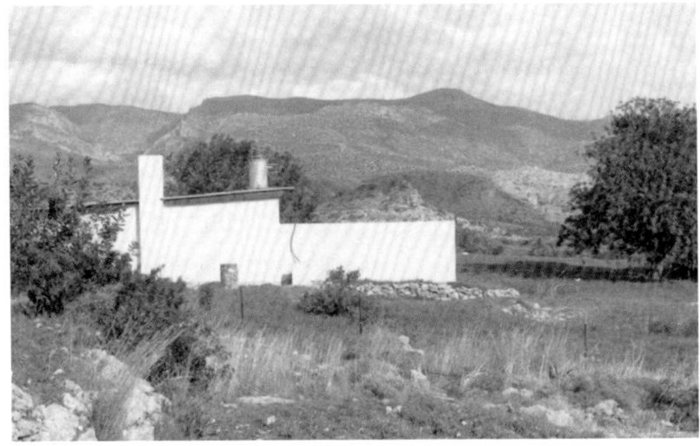

The local population rarely owned cameras in this period. Yet photographs of family events and photographs for ID and passports were becoming increasingly important. By meeting this need, Poul, a foreigner, gained an unusually intimate access to the local people and was well loved. His passion for photography was taken to new heights when, in 1989, he won first prize in the BBC World Service Photographic Competition entitled 'Home', with the photograph of Lina Andrianopoulou featured on the front cover.

Poul died in 1993. He left this important collection as a legacy to the place he loved. If you stroll around the Castro and the local villages, you will see his photographs in homes, restaurants and shops. You will also appreciate the lives and society he captured *through his lens.*

Thank you for taking an interest in my father's work. I hope you enjoy his photographs as much as I do.

Lis Rasmussen

Προλεγόμενα
LIS RASMUSSEN

Ο πατέρας μου, Poul Rasmussen γεννήθηκε το 1929 και μεγάλωσε κοντά στην Κοπεγχάγη. Το παθιασμένο του ενδιαφέρον για τη φωτογραφία καθώς και η λαχτάρα του για περιπέτεια εκδηλώθηκαν από νωρίς. Στον Β' παγκόσμιο πόλεμο κατατάχθηκε στο Ναυτικό και αυτό του έδωσε την ευκαιρία να εξερευνήσει τον κόσμο και να μάθει να πετάει. Το 1966 ο Poul γνώρισε έναν διάσημο Δανό δημοσιογράφο και συγγραφέα, τον Hakon Mielche, και ταξίδεψαν μαζί στην Πελοπόννησο, κάτι που άλλαξε τη ζωή του για πάντα. Πριν επιστρέψει στη Δανία αγόρασε ένα κομμάτι γης στην παραλία Πορί. Εκεί έχτισε το σπίτι του και πέρασε τον περισσότερο χρόνο του για την επόμενη δεκαετία.

Ο πατέρας μου και η Thea γνωρίστηκαν στην Κοπεγχάγη το 1972. Το 1978 μετακόμισαν μόνιμα στο Πορί. Αγαπούσαν το κλίμα, τη ζωή και κυρίως τους ανθρώπους. Όντας καλλιτέχνης και δημιουργικός, ο πατέρας μου έγινε ιδιοφυΐα στην ξυλουργική, στη μηχανική καθώς και στη φωτογραφία. Η Thea ήταν μια ταλαντούχα υφάντρια. Ο πατέρας μου της έφτιαξε τους αργαλειούς με τους οποίους δημιούργησε όμορφα έργα και επανέφερε την παράδοση της υφαντικής στις ντόπιες γυναίκες.

Ο ντόπιος πληθυσμός σπάνια διέθετε φωτογραφικές μηχανές αυτή την περίοδο. Ωστόσο, οι φωτογραφίες ταυτότητας και διαβατηρίου, καθώς και οικογενειακών γιορτών, ήταν όλο και πιο σημαντικές. Ανταποκρινόμενος σε αυτή την ανάγκη ο Poul, ένας ξένος, απέκτησε μια ασυνήθιστη οικειότητα με τους ντόπιους και αγαπήθηκε πολύ. Το πάθος του για τη φωτογραφία απογειώθηκε όταν, το 1989, κέρδισε το πρώτο βραβείο στον διαγωνισμό φωτογραφίας BBC World Service Photographic Competition, με τίτλο 'Home', με τη φωτογραφία της Λίνας Ανδριανοπούλου στο σπίτι της.

Ο Poul πέθανε το 1993. Άφησε αυτή τη σημαντική συλλογή ως κληρονομιά στον τόπο που αγάπησε. Αν κάνετε μια βόλτα στο Κάστρο και στα γύρω χωριά, μπορείτε να δείτε τις φωτογραφίες του σε σπίτια, εστιατόρια και καταστήματα. Θα κατανοήσετε έτσι τις ζωές και την κοινωνία που απαθανάτισε με το φακό του.

Σας ευχαριστώ για το ενδιαφέρον σας για τη δουλειά του πατέρα μου. Ελπίζω να απολαύσετε τις φωτογραφίες του όσο κι εγώ.

Lis Rasmussen

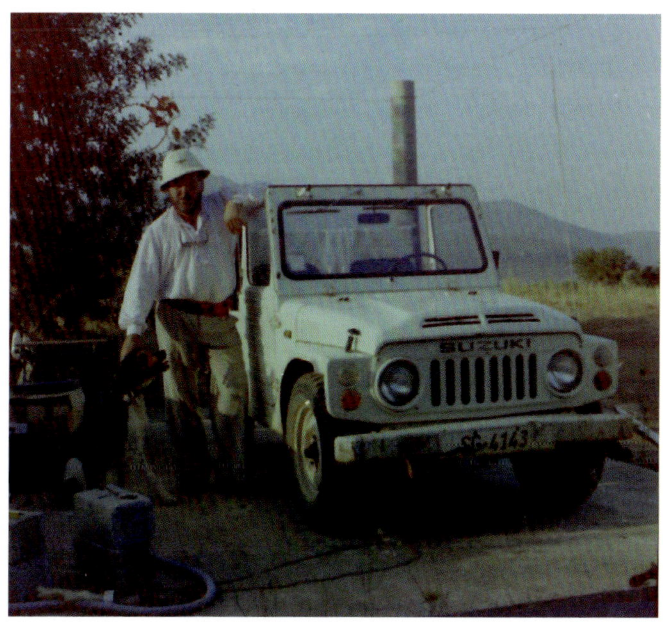

CHAPTER 1 · THE LANDSCAPE · ΤΟ ΠΕΡΙΒΑΛΛΟΝ

Arrival

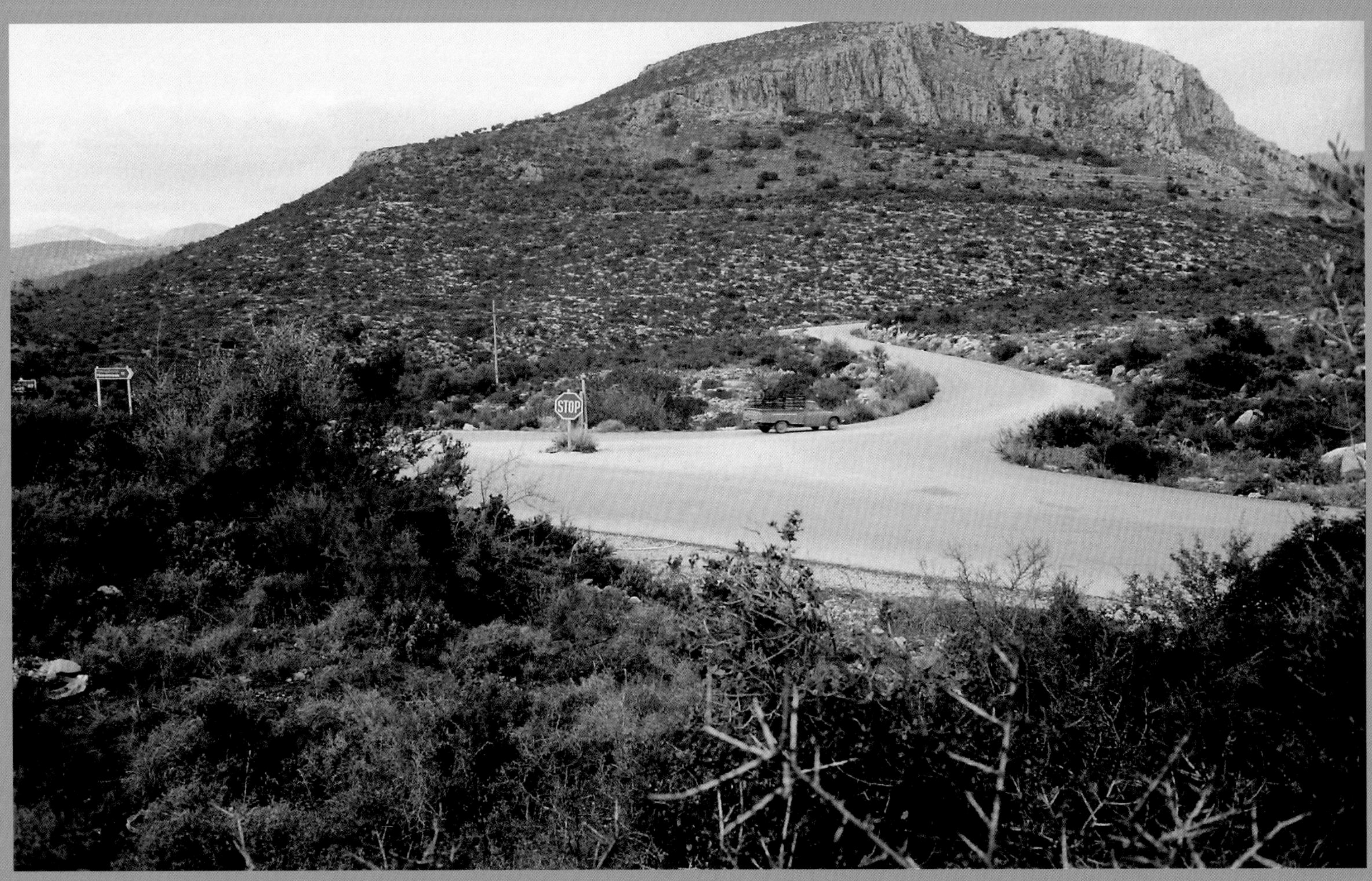

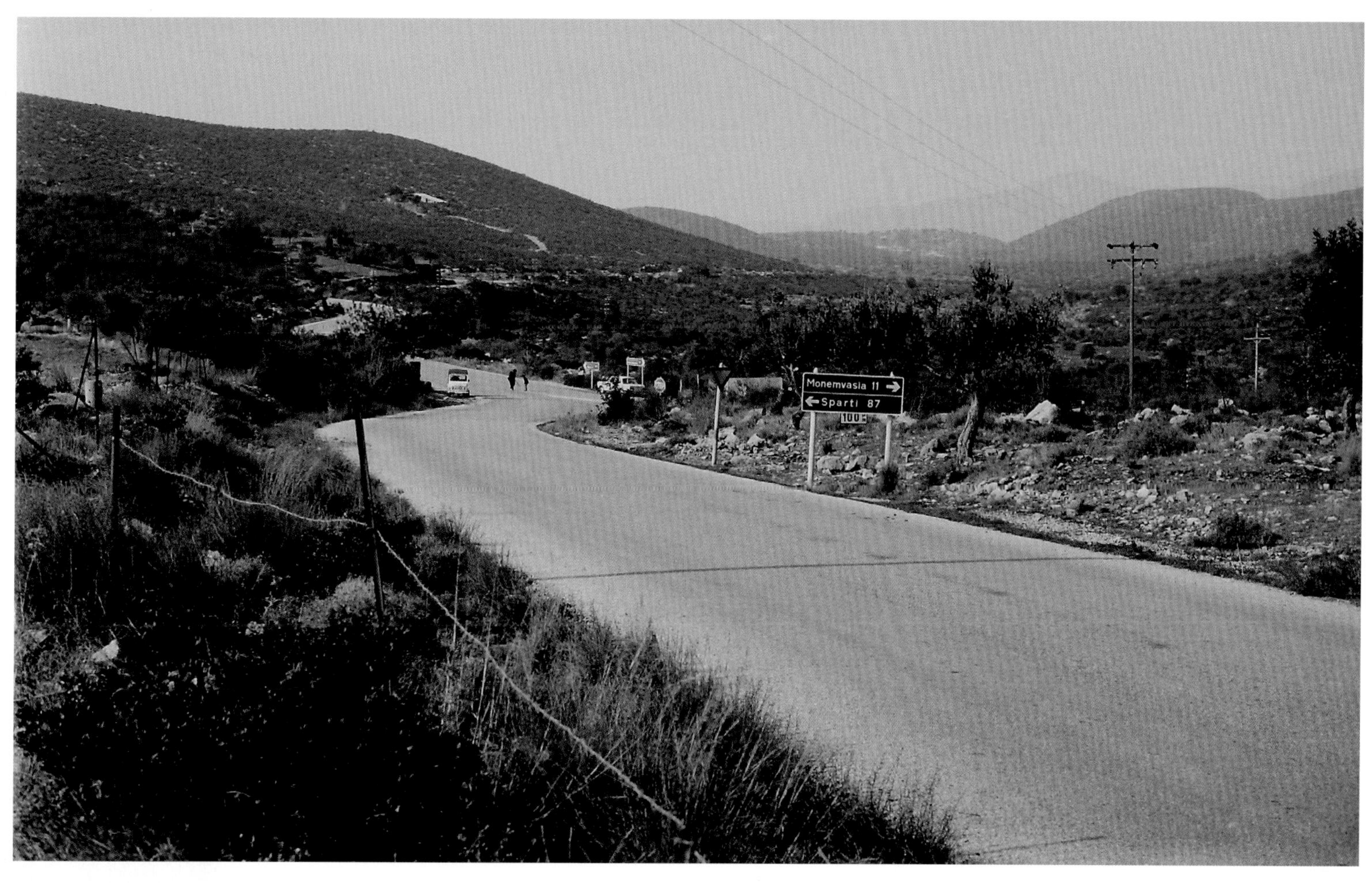

There was something timelessly grand about those hills and declivities, the antique groves, the old Ottoman farms, the Byzantine and Venetian influence of Monemvasia itself…

KEVIN McGRATH, *ON FRIENDSHIP*, 2024

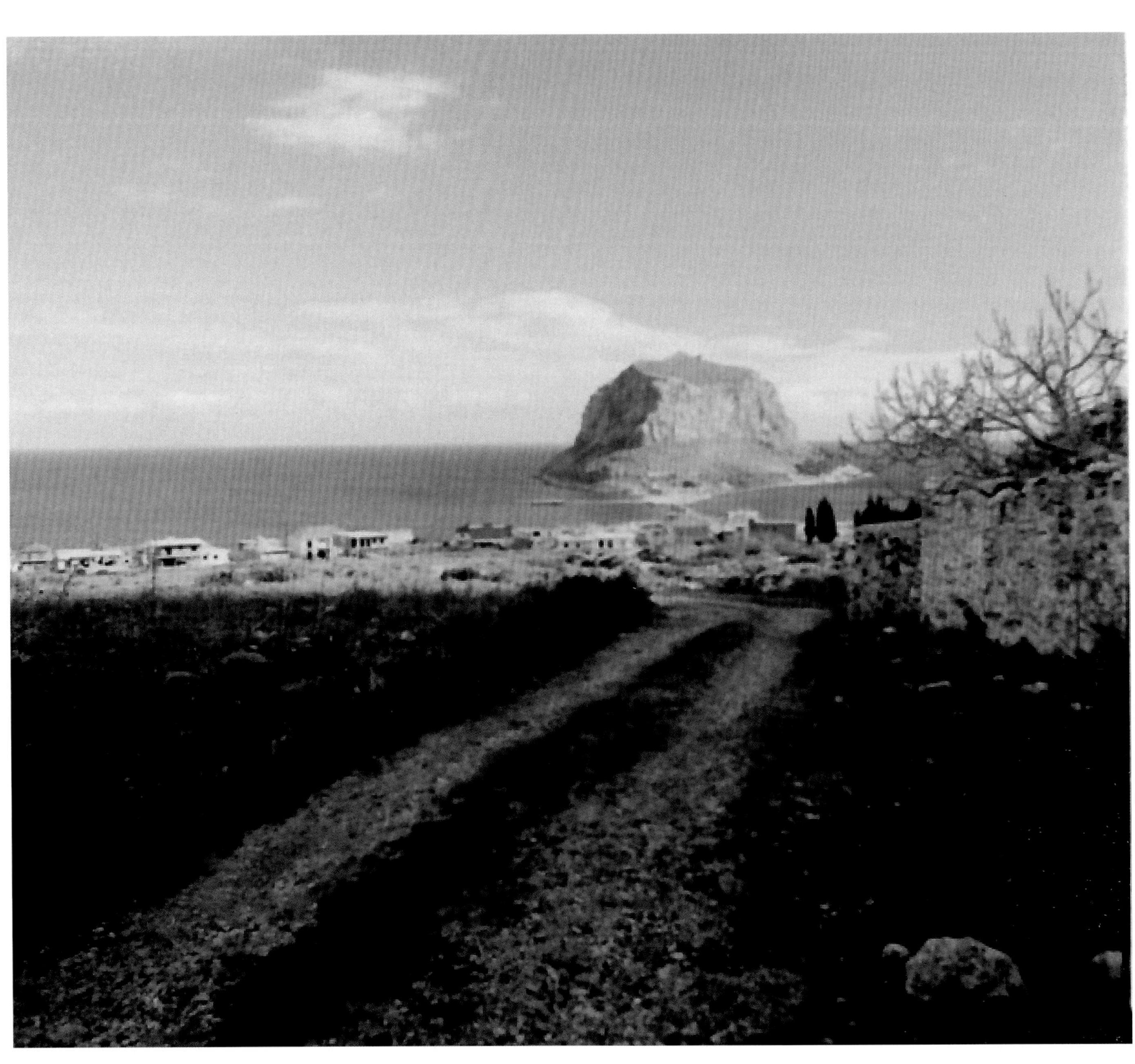

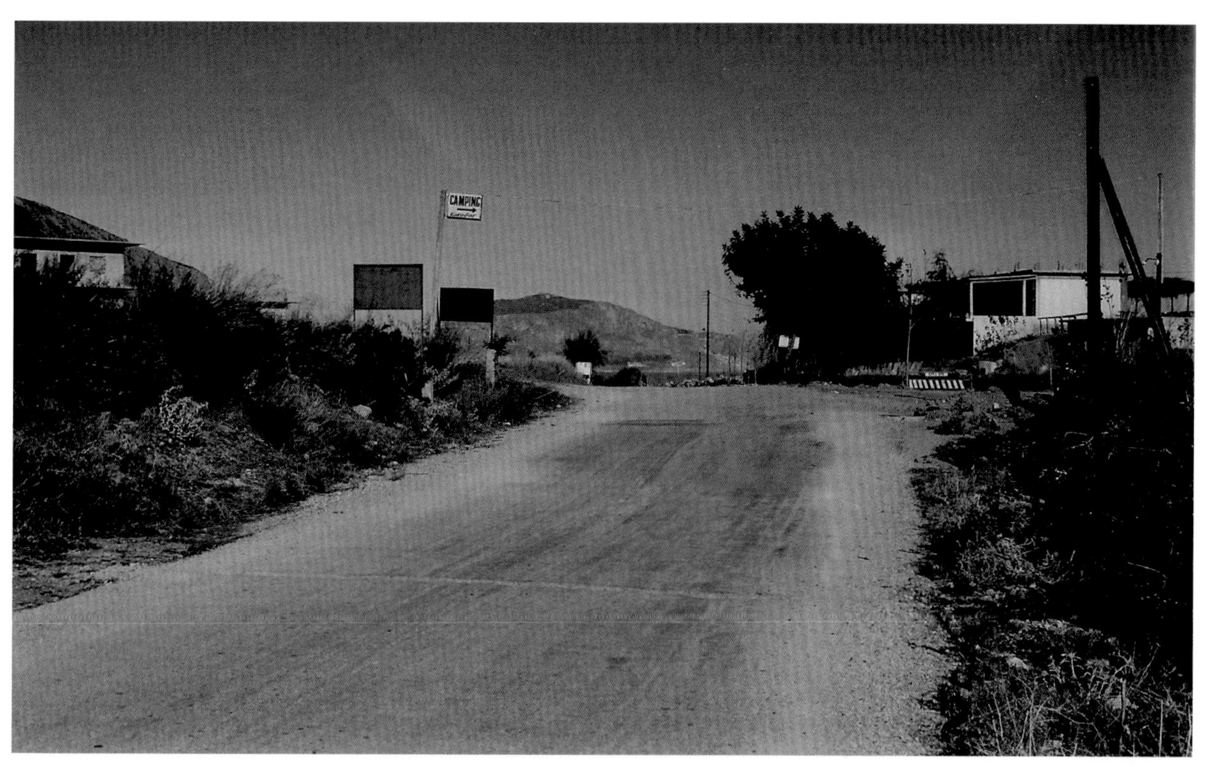
CAMPING

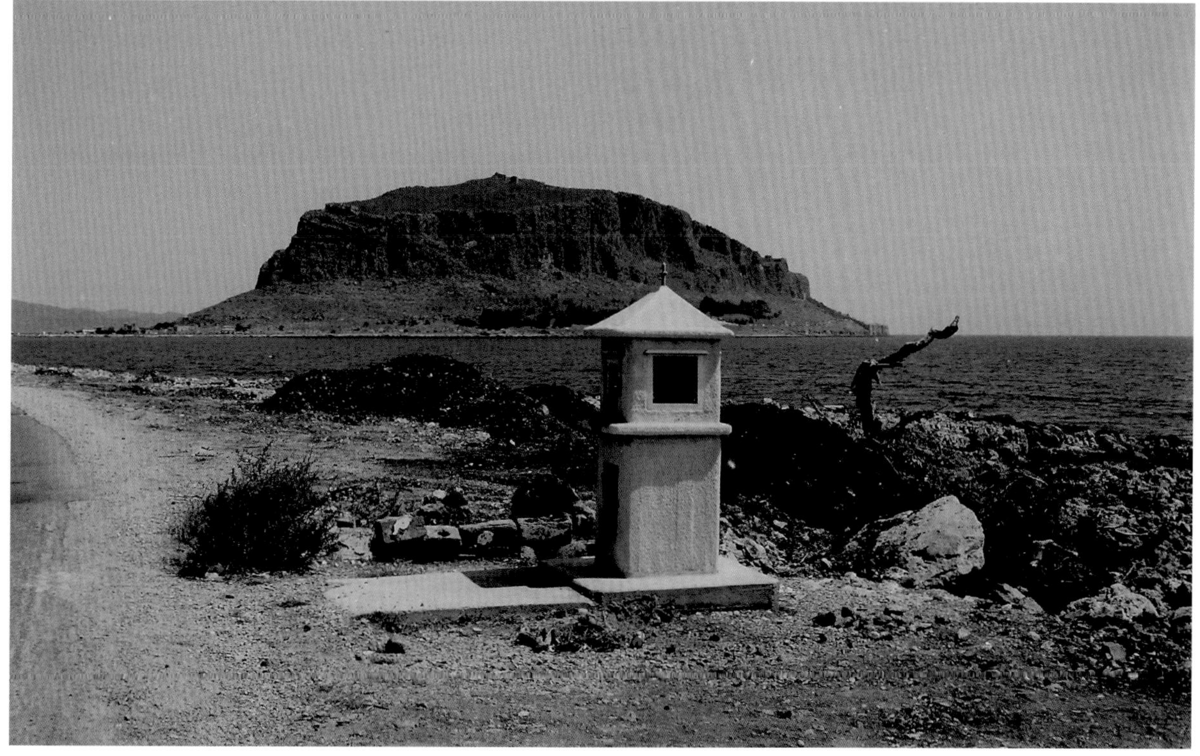

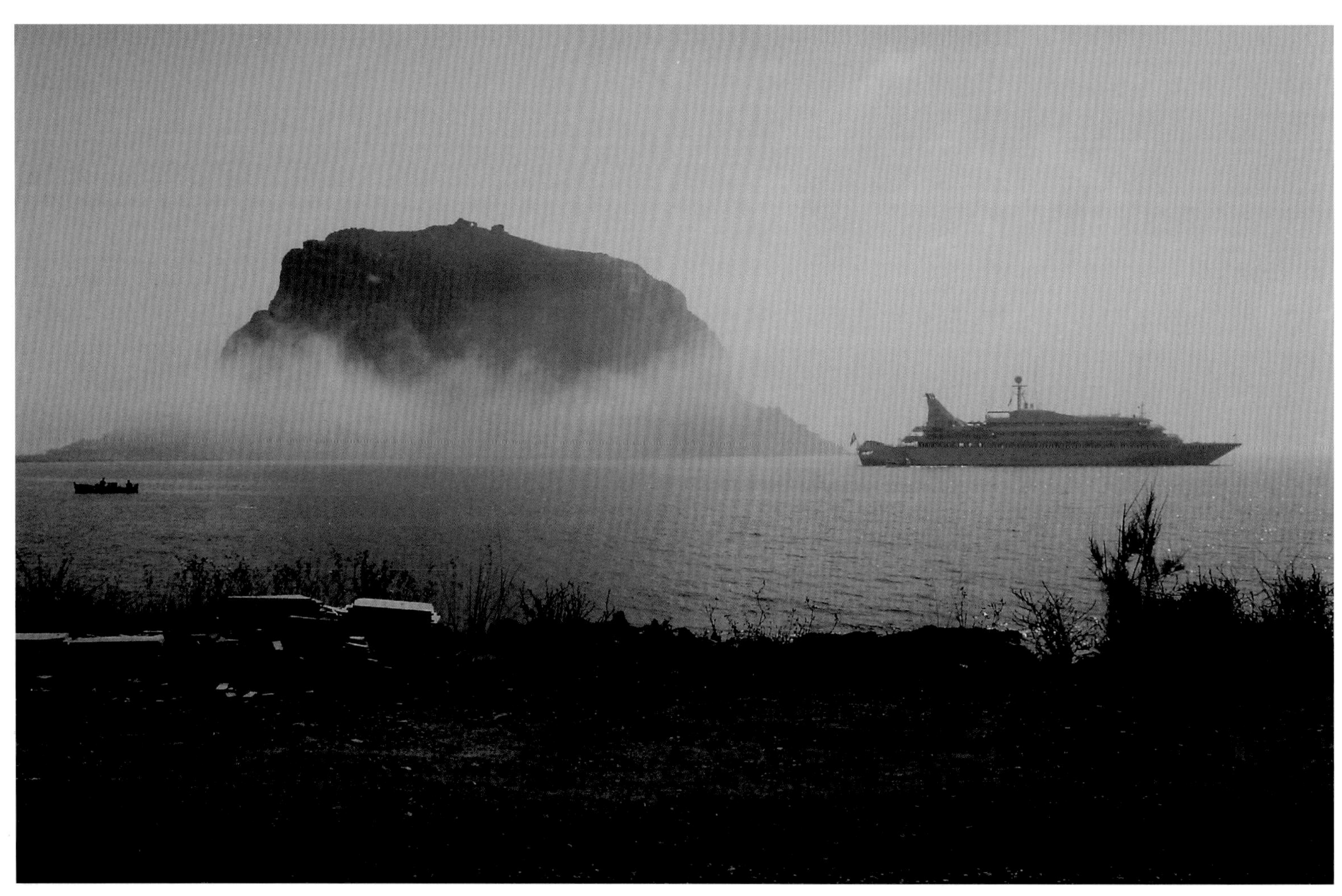

Monemvasia – waves were breaking at my feet, and a huge, menacing mass, silent and without a light, appeared resting on the sea.

NIKOS KAZANTZAKIS, *JOURNEY TO THE MOREA*, 1965

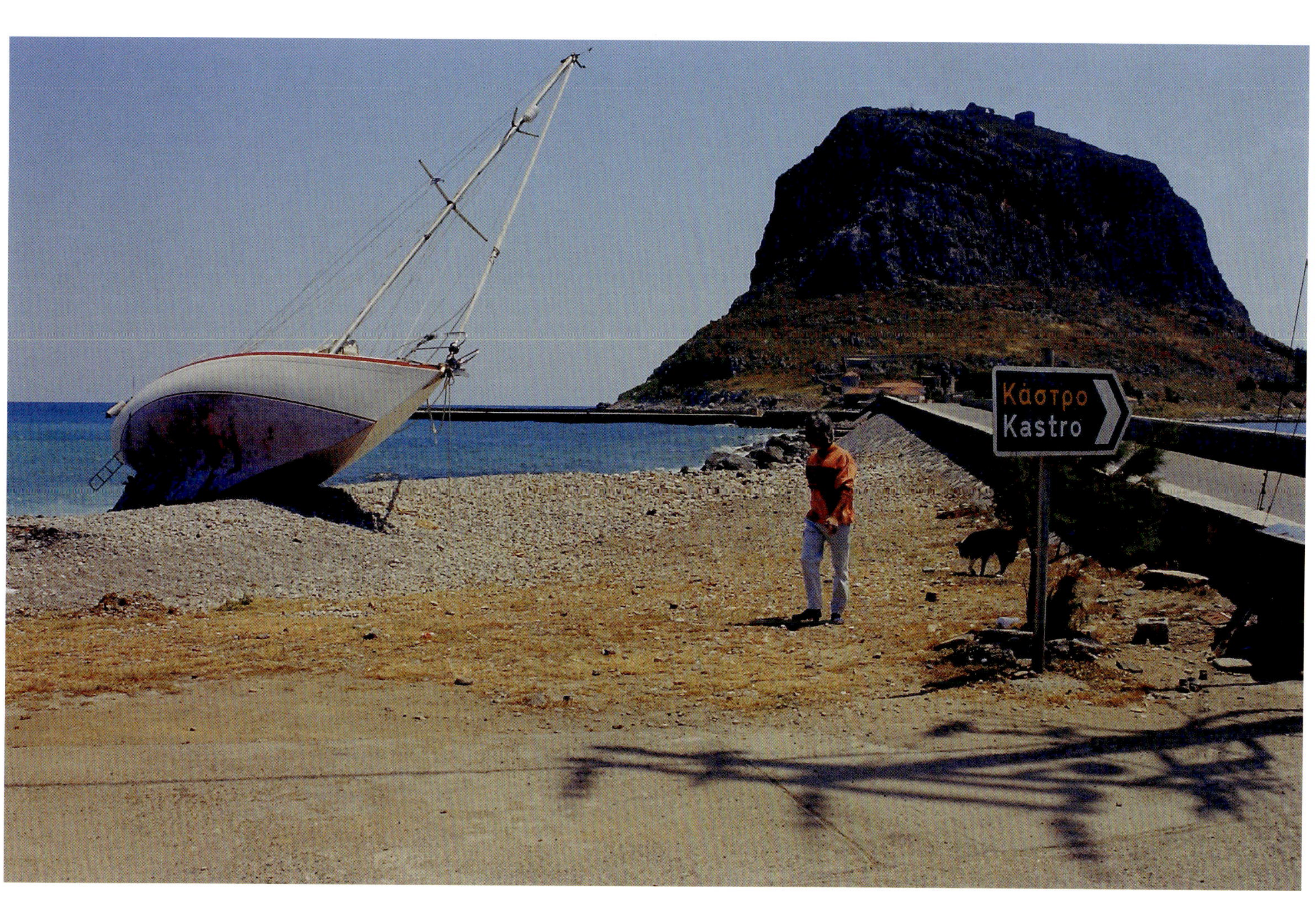
Κάστρο
Kastro

Castro

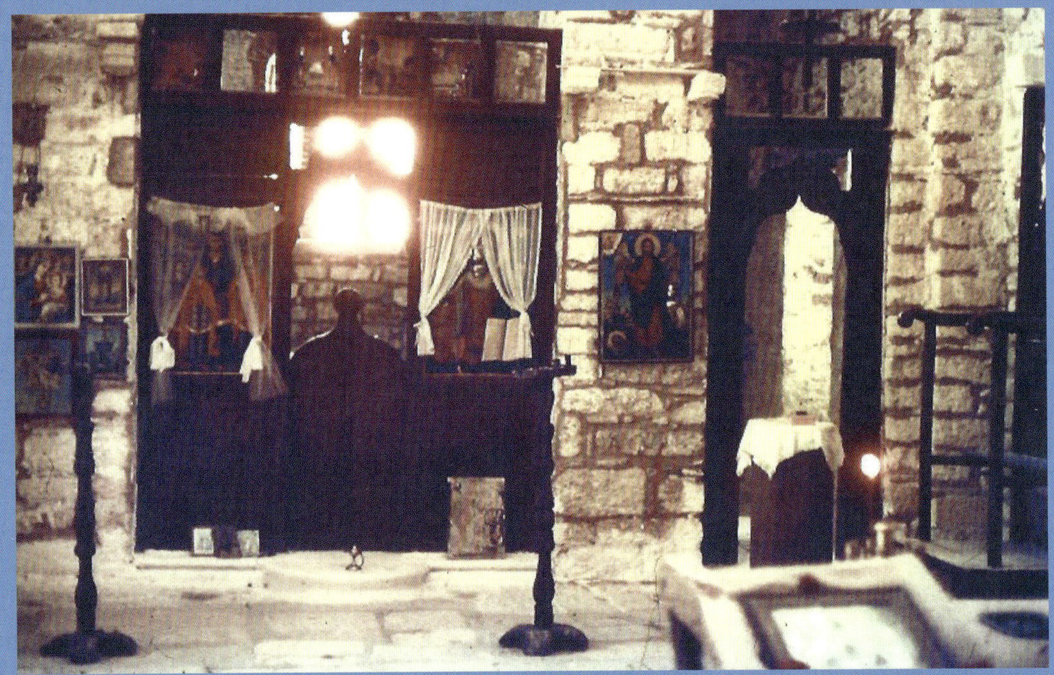

One building stood intact, the church of St Sophia, built on the edge of the northern cliff at the end of the thirteenth century on the orders of the pious Emperor Andronicus II. It was in good repair, though the frescoes in the interior were fragmentary and fading. It stood solid and dignified among the desolation.

STEVEN RUNCIMAN, *A TRAVELLER'S ALPHABET: PARTIAL MEMOIRS*, 1991

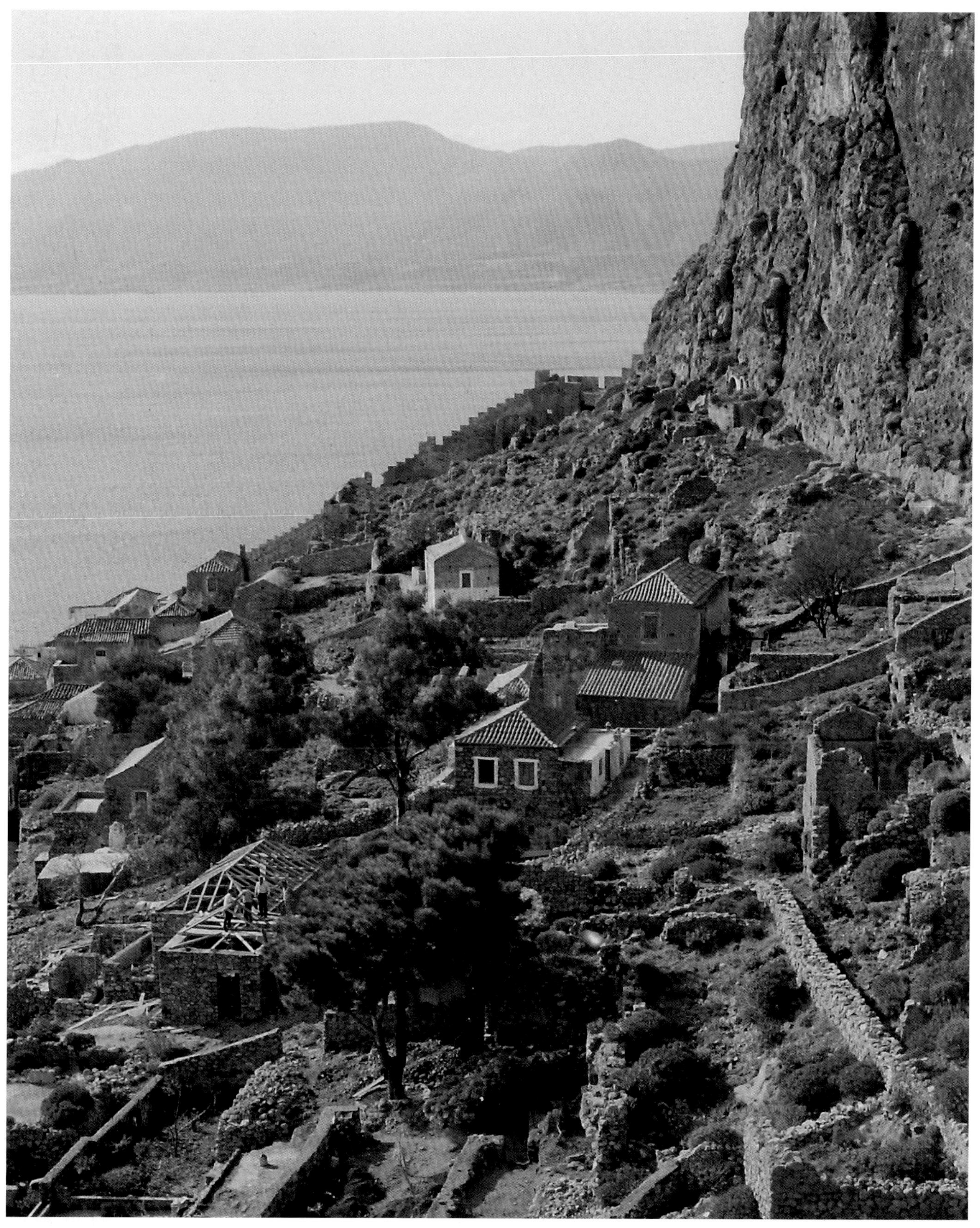

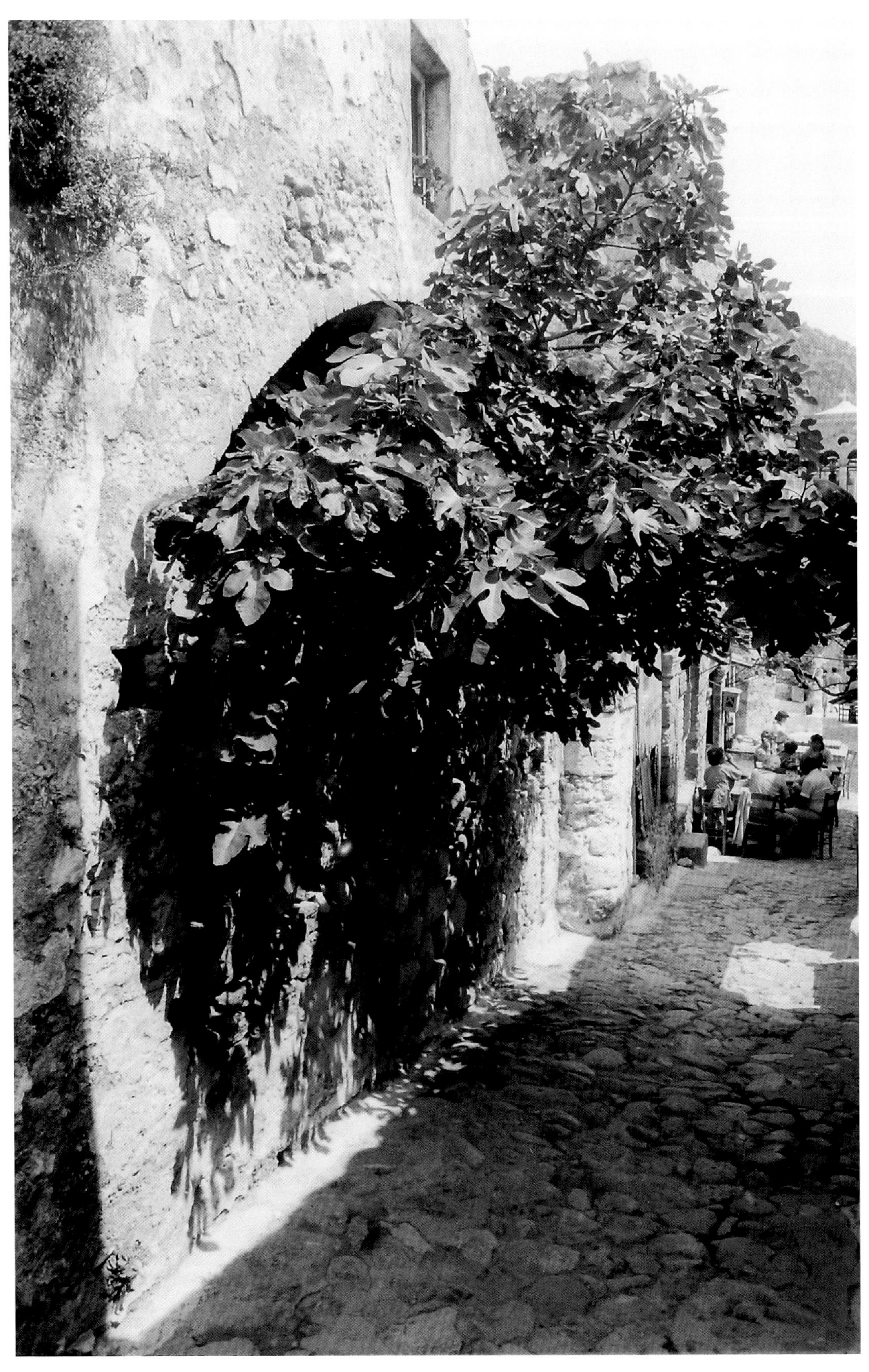

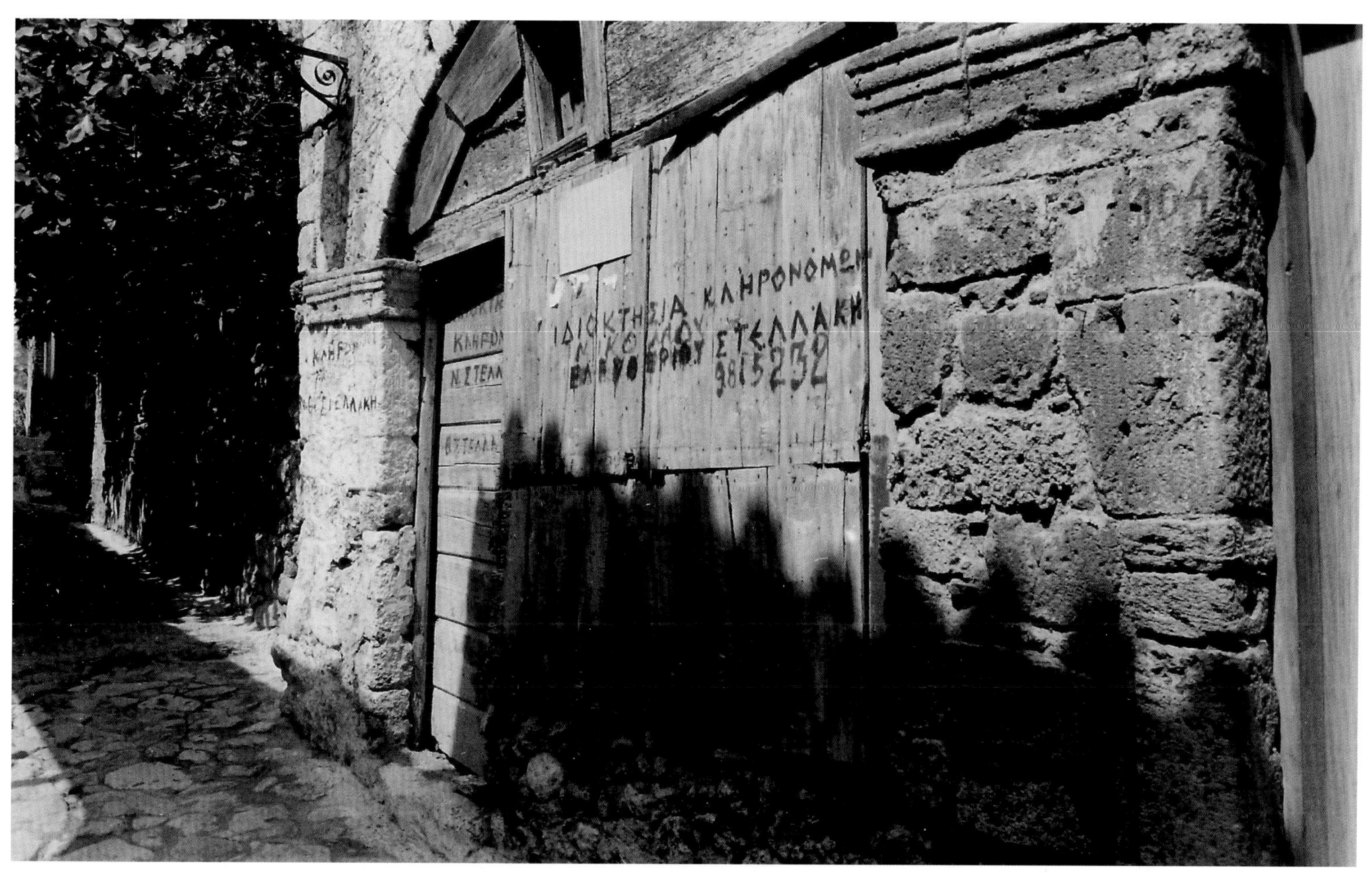

Walking downhill towards the two cafés near the central square twenty shop-fronts have been counted, but very few of them open their flaps nowadays and reveal their secrets to the curious passer-by.

W.R. ELLIOTT, *MONEMVASIA, THE GIBRALTAR OF GREECE*, 1971

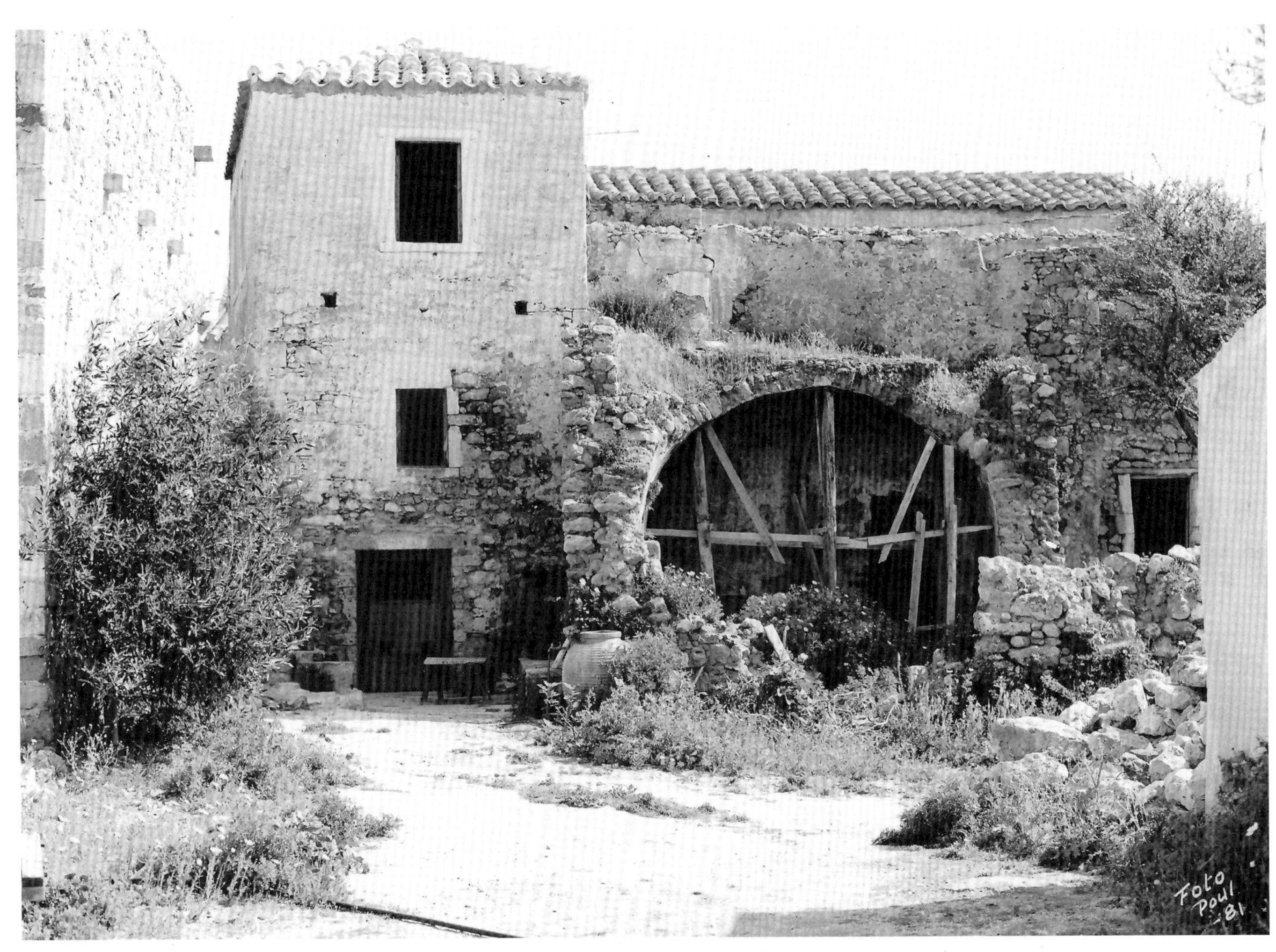

Shadowy arcades, labyrinthine medieval lanes, ruined churches; life again entwines among the ruins, deep rooted like ivy.

NIKOS KAZANTZAKIS, *JOURNEY TO THE MOREA*, 1965

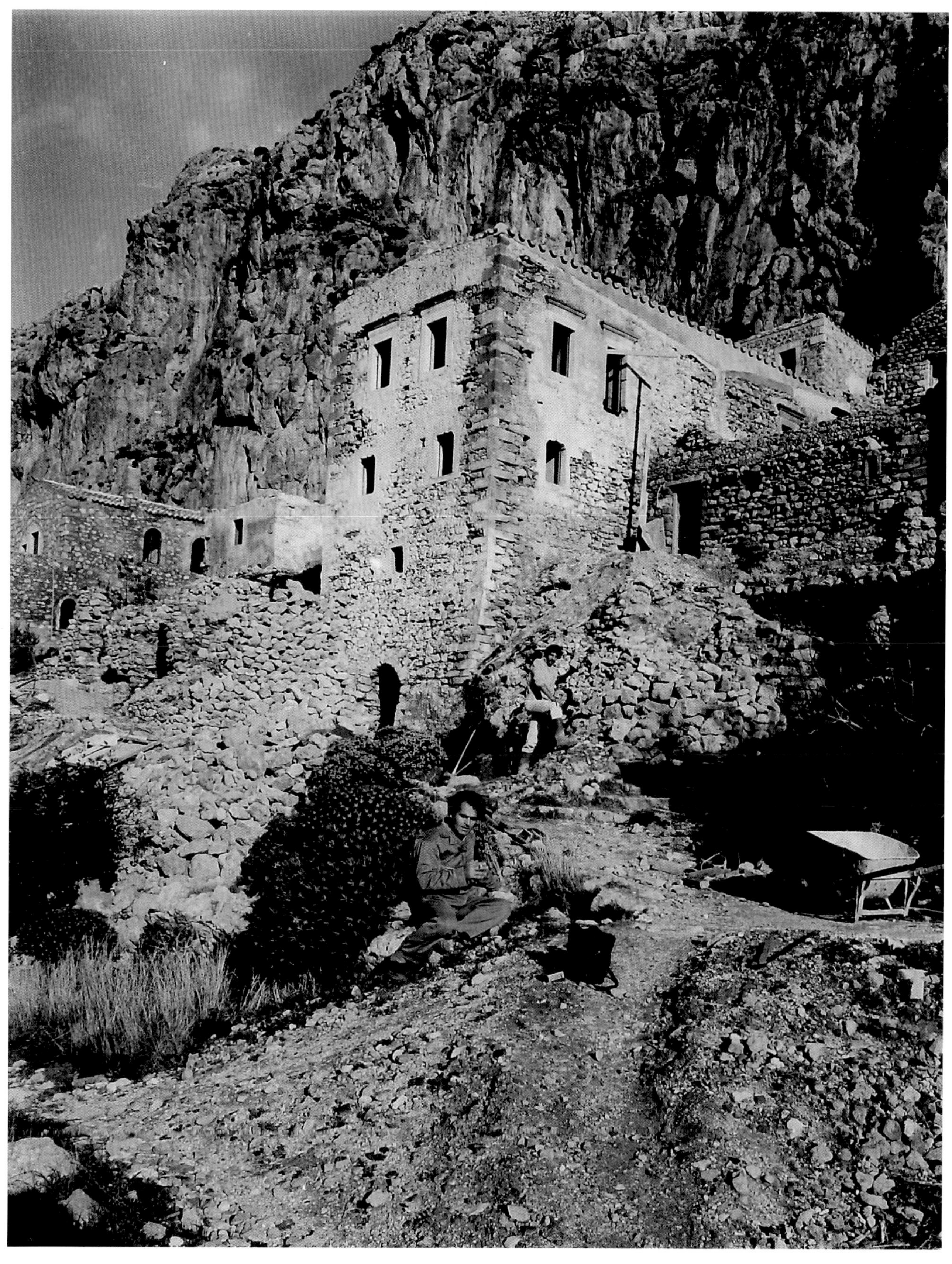

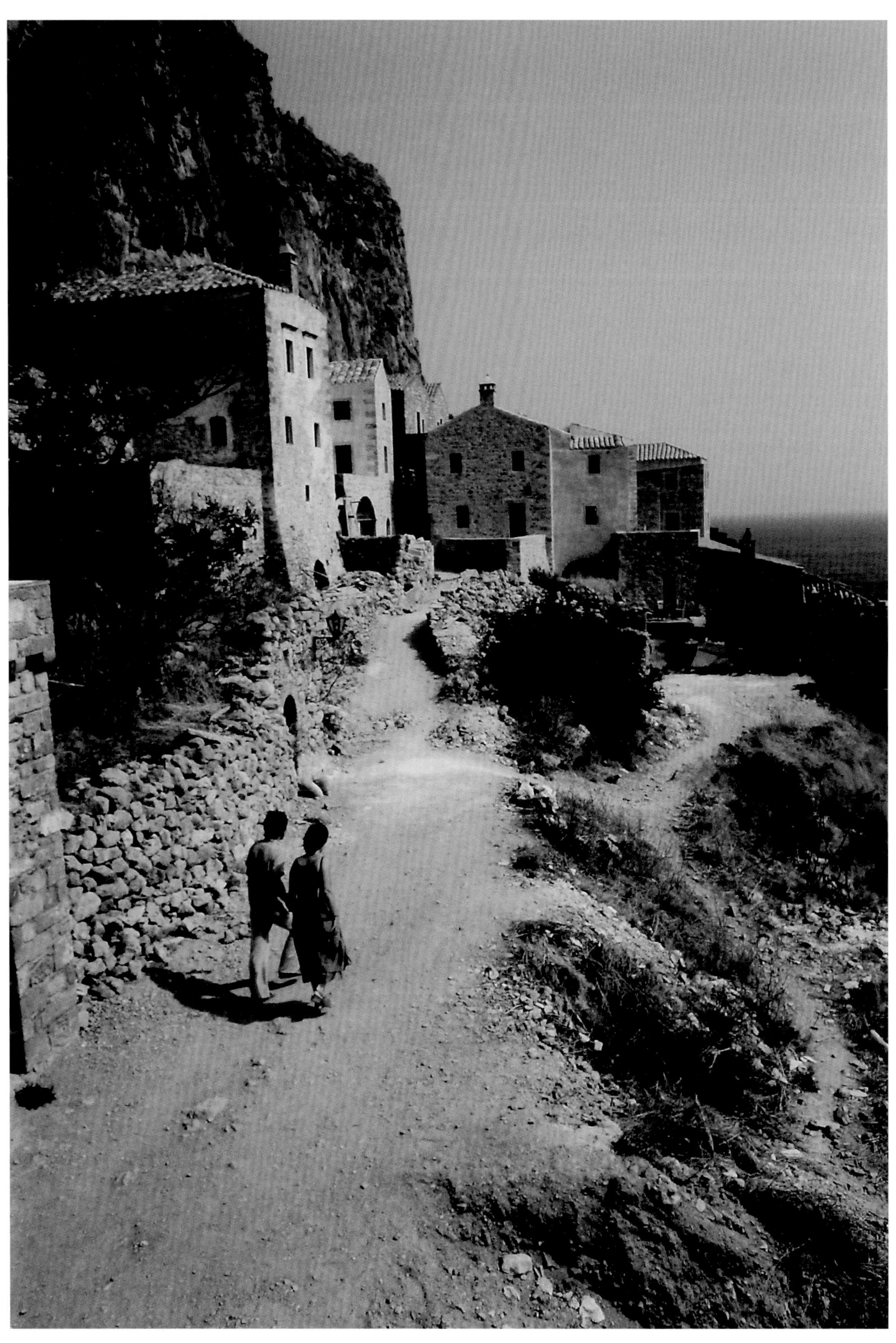

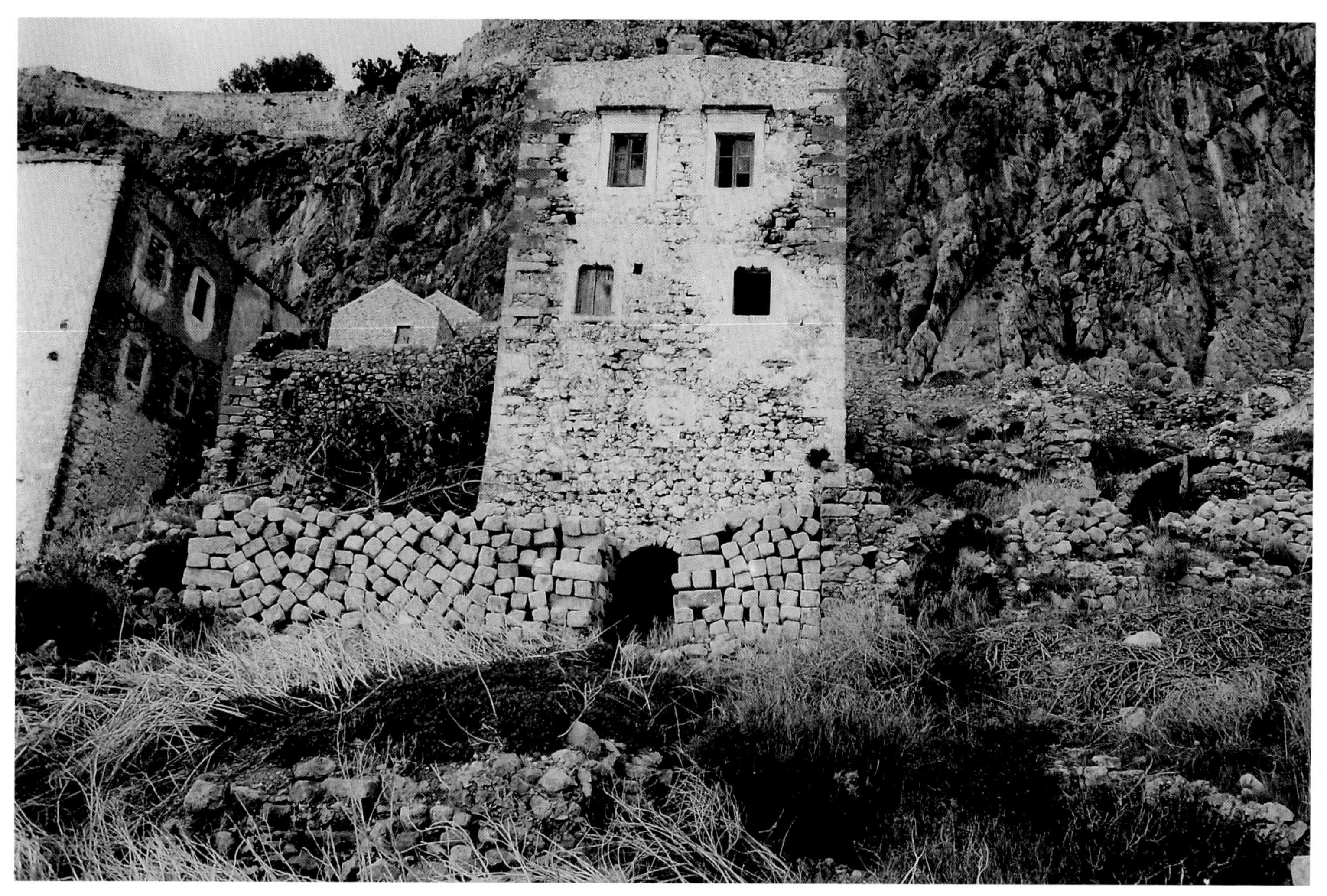

This region
betrays nothing of its ancient magnificence. Rusty lamposts,
houses riddled with thousands of holes, time eaten balustrades,
fallen balconies…

YANNIS RITSOS, *XXI*, *TIME*, 1975

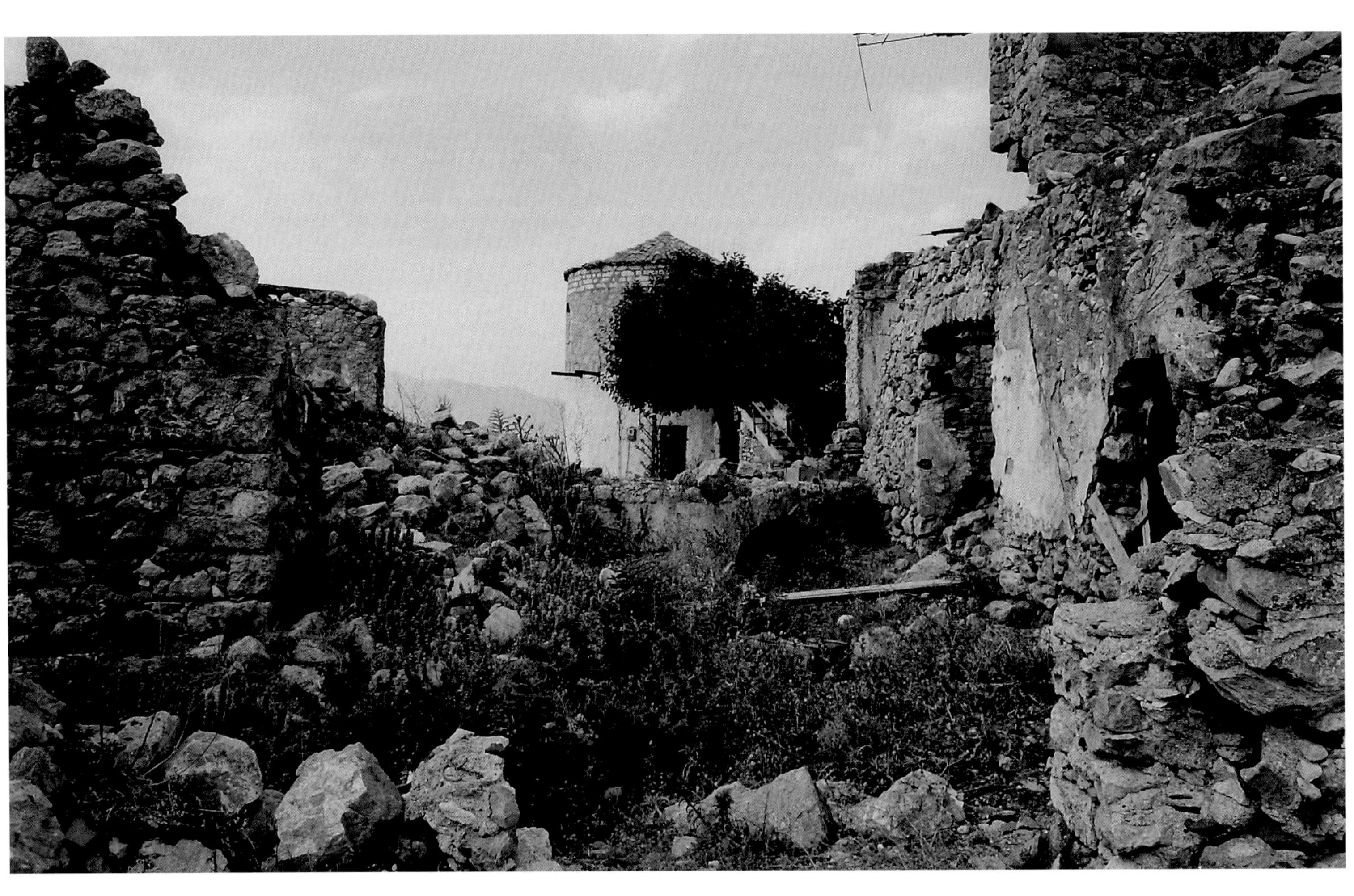

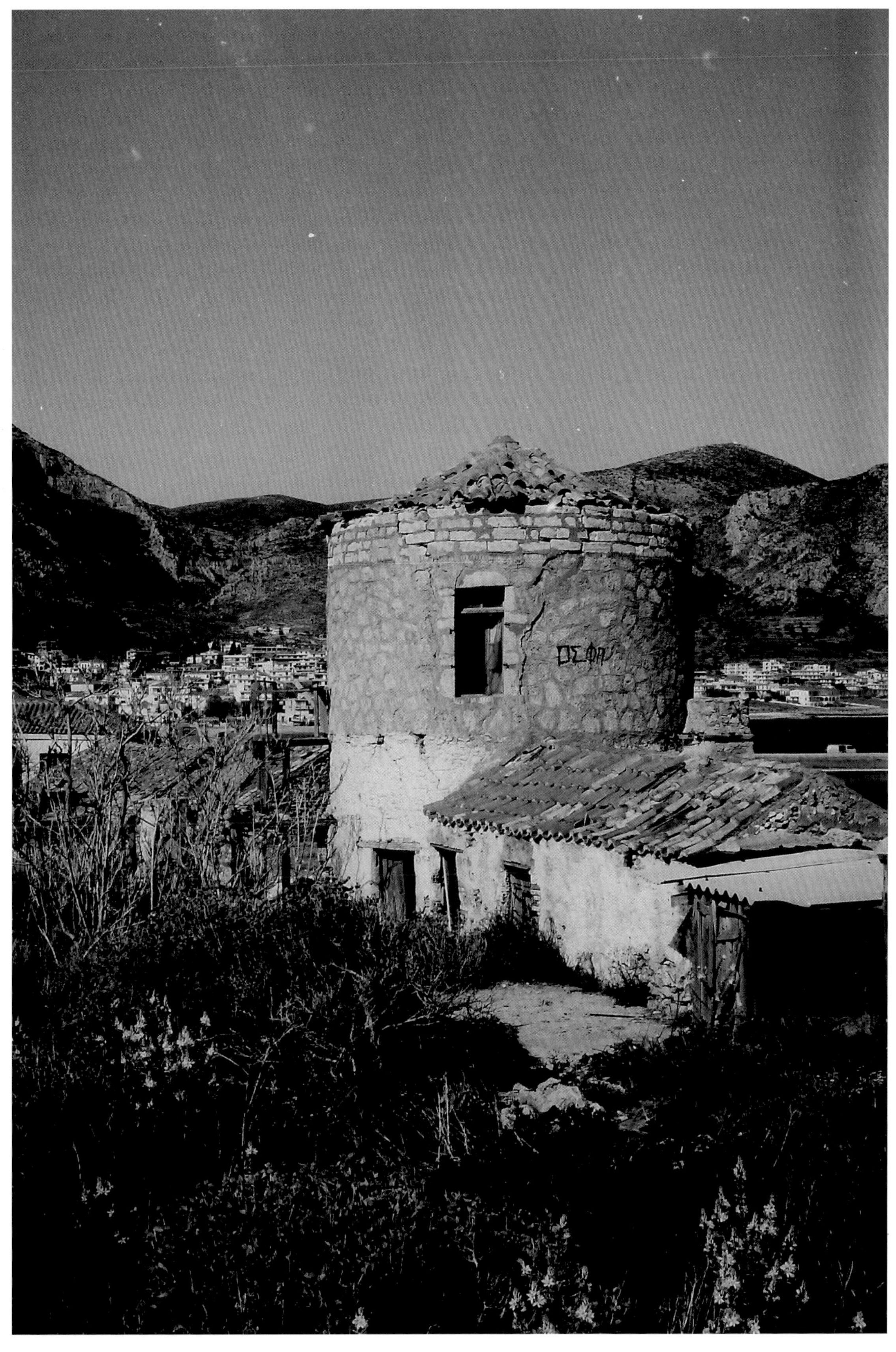

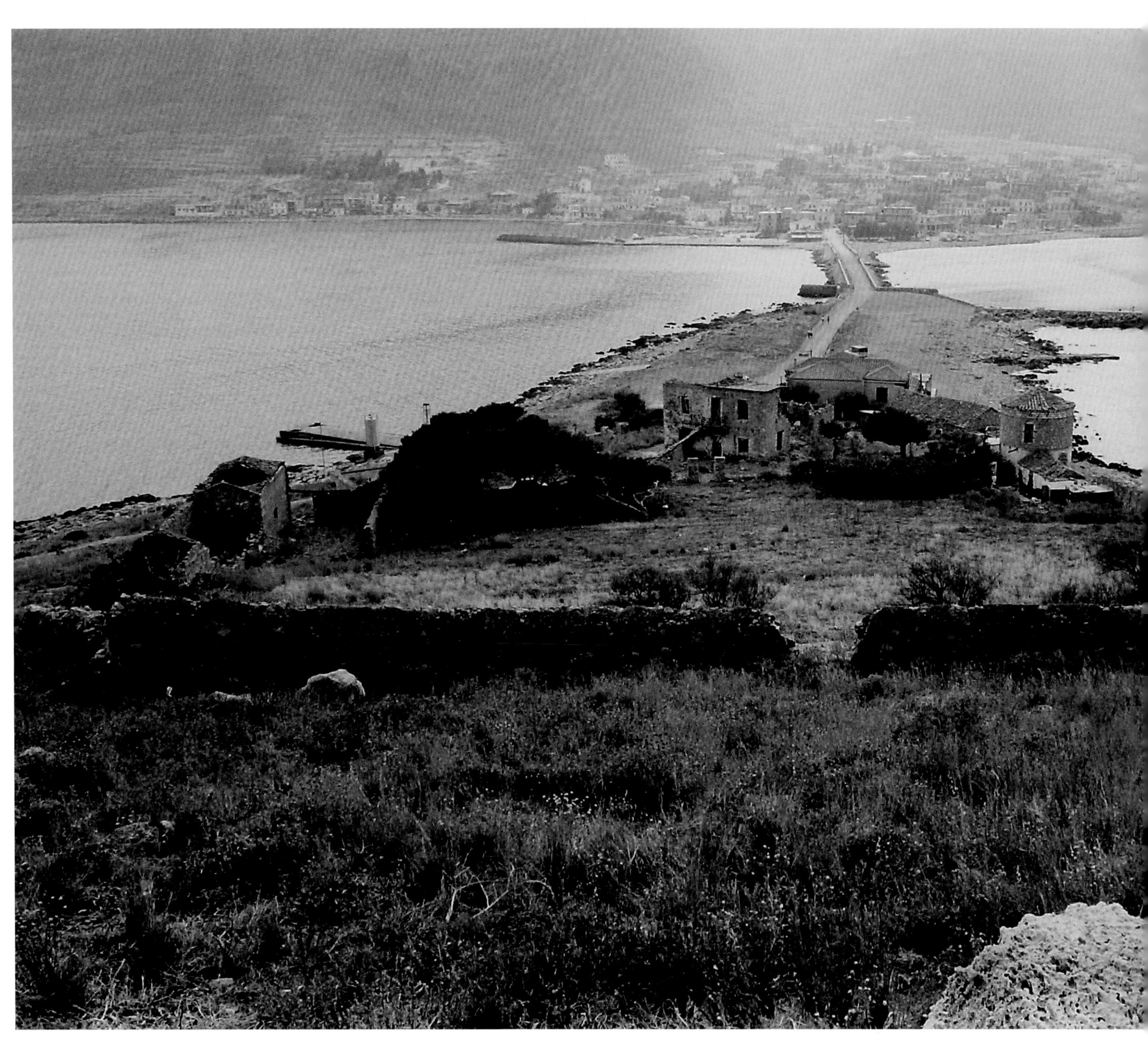

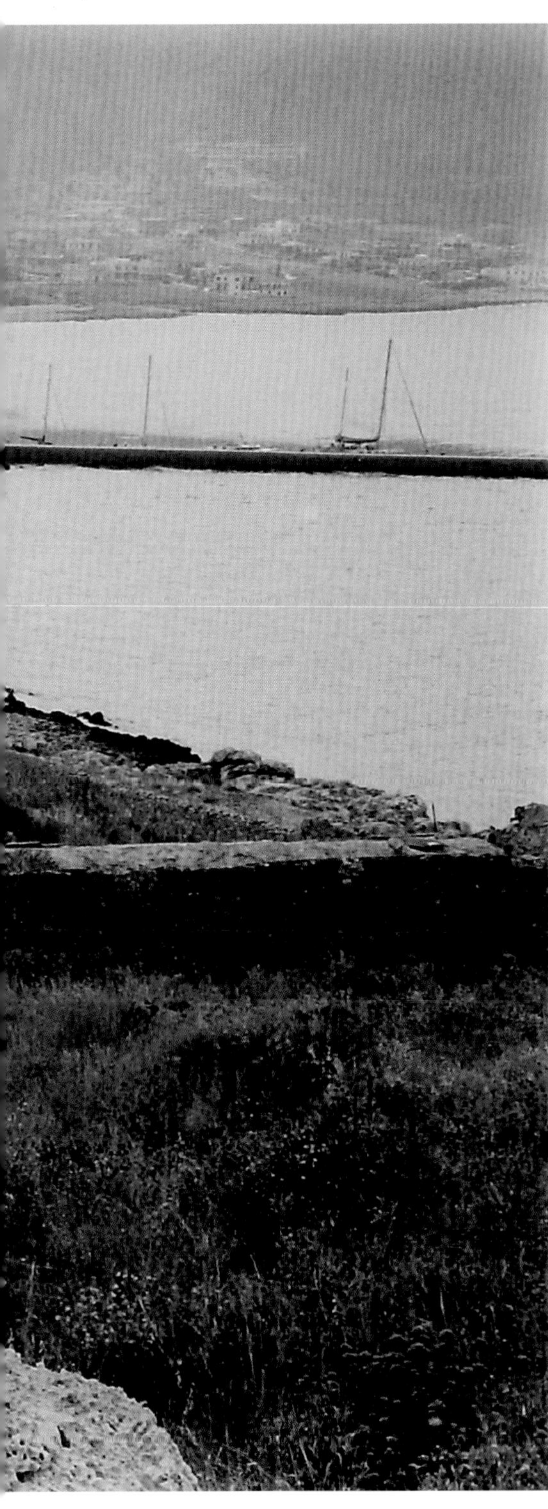

Towards the land sloping, but not gradually, and linked by a long apparently ill constructed, bridge, with the opposite hill, arising more meekly and greenly from the shore.

W.R. ELLIOTT, *MONEMVASIA THE GIBRALTAR OF GREECE*, 1971

Yefira

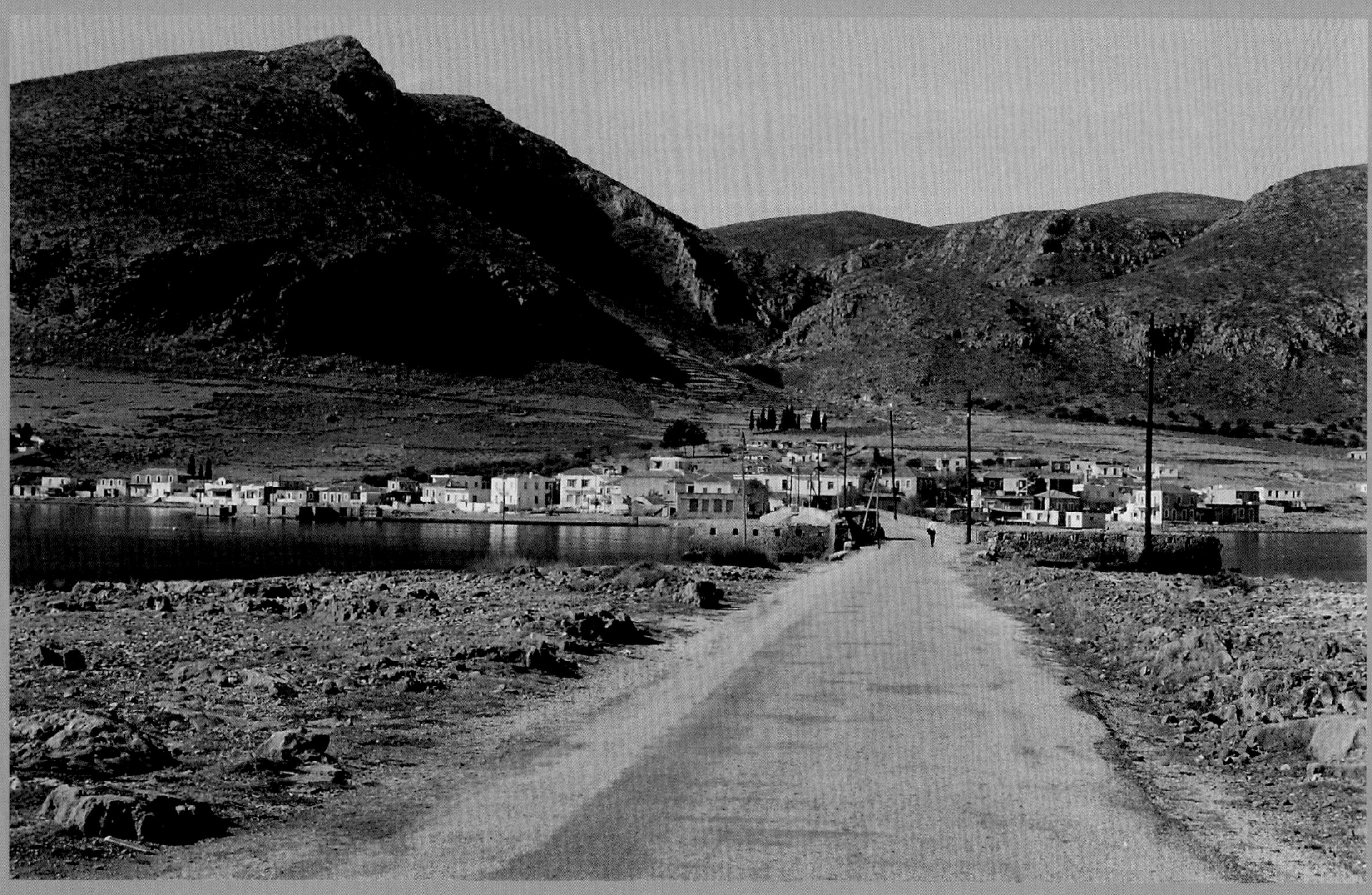

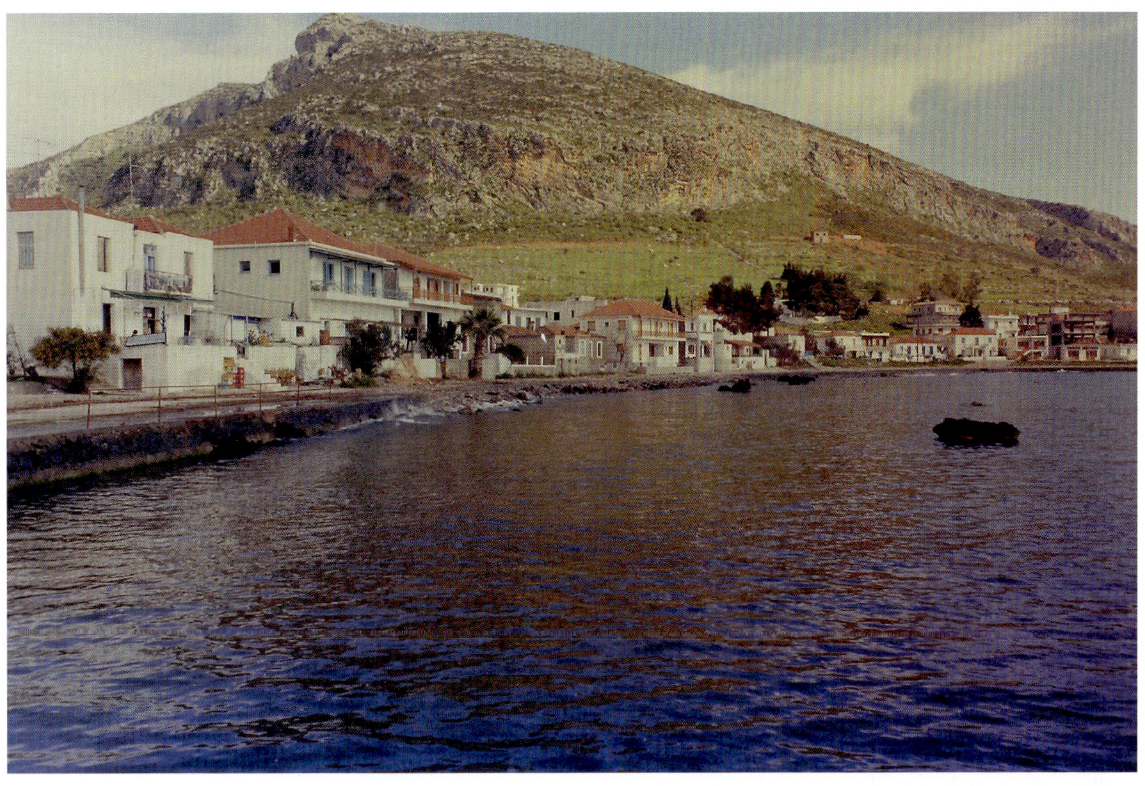

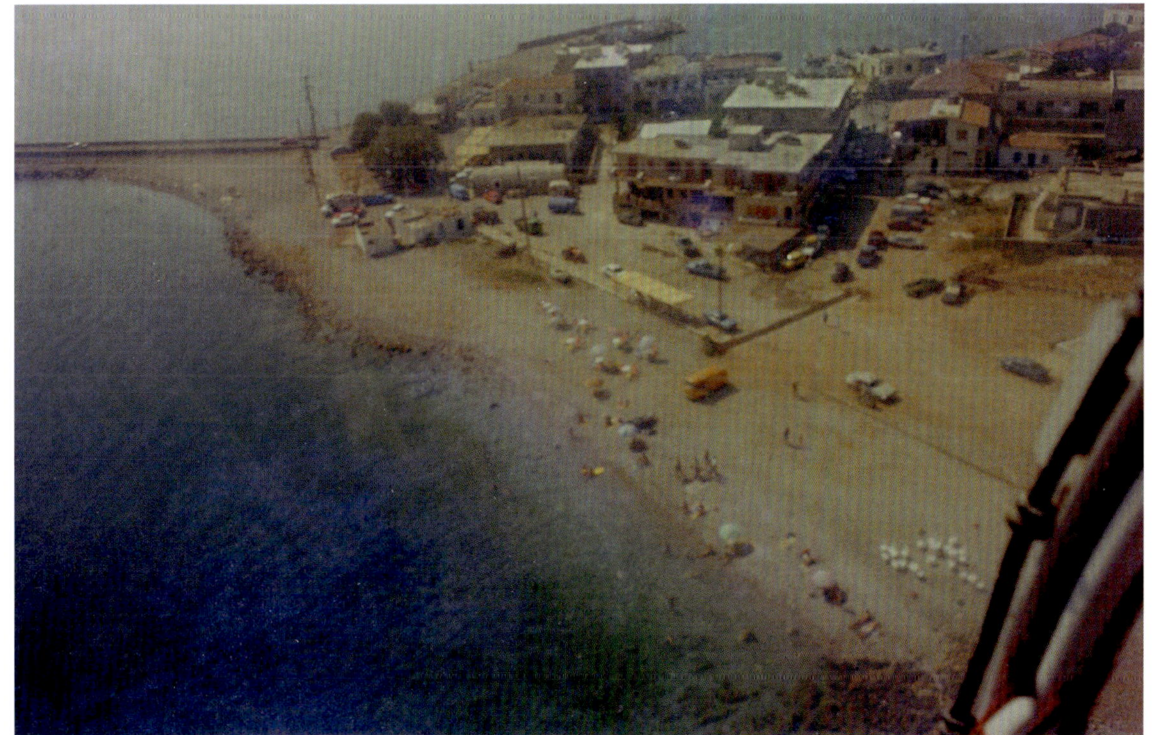

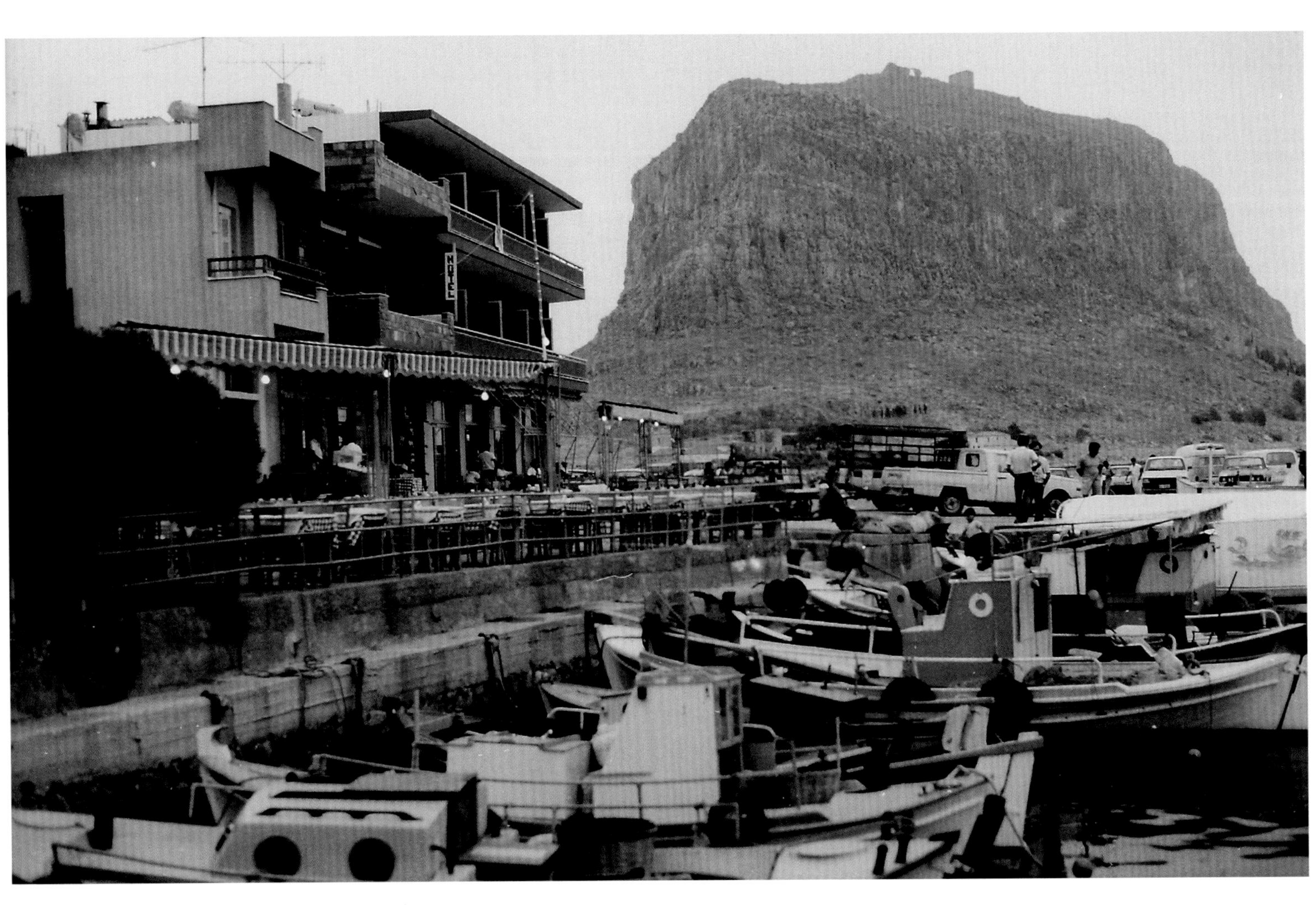

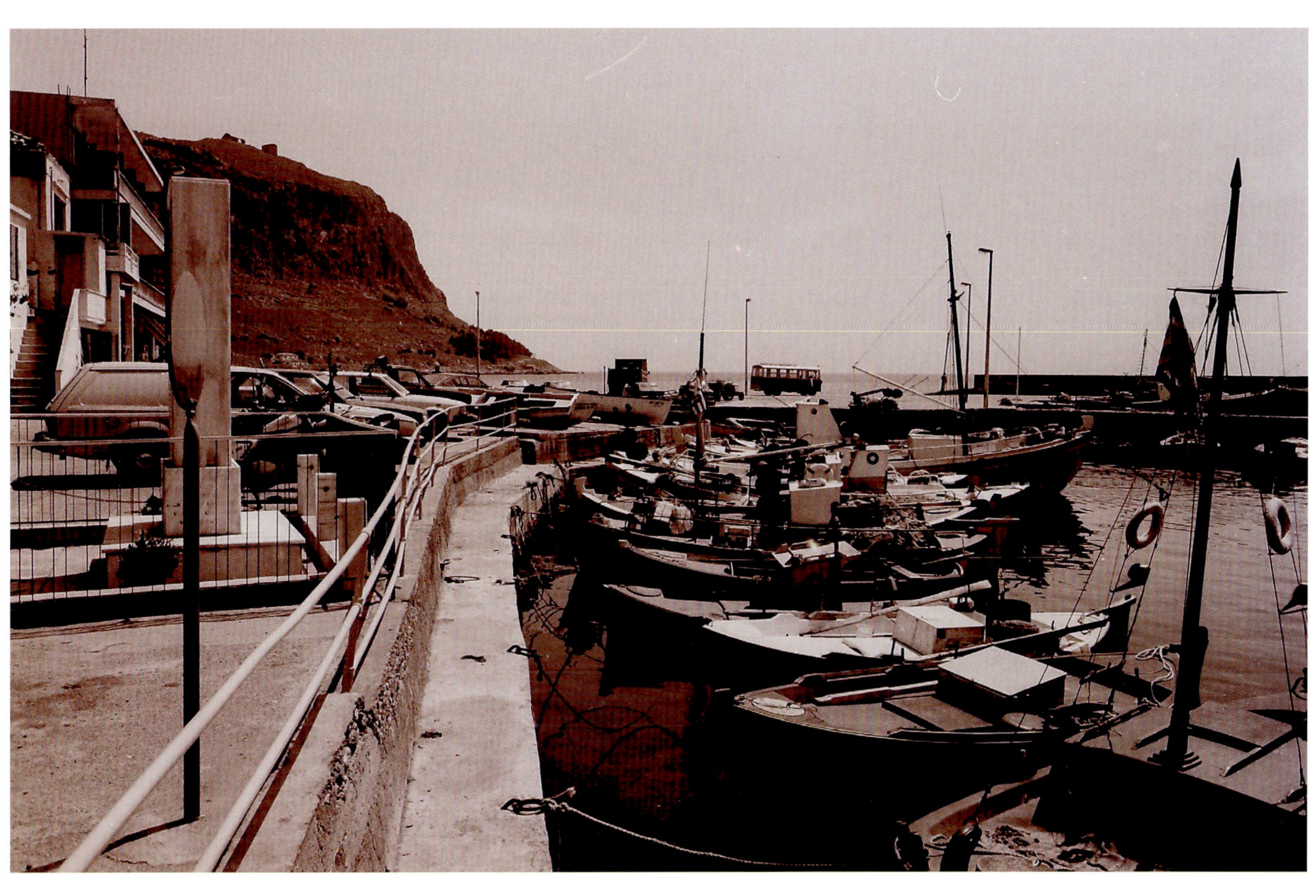

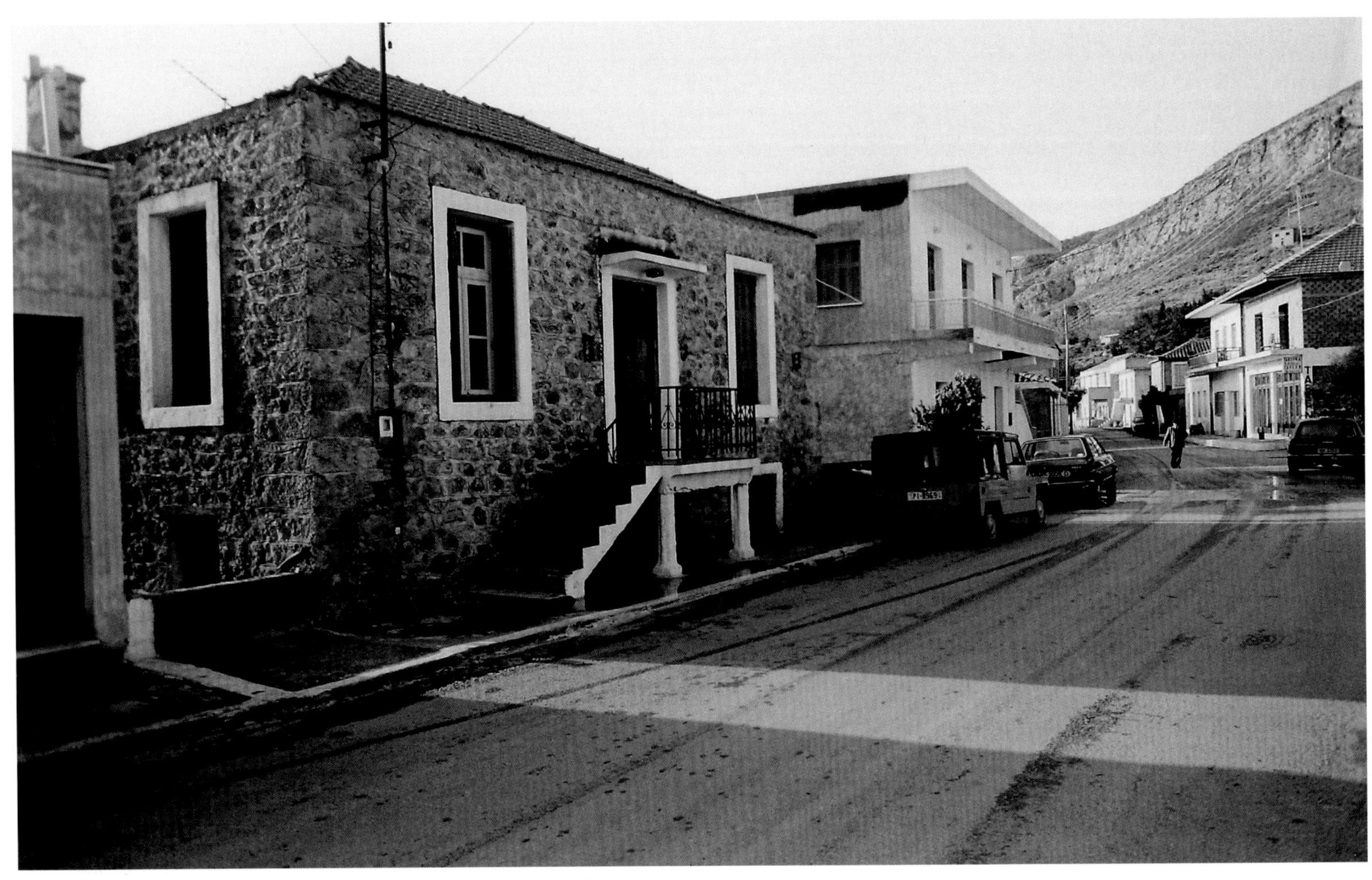

... and there are now houses and roads and affluence, yet the deep old culture remains as it was, almost: that was wonderful to re-enter.

KEVIN McGRATH, *CONSCIOUSNESS*, 2023

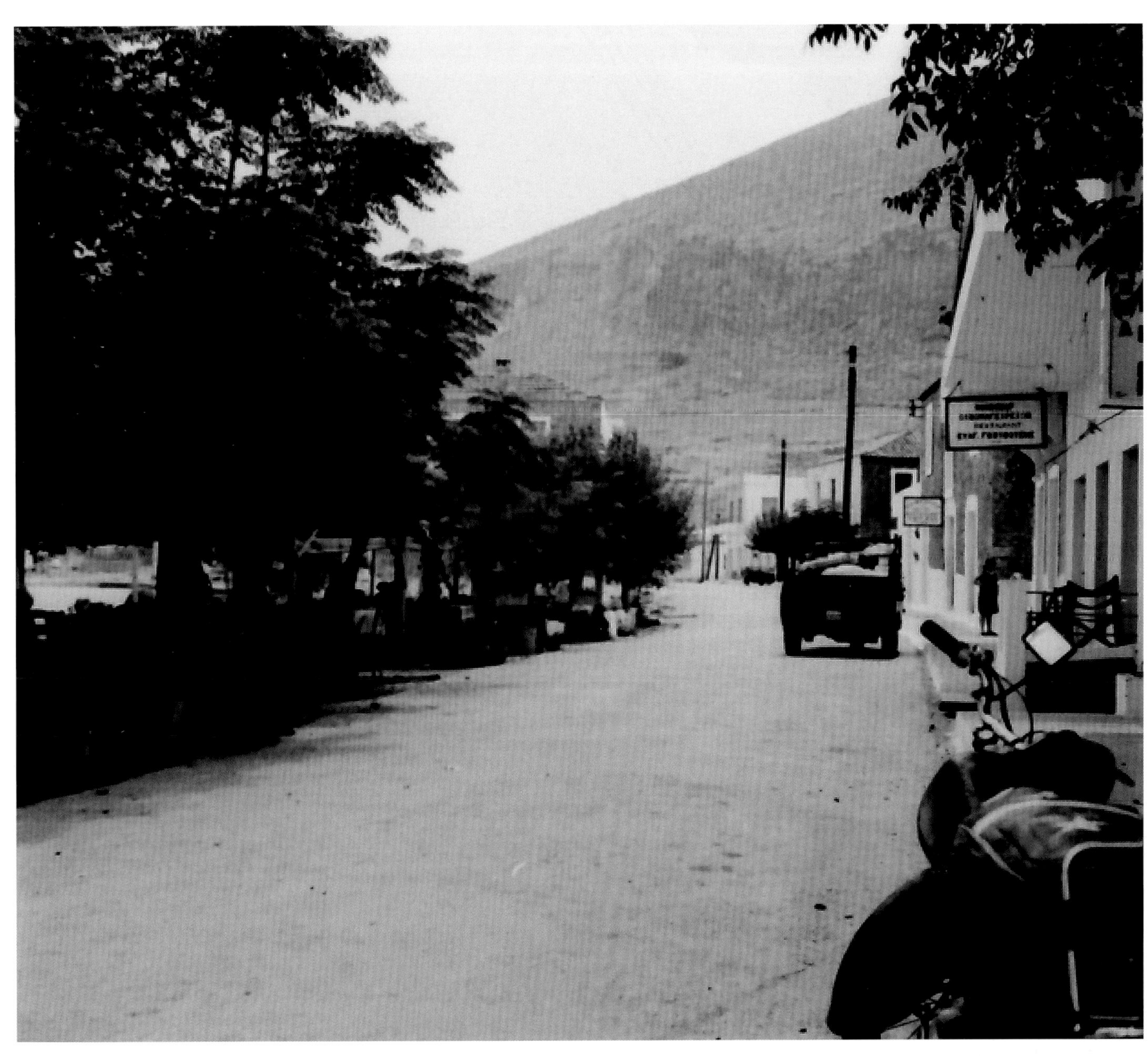

Villages

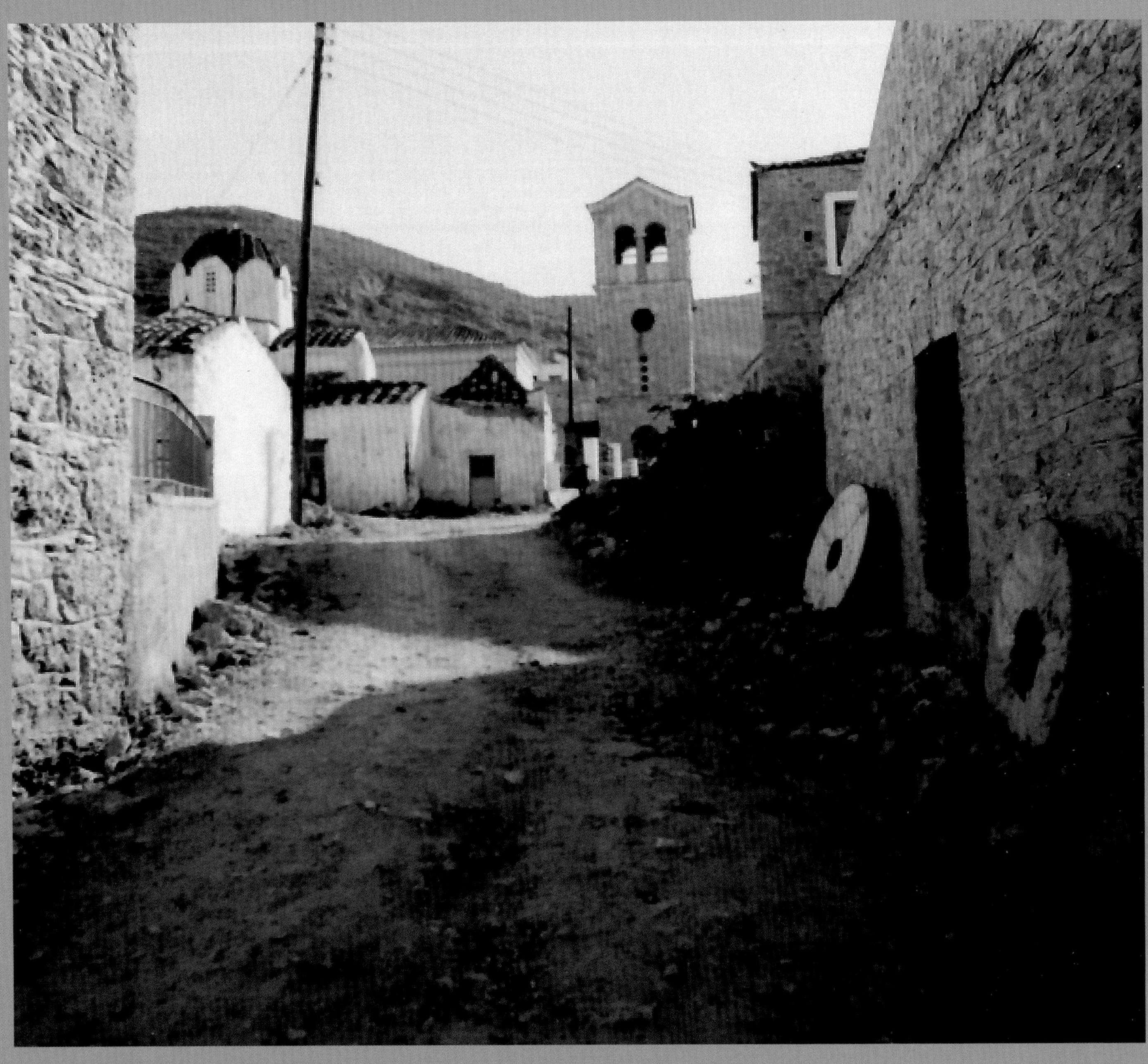

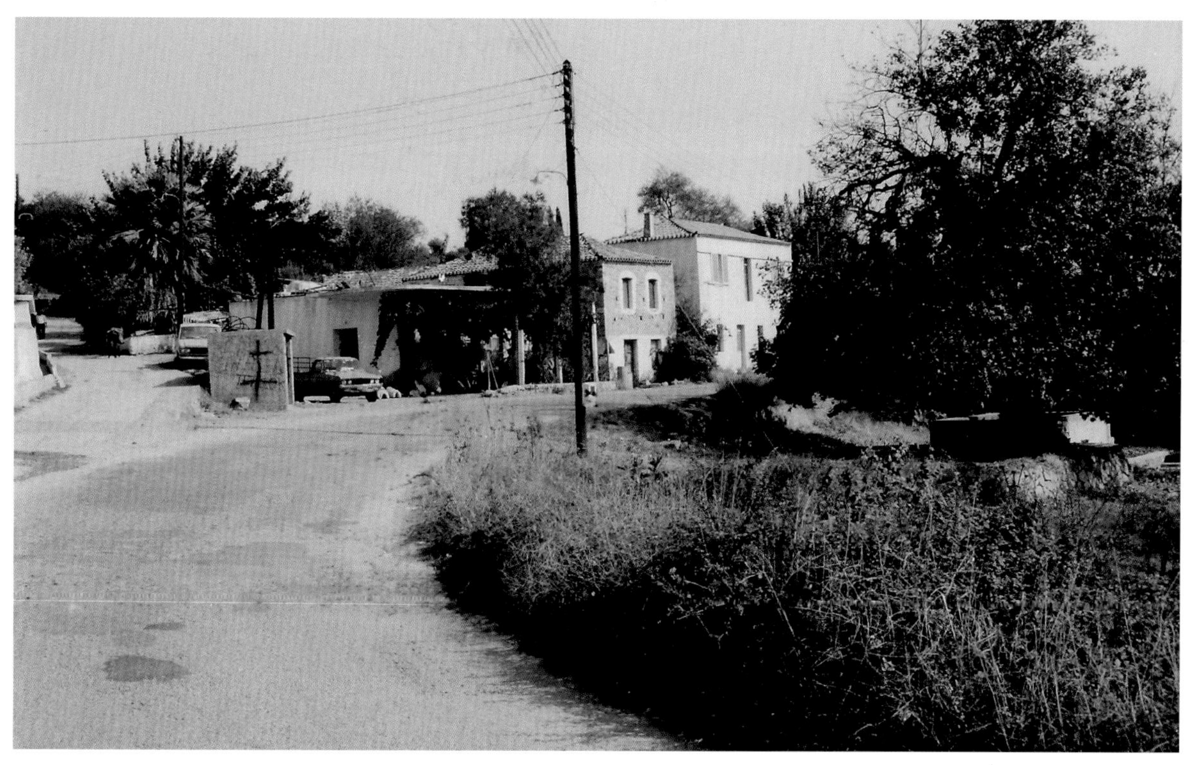

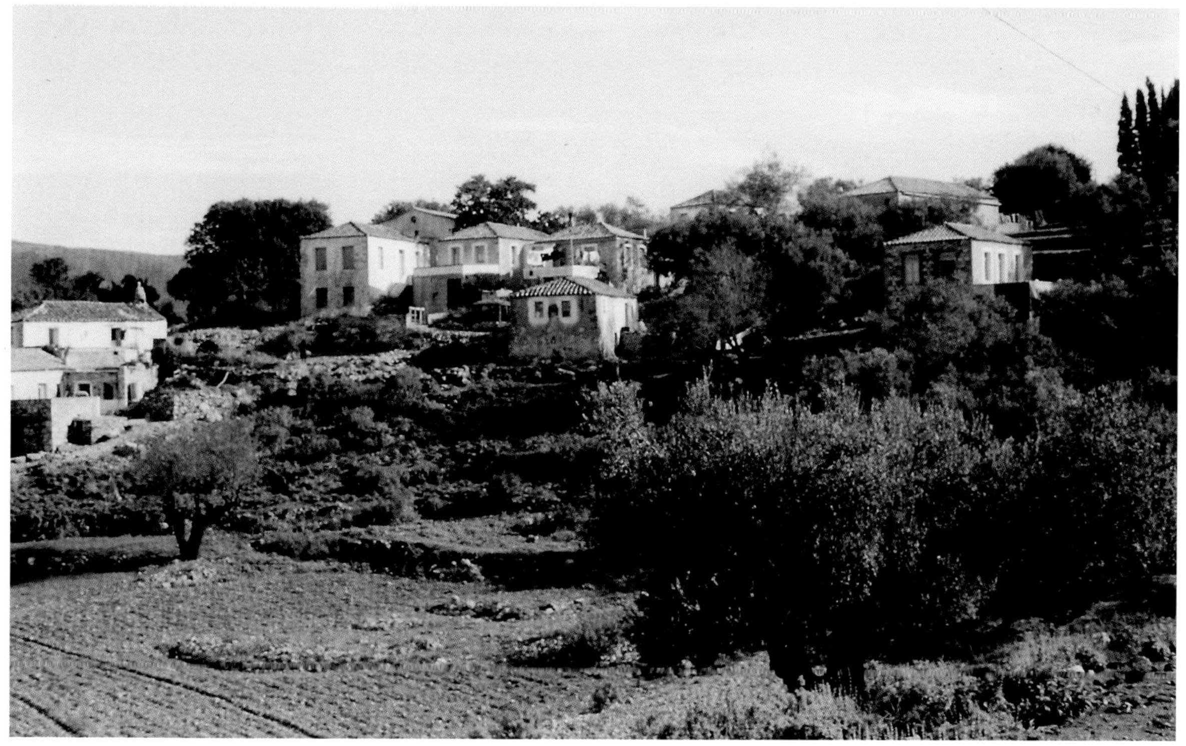

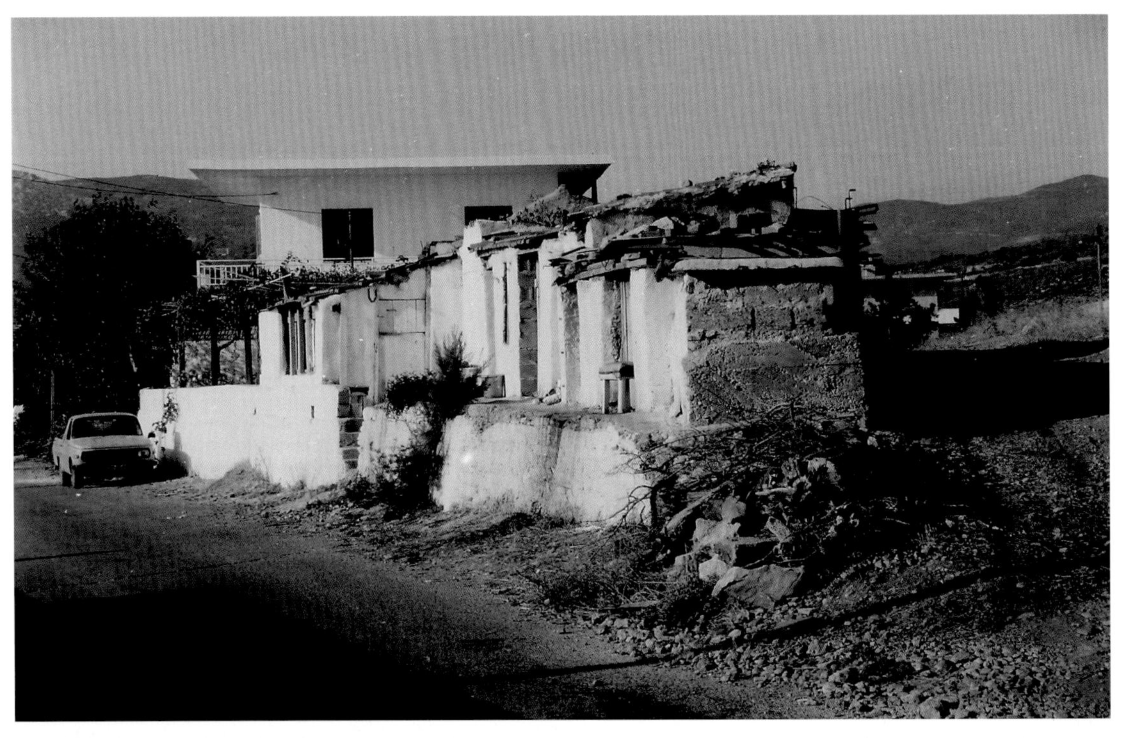

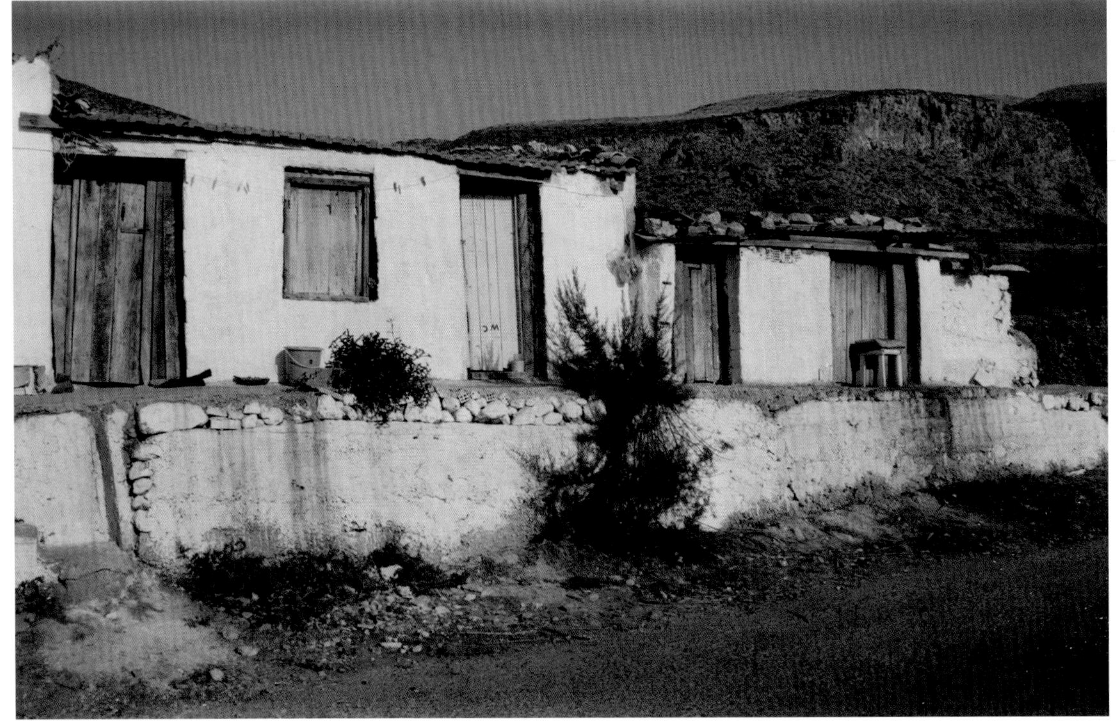

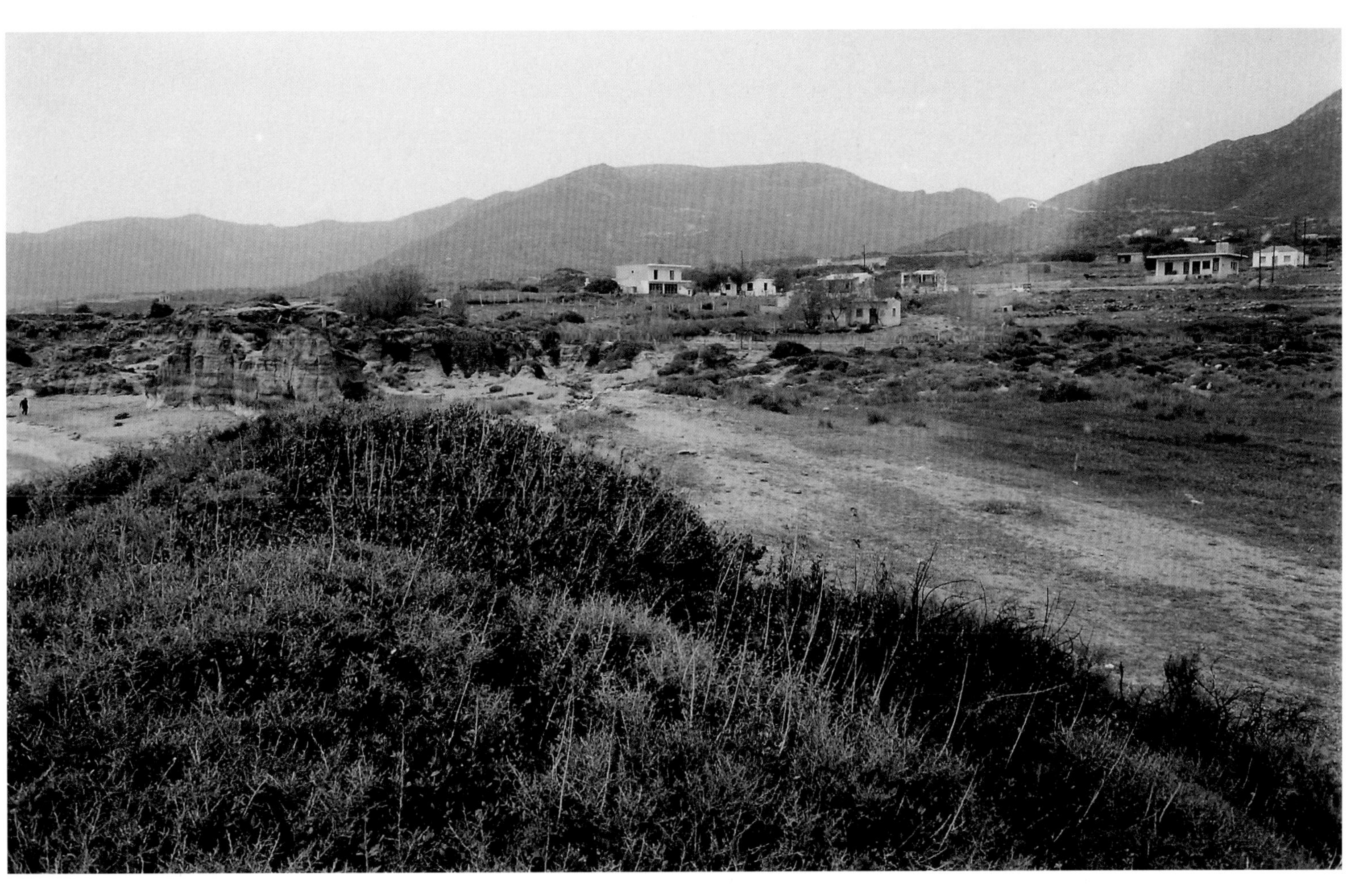

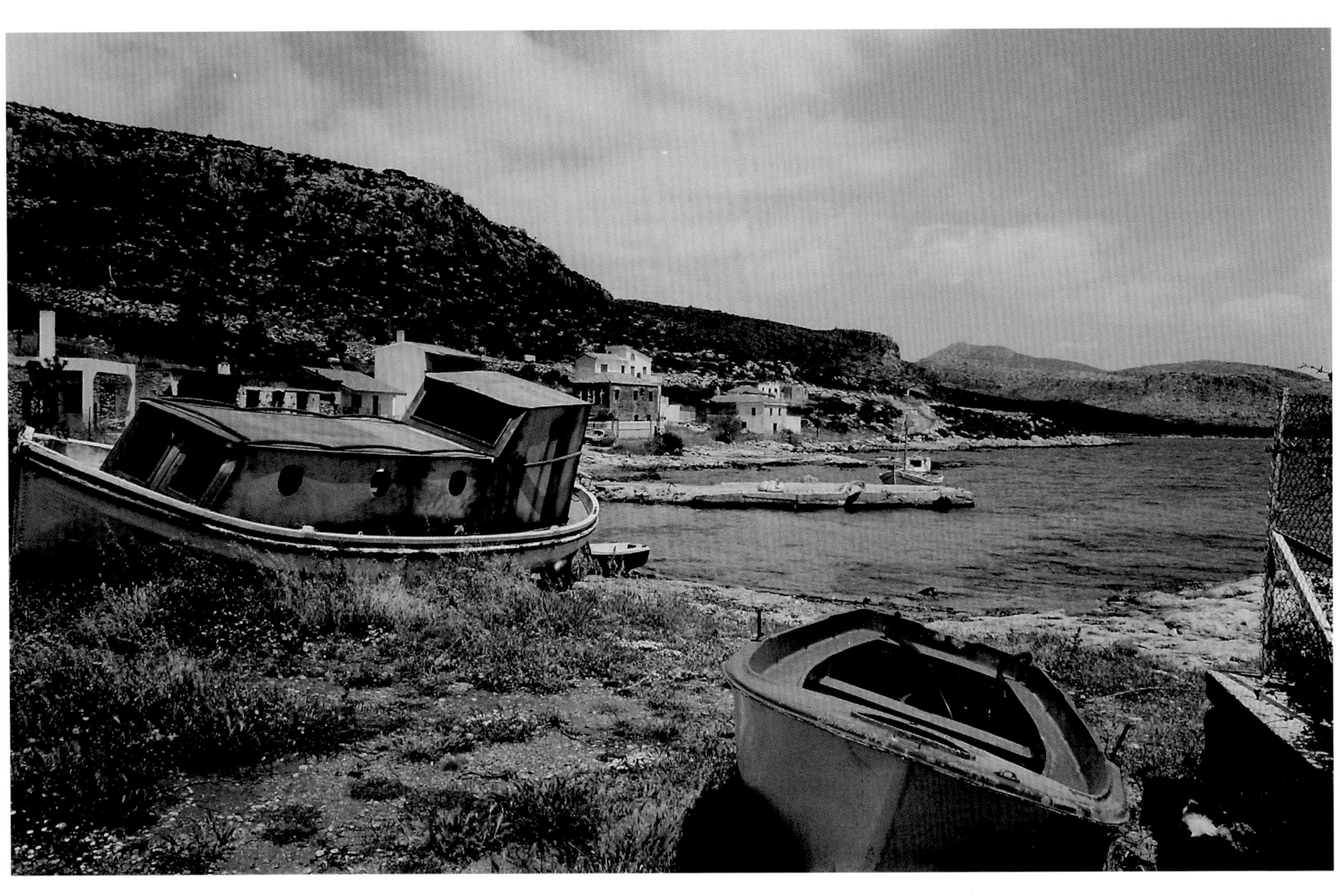

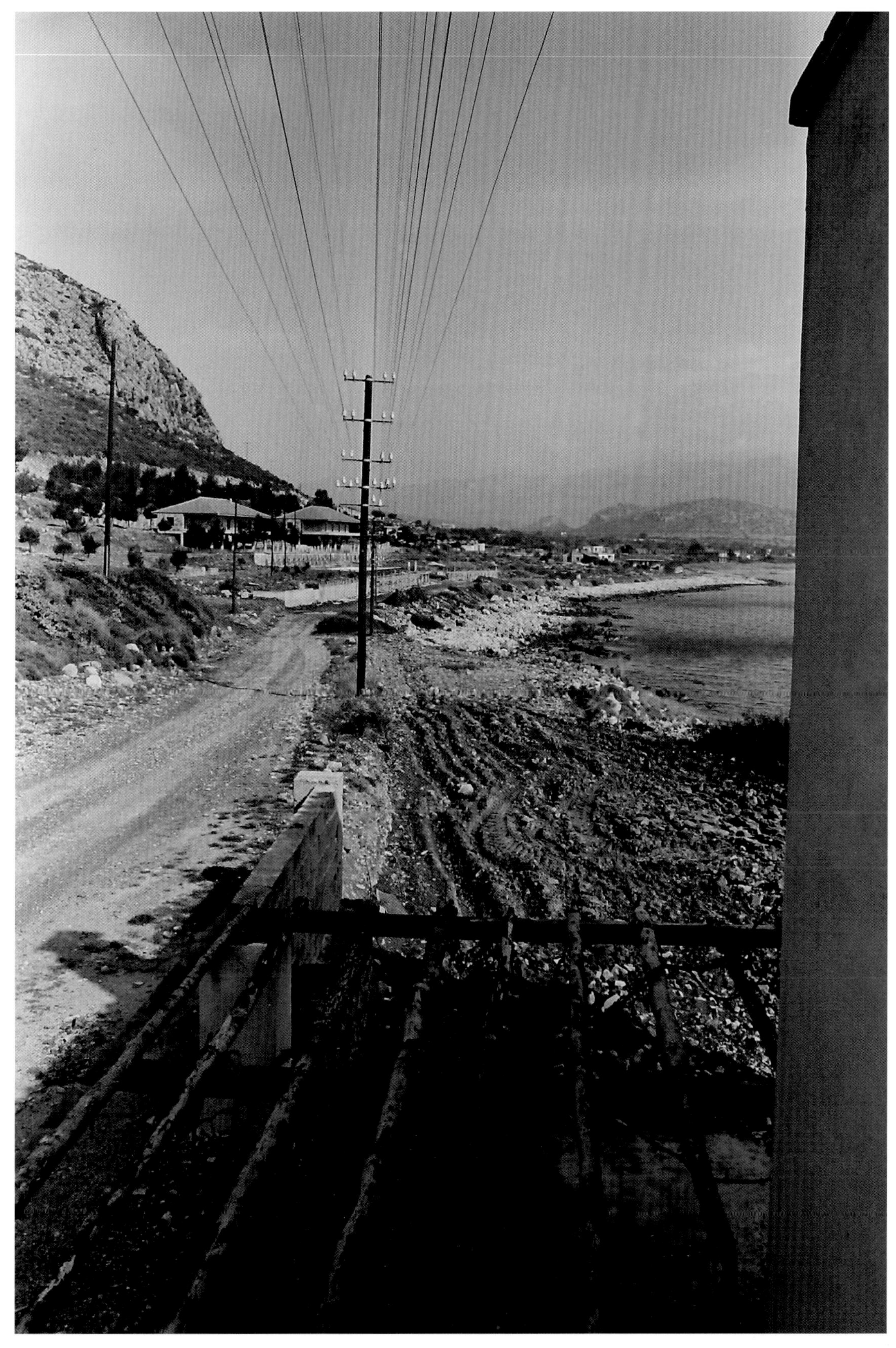

Castro

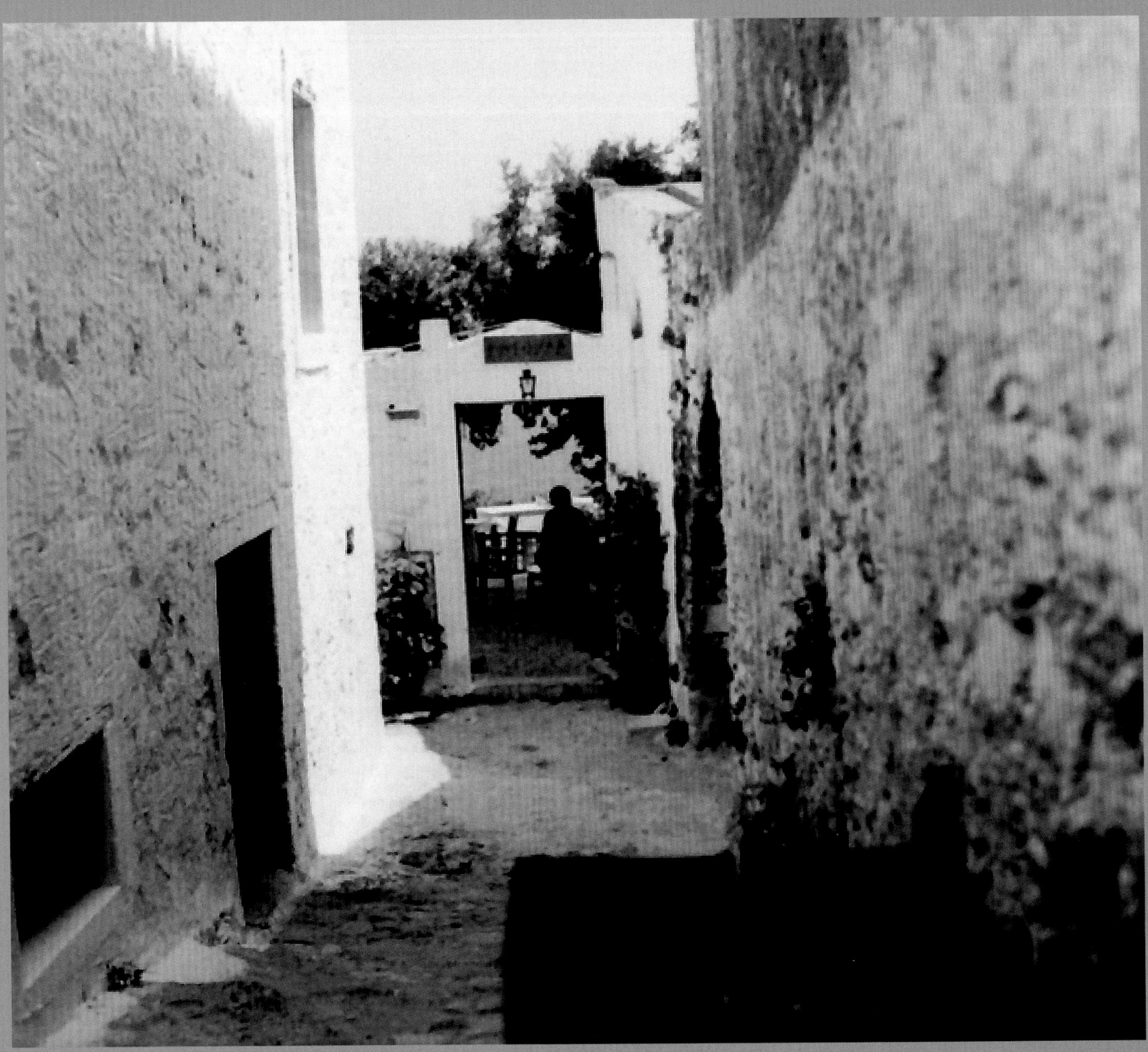

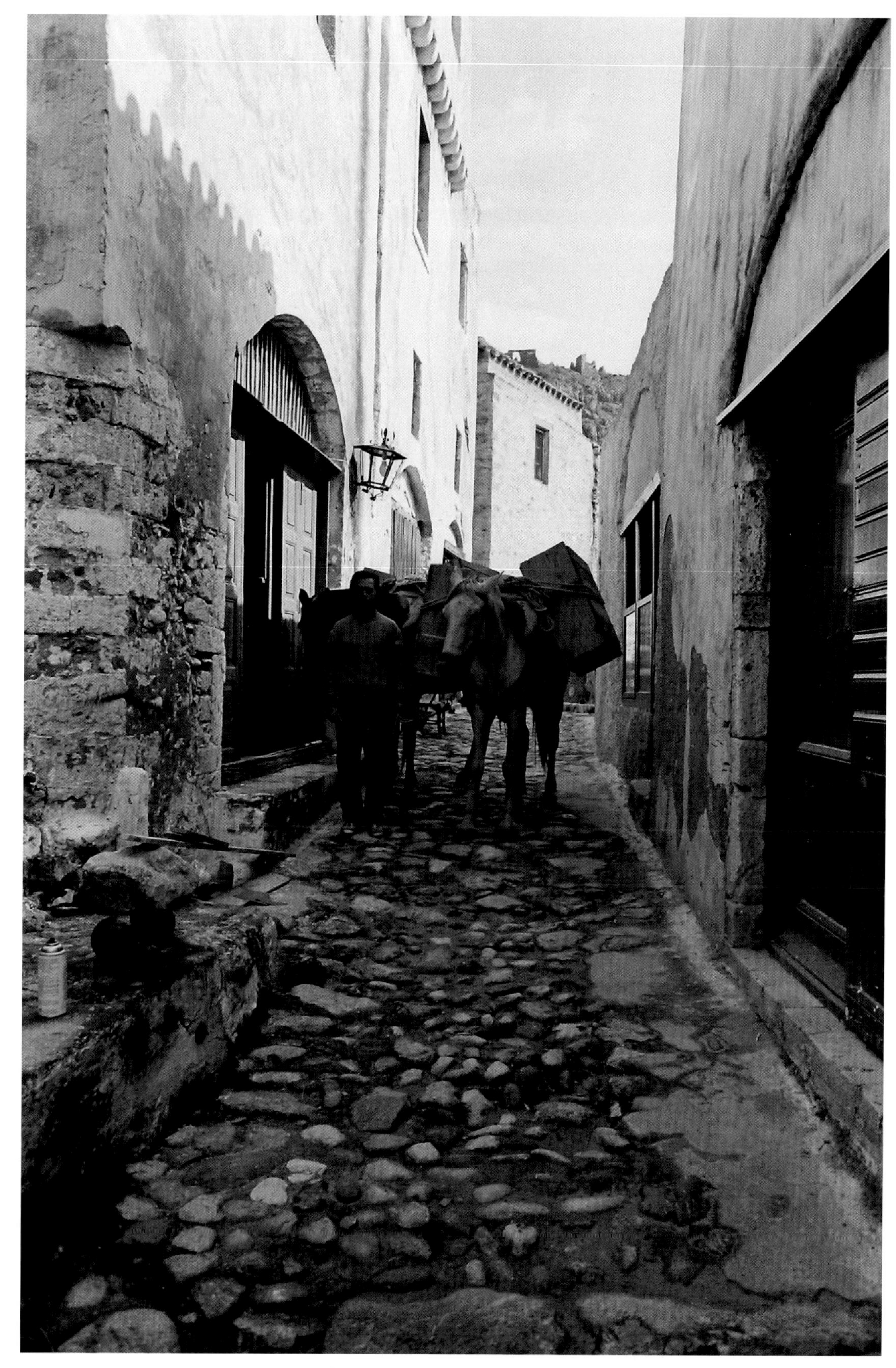

Old, low houses, cobblers, grocers, a barber's shop… Two or three men were seated on doorsteps, a donkey laden with dried twigs went by.

NIKOS KAZANTZAKIS, *JOURNEY TO THE MOREA*, 1965

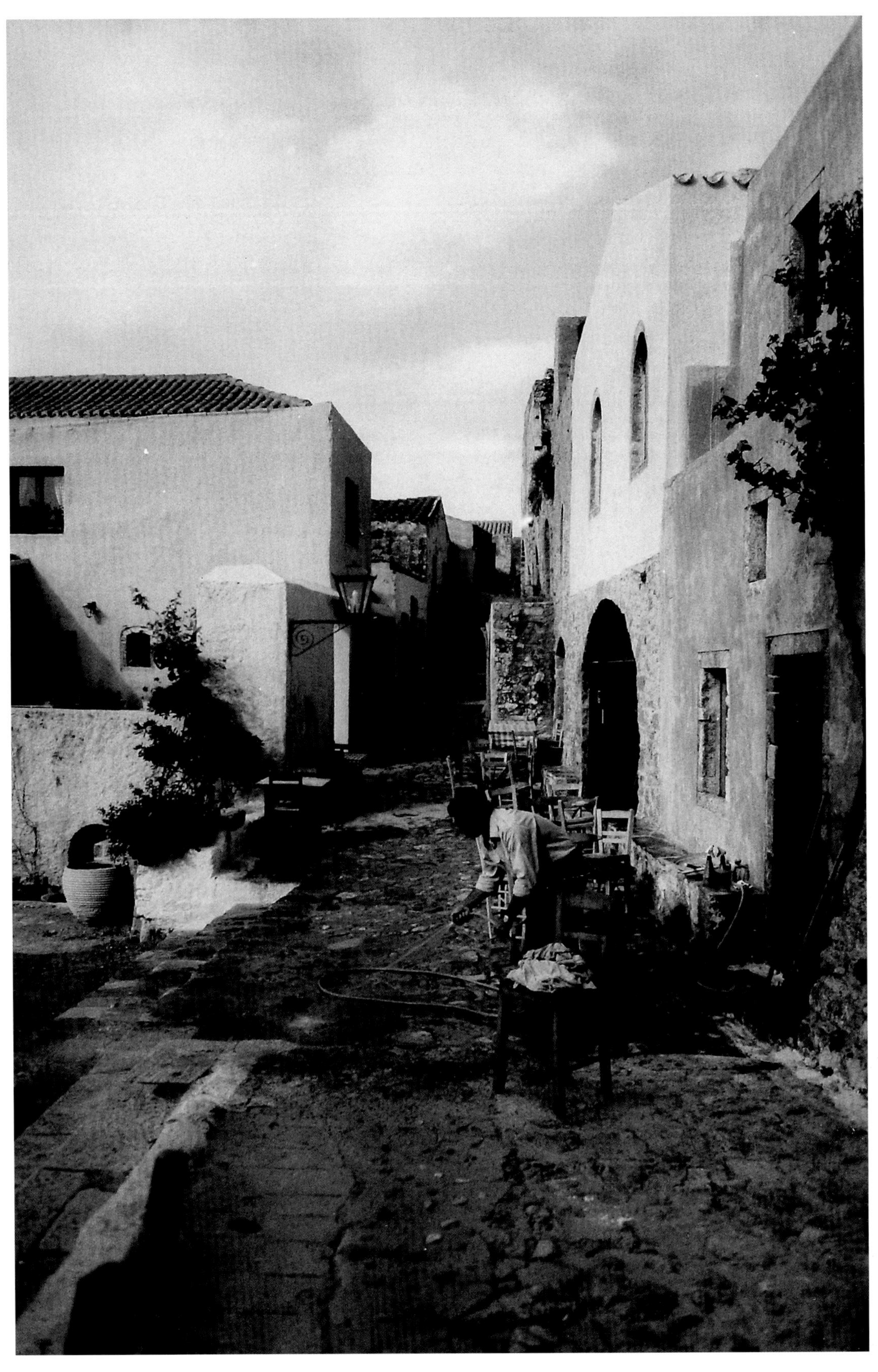

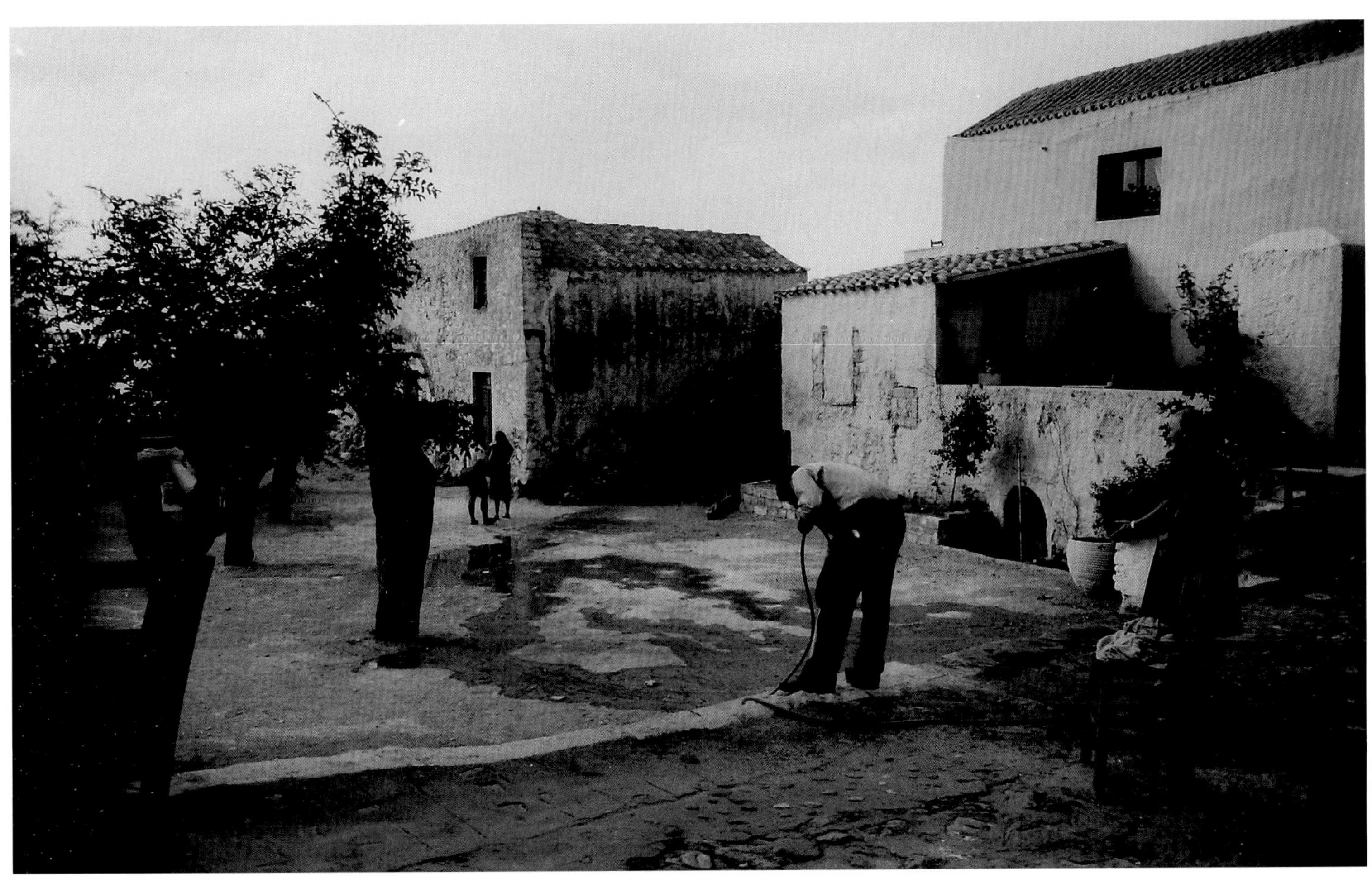

Seeing your shadow grow and diminish,
Lose itself in the other shadows…

GEORGE SEFERIS, 'MYTHISTOREMA', 1935

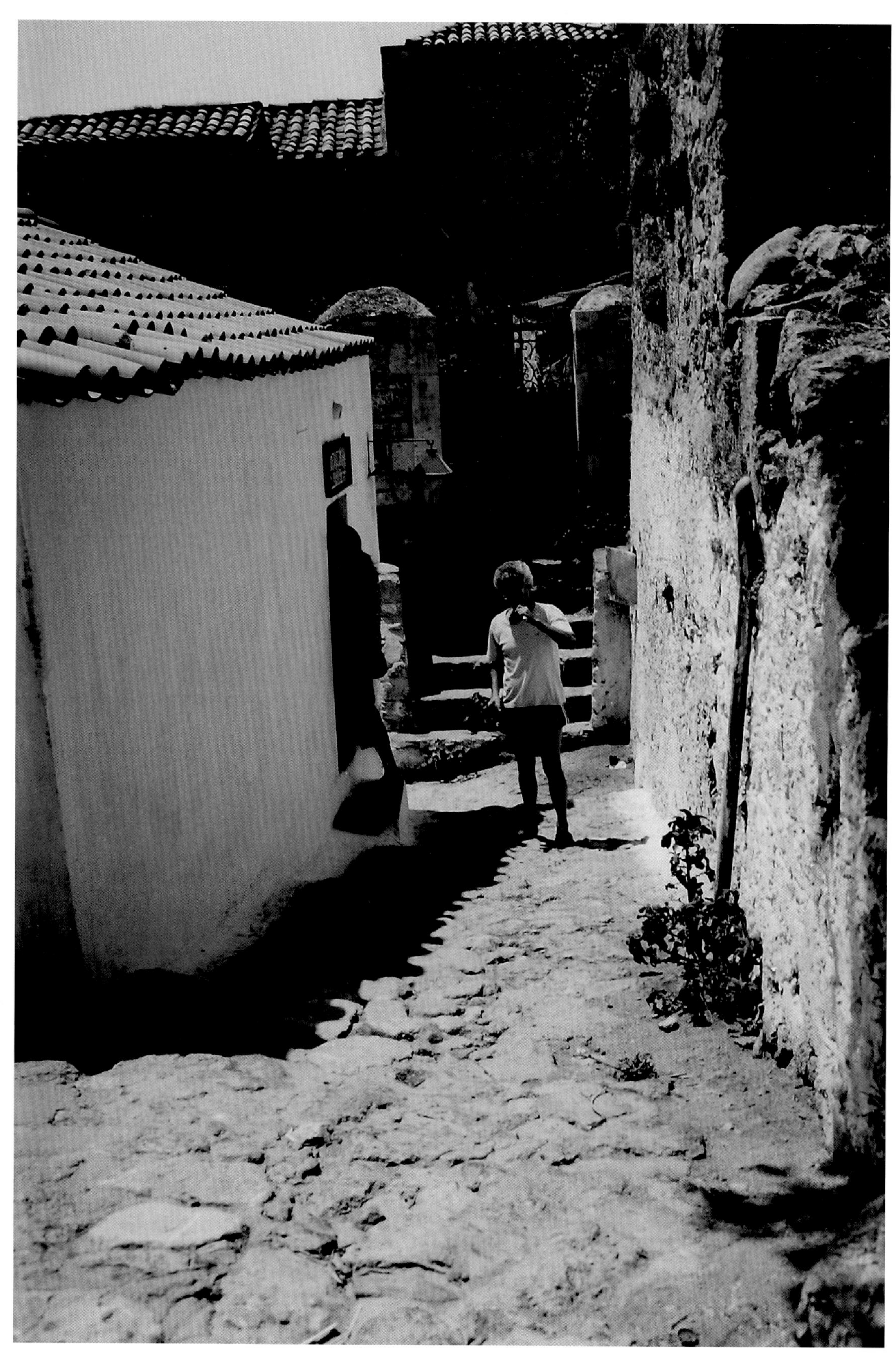

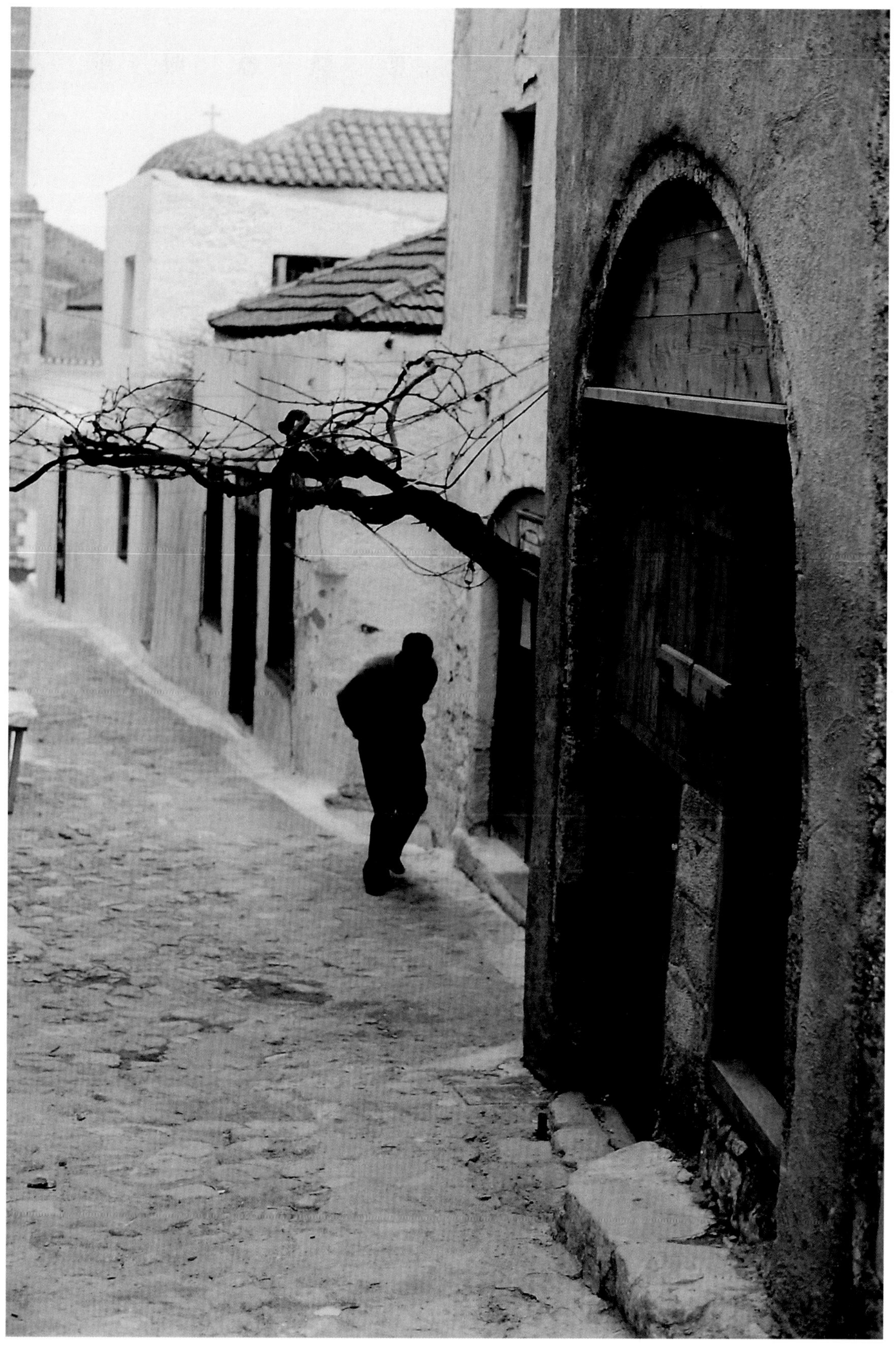

Yefira

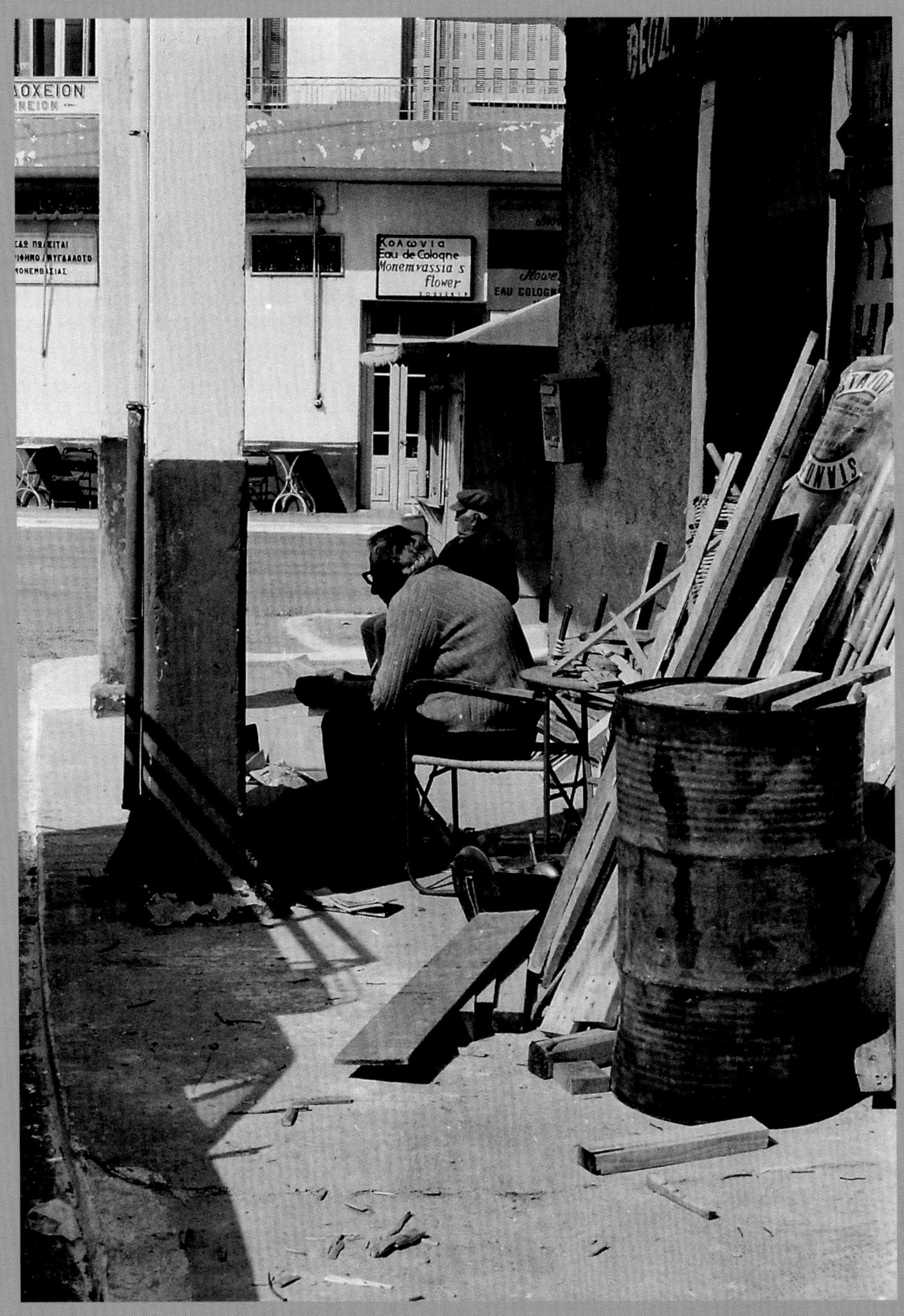

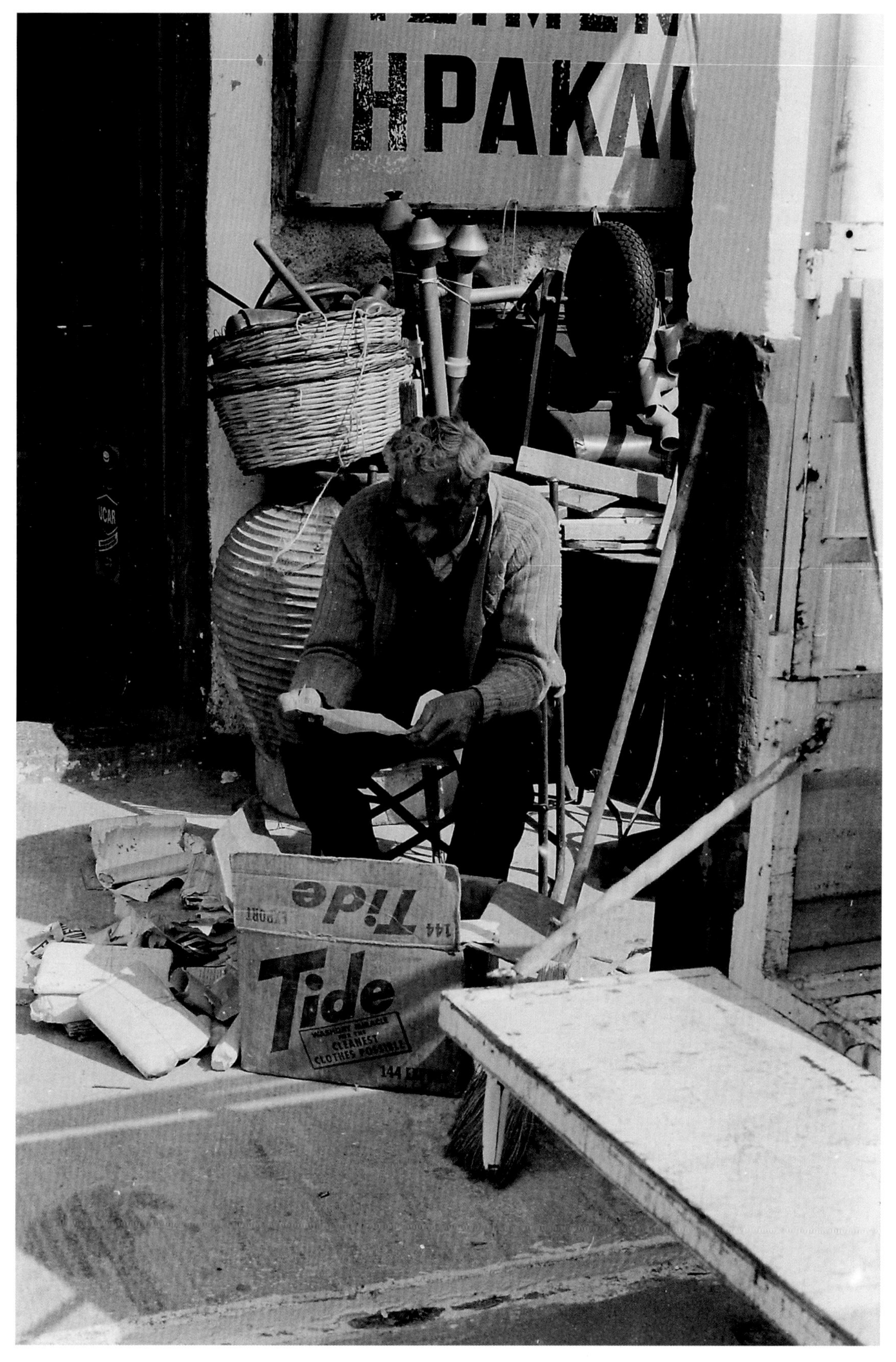
ΗΡΑΚΛ
Tide
Tide
CLEANEST
CLOTHES POSSIBLE

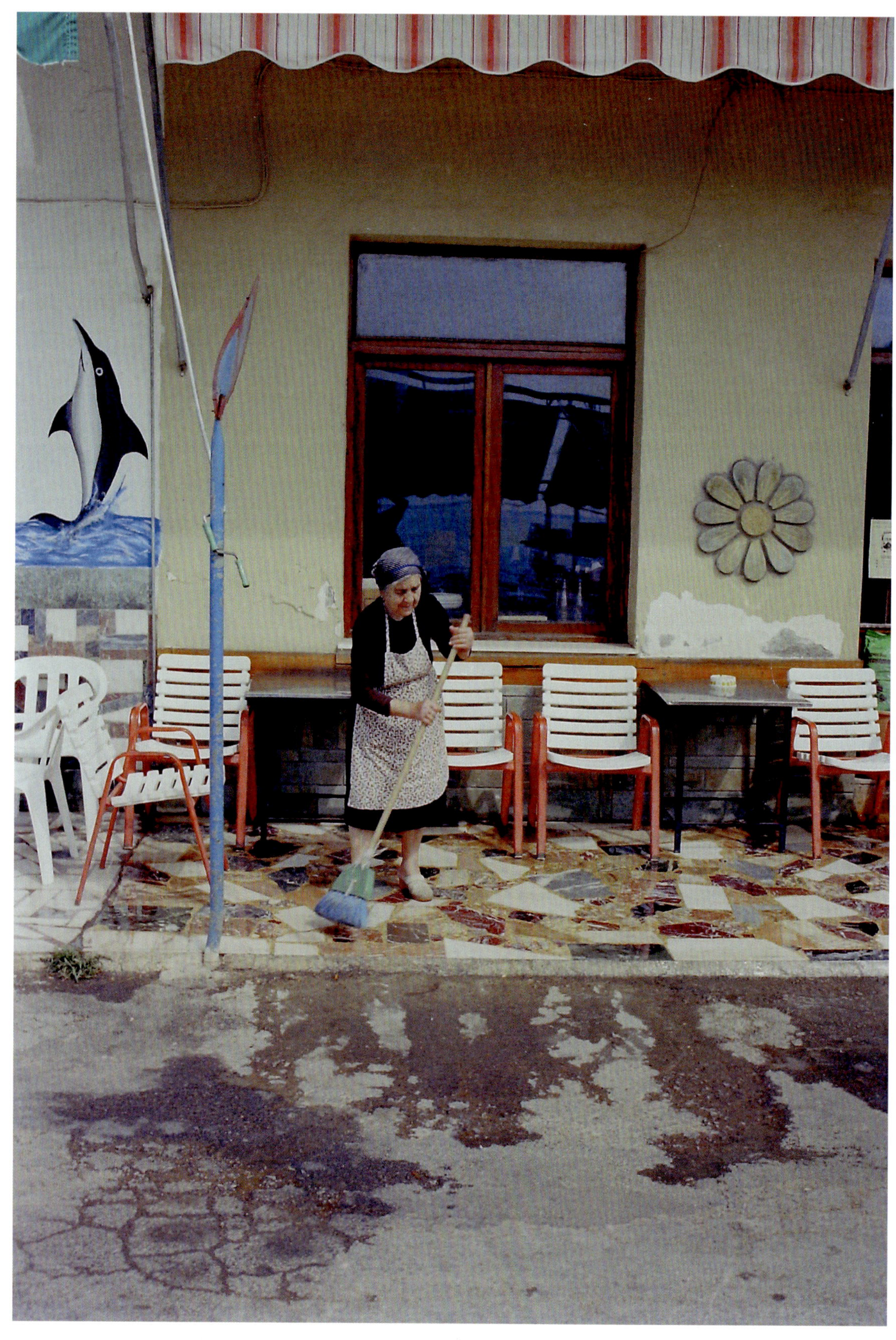

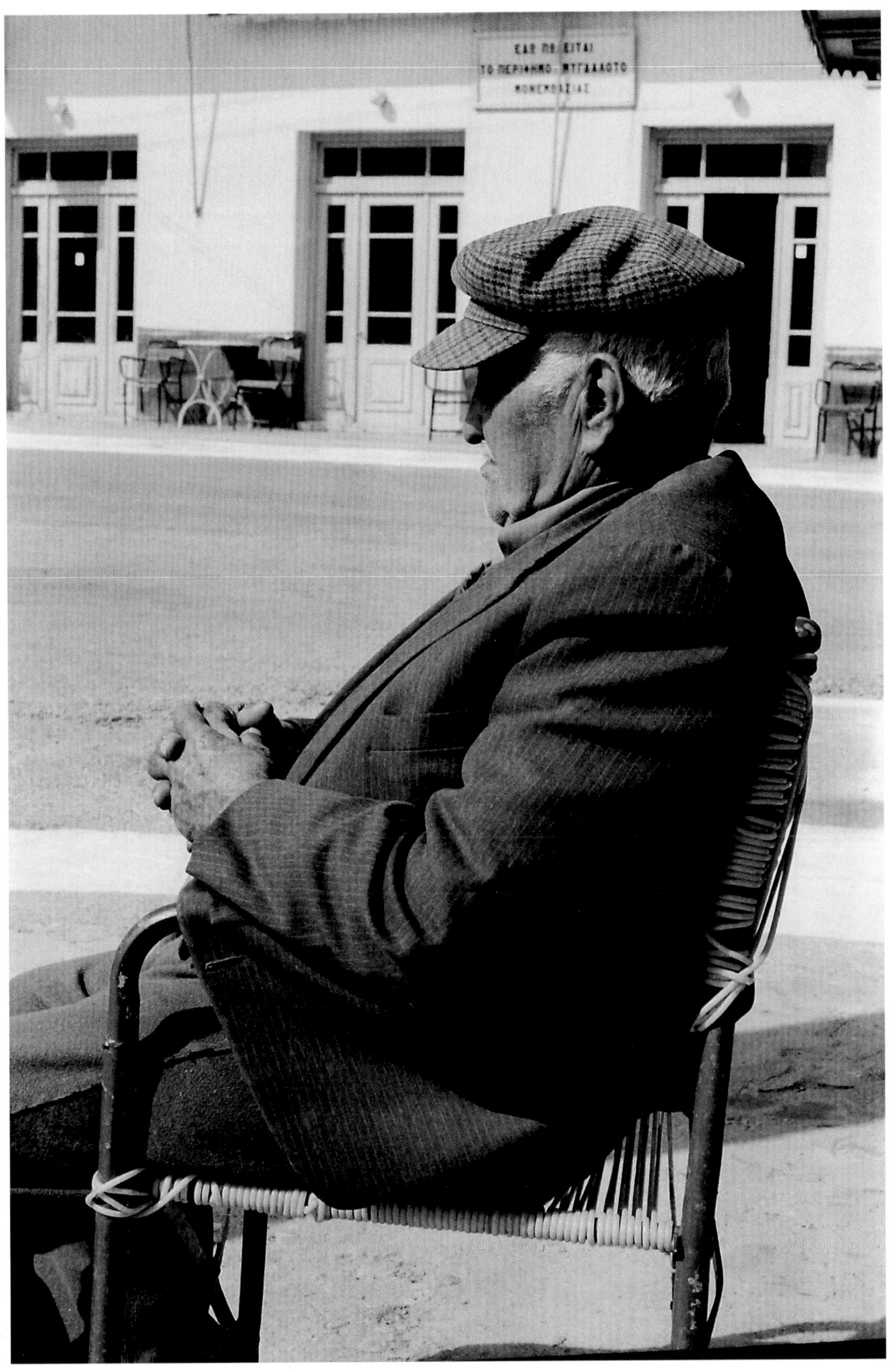

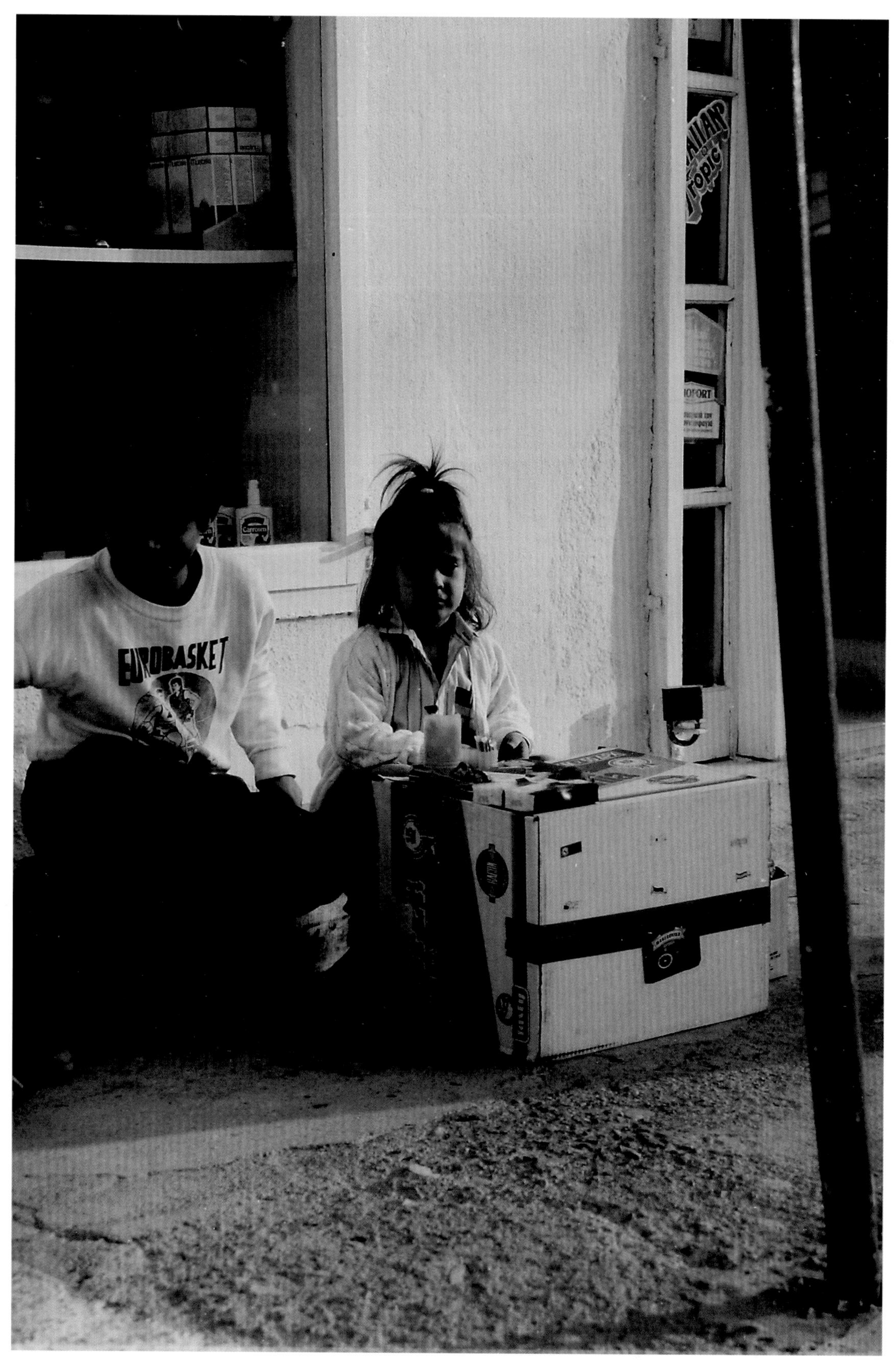
EUROBASKET
Tropic

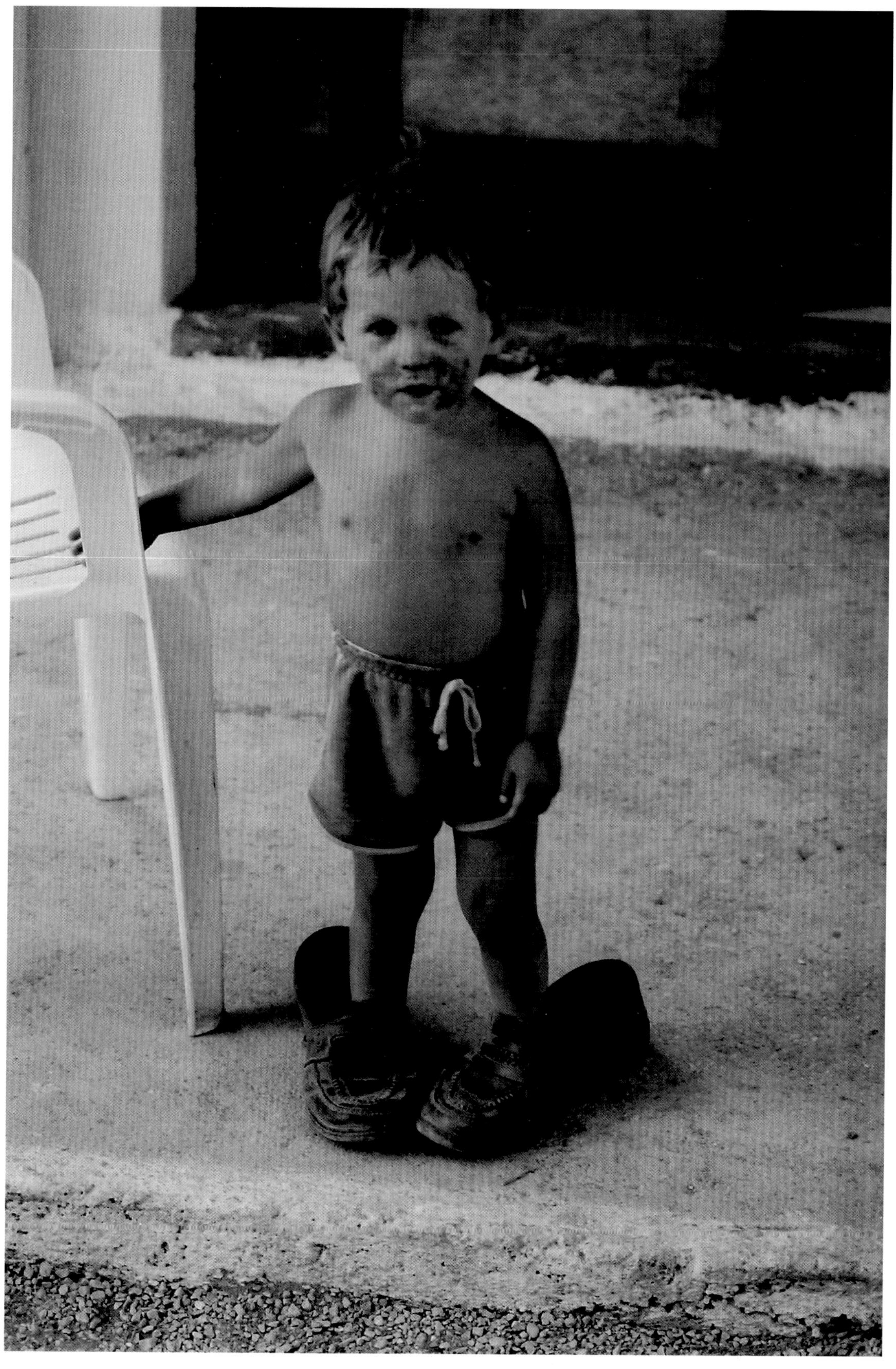

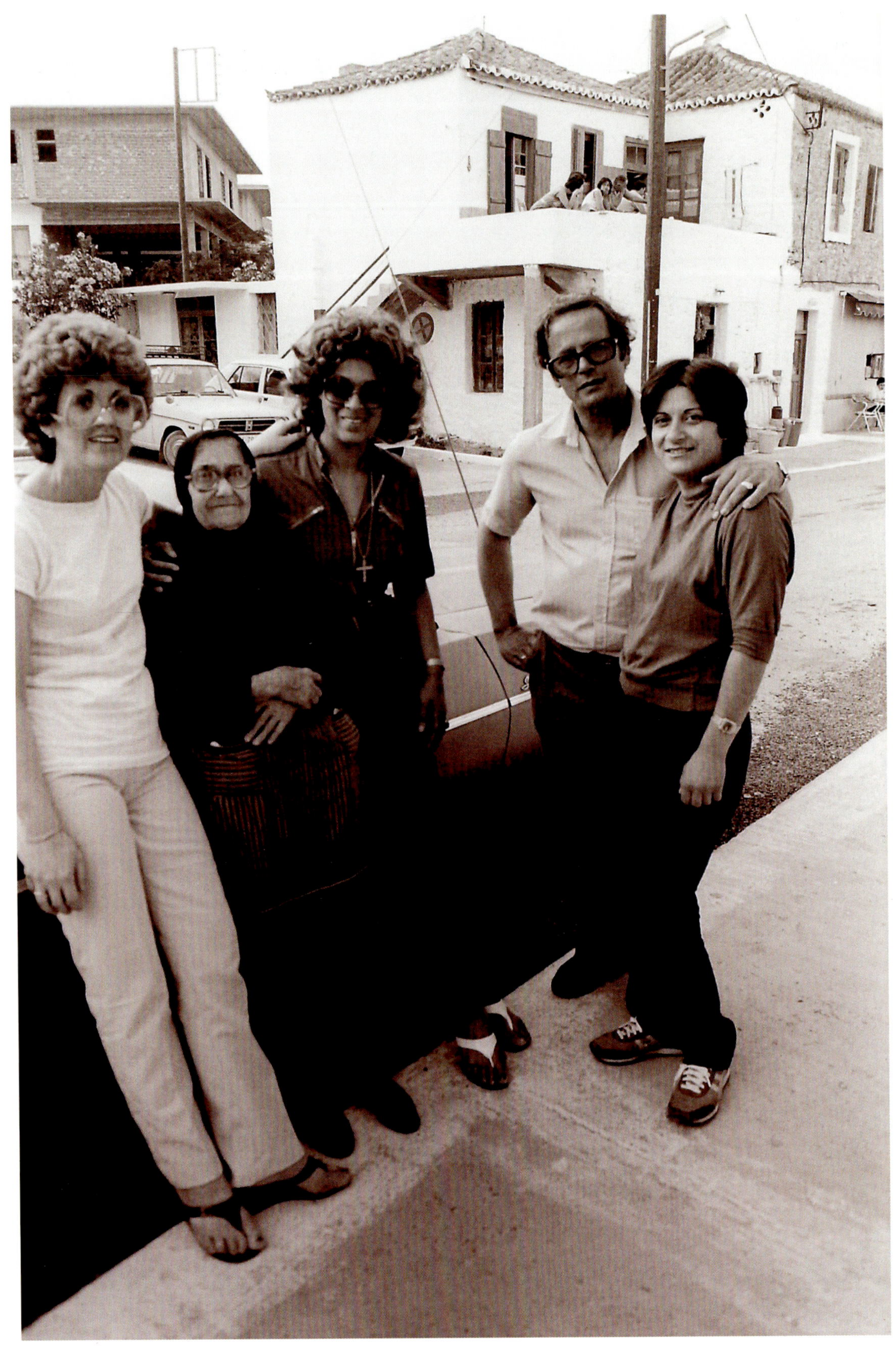

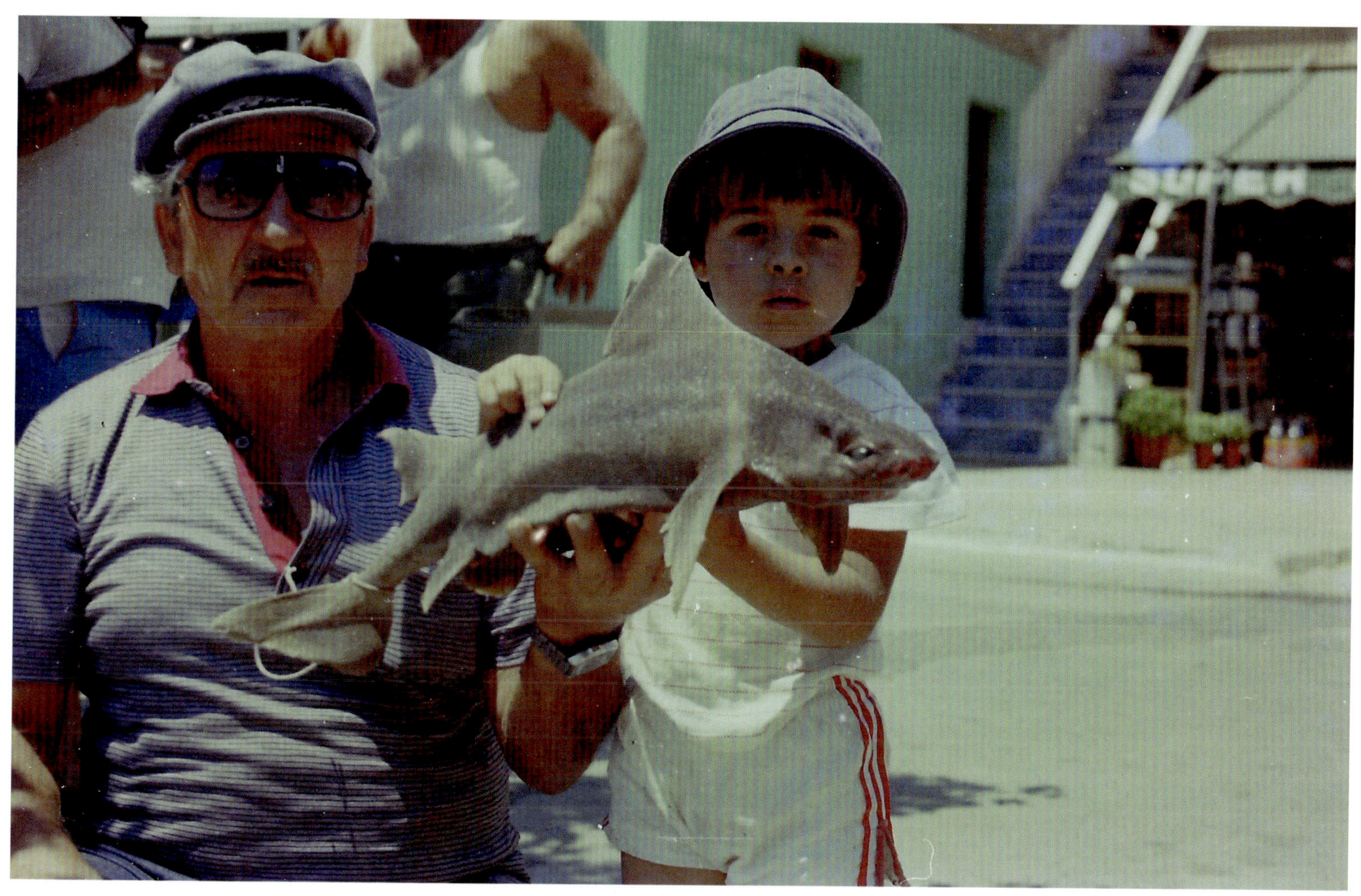

More and more, we were told, the population was moving across to the new settlement on the mainland where modern amenities such as drainage and electric light were promised.

STEVEN RUNCIMAN, *A TRAVELLER'S ALPHABET: PARTIAL MEMOIRS*, 1991

Villages

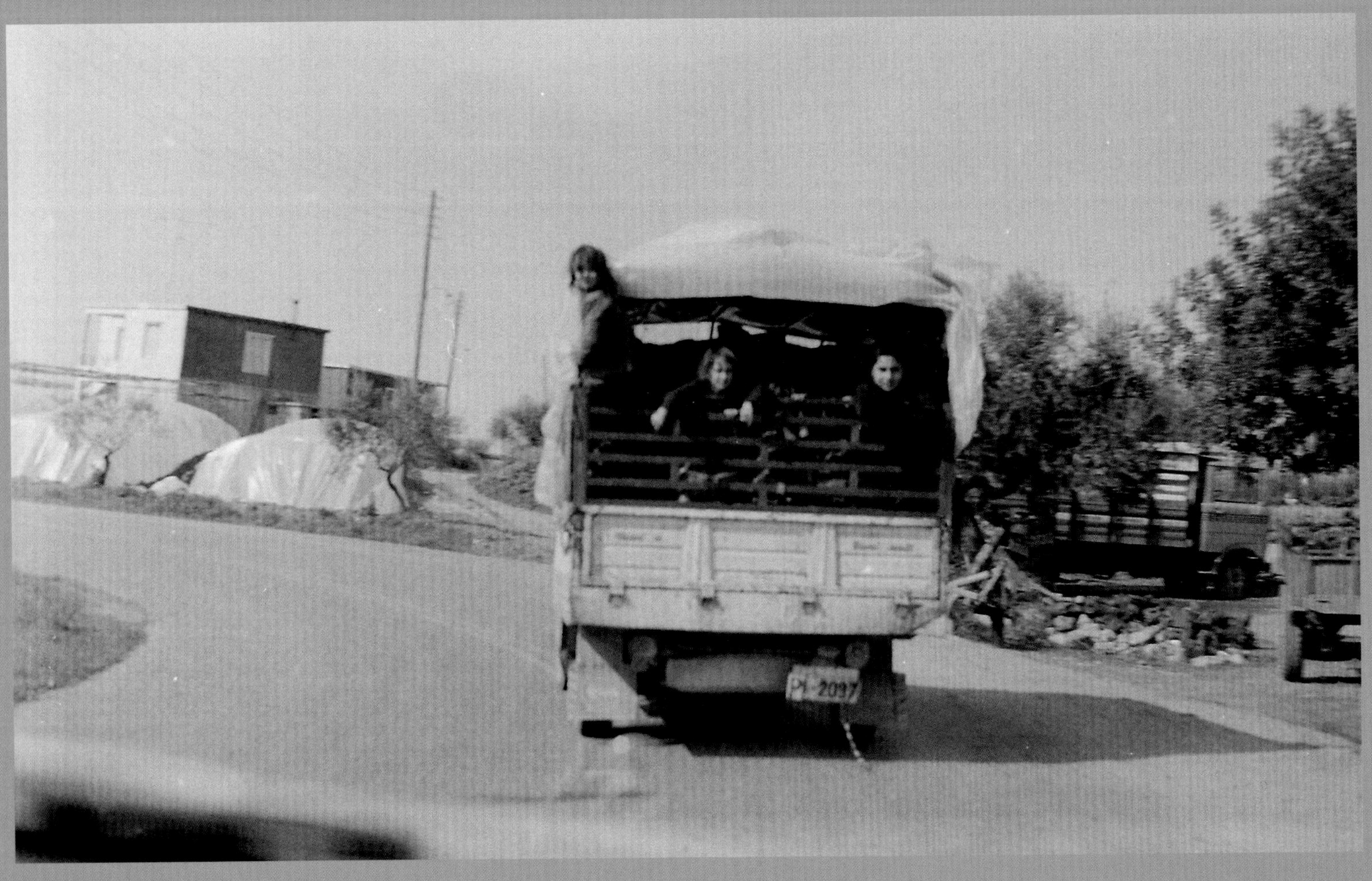

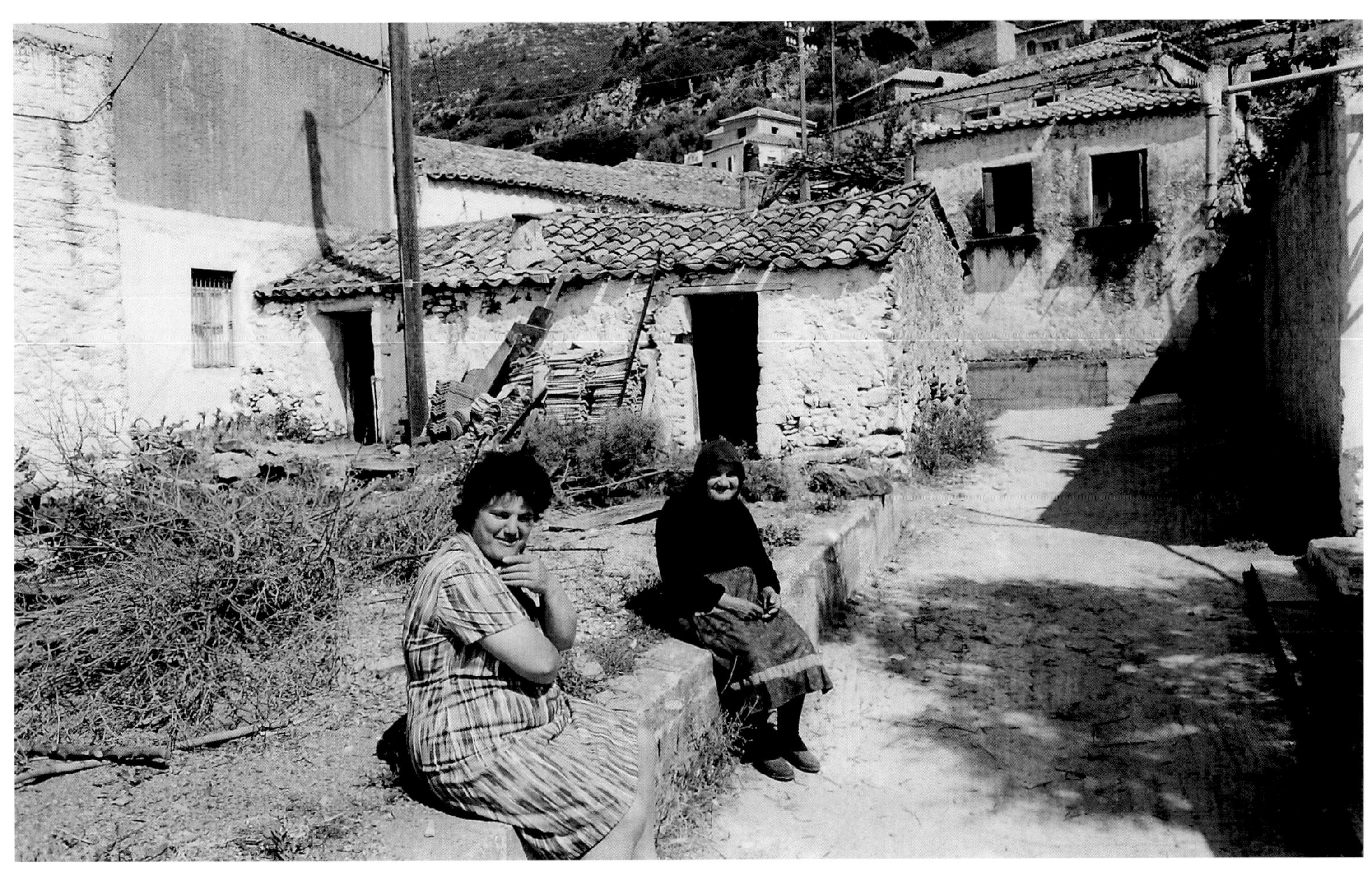

However, at the end of the 1980s there was a sudden small boom in new house construction and in renovation; private telephones were installed in nearly all houses, and televisions were acquired. All of this lightened, to some extent, the atmosphere of decline.

LAURIE KAIN HART, *TIME, RELIGION AND SOCIAL EXPERIENCE IN RURAL GREECE*, 1992

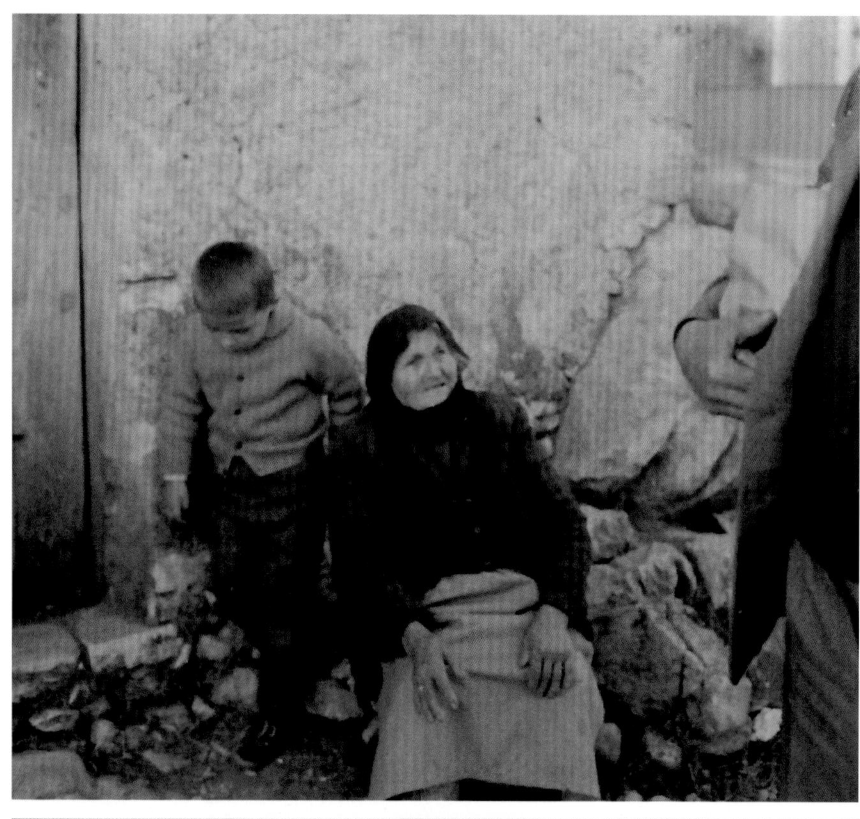

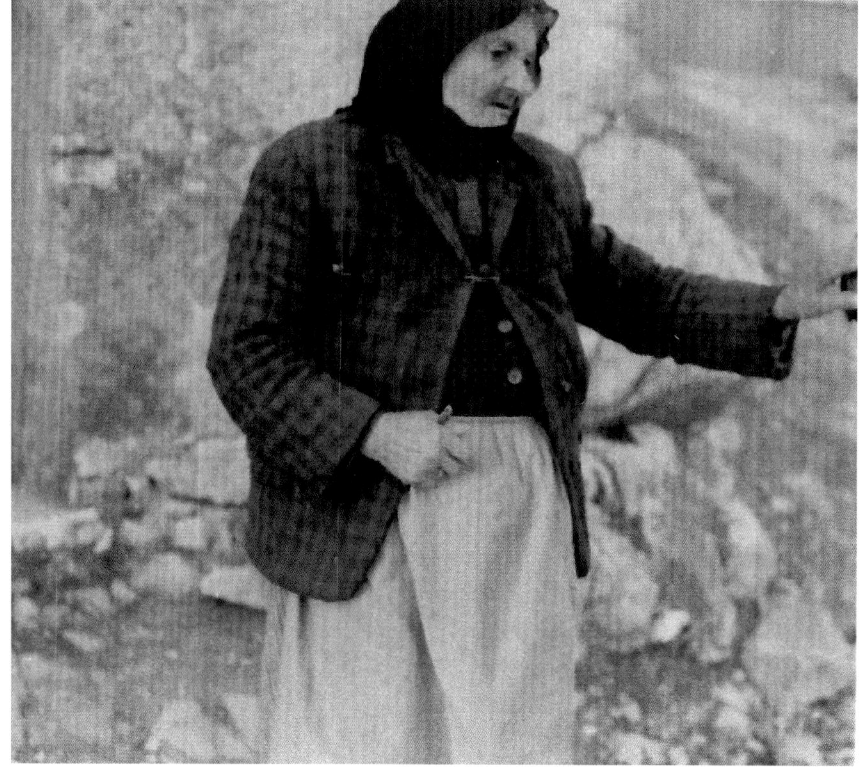

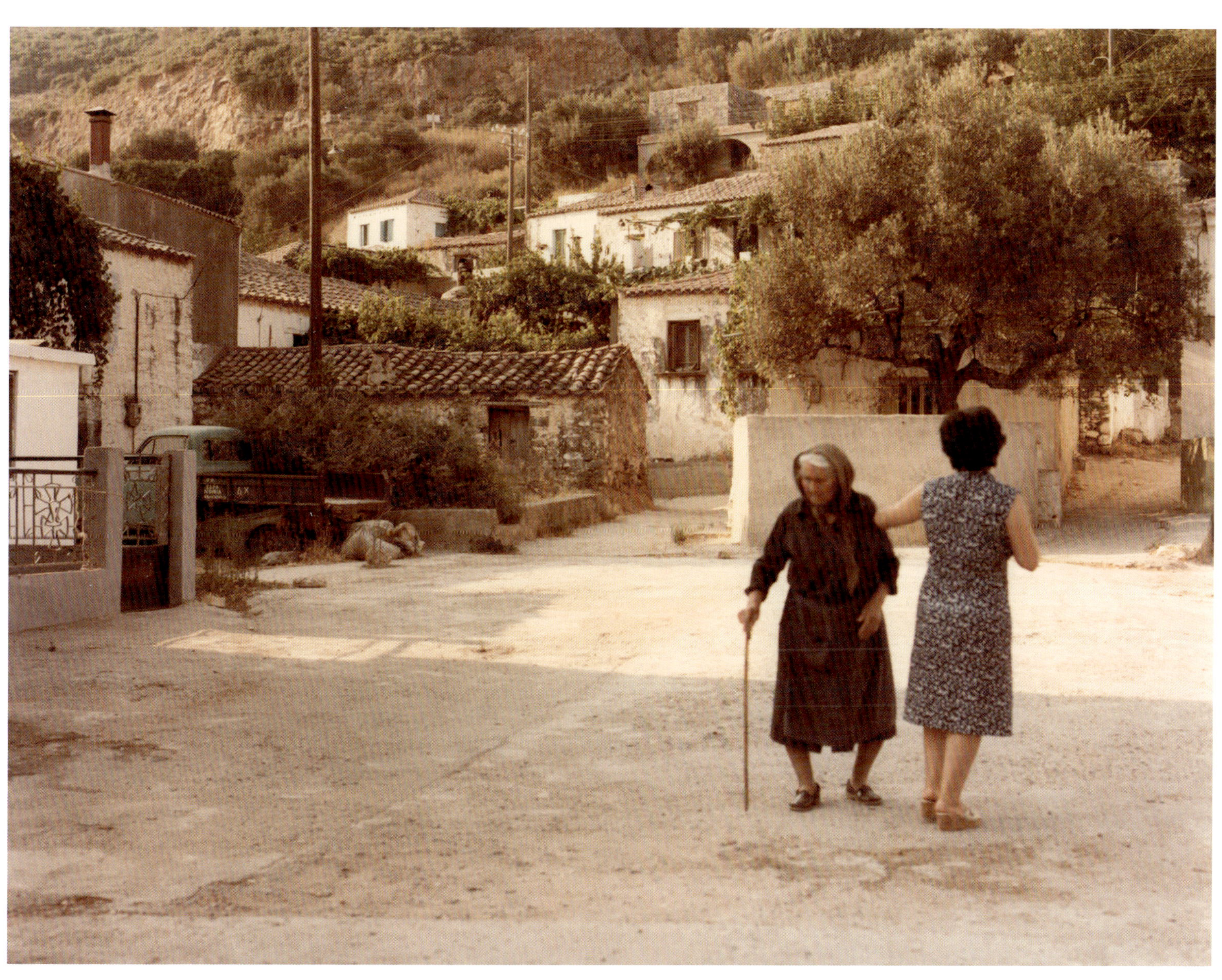

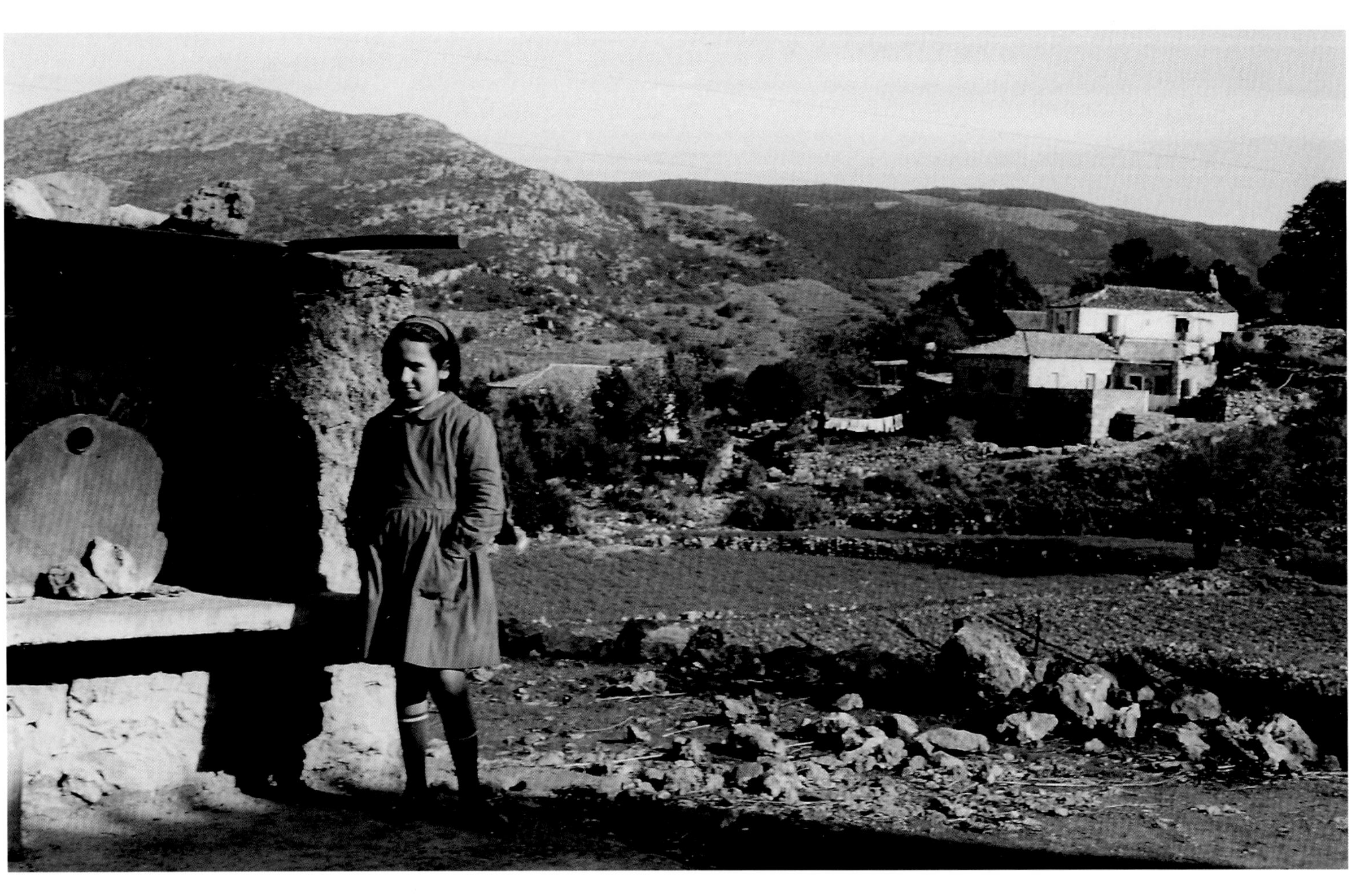

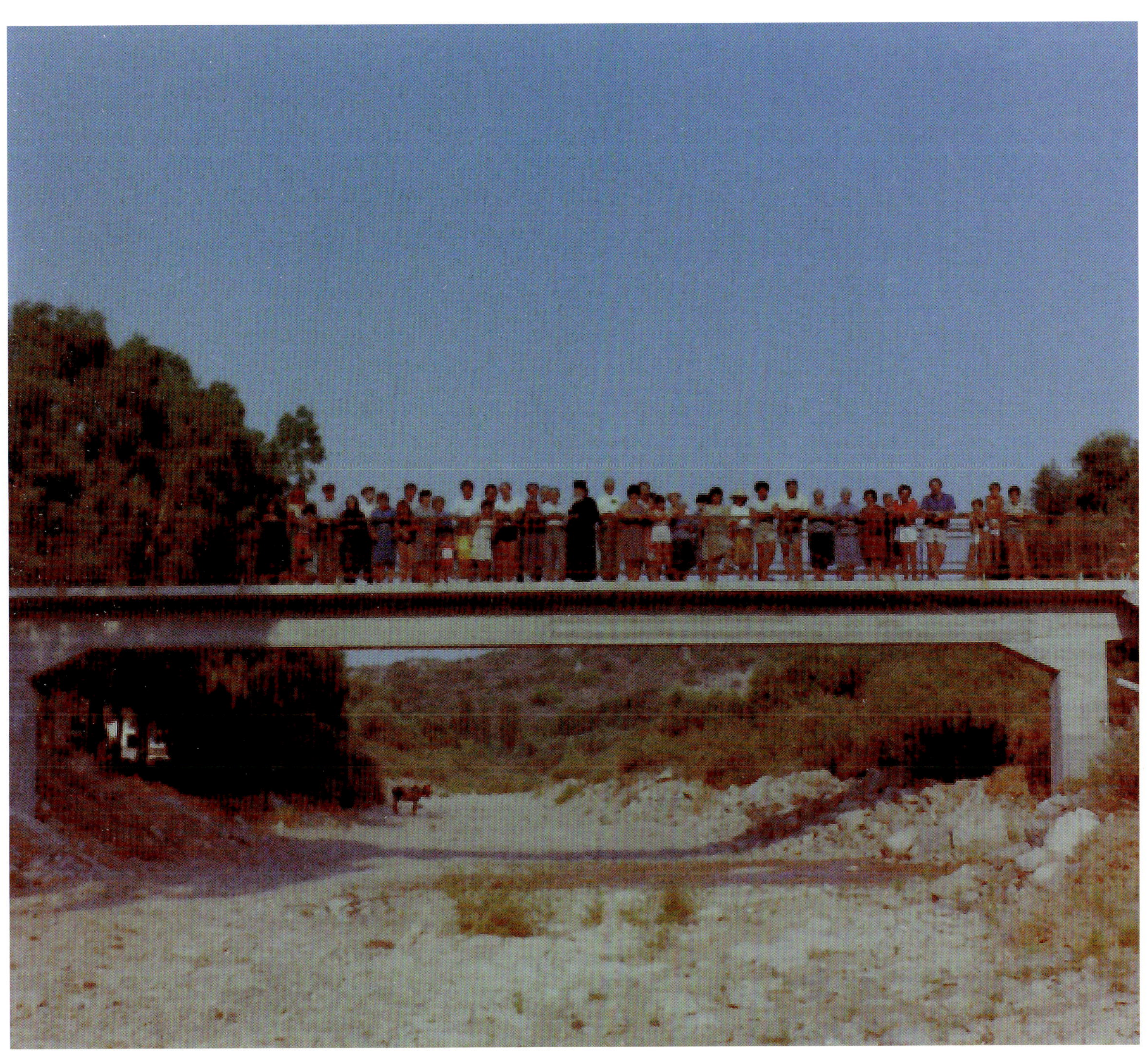

Shops and Offices

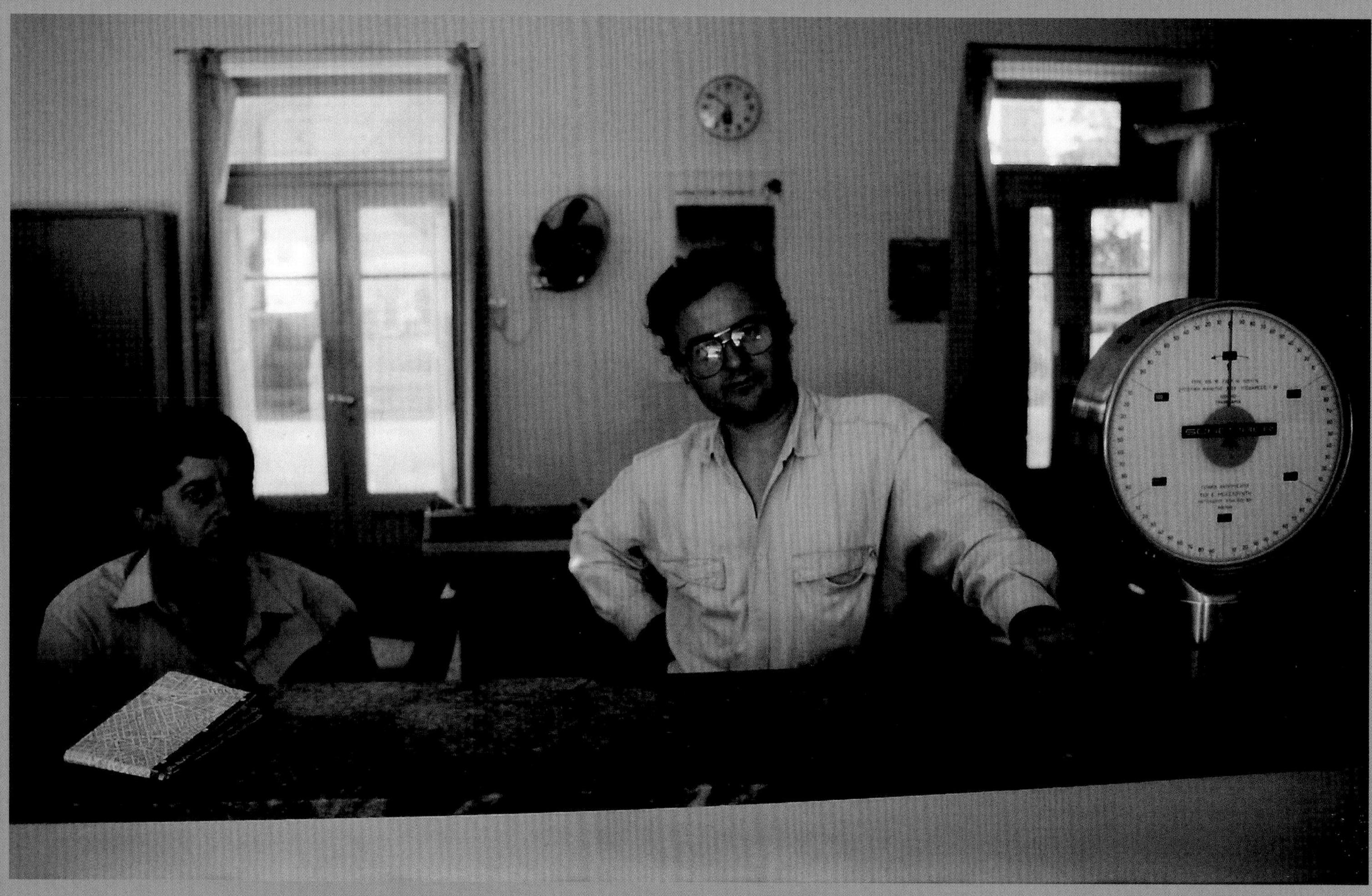

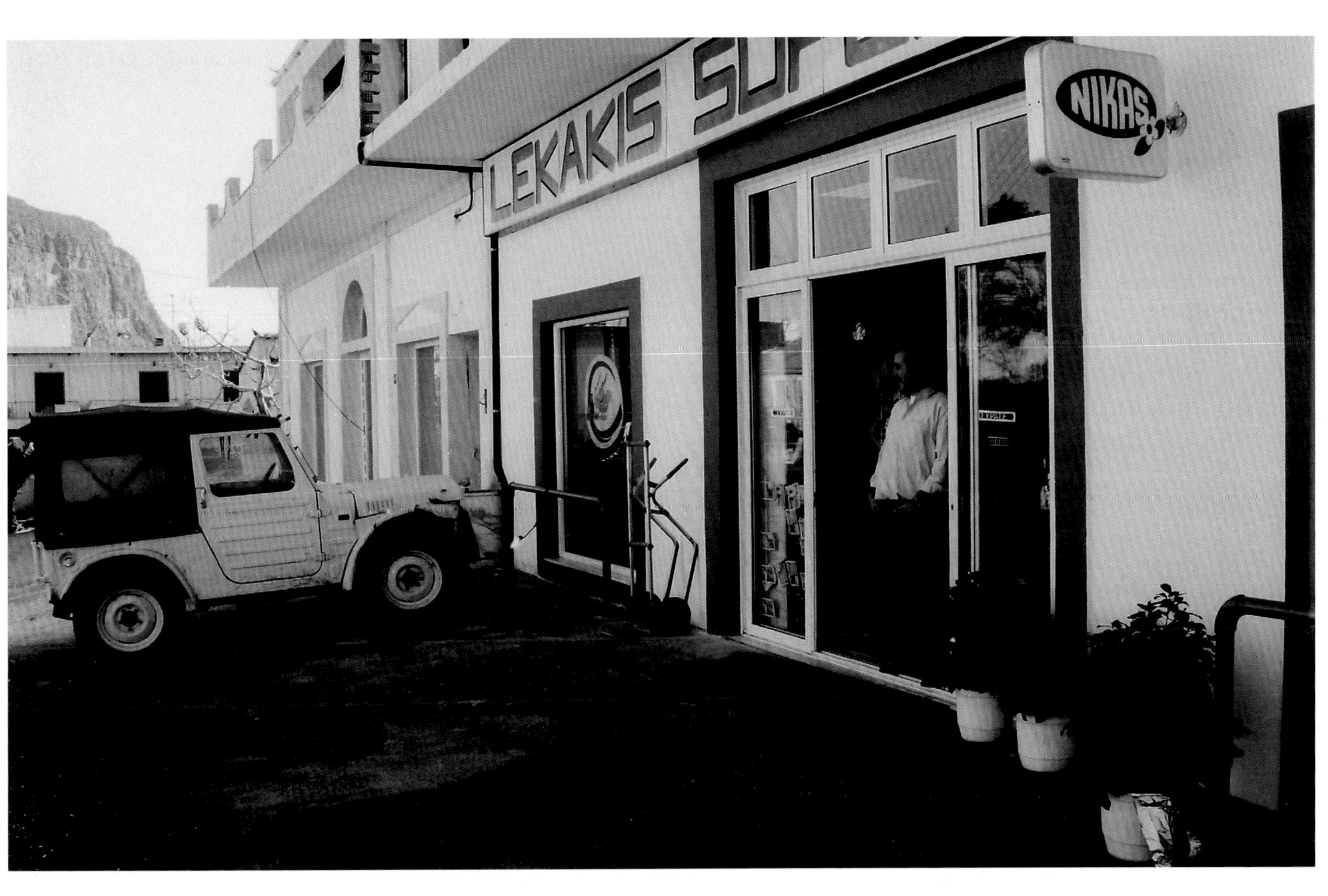
LEKAKIS SUP
NIKAS

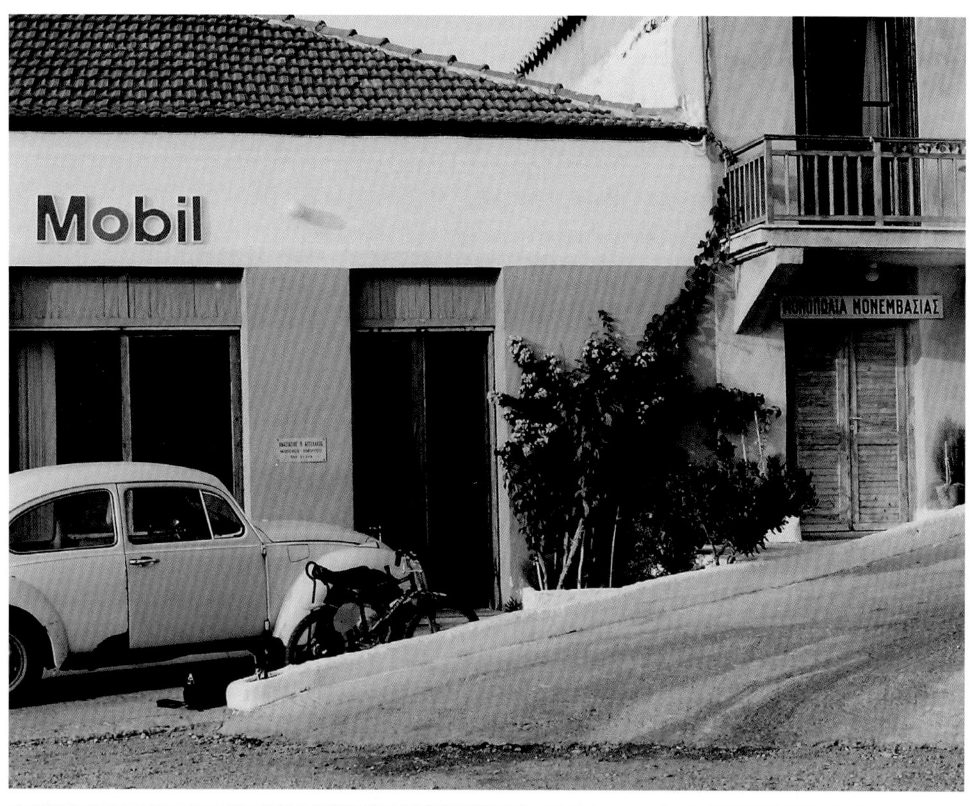
Mobil
ΜΟΝΟΠΩΛΙΑ ΜΟΝΕΜΒΑΣΙΑΣ

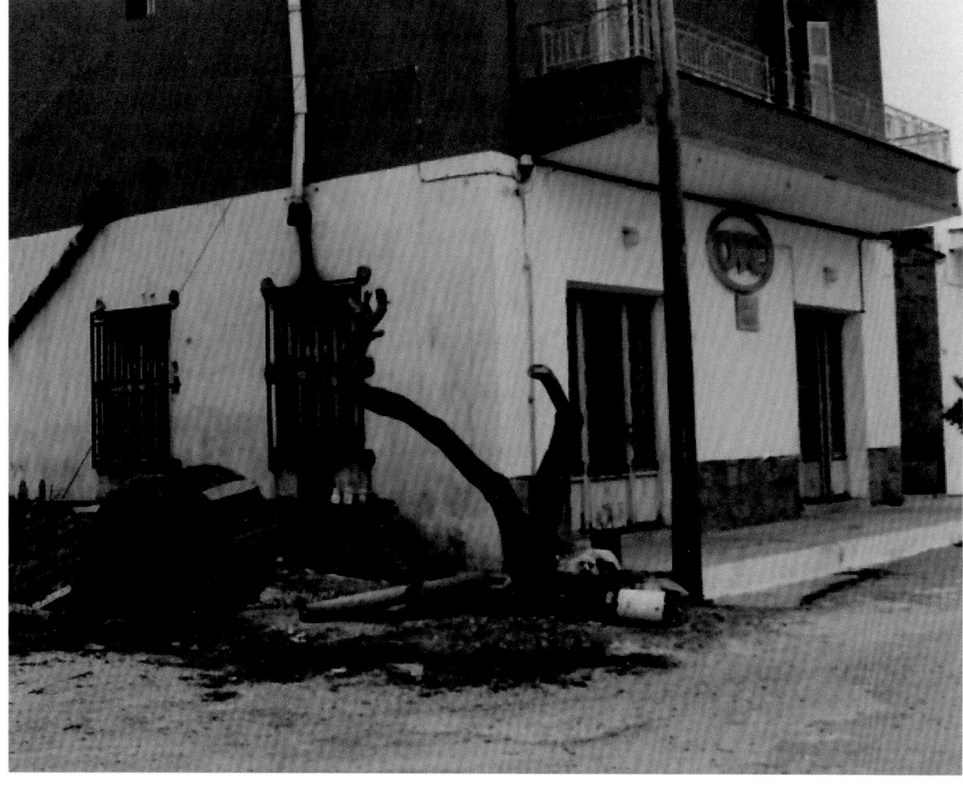

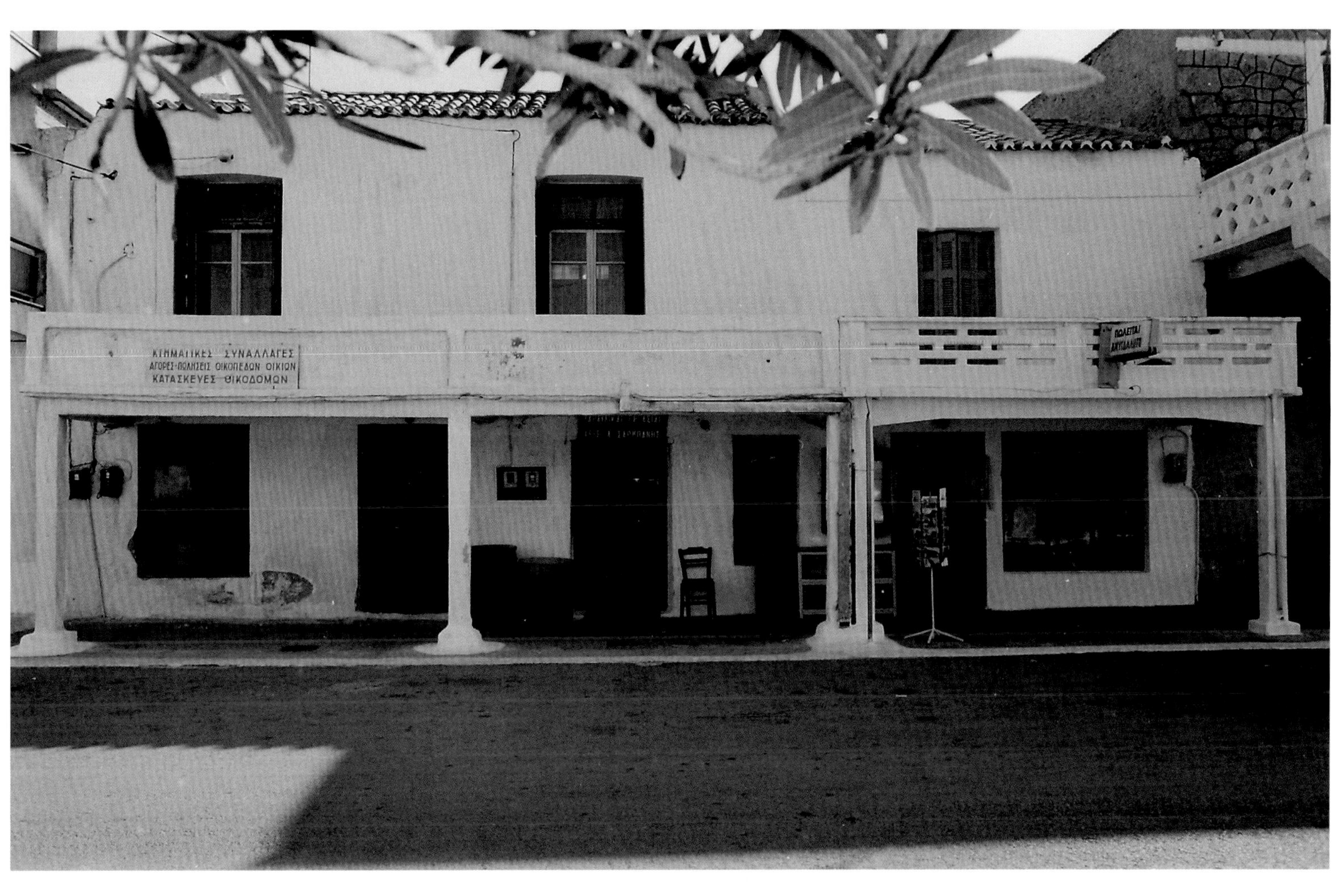
ΚΤΗΜΑΤΙΚΕΣ ΣΥΝΑΛΛΑΓΕΣ
ΑΓΟΡΕΣ-ΠΩΛΗΣΕΙΣ ΟΙΚΟΠΕΔΩΝ ΟΙΚΙΩΝ
ΚΑΤΑΣΚΕΥΕΣ ΟΙΚΟΔΟΜΩΝ
ΠΩΛΕΙΤΑΙ

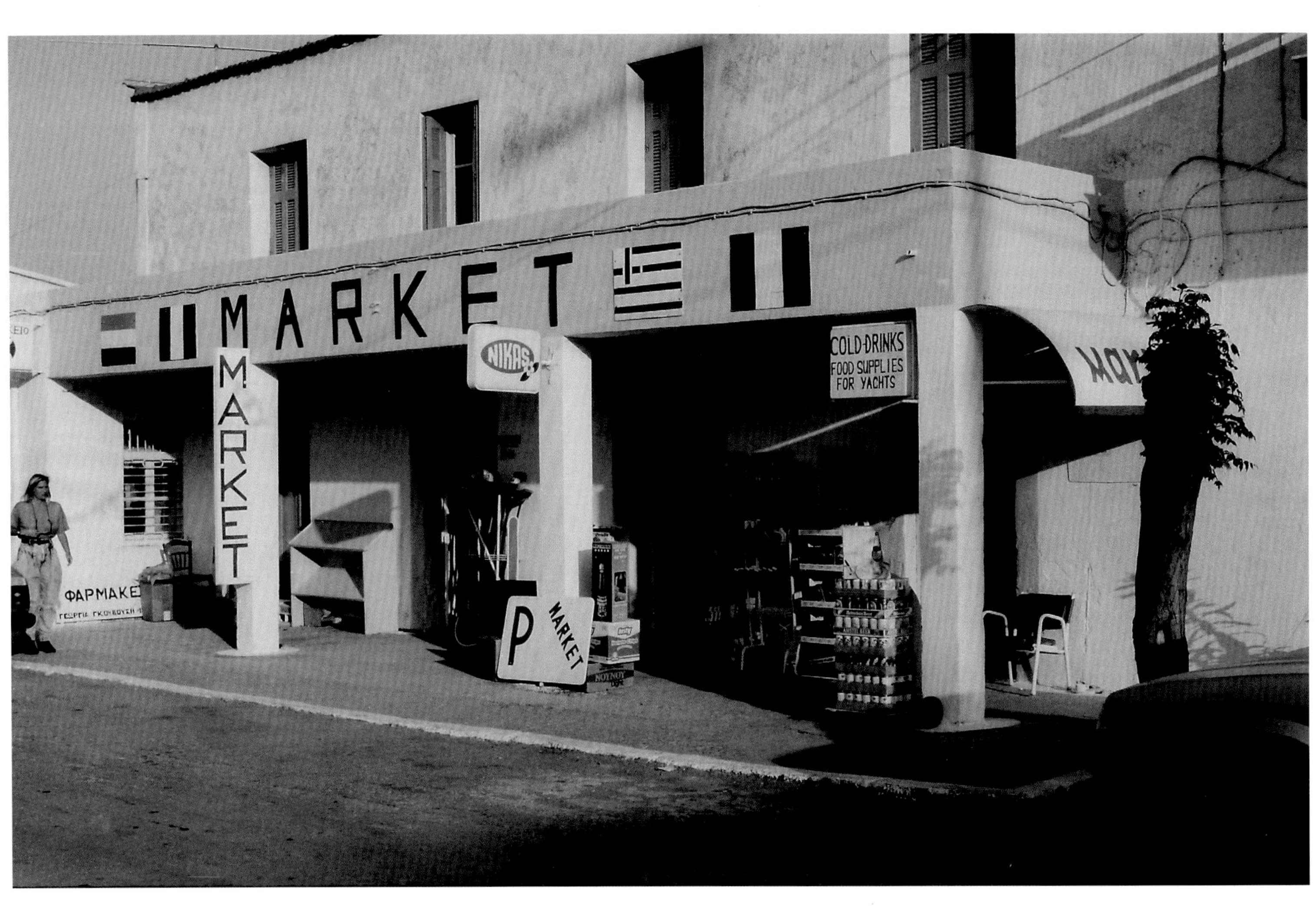
MARKET
MARKET
NIKAS
COLD DRINKS
FOOD SUPPLIES
FOR YACHTS
ΦΑΡΜΑΚΕ
P
MARKET

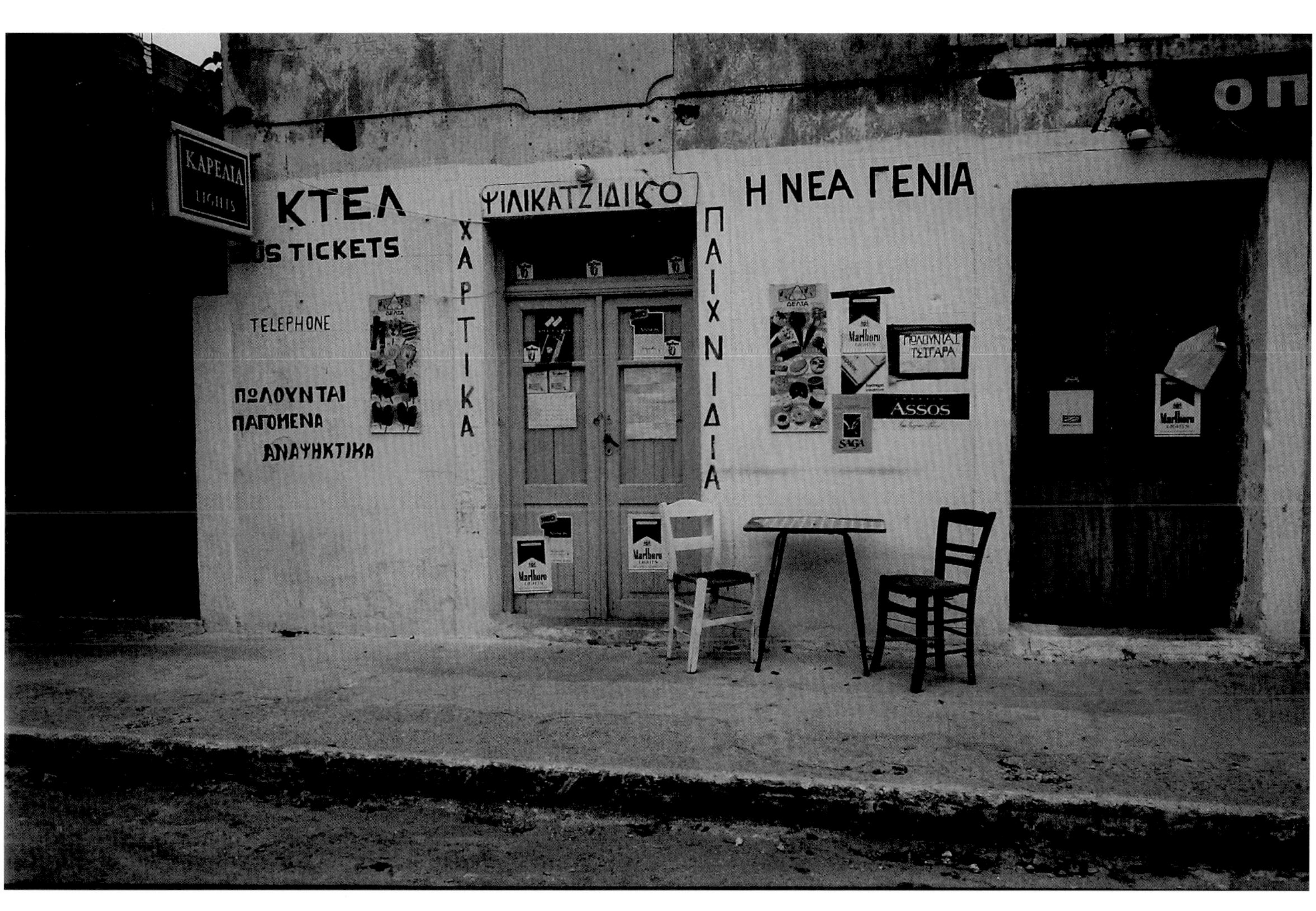
ΚΑΡΕΛΙΑ
LIGHTS
ΚΤΕΛ
TICKETS
ΨΙΛΙΚΑΤΖΙΔΙΚΟ
Η ΝΕΑ ΓΕΝΙΑ
ΧΑΡΤΙΚΑ
ΠΑΙΧΝΙΔΙΑ
TELEPHONE
ΠΩΛΟΥΝΤΑΙ
ΠΑΓΟΜΕΝΑ
ΑΝΑΨΗΚΤΙΚΑ
ΠΩΛΟΥΝΤΑΙ
ΤΣΙΓΑΡΑ
Marlboro
ASSOS
SAGA

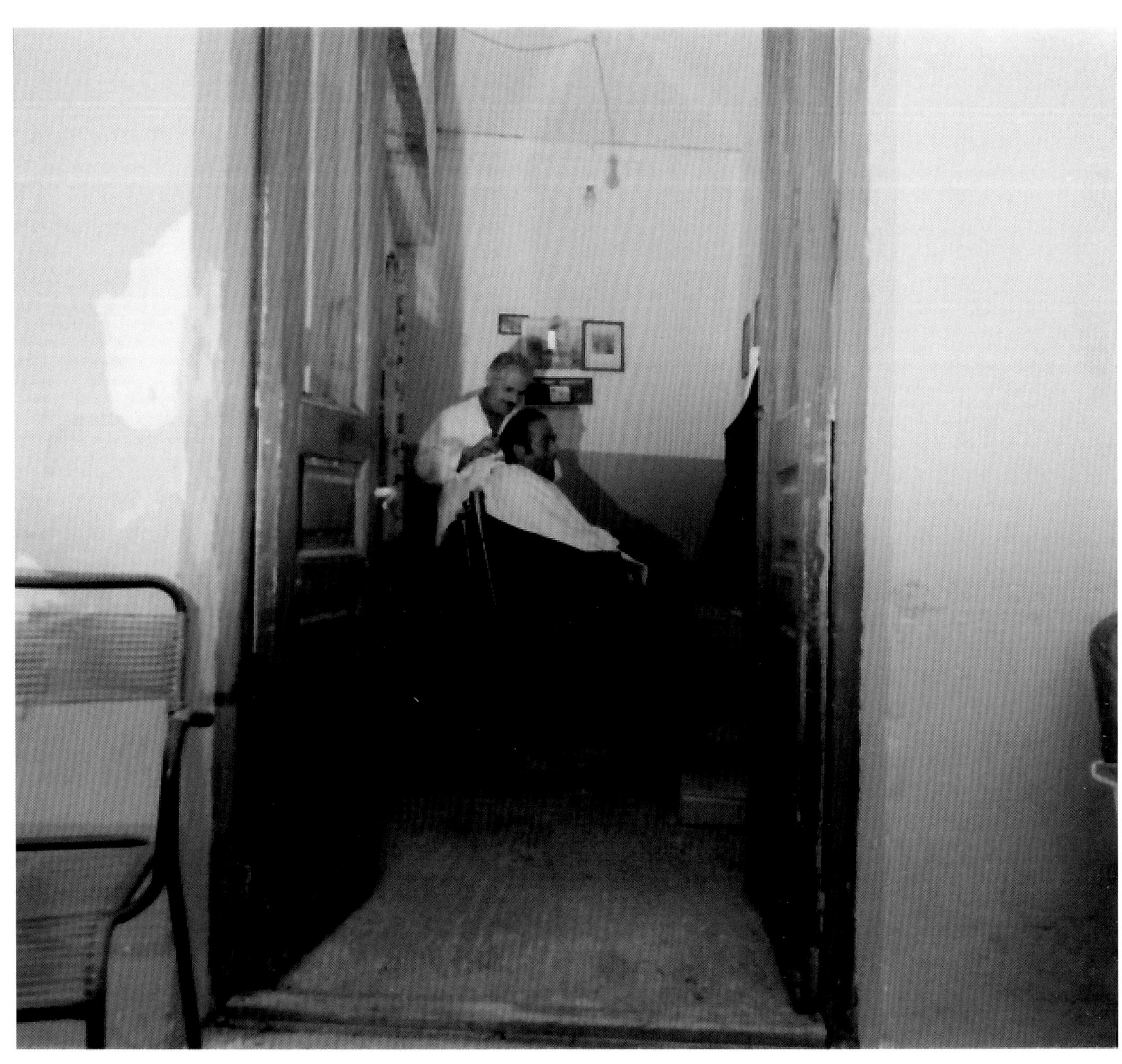

Like the worker who comes out of the neighbourhood barbershop
Freshly shaven at a weekend,
This is peace.

YANNIS RITSOS, 'PEACE', 1953

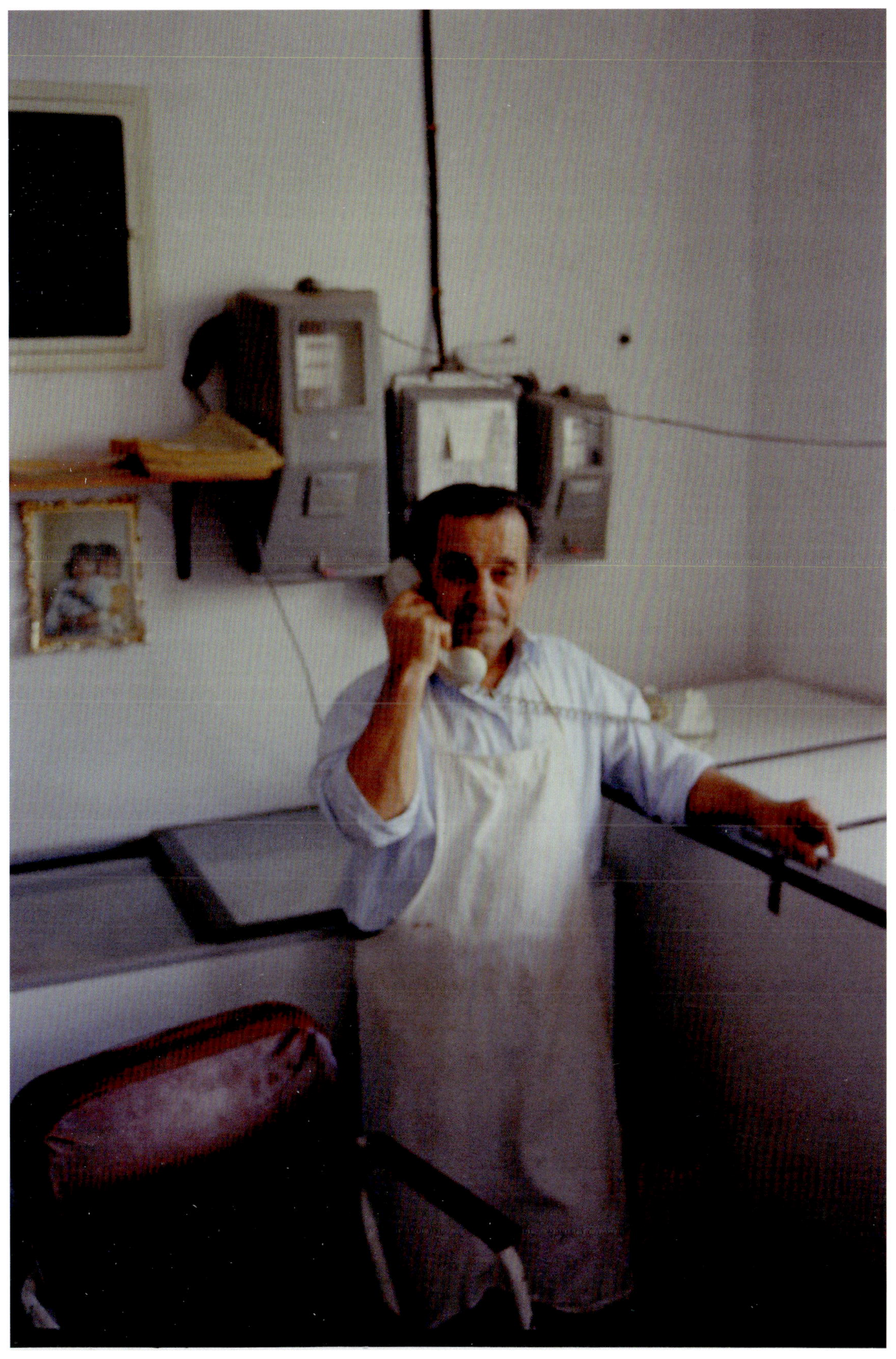

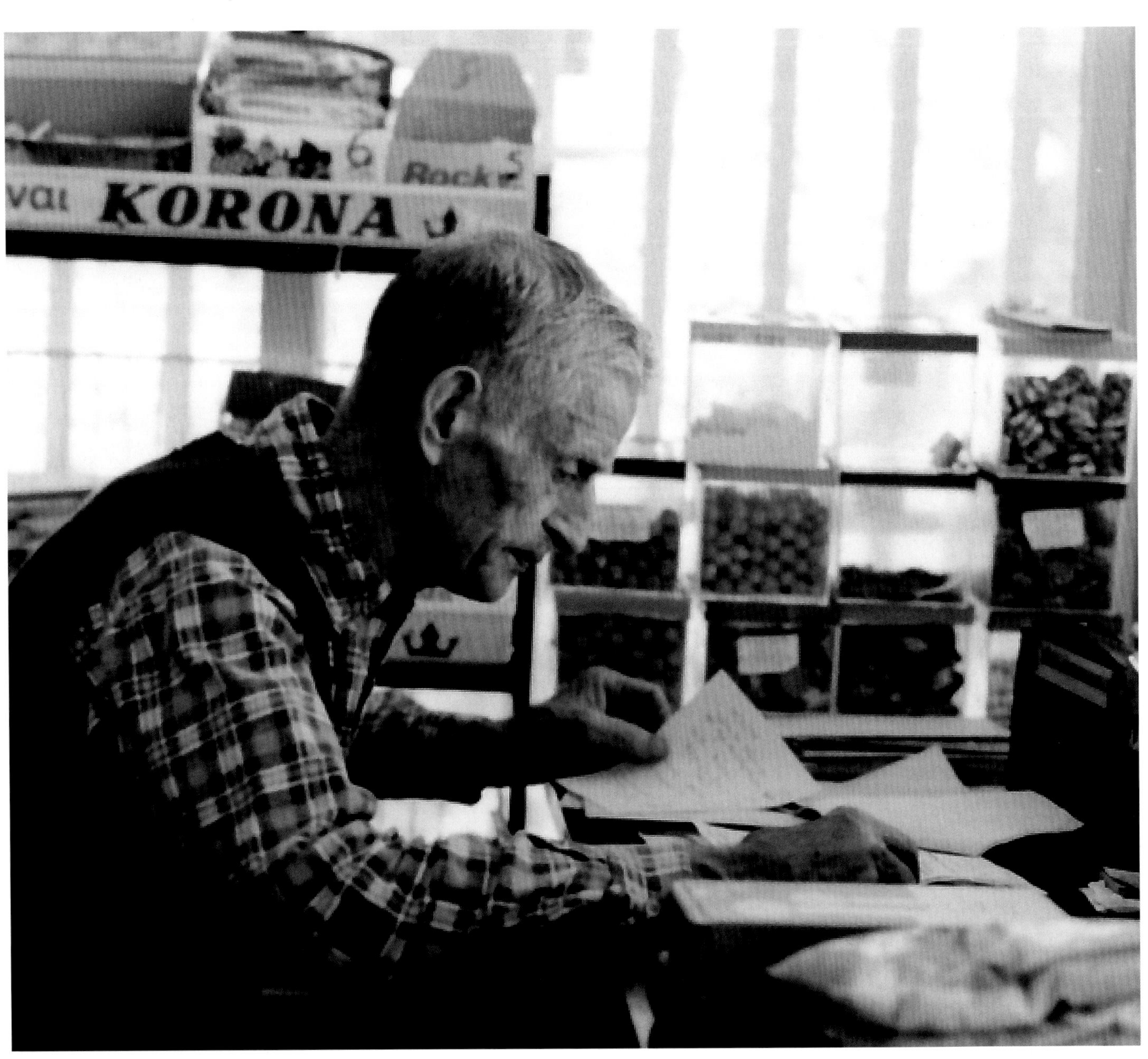
KORONA

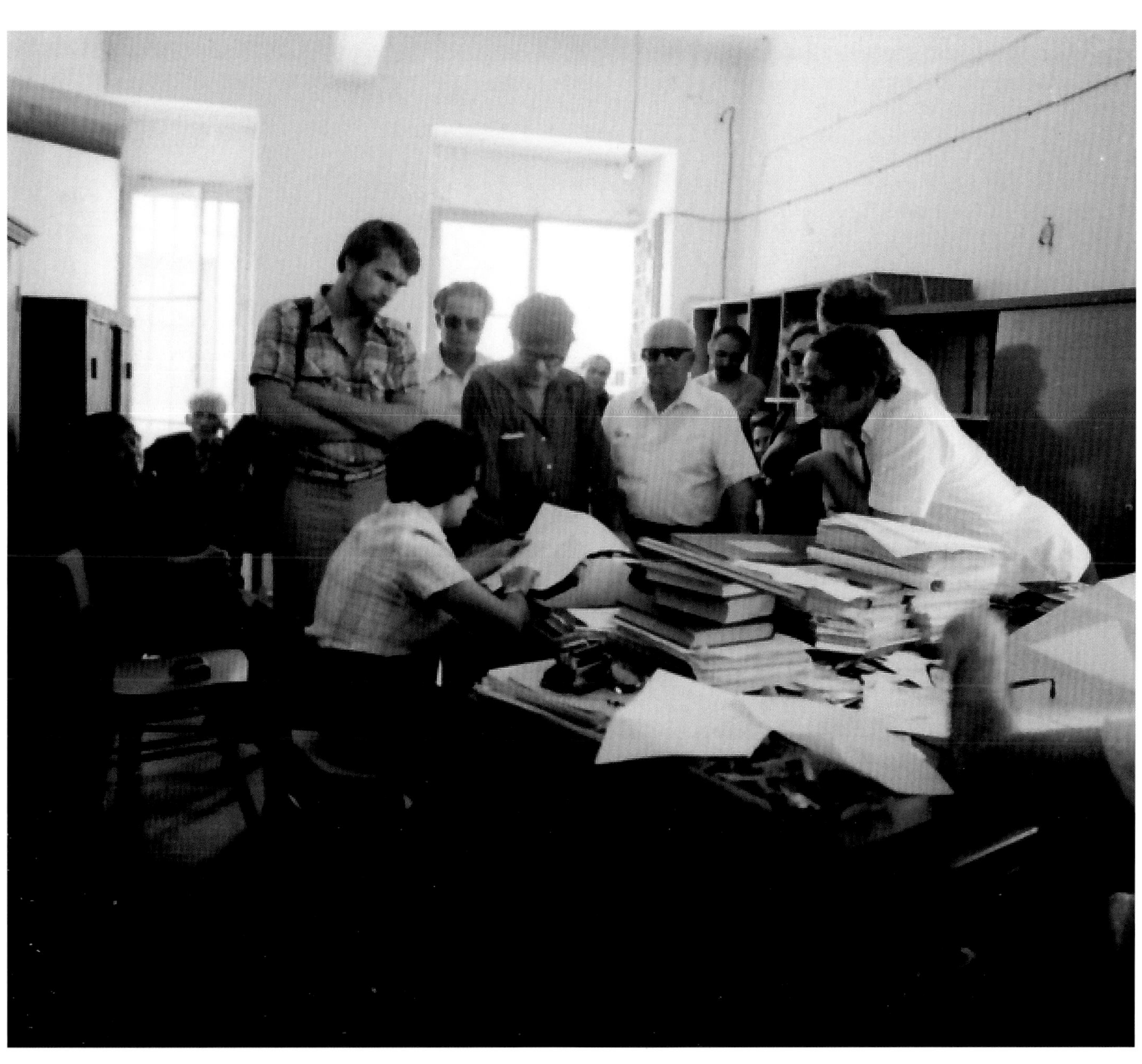

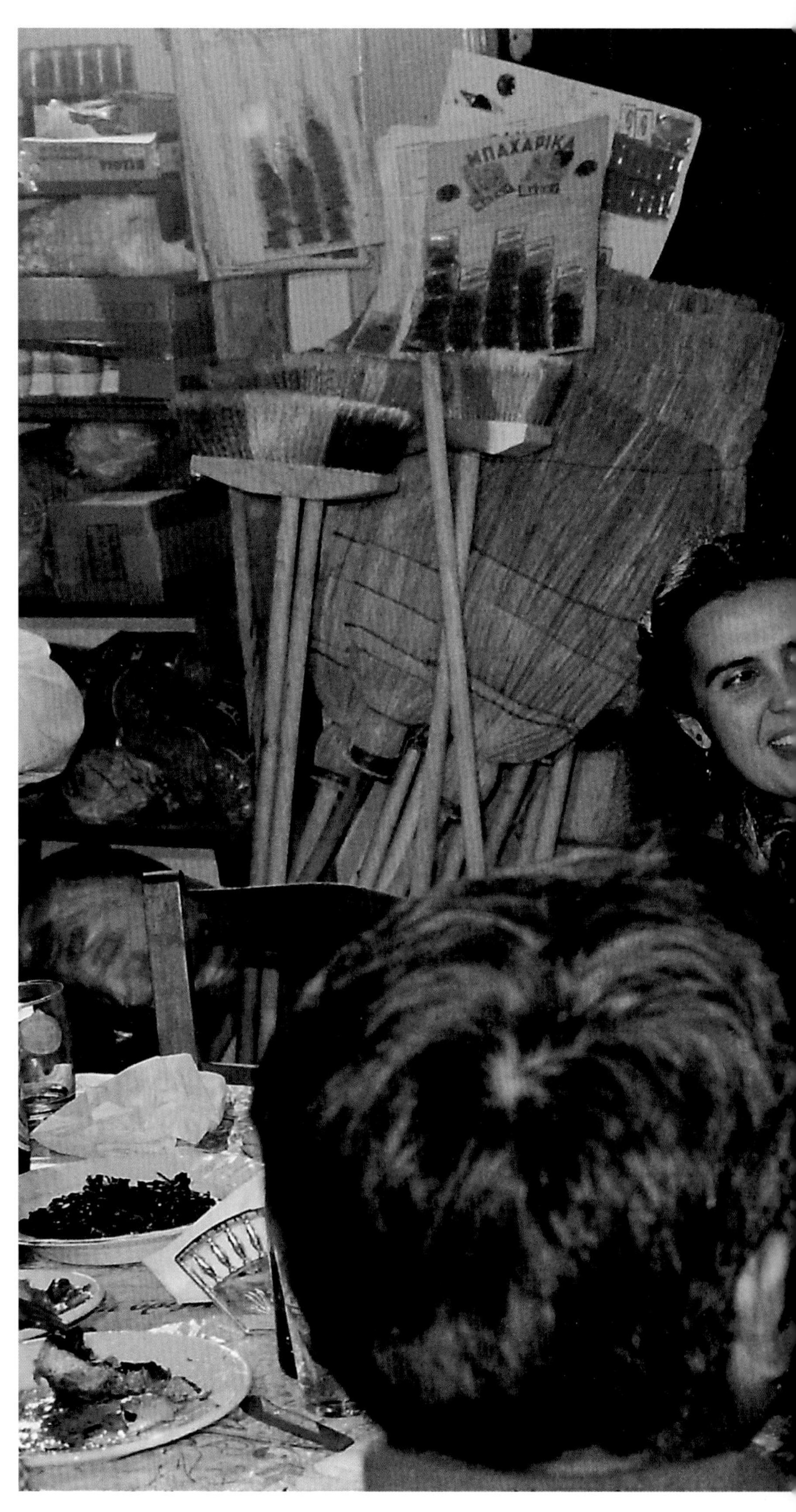

For the majority of Greeks,
life was becoming more
comfortable than it had ever been.

RODERICK BEATON, *GREECE:*
BIOGRAPHY OF A MODERN NATION, 2019

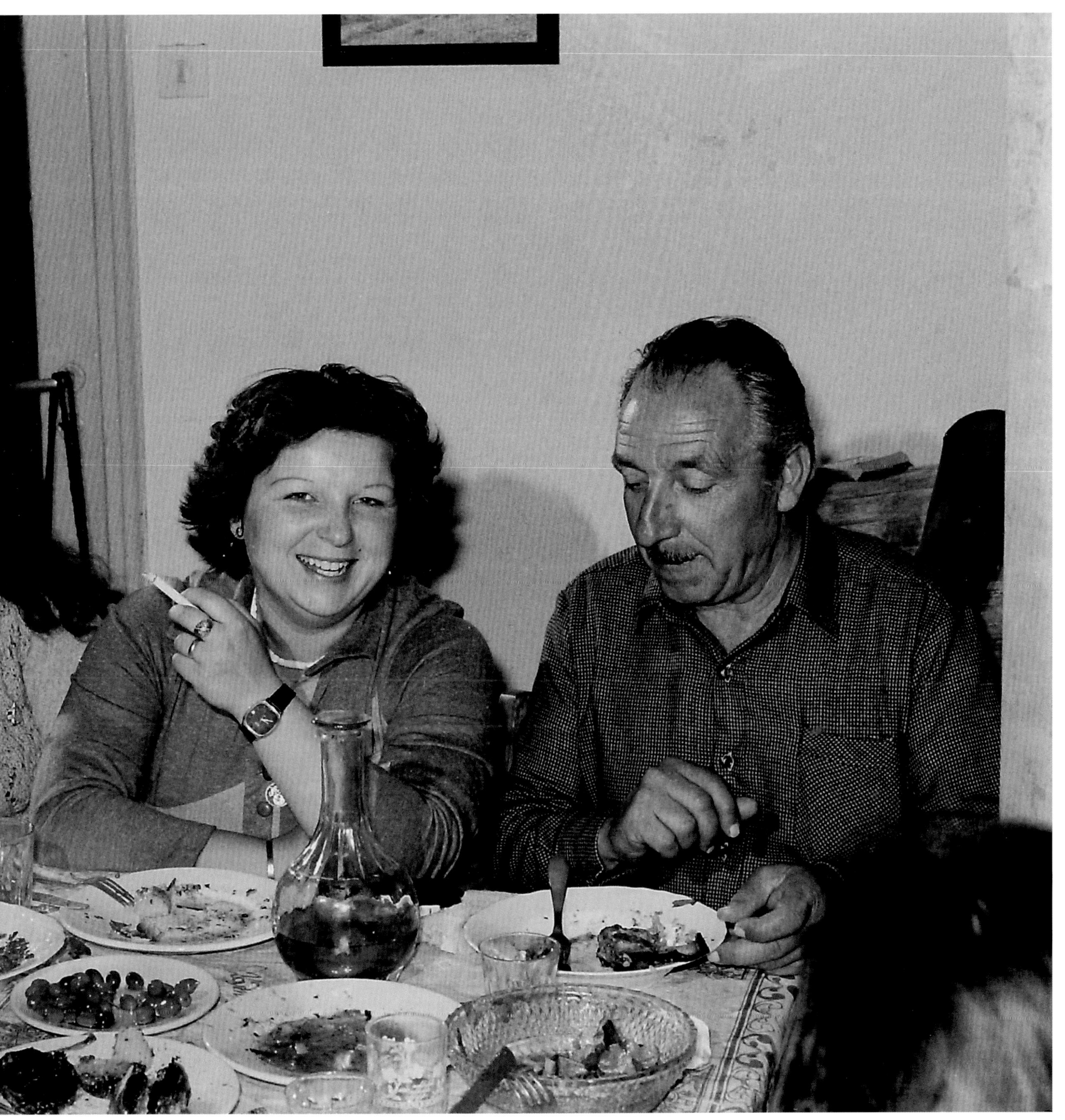

Fishing

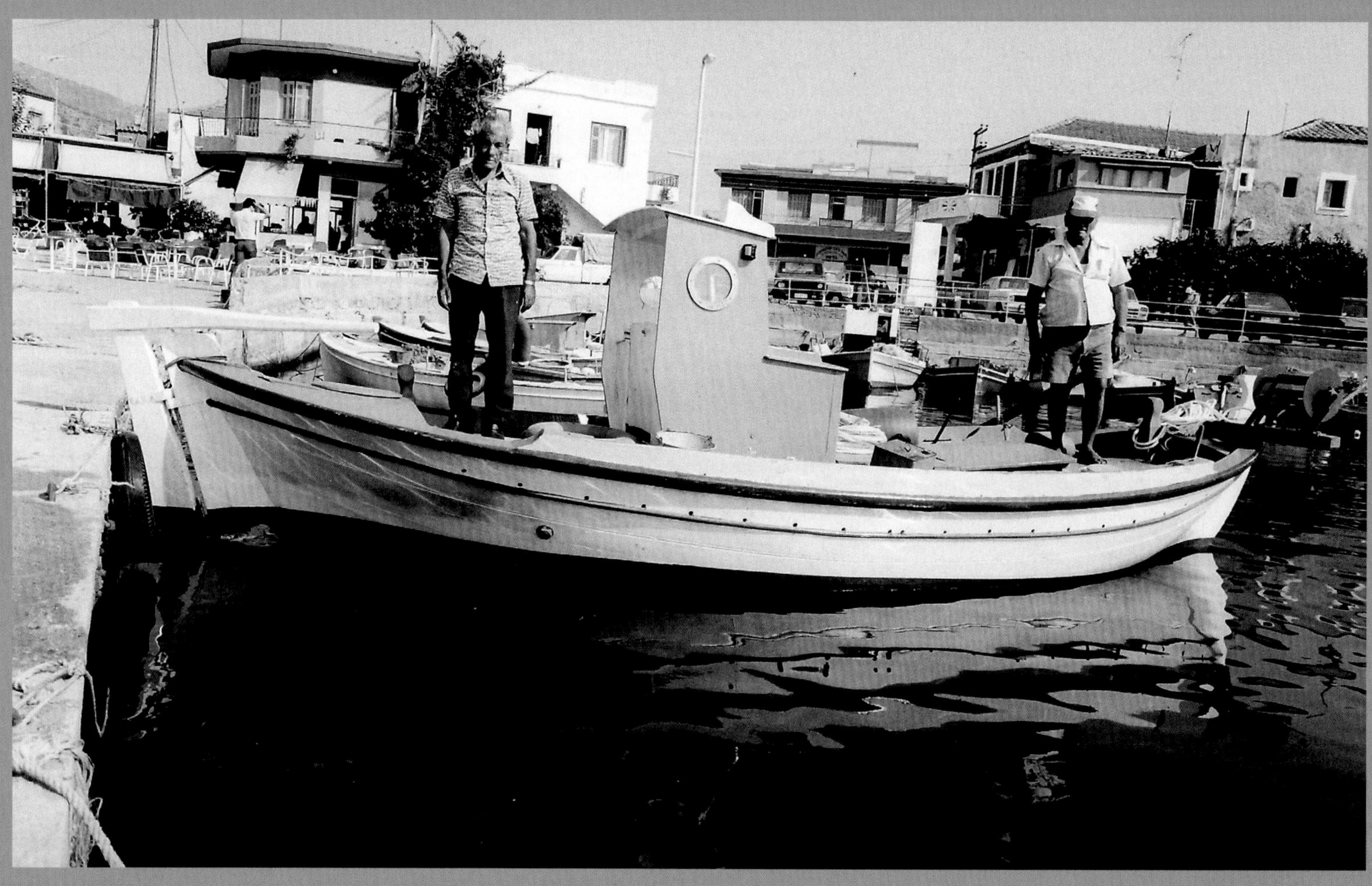

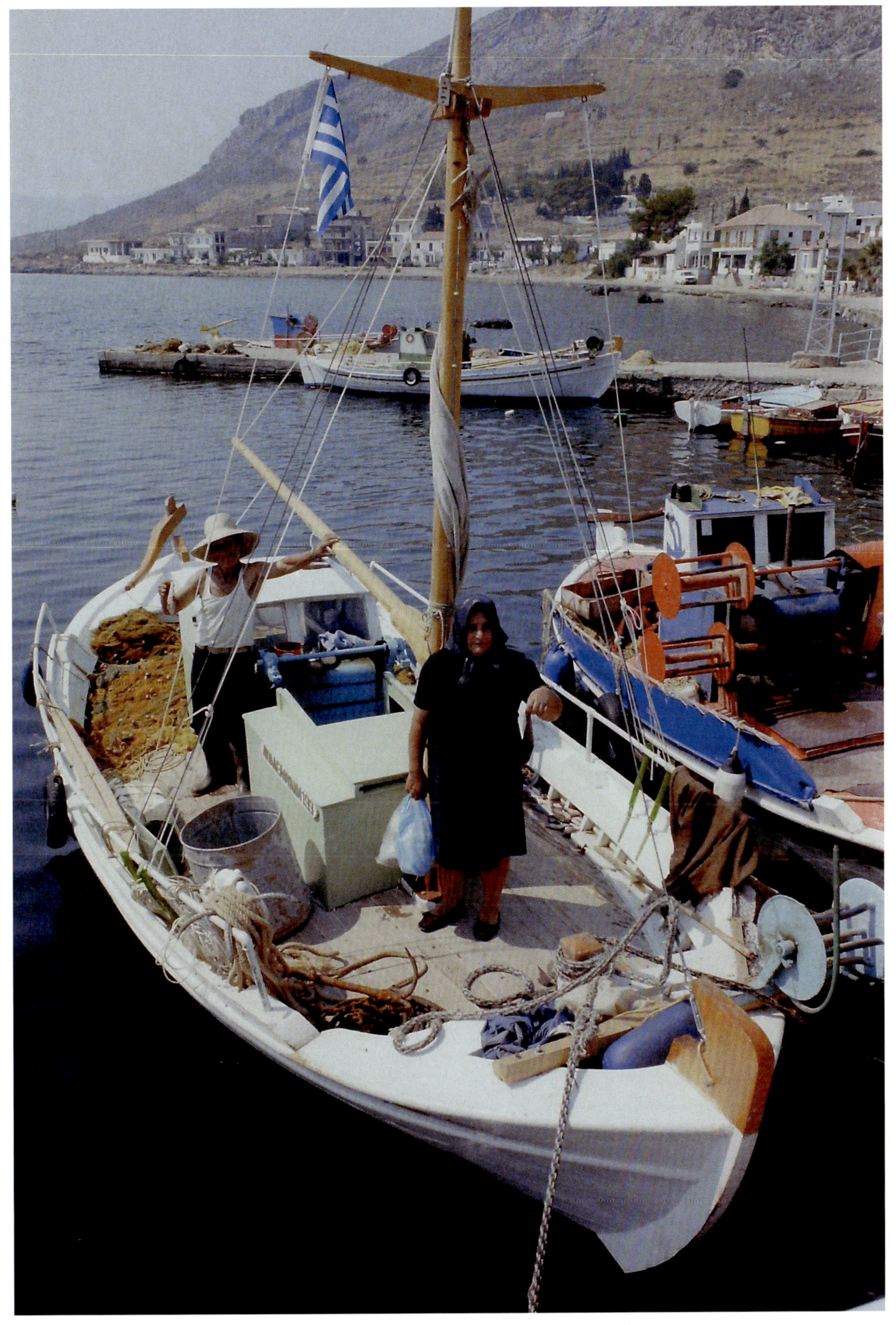

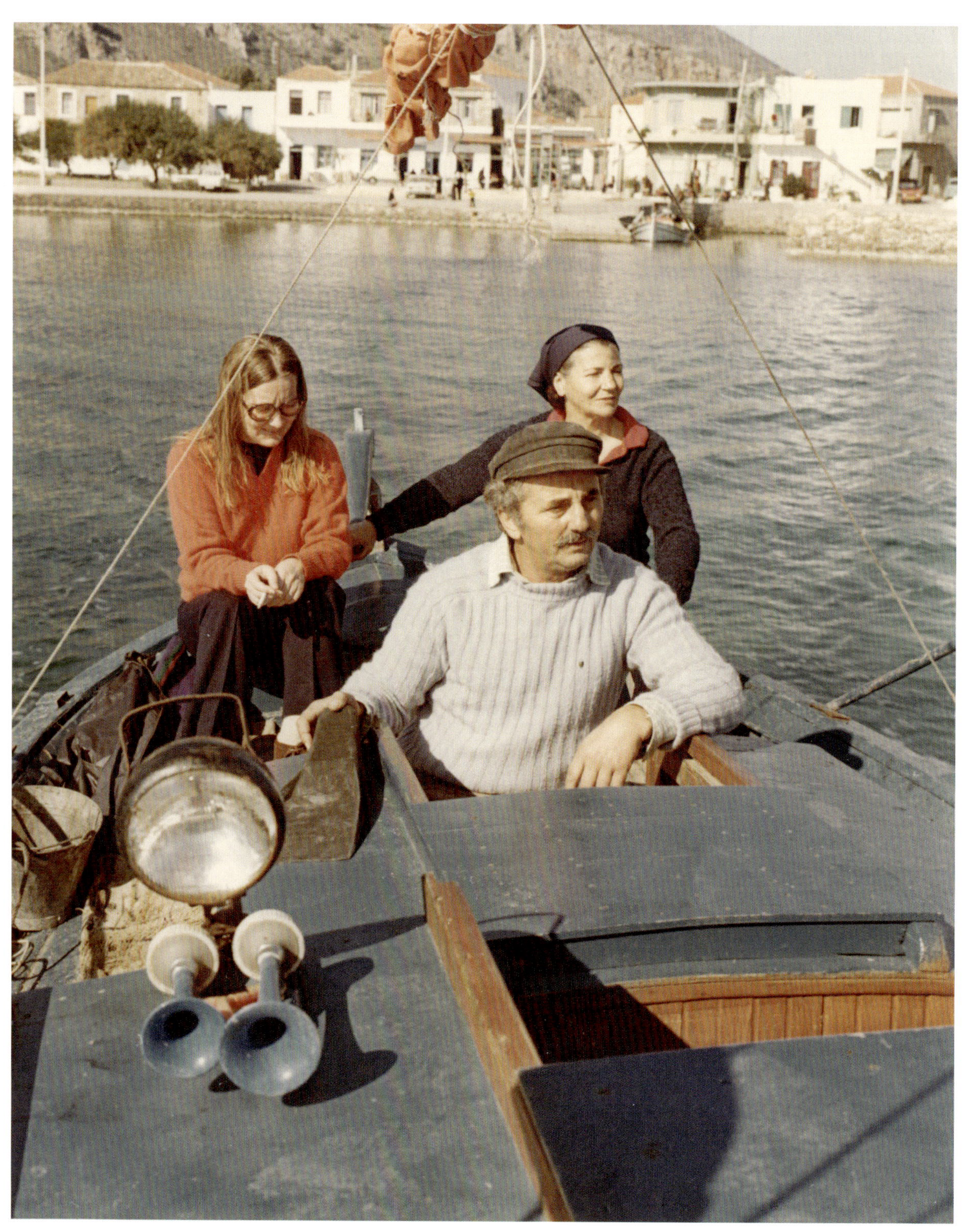

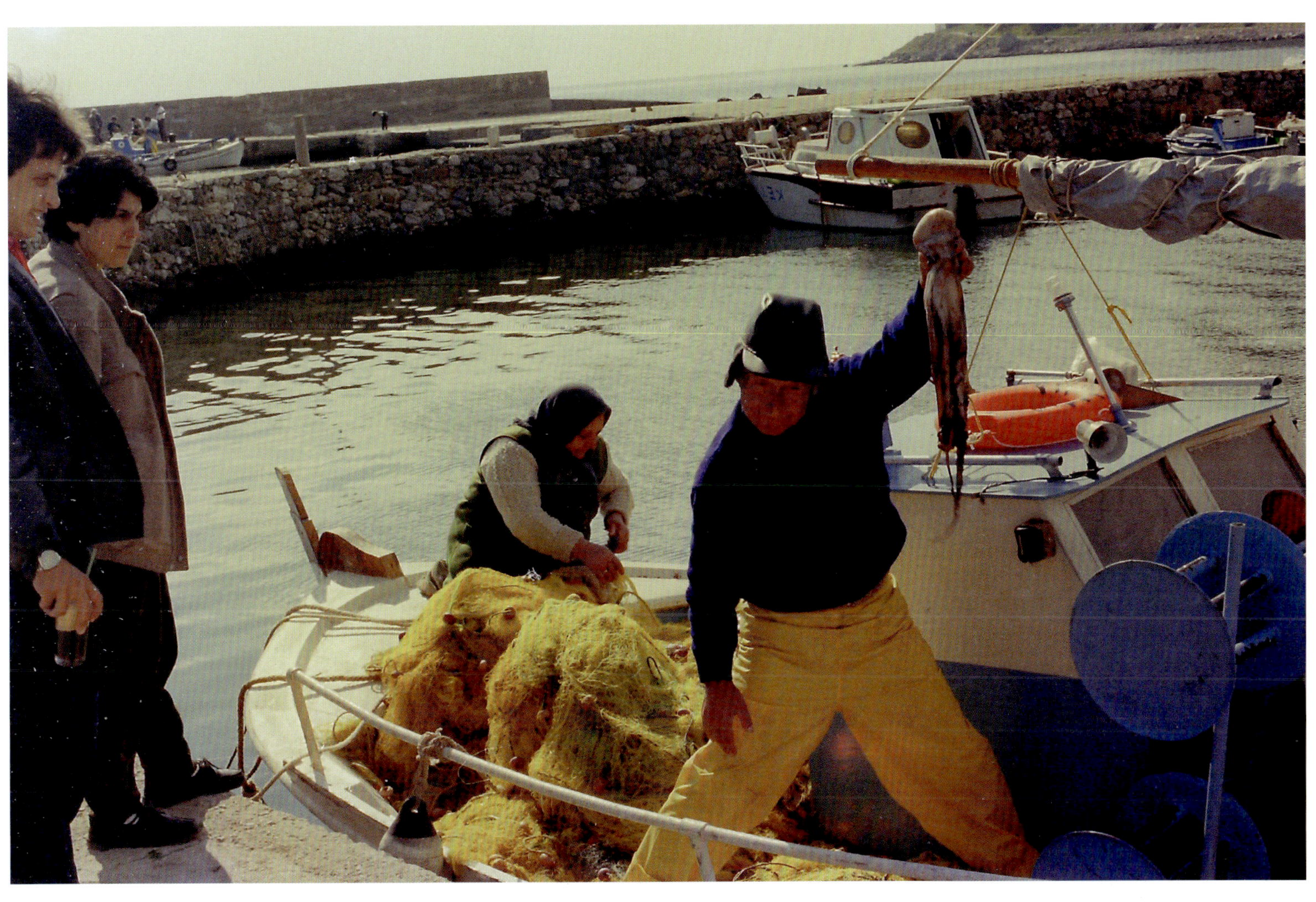

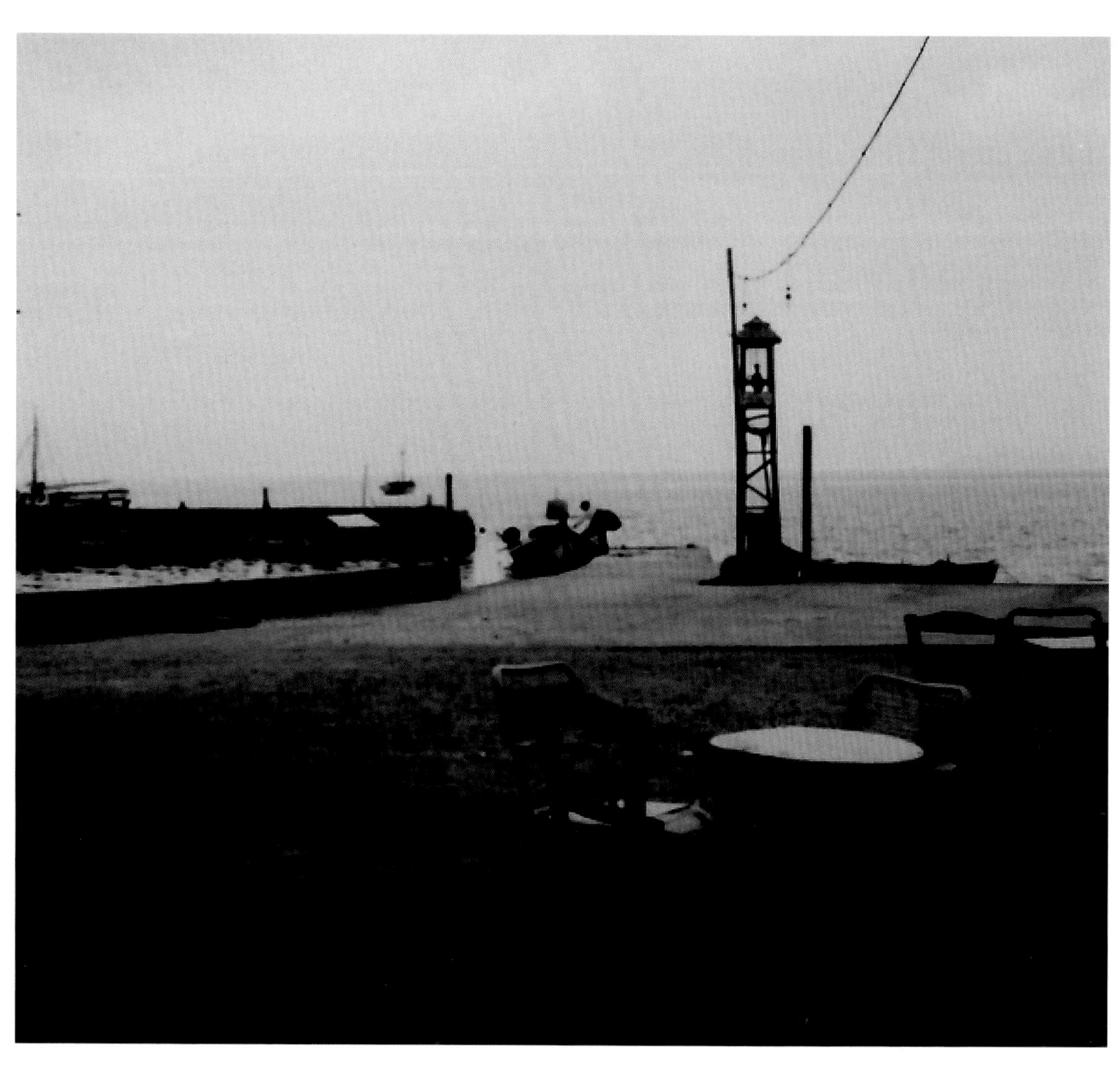

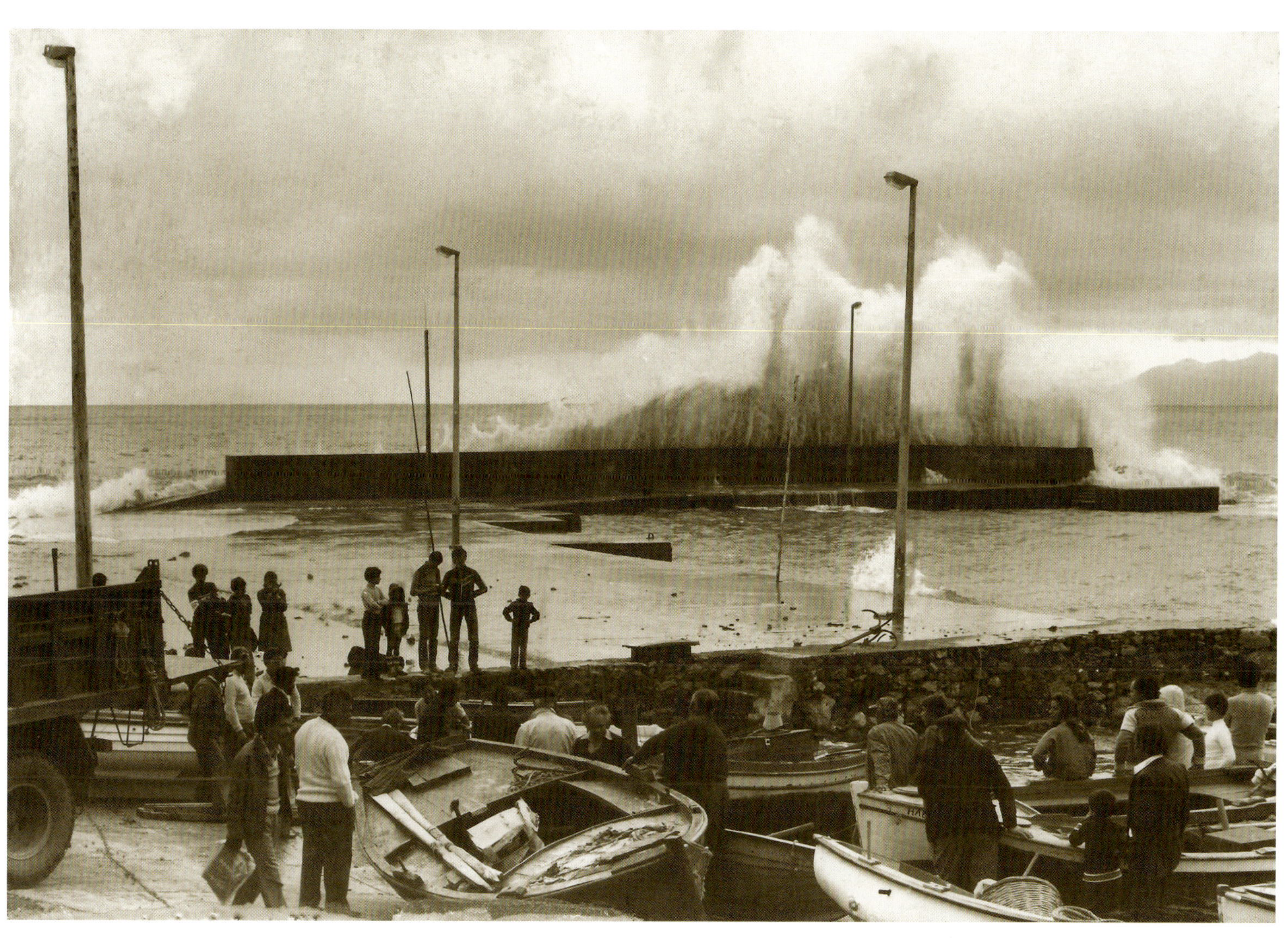

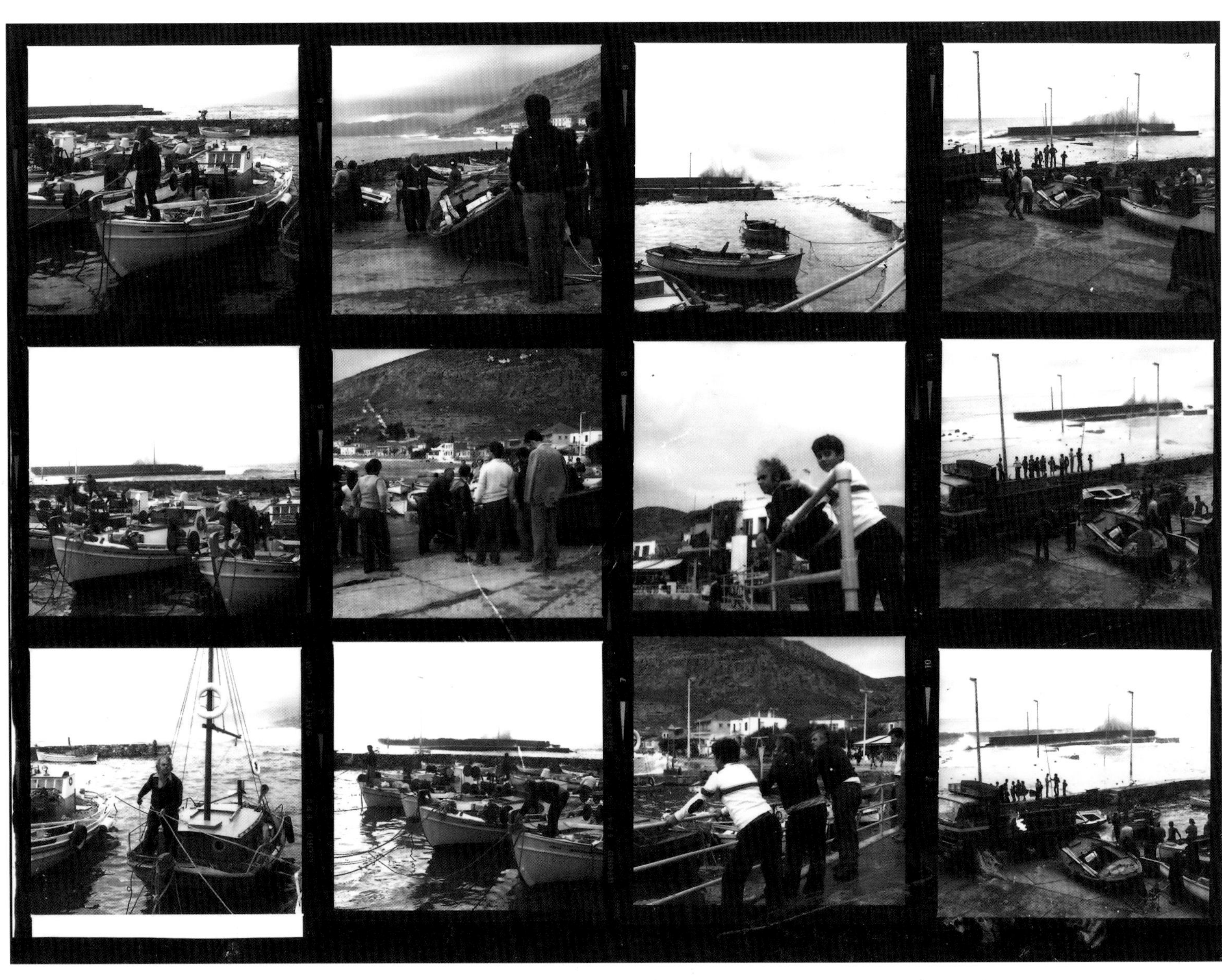

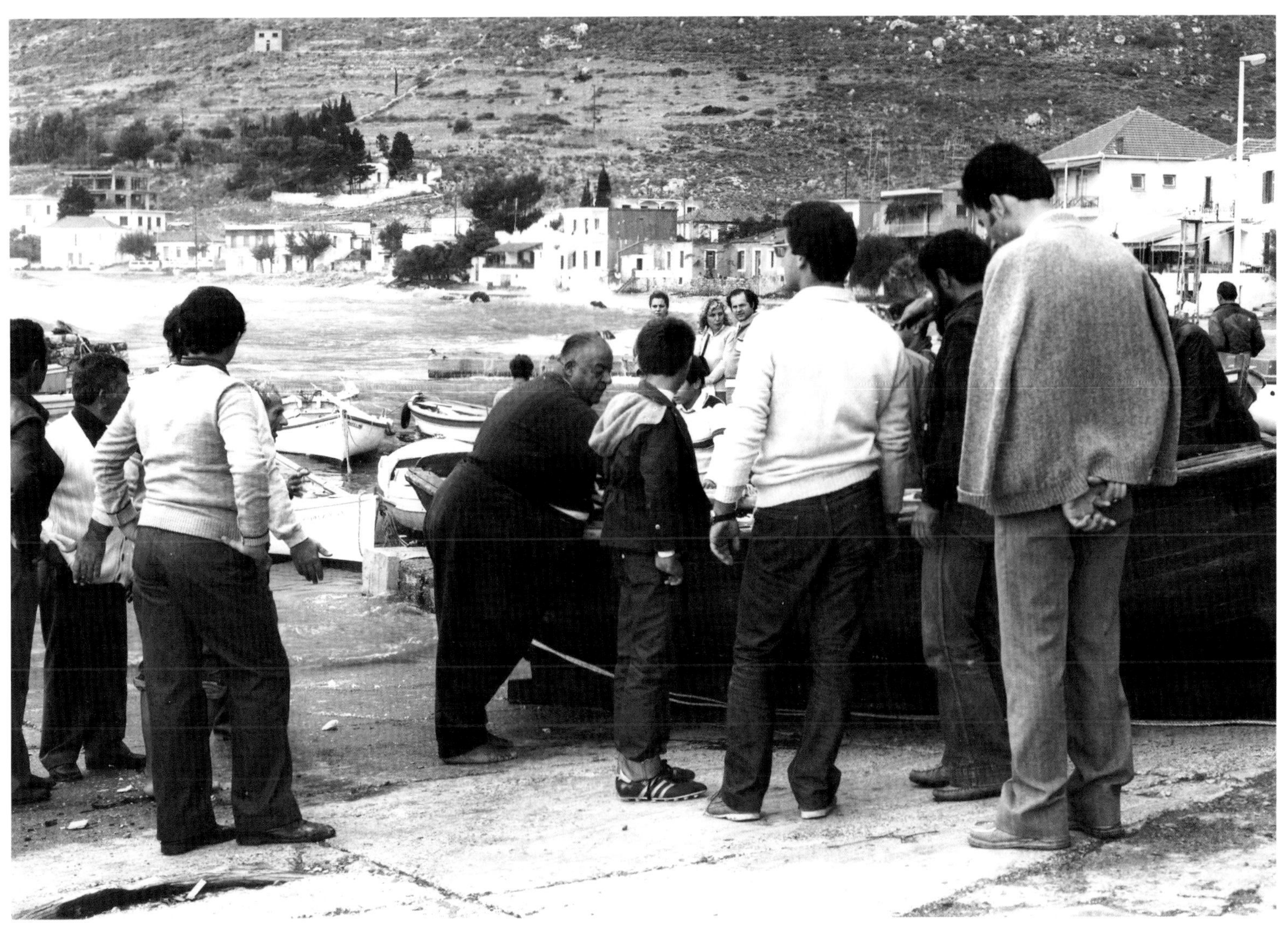

Many of the inhabitants (are) good sailors and work at sea, and have vigour and an active and practical spirit.

EMPEROR ANDRONIKOS II, CHRYSOBULL, ISSUED JUNE 1301

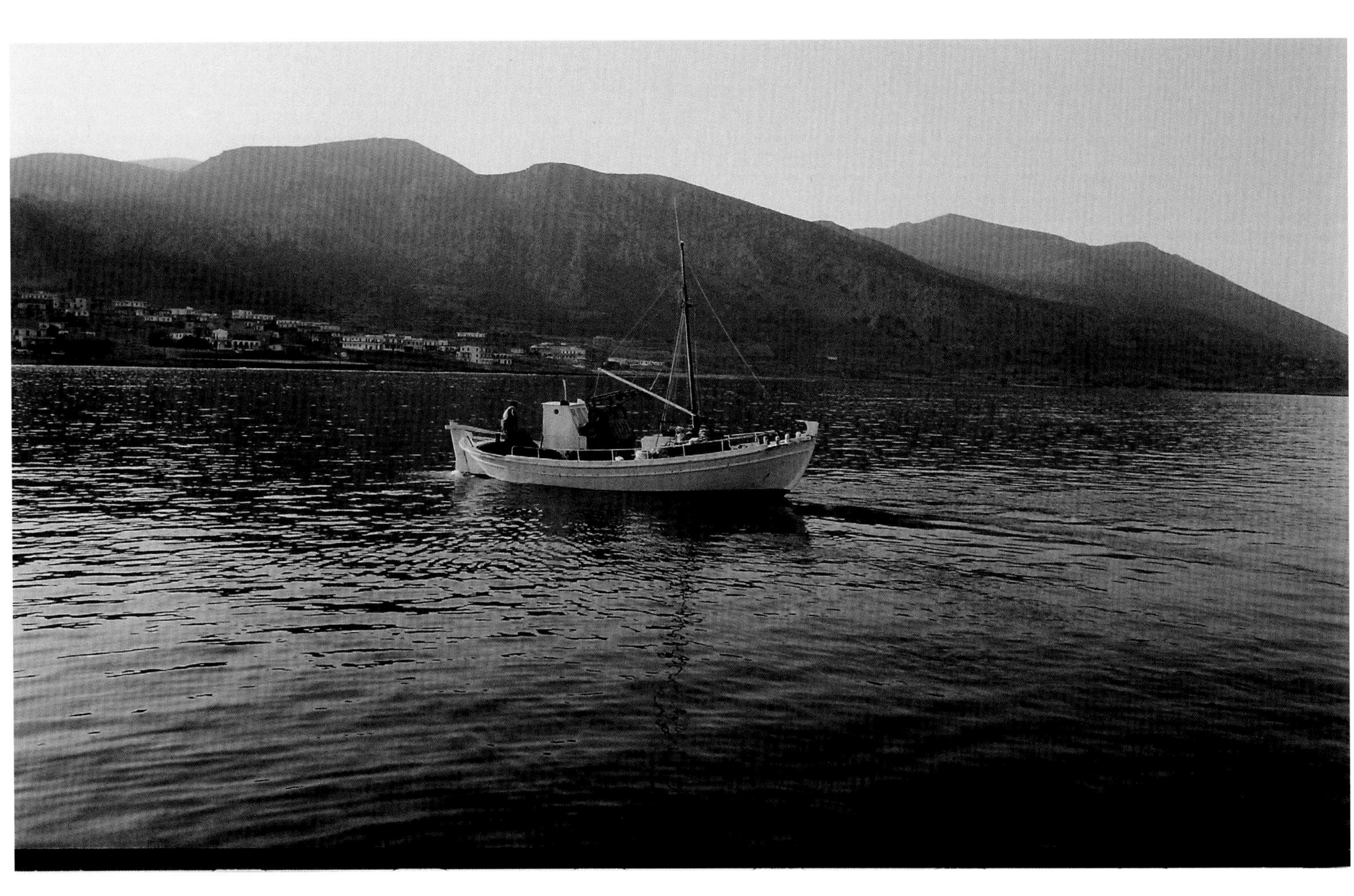

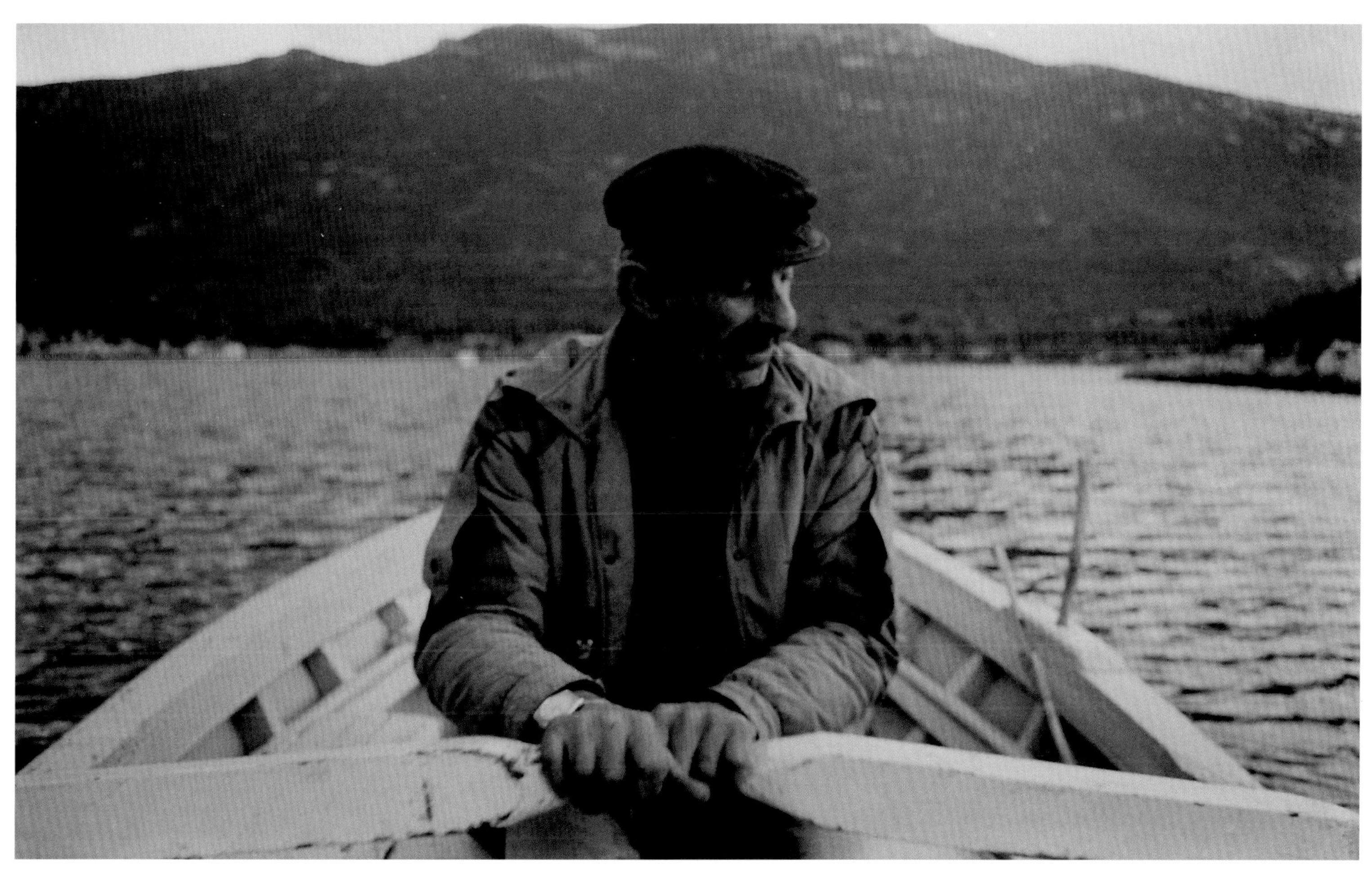

Now that we embark
Leave the coast and set out
Upon one more voyage
We are free at last to be alone.

KEVIN McGRATH, *HELLAS*, 2023

Agriculture

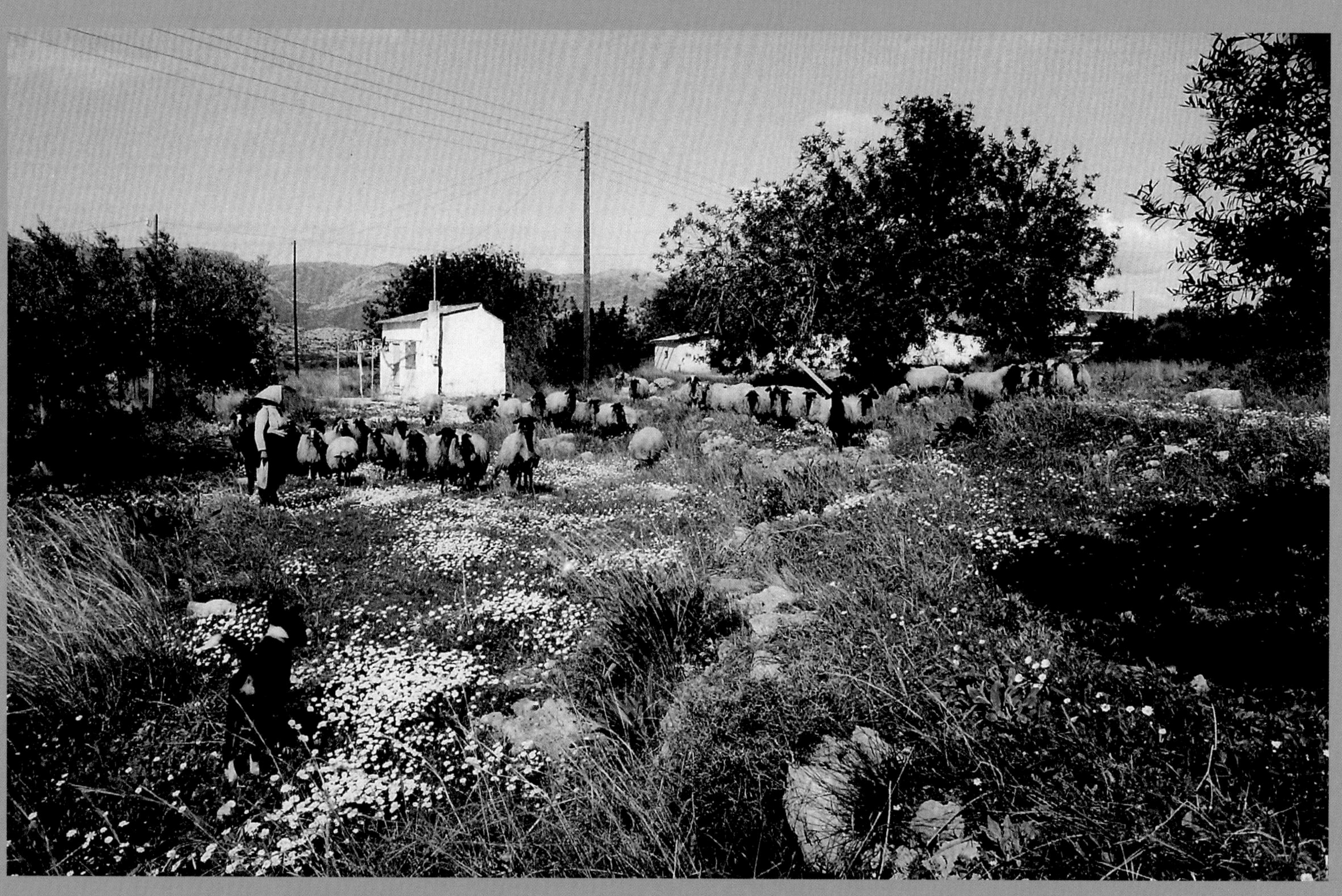

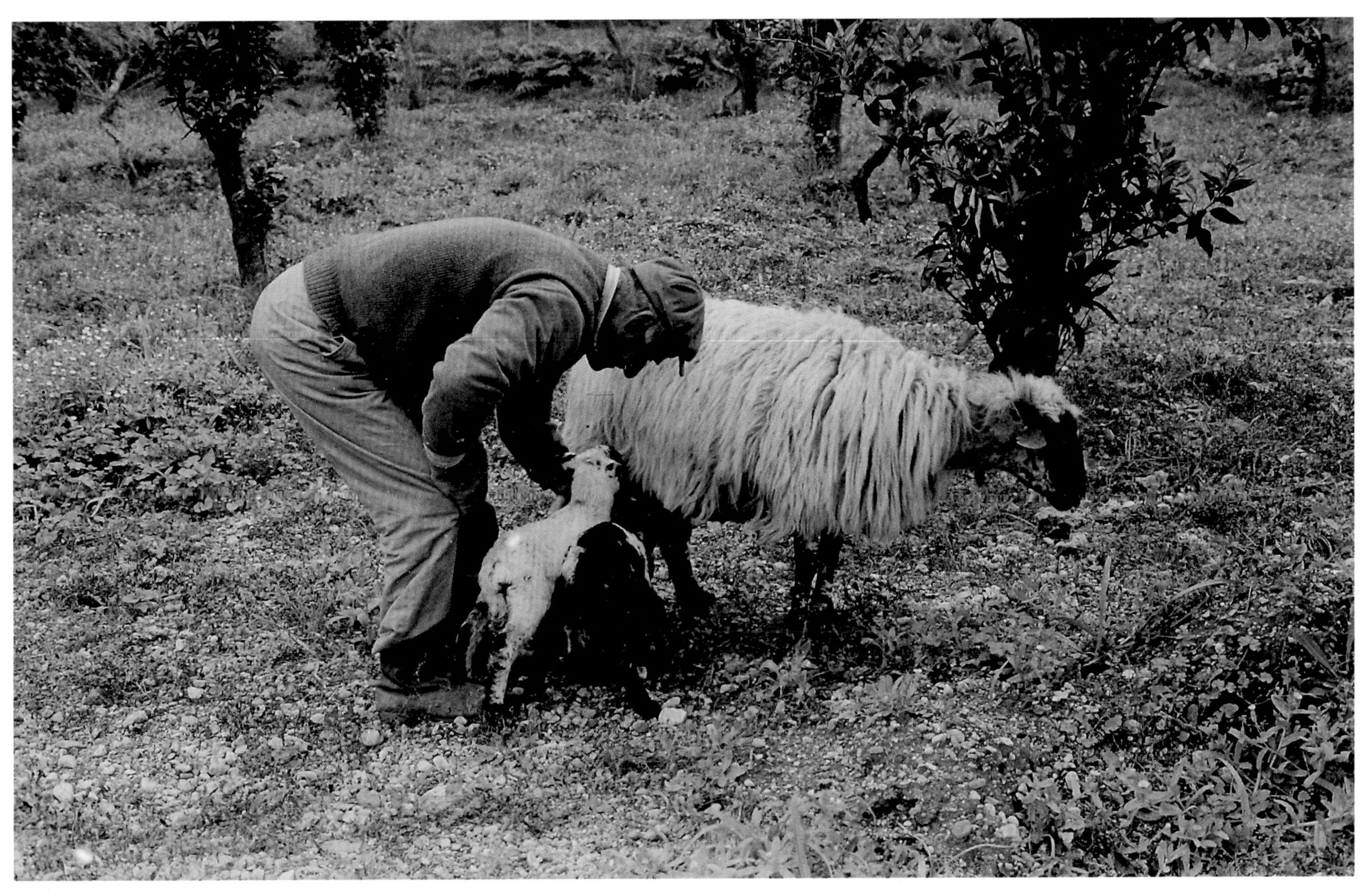

On these hillsides forever there will be the shepherd with his flock: he will survive everything, including the tradition of all that ever was.

HENRY MILLER, *THE COLOSSUS OF MAROUSSI*, 1941

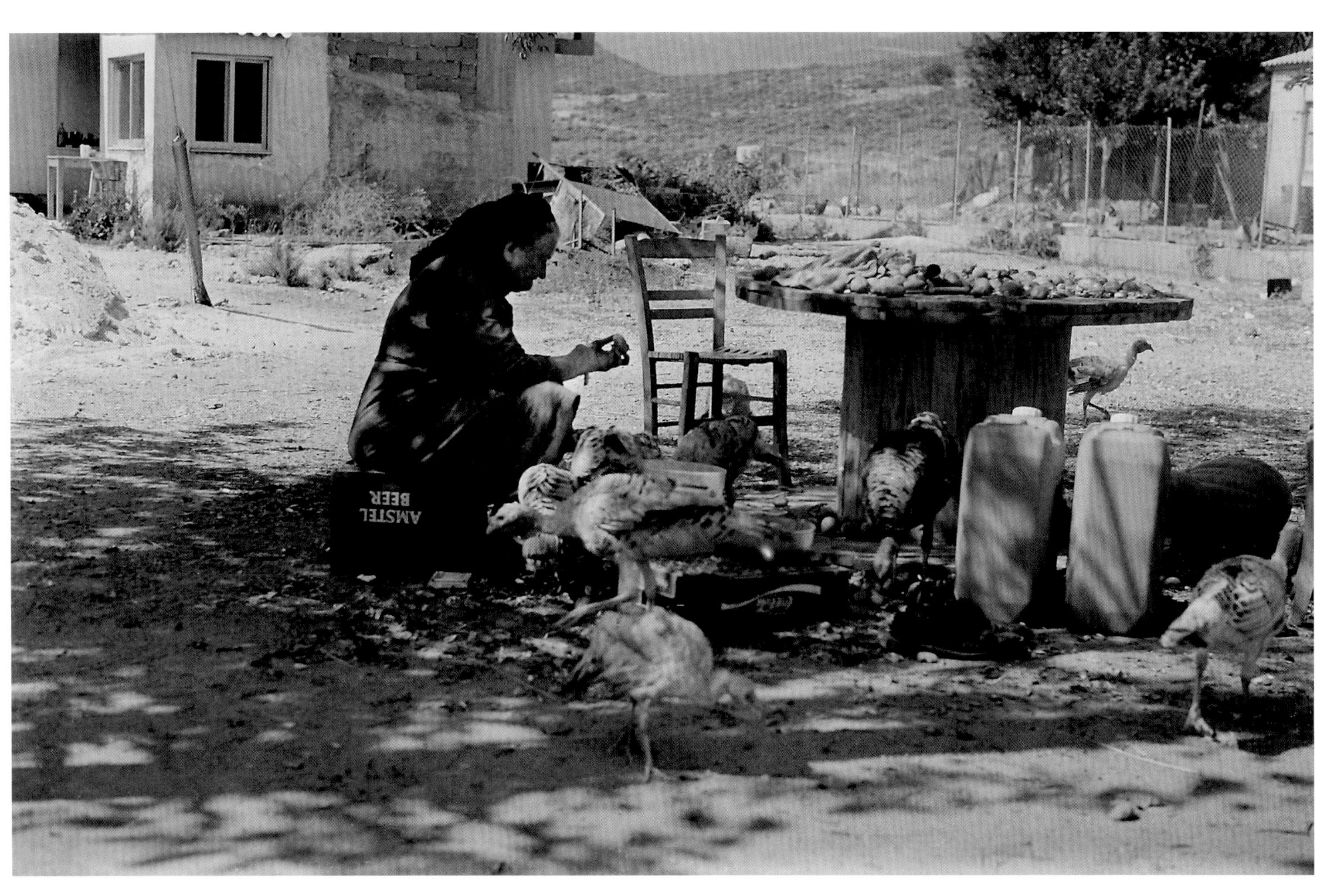
AMSTEL
BEER

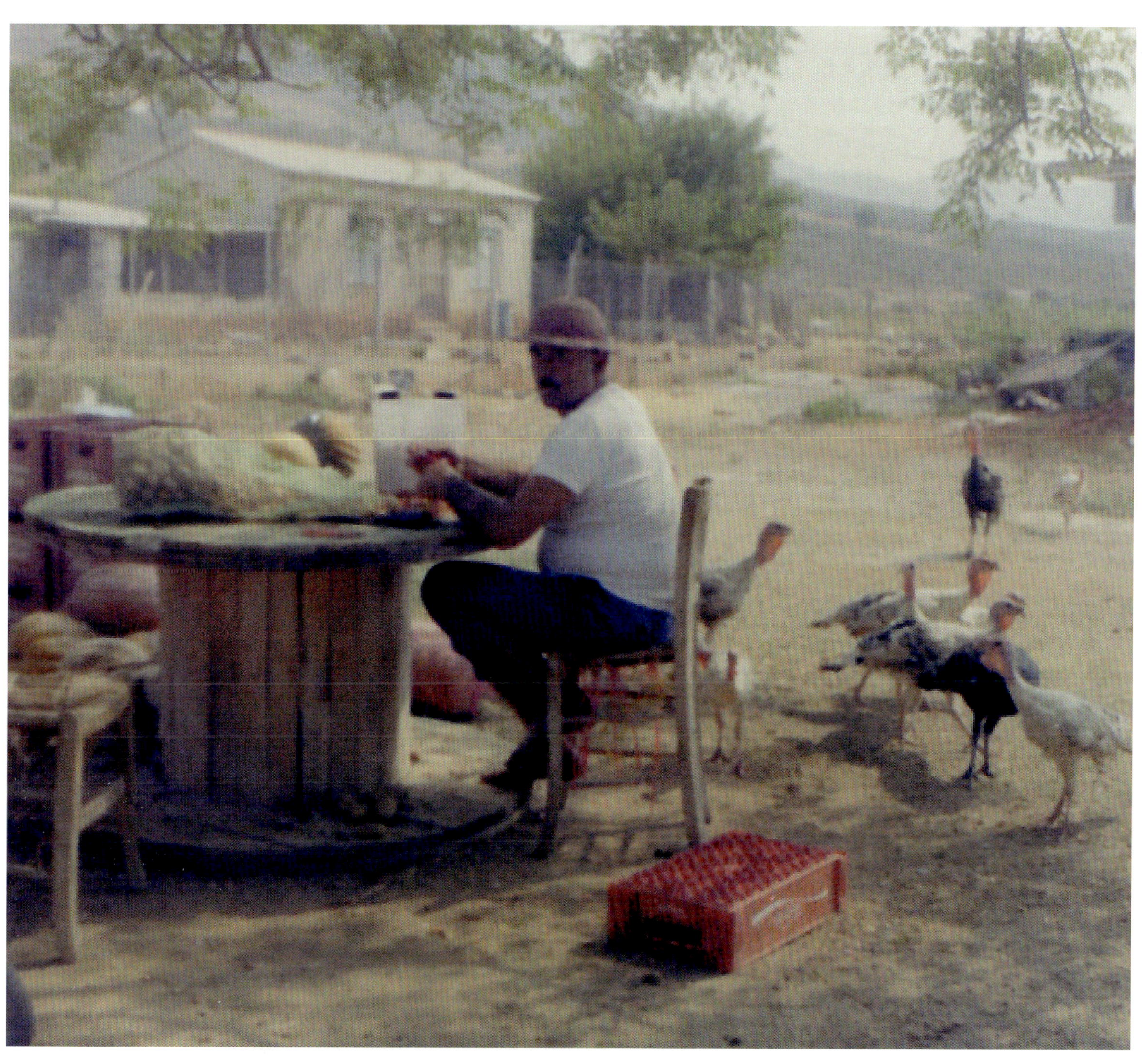

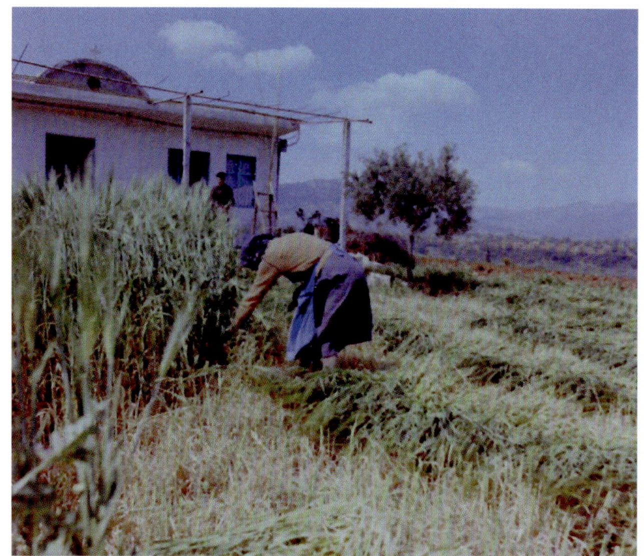

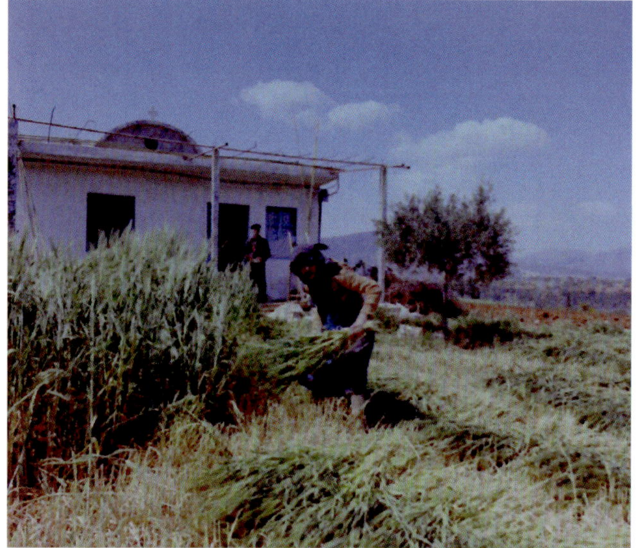

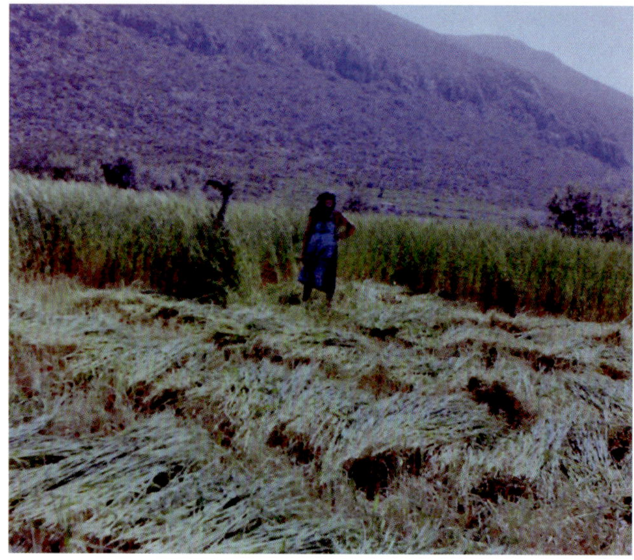

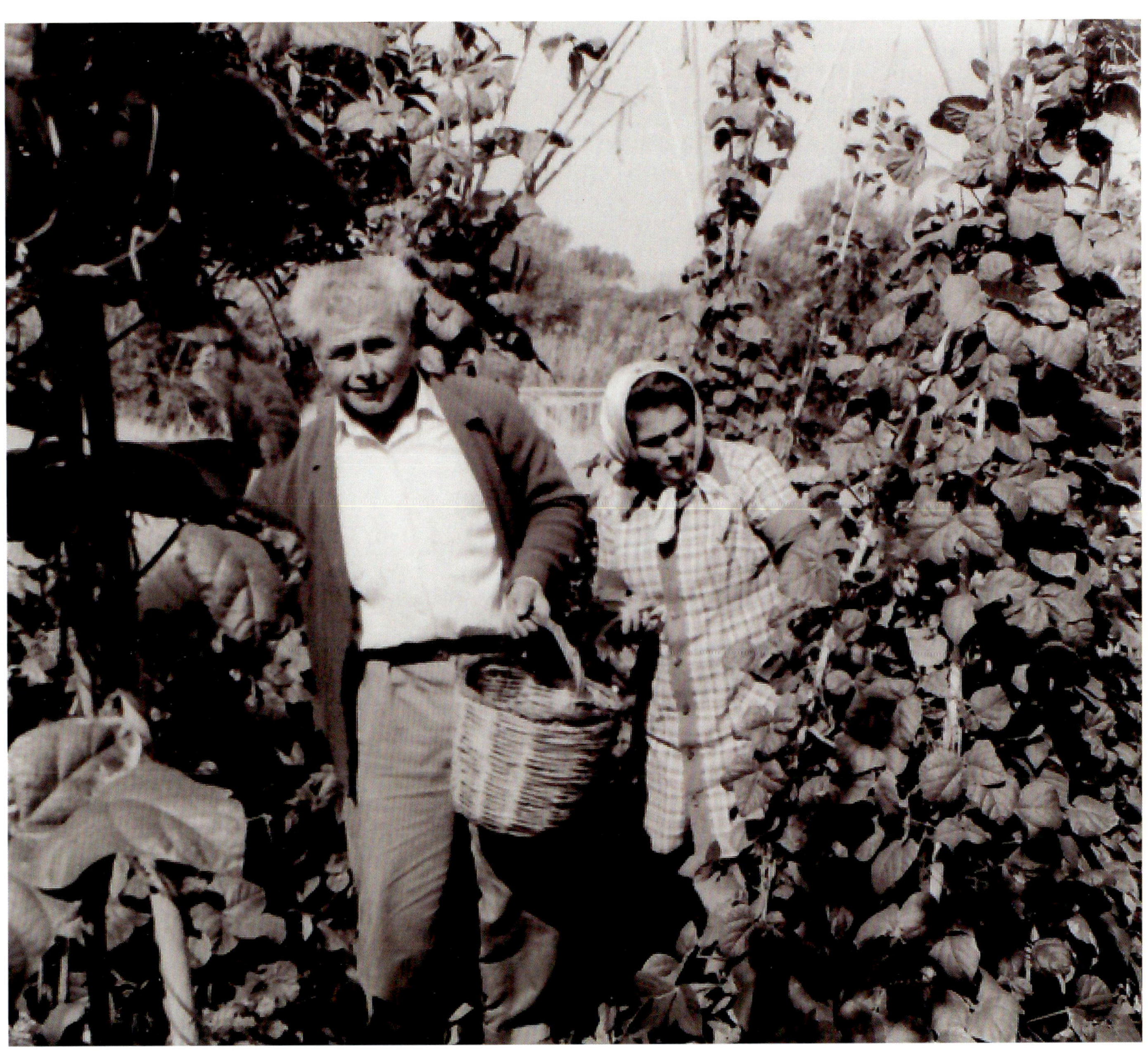

You should embrace work – tasks in their due order,
so that your granaries may be full of substance in its season.
It is from work that men are rich in flocks. and wealthy,
and a working man is much dearer to the immortals.

HESIOD, *WORKS AND DAYS*, 8TH CENTURY BC

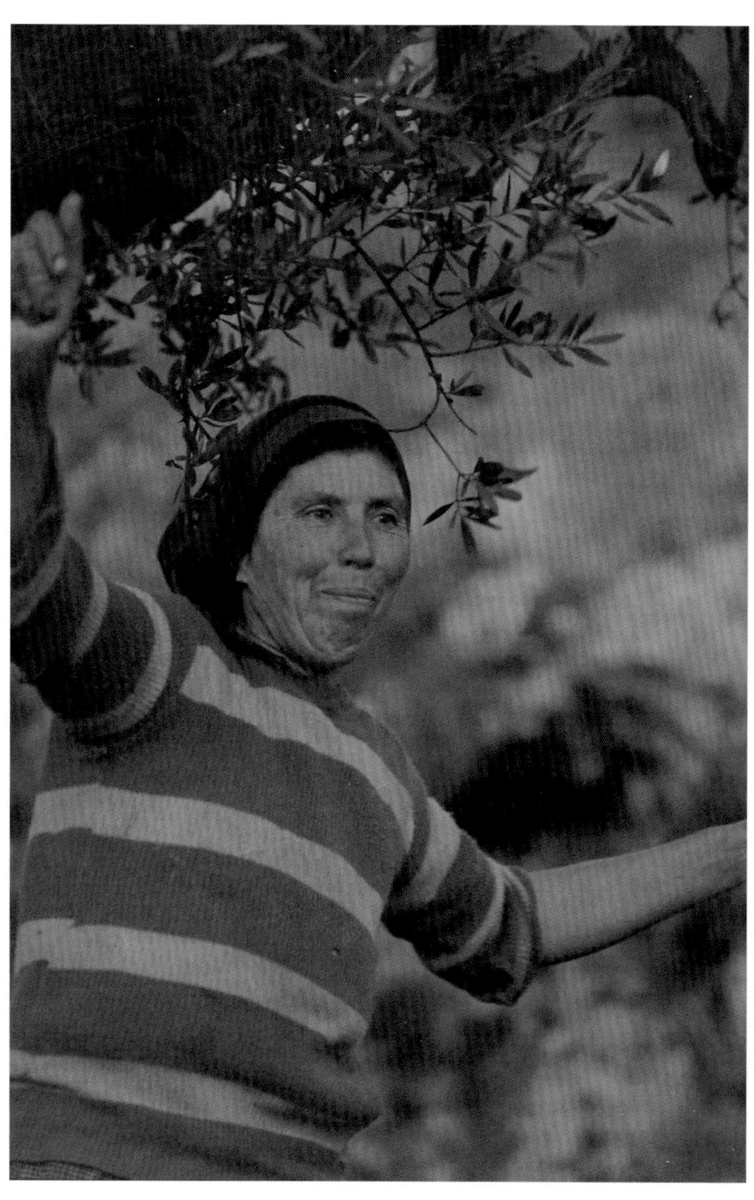

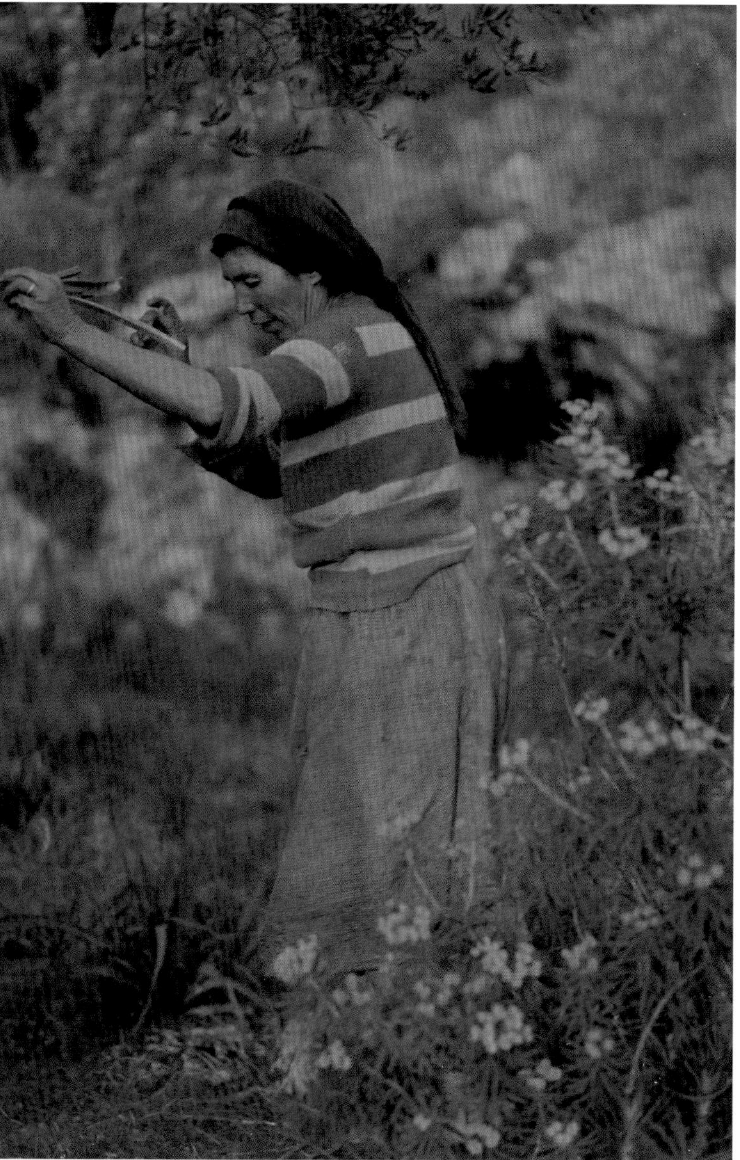

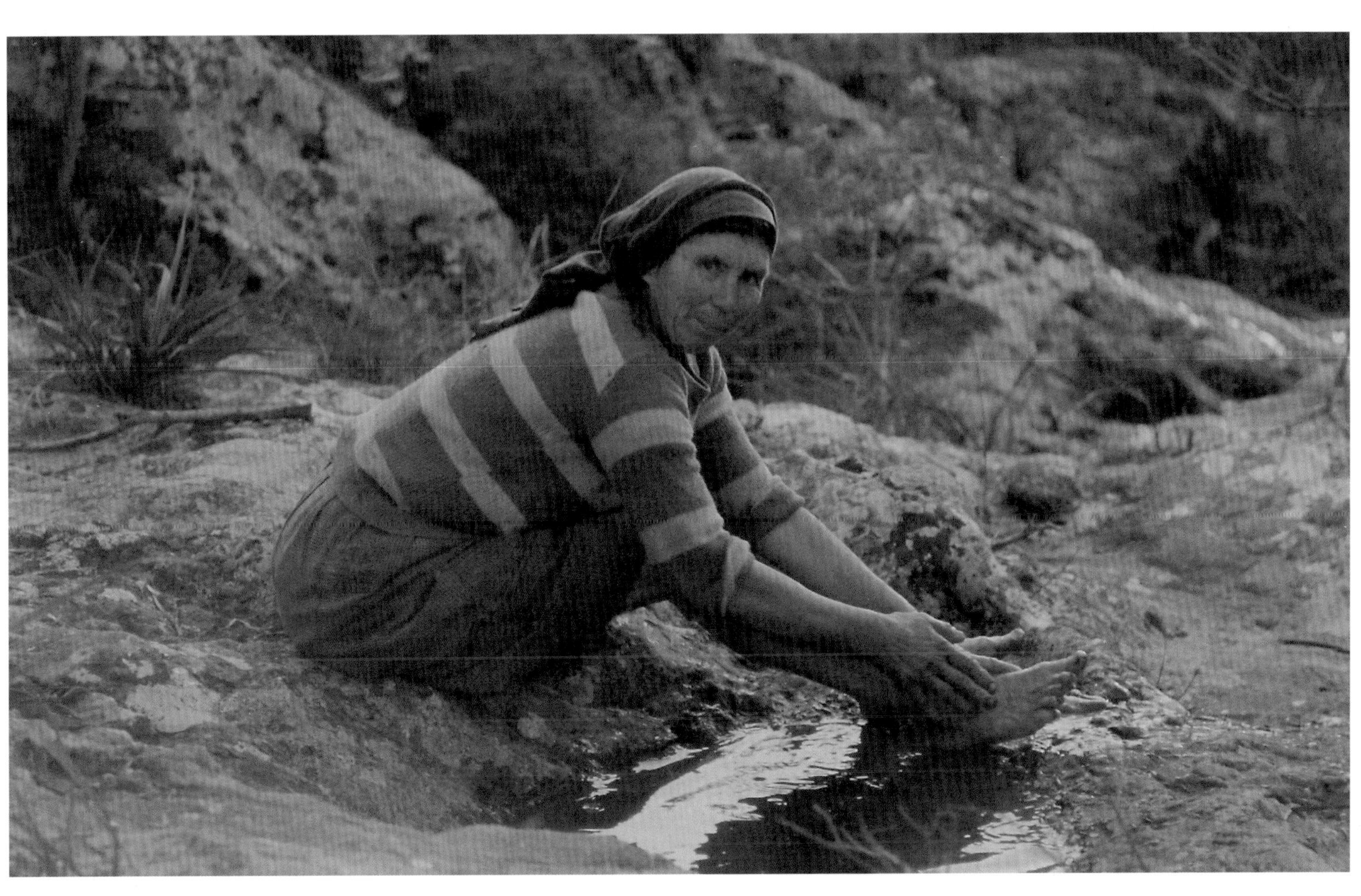

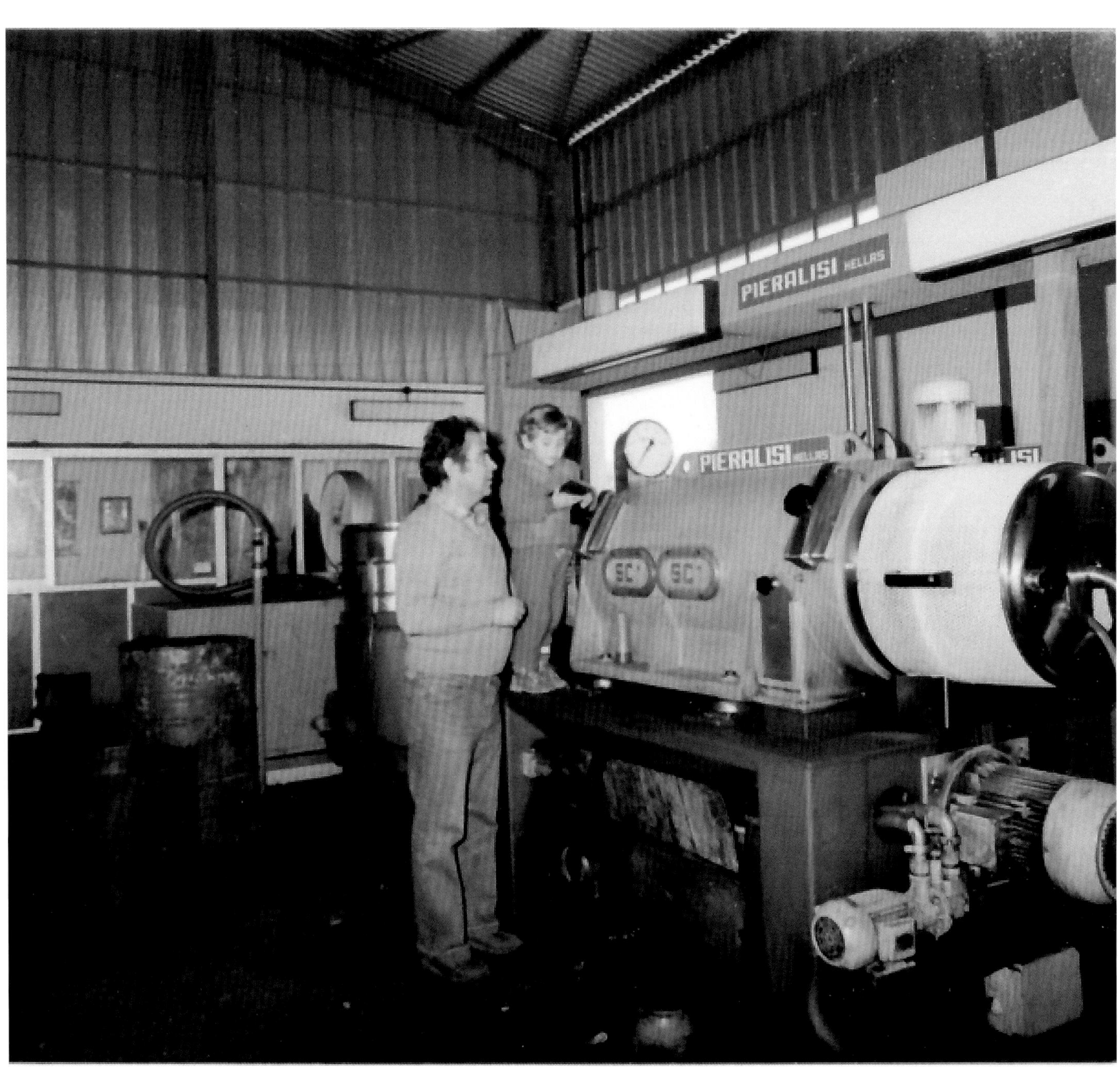
PIERALISI HELLAS
PIERALISI HELLAS

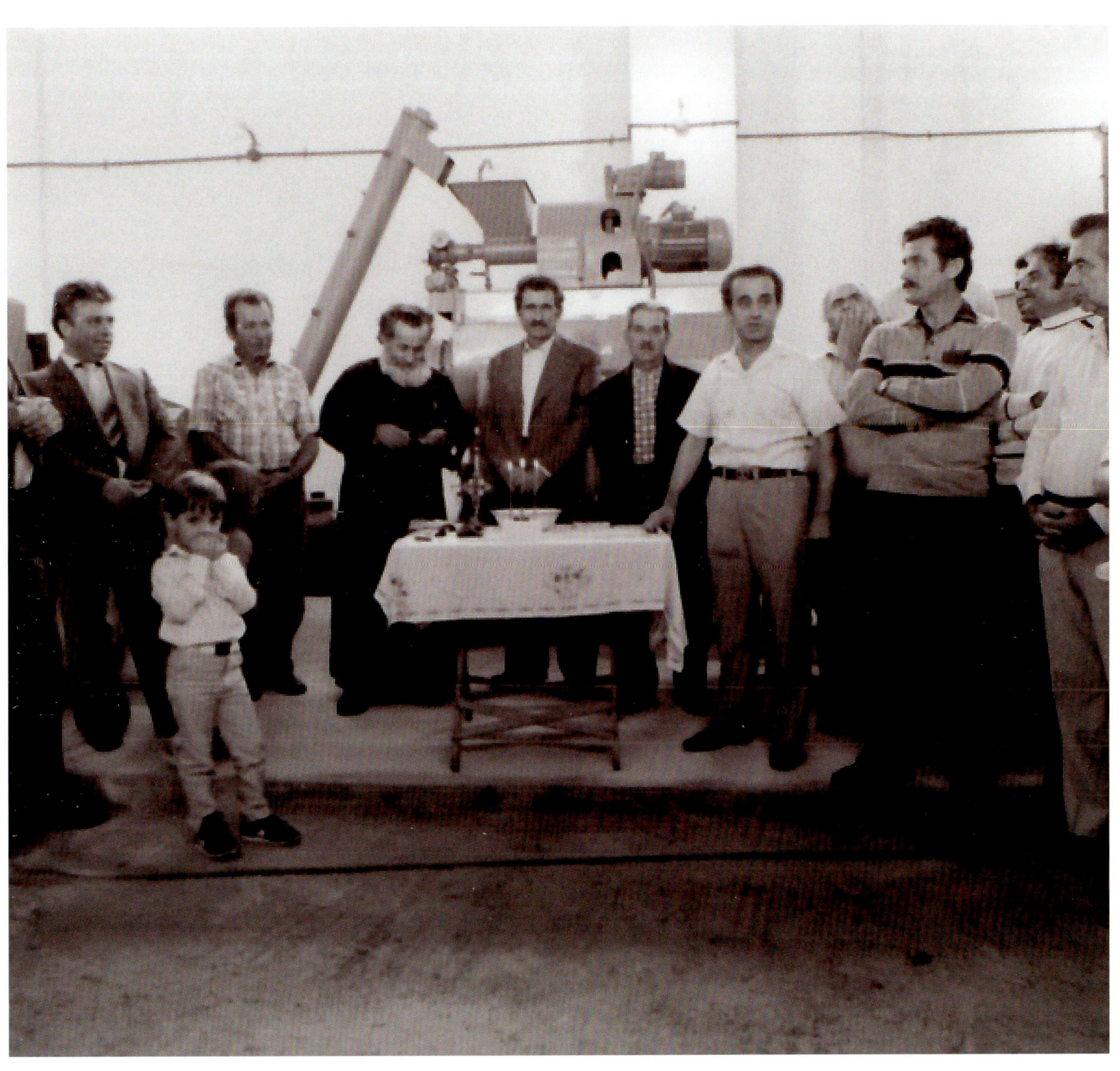

Construction

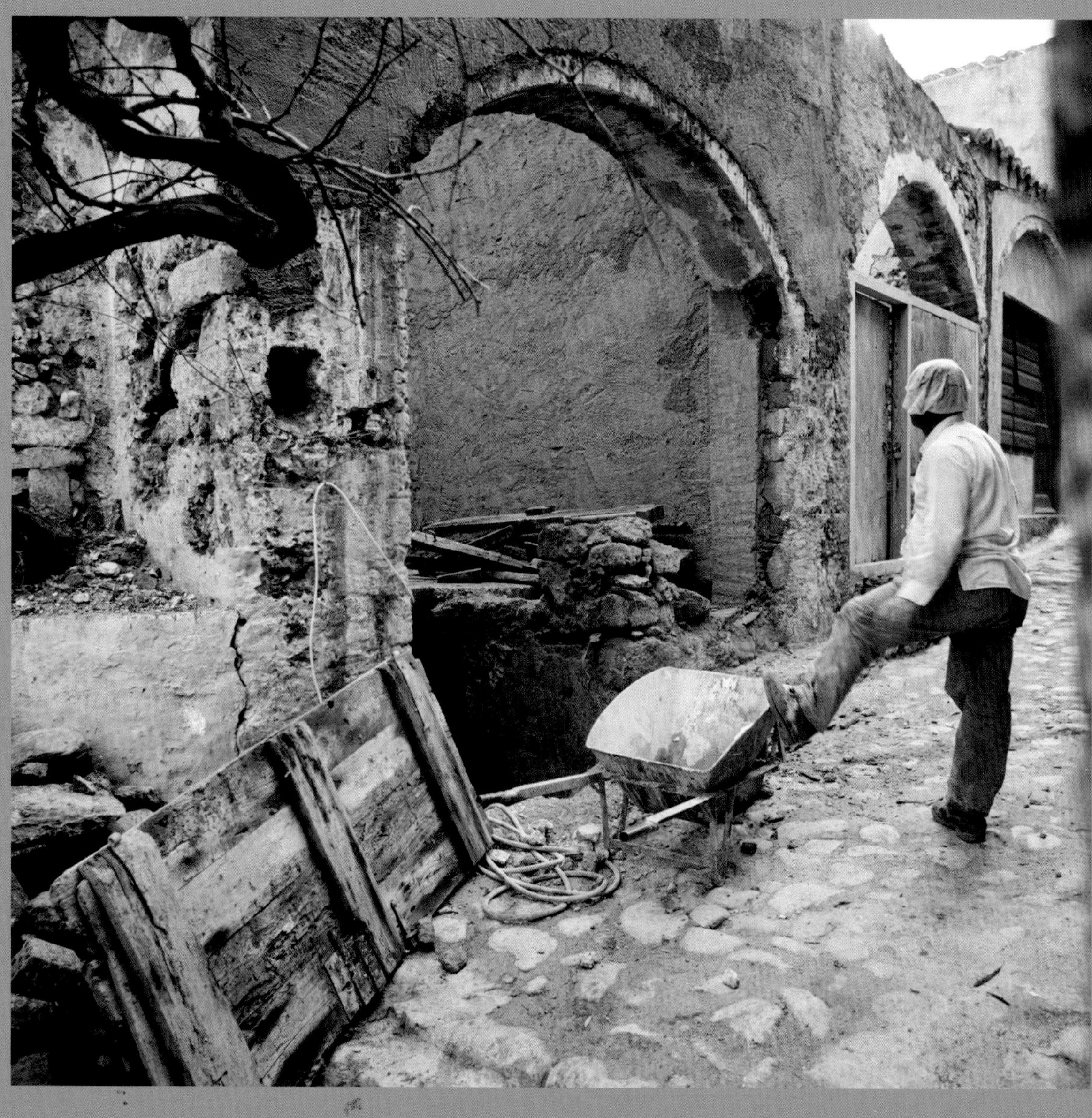

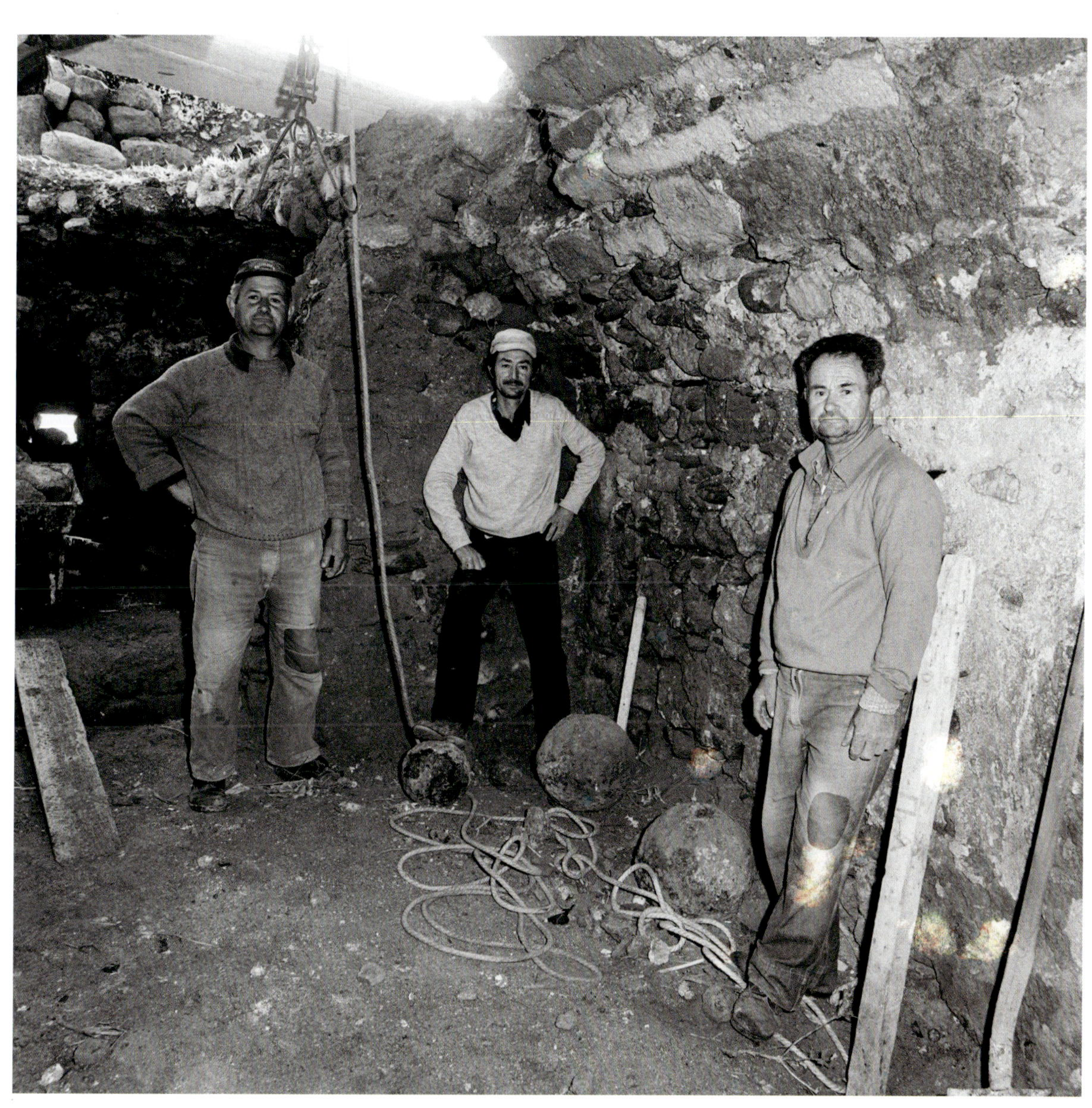

The beauty and the preservation of the area interests us too.

YIANNIS CHARAMIS, BUILDING CONTRACTOR, *GREECE IS*, 2016

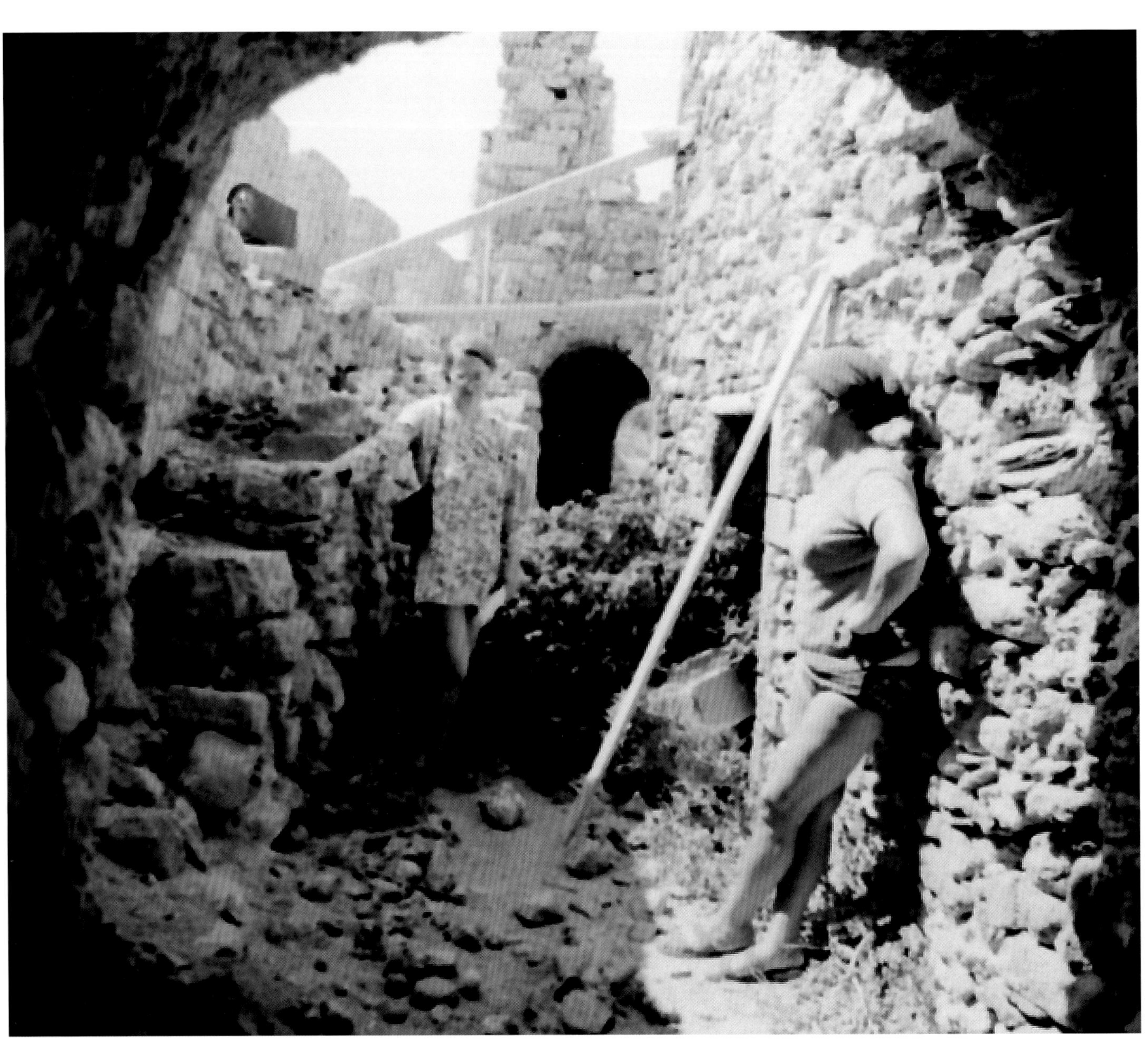

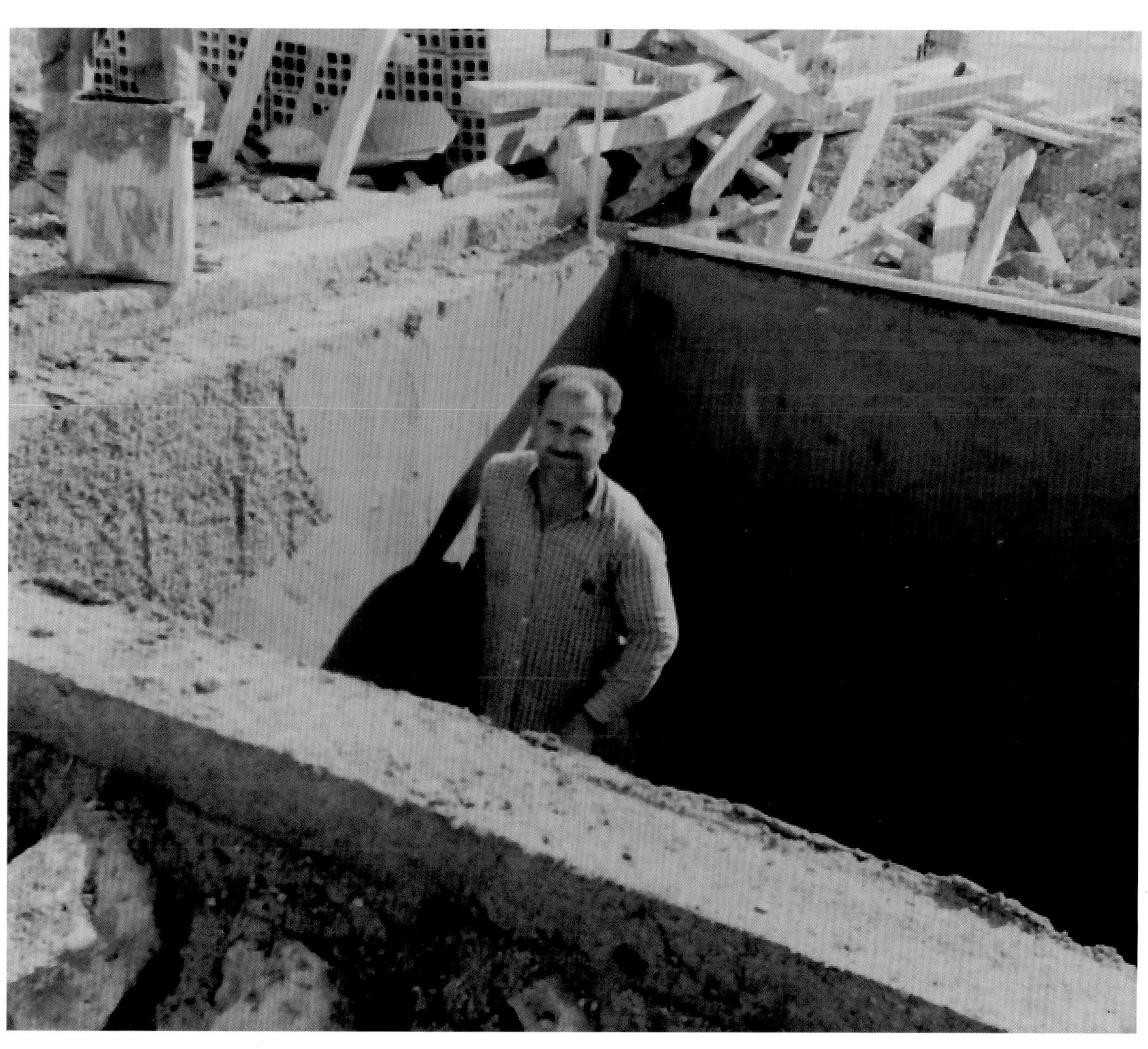

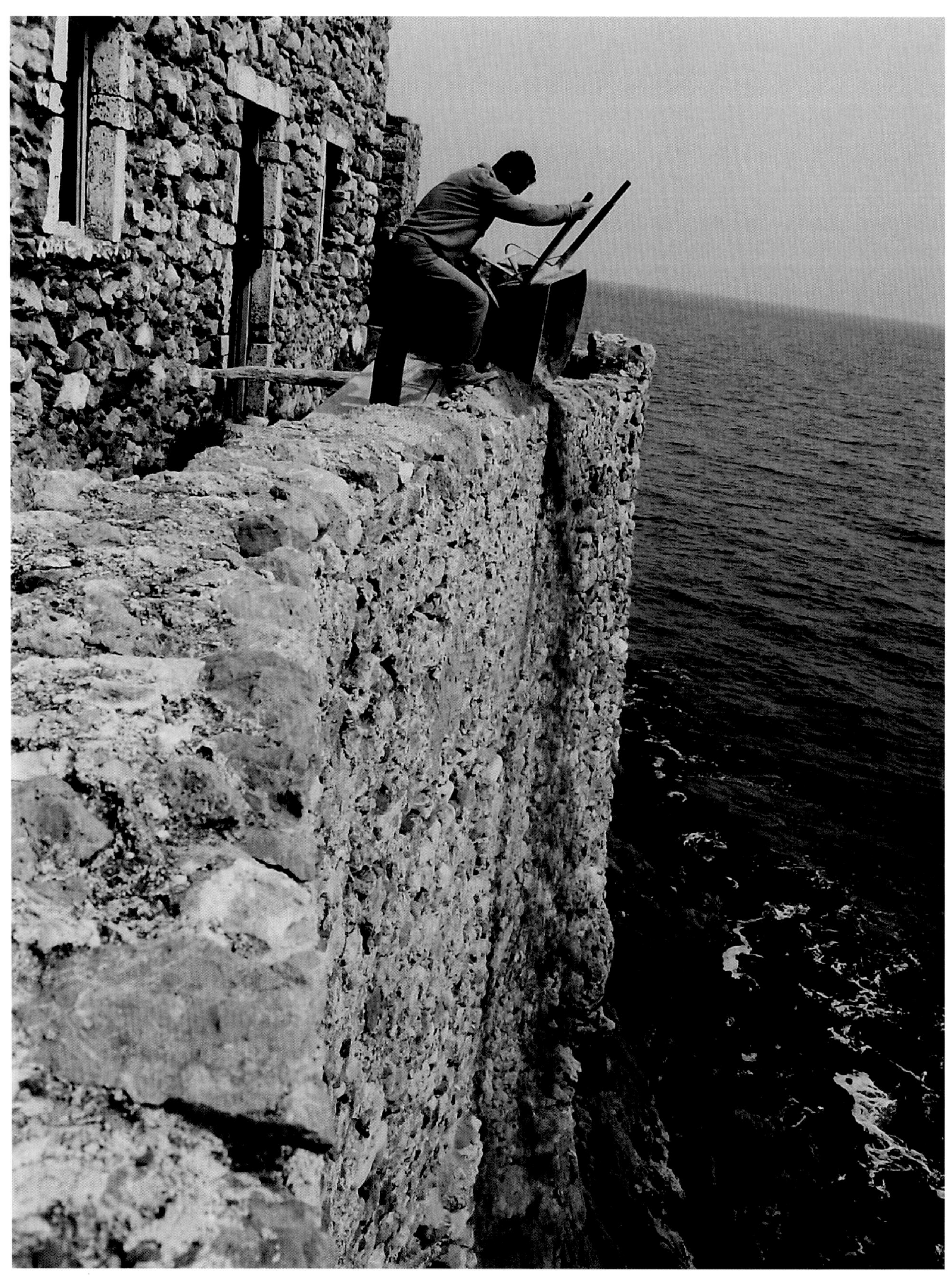

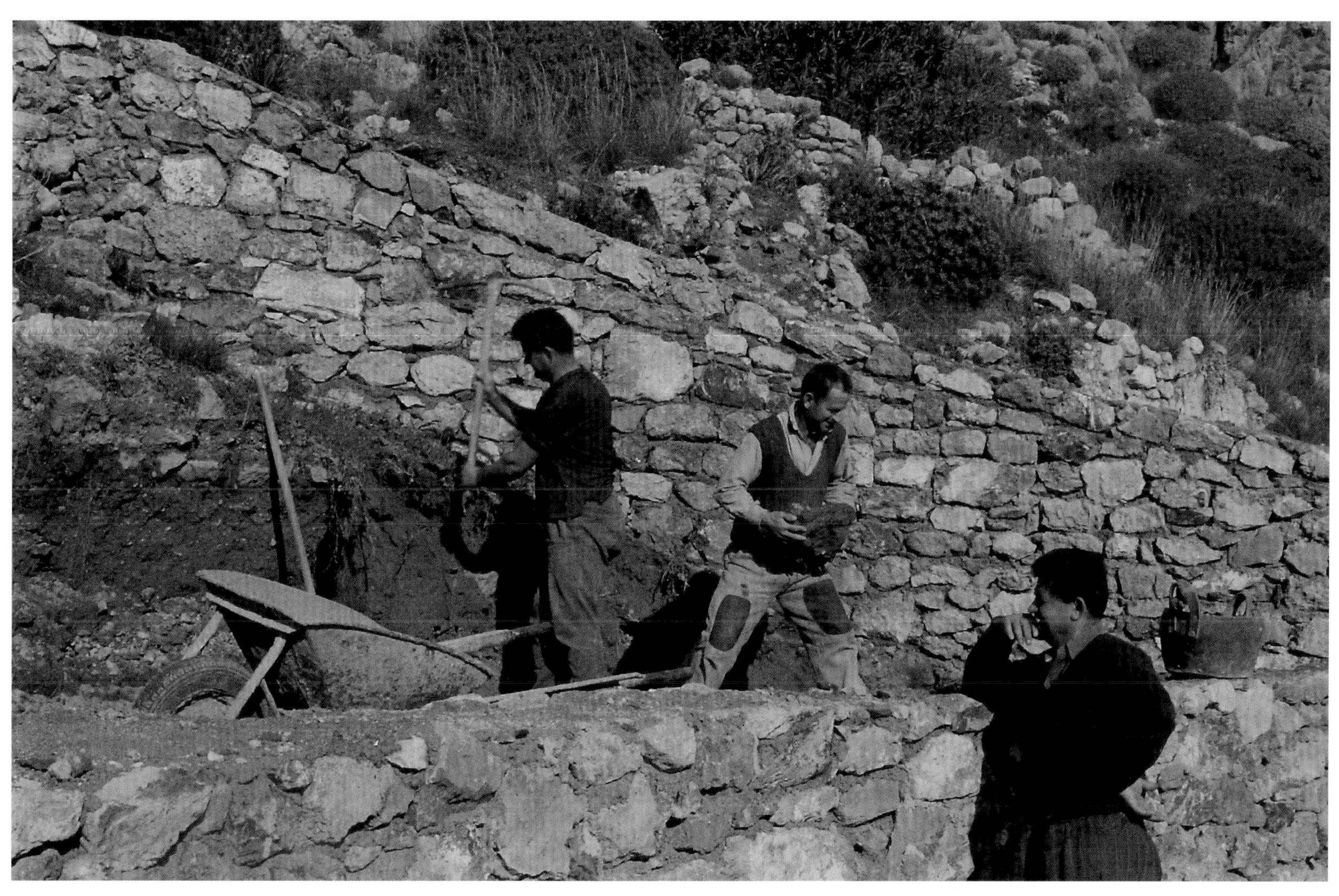

When you say my brother: my brother – when we say: tomorrow we will build,
When we build and sing,
This is peace.

YANNIS RITSOS, 'PEACE', 1953

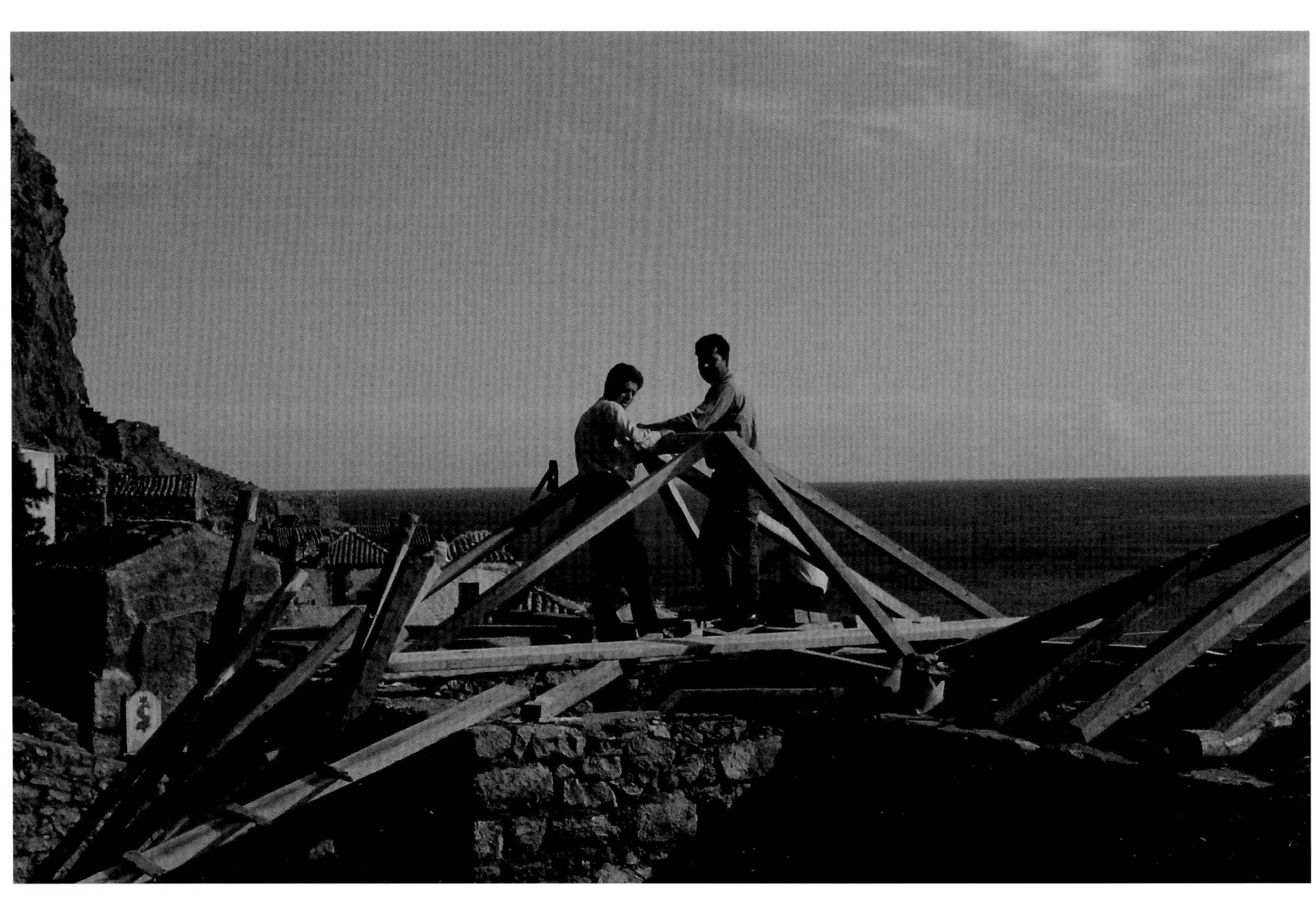

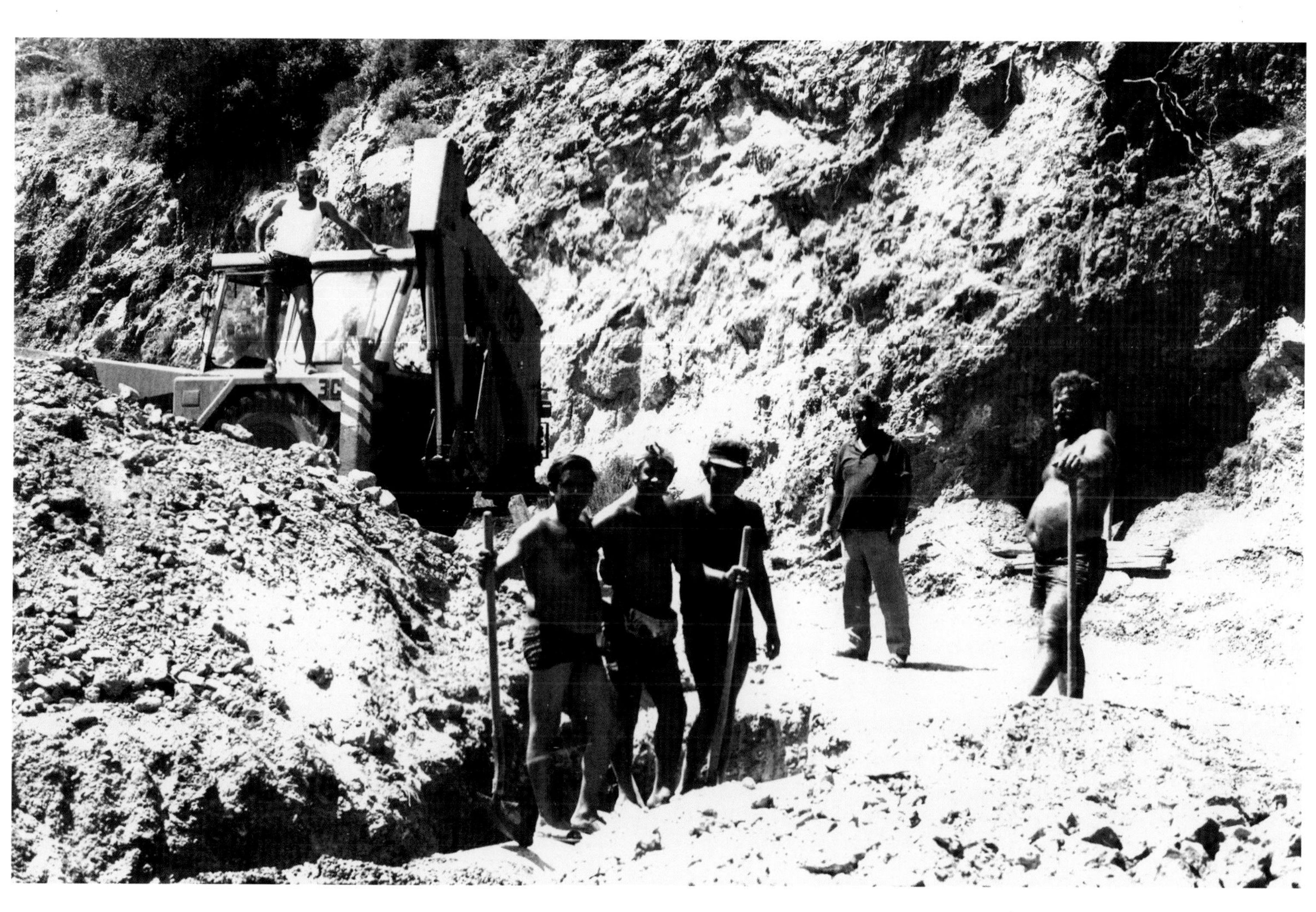

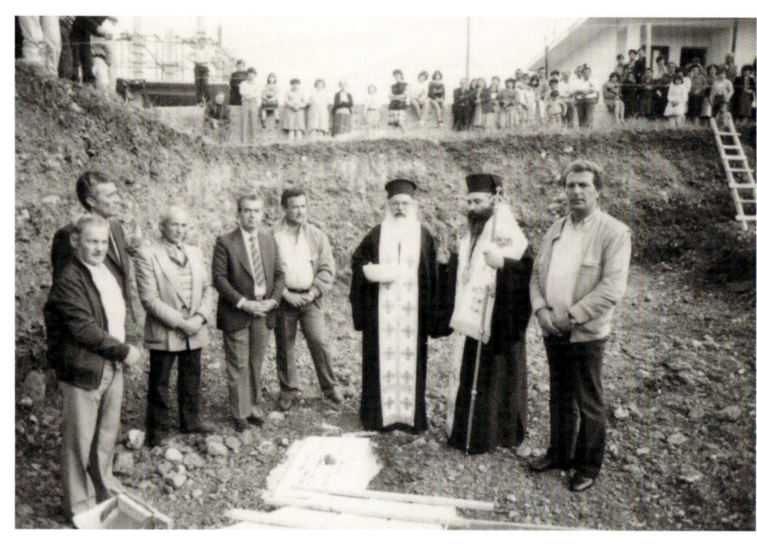

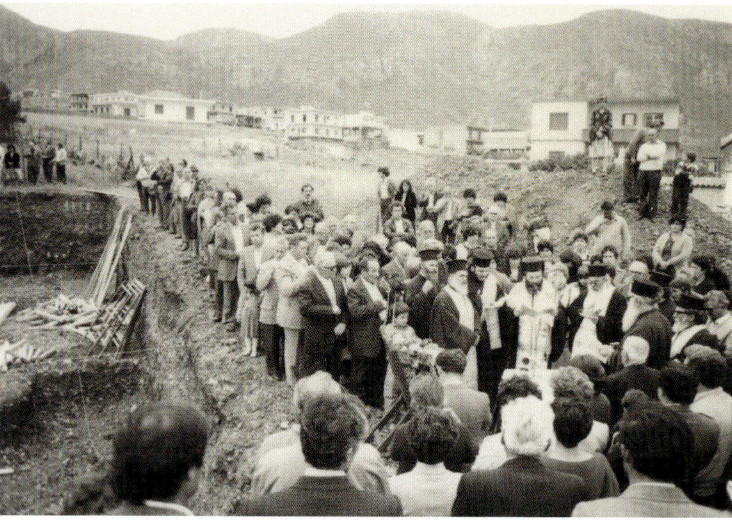

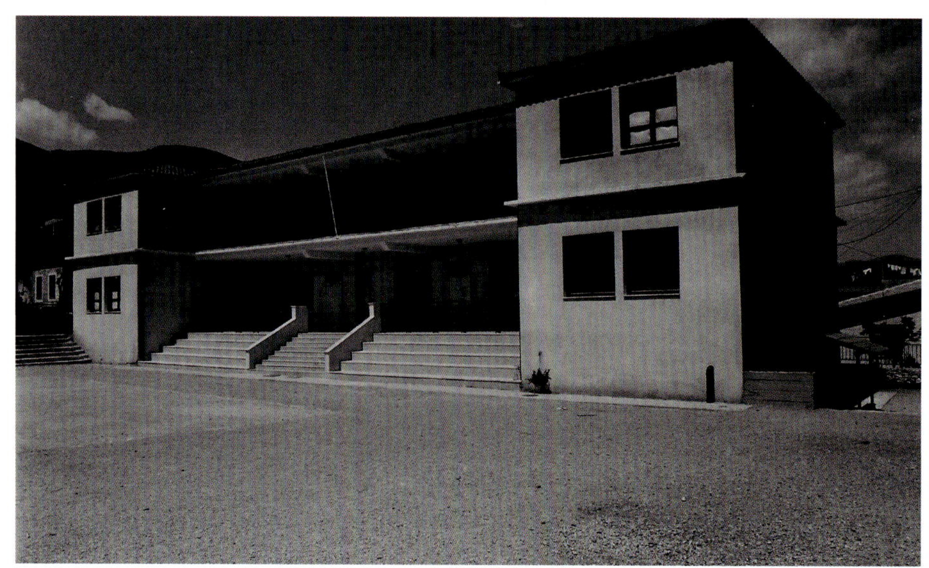

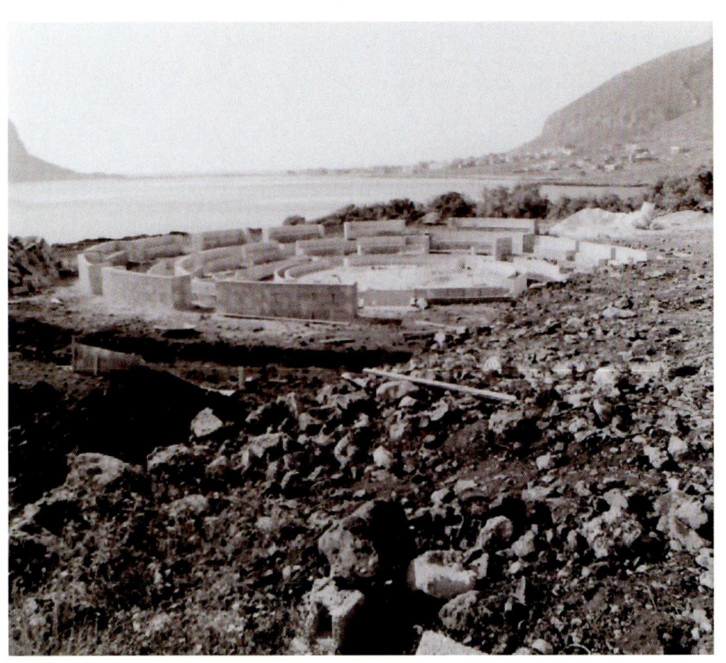

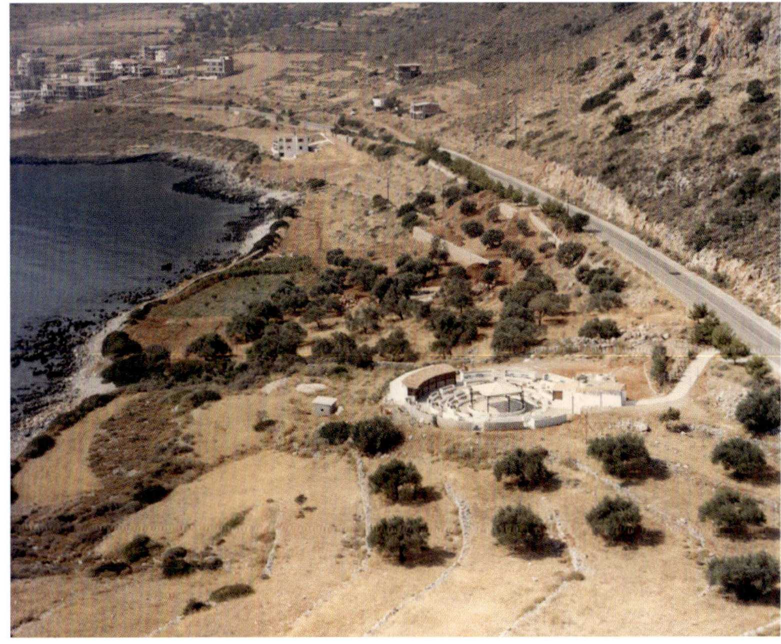

Development has its downside and foreigners who enjoyed the environment and society of Greece when it was relatively undeveloped are now faced with a great new Greek phenomenon that is close to the Western norm.

JOHN S. KOLIOPOULOS AND THANOS VEREMIS, *GREECE: THE MODERN SEQUEL FROM 1821 TO THE PRESENT*, 2007

CHAPTER 4 · THE TRADITION · Η ΠΑΡΑΔΟΣΗ

Church and National Occasions

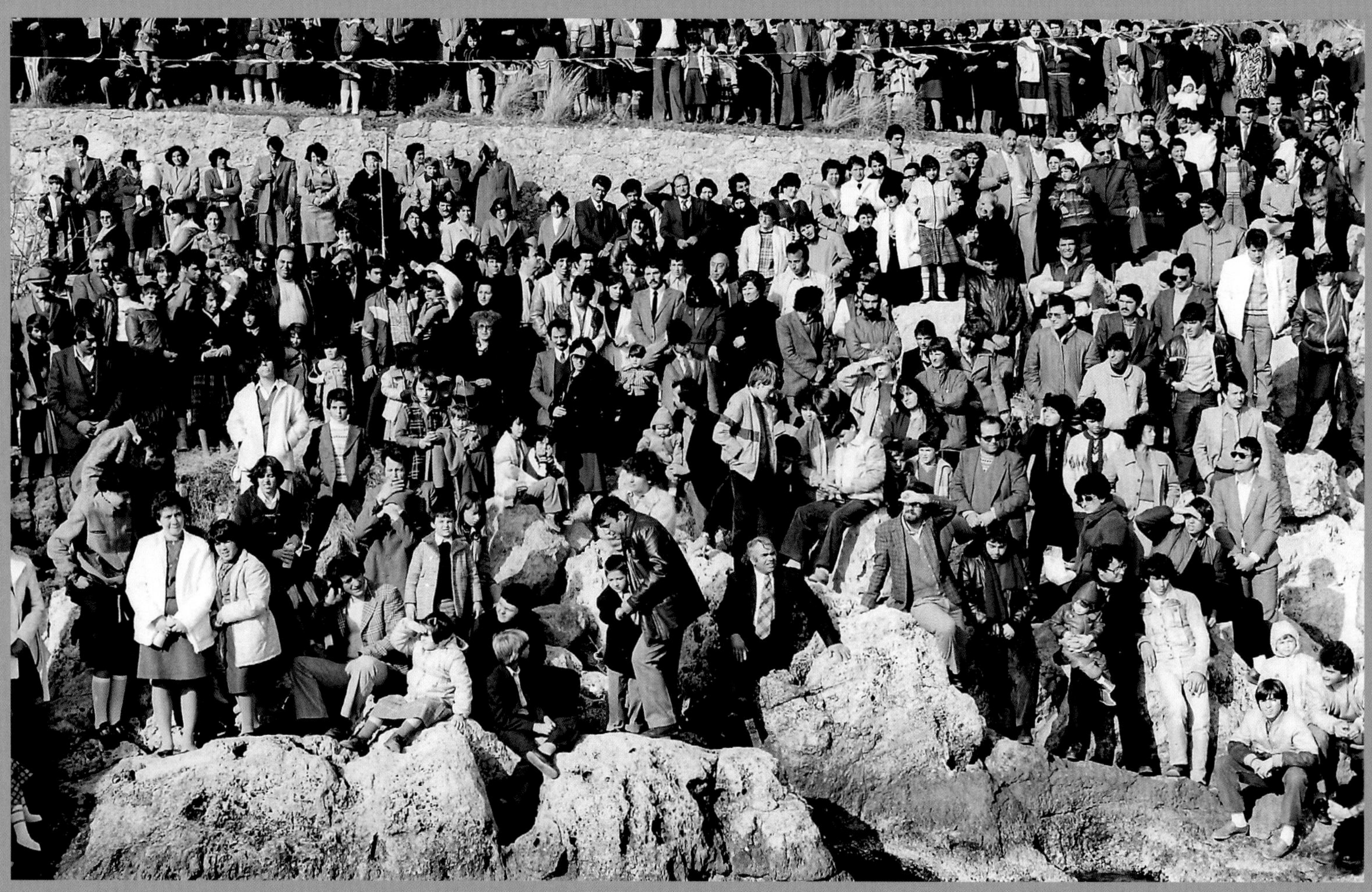

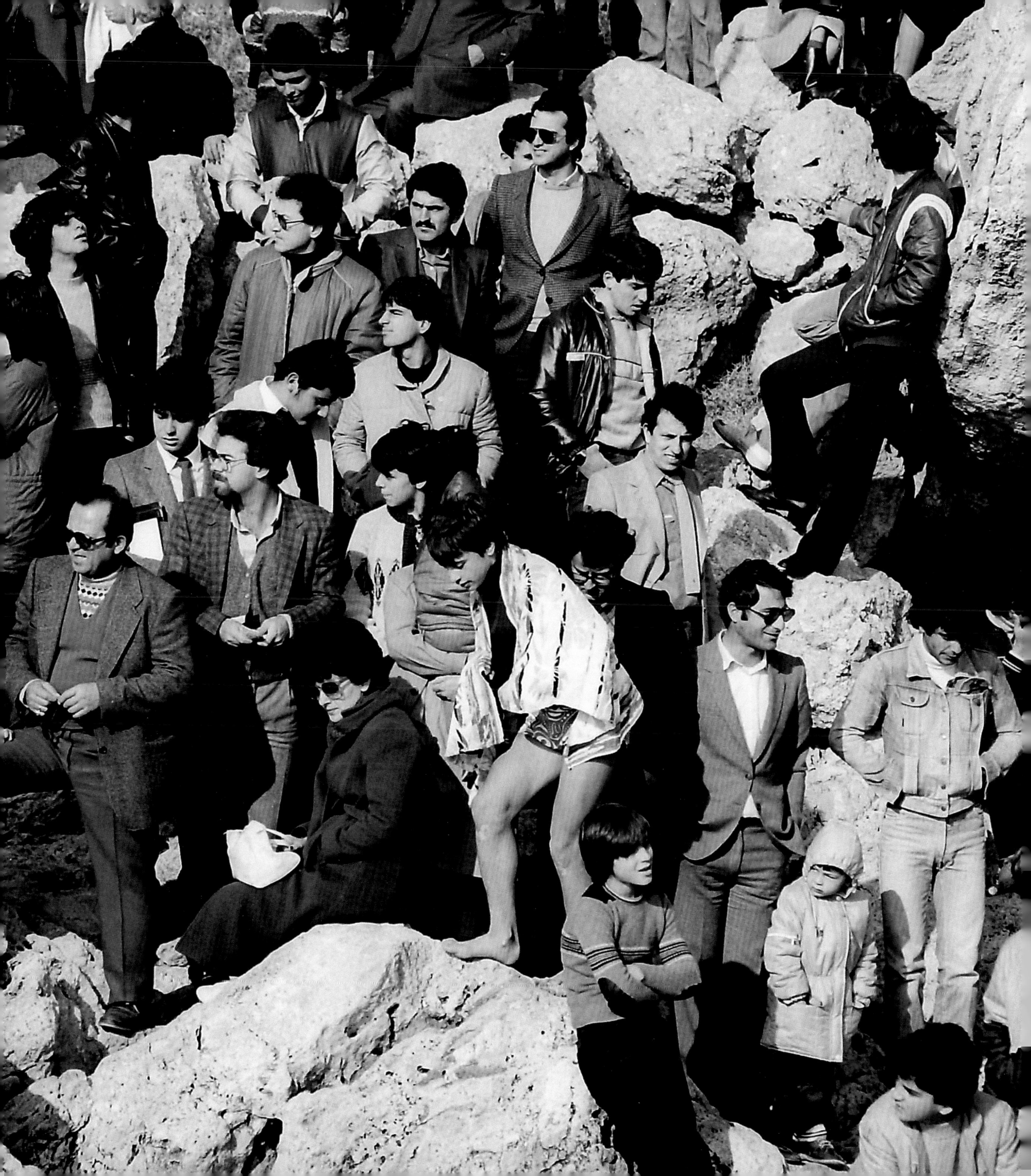

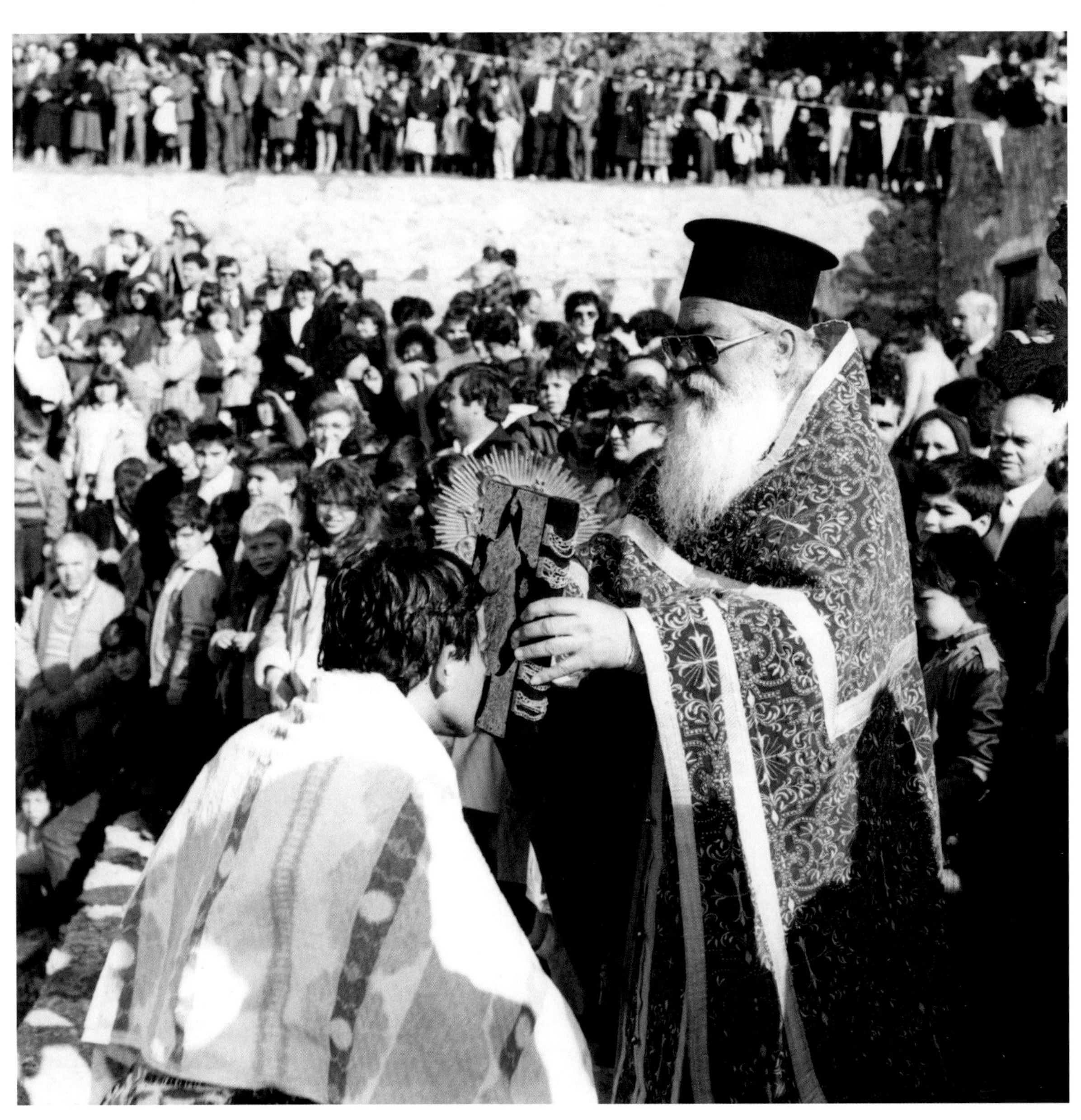

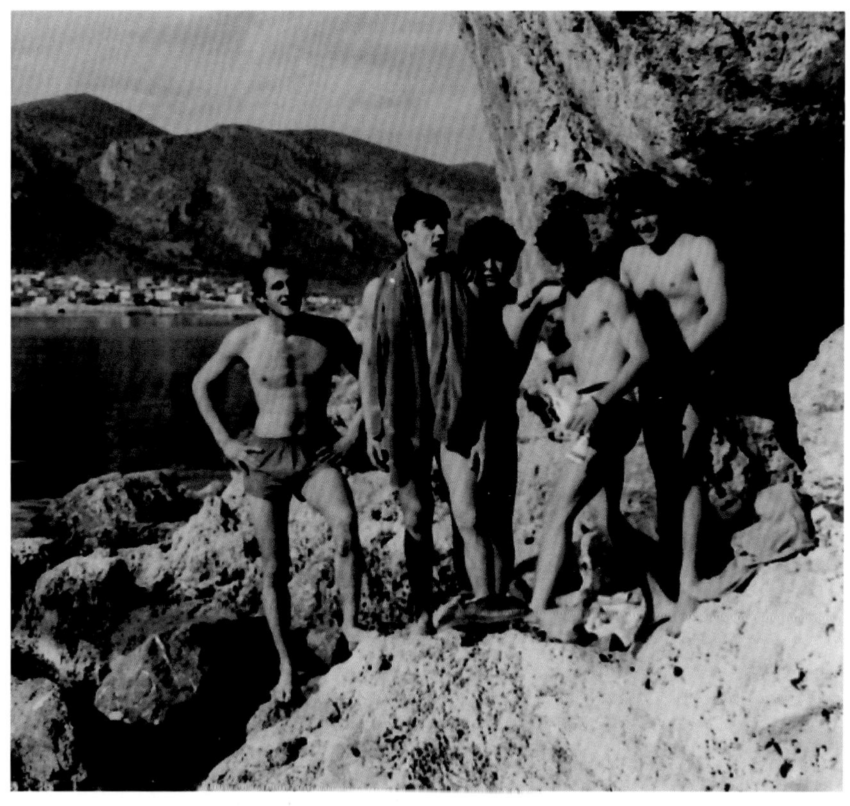

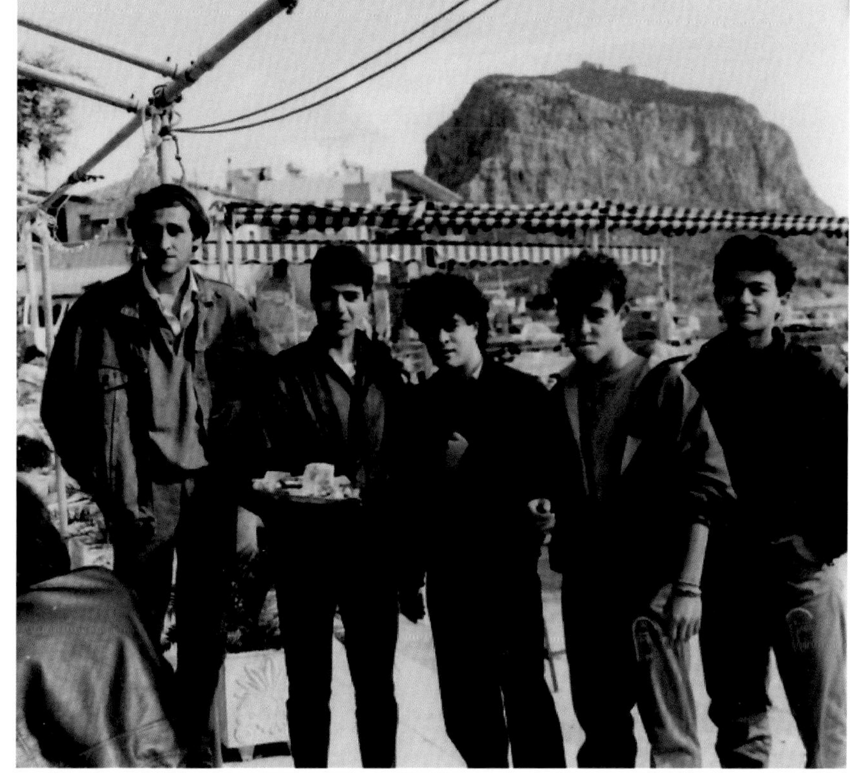

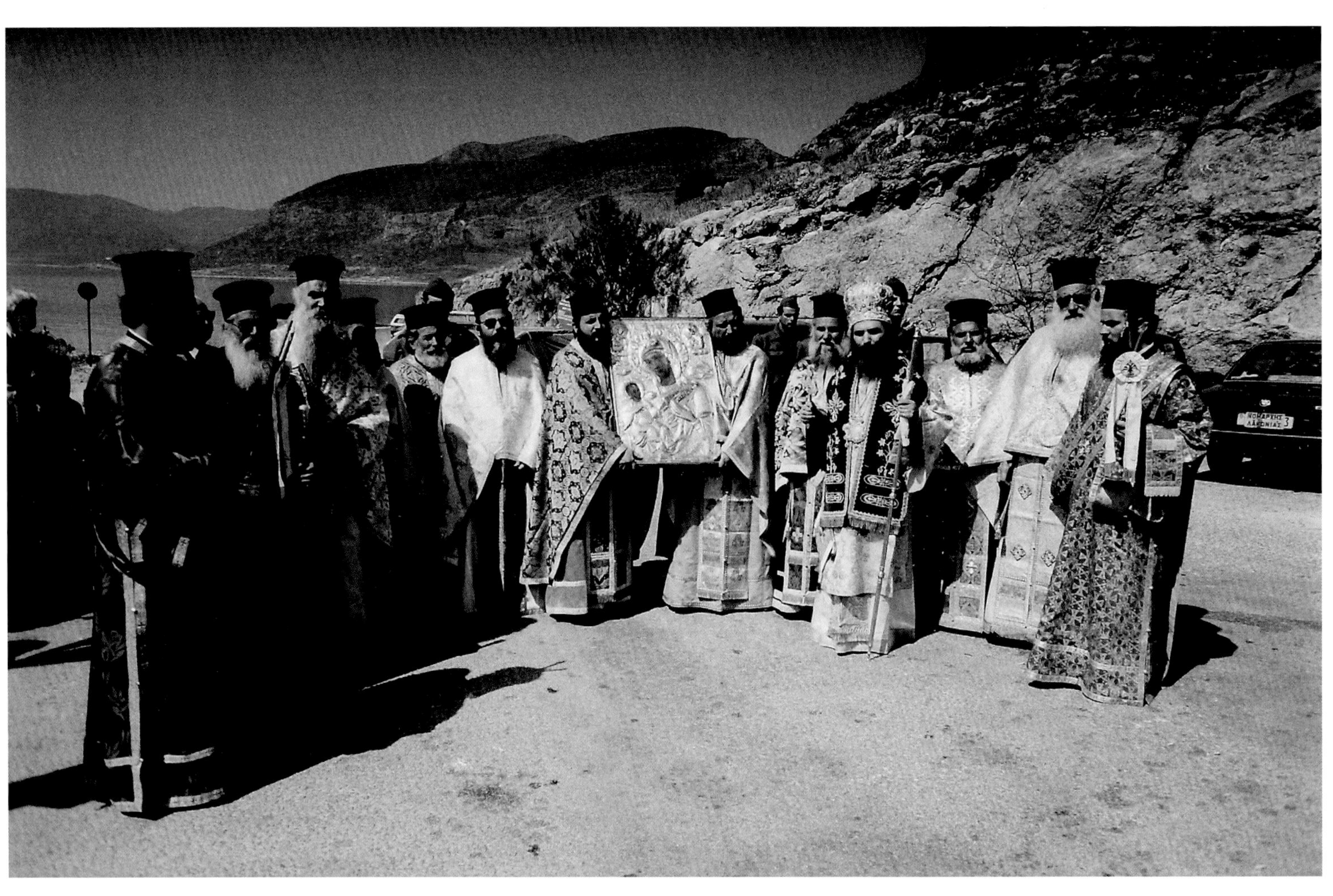

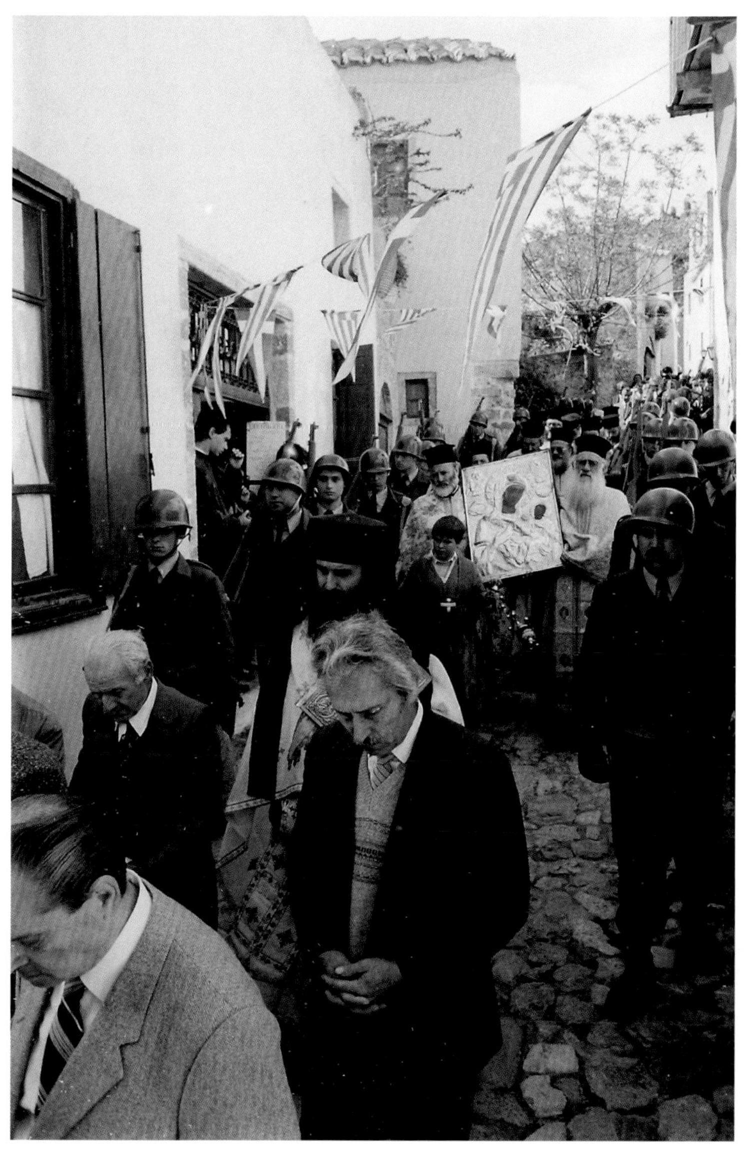

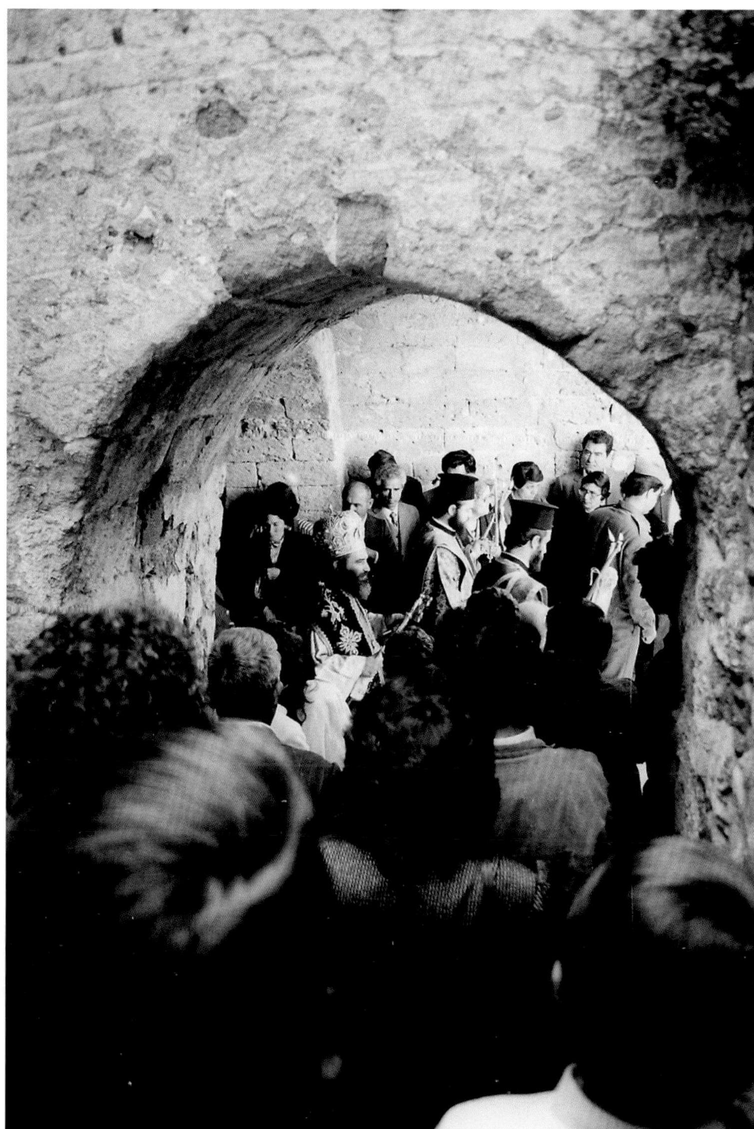

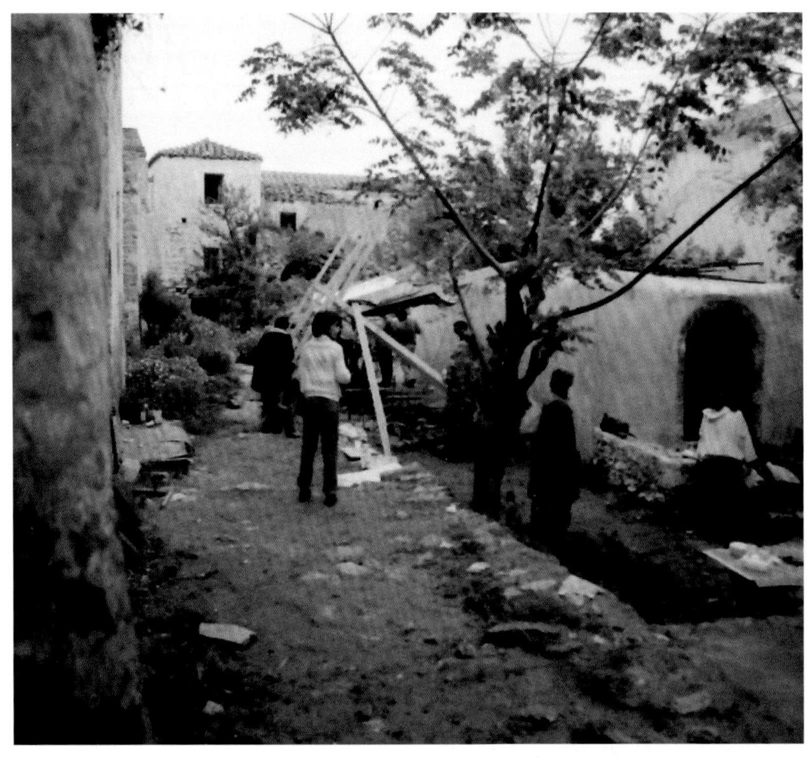

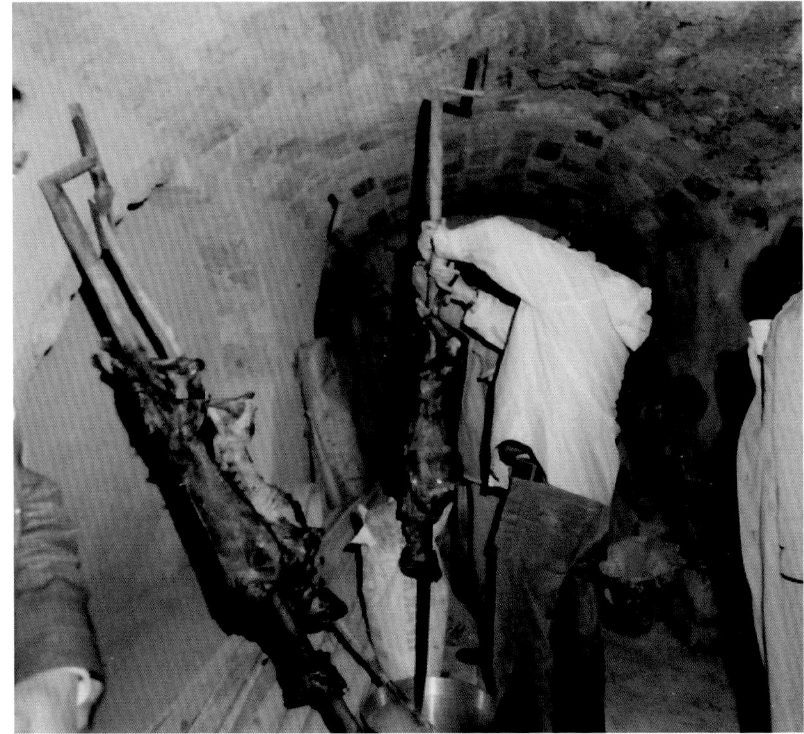

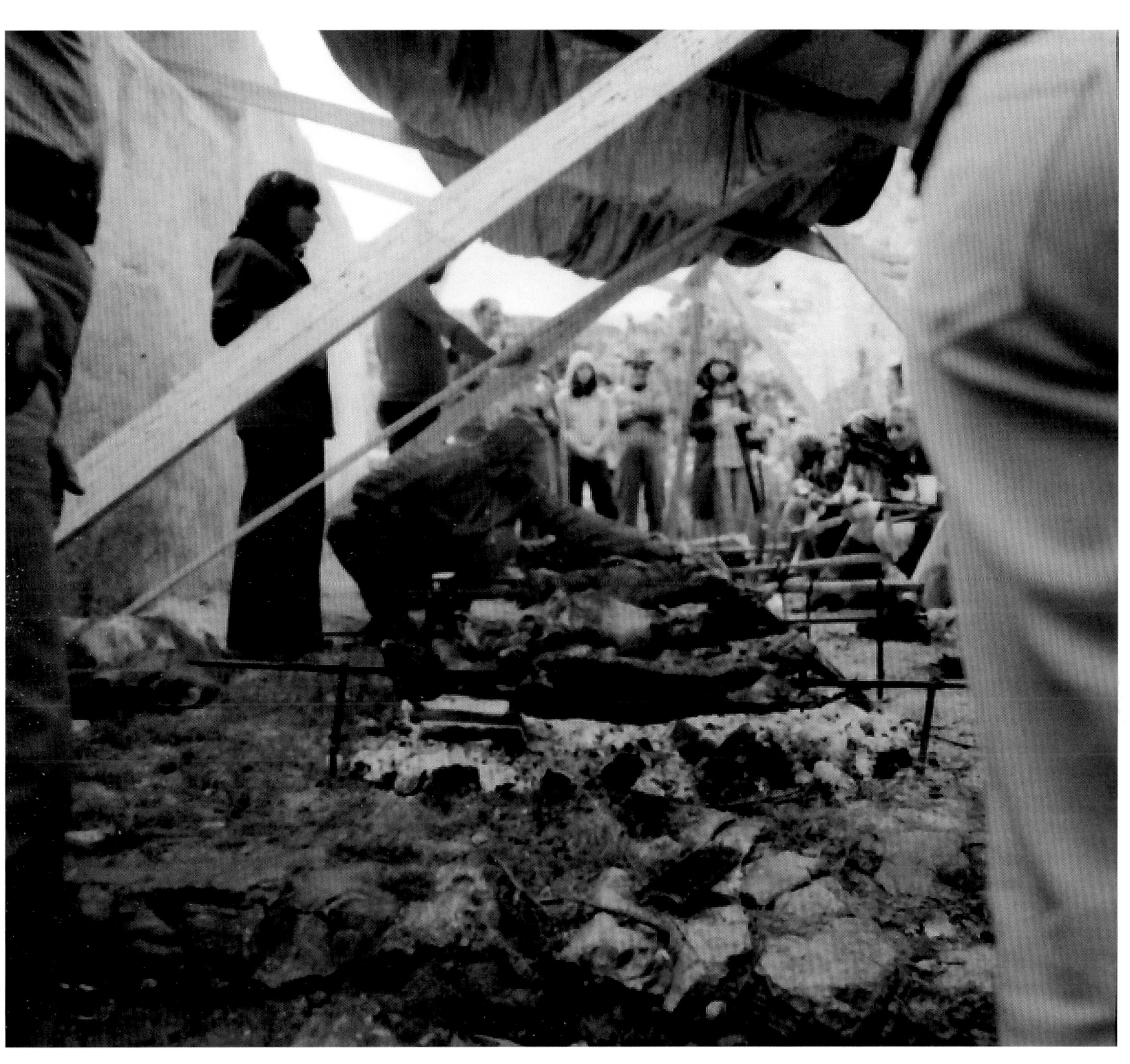

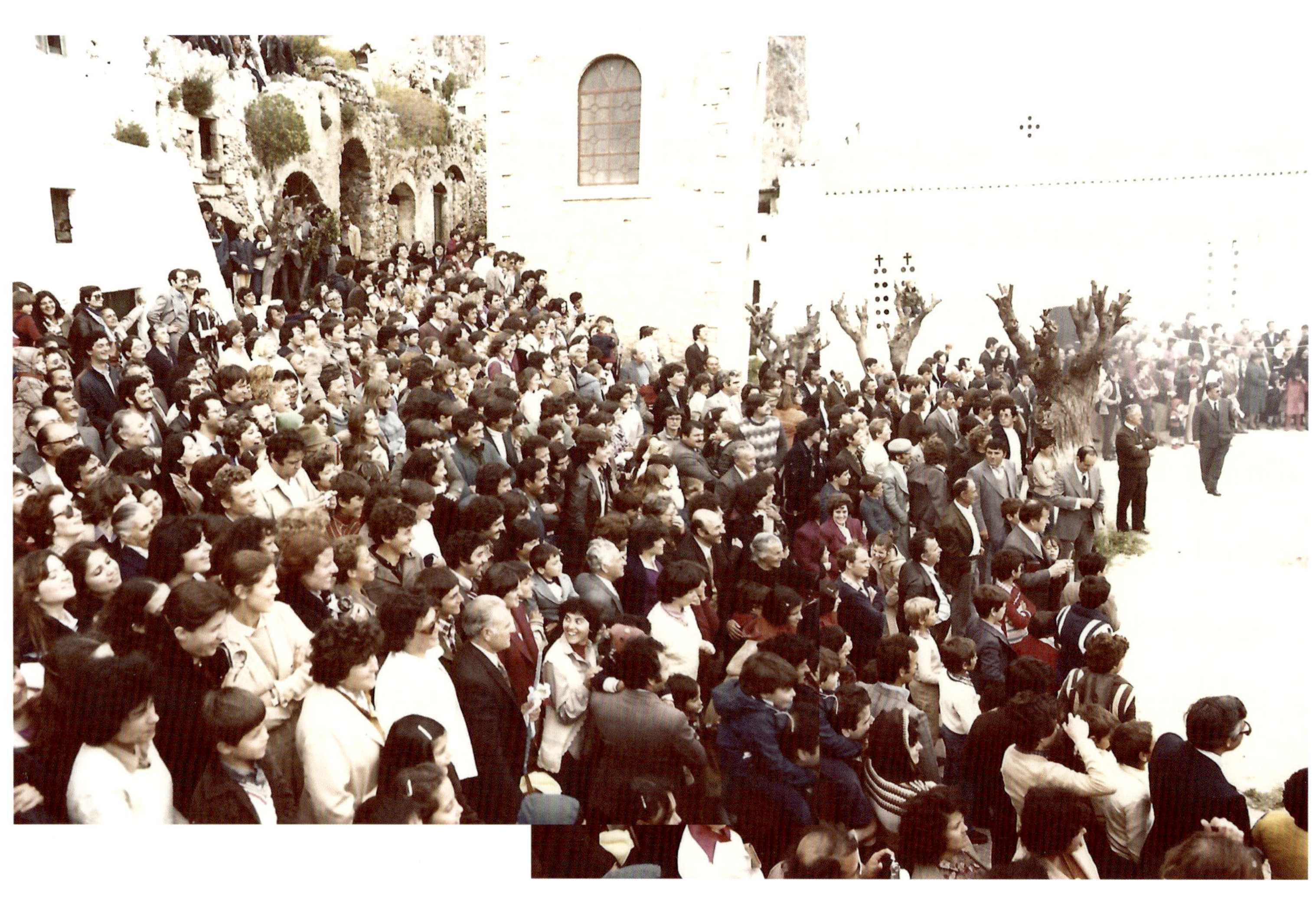

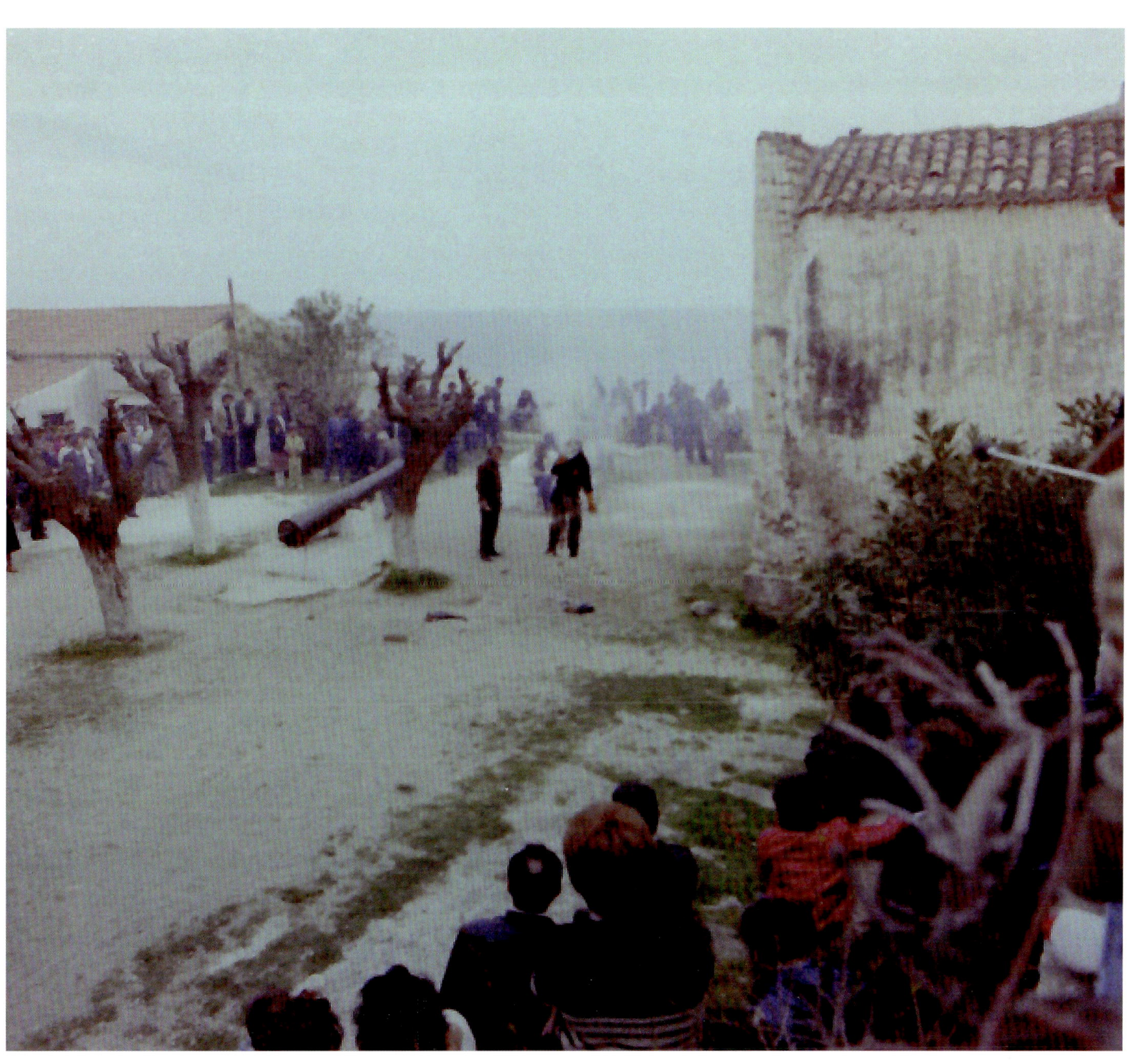

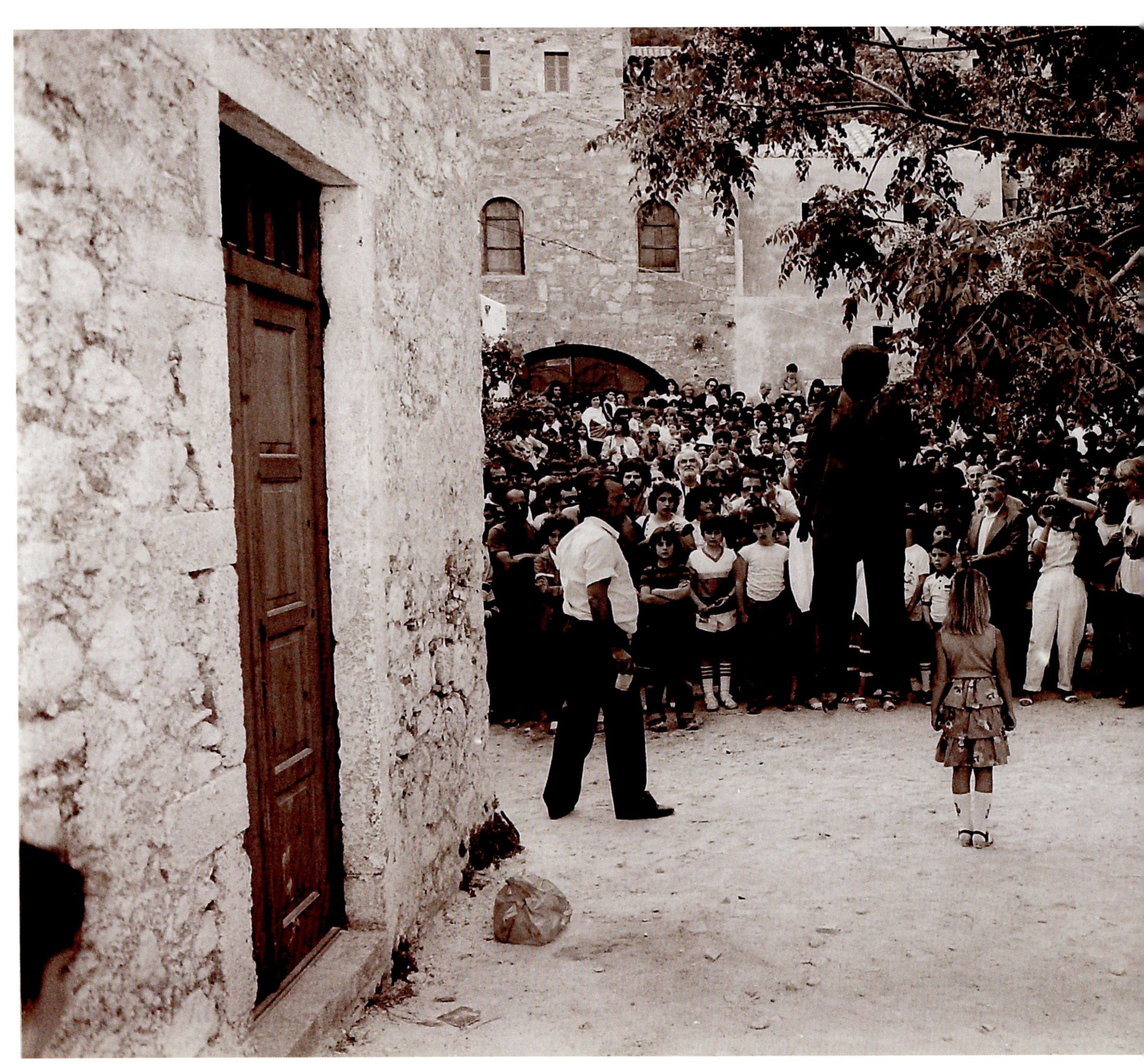

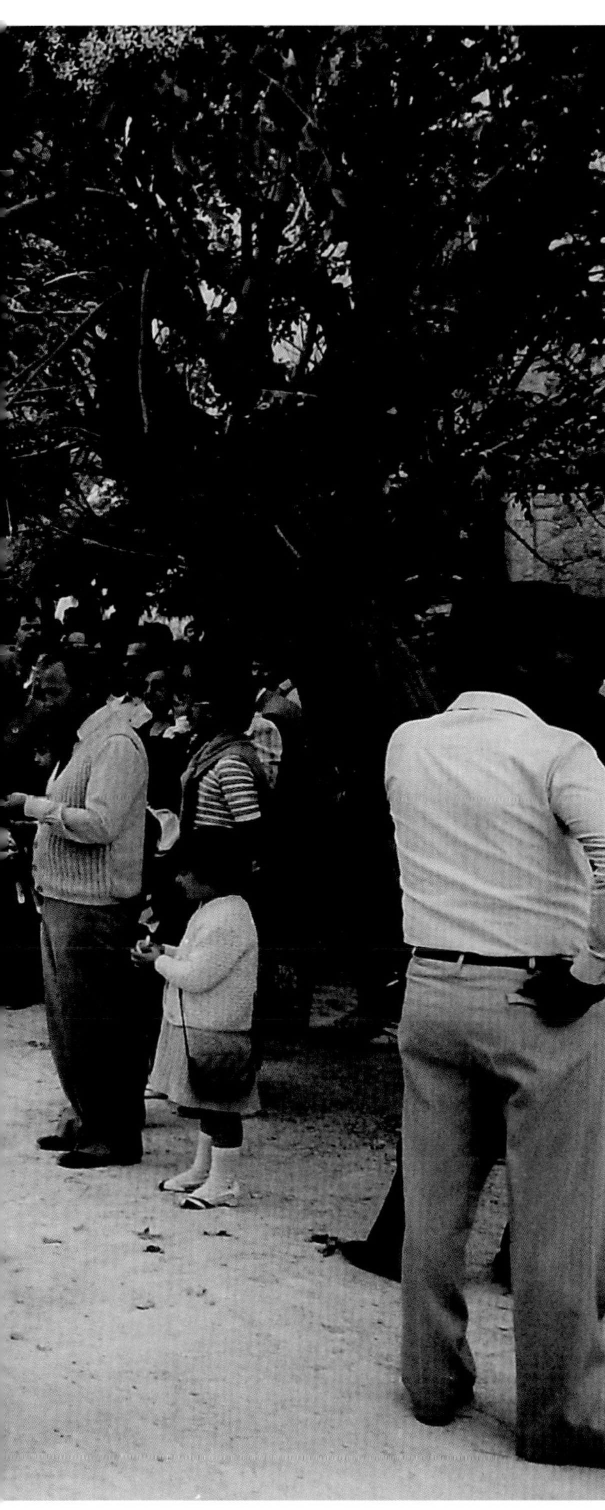

Those who filled an effigy of Judas with gunpowder and straw for the boys to burn in the village square...

YANNIS RITSOS,
'THE WOMEN OF MONEMVASIA', 1975

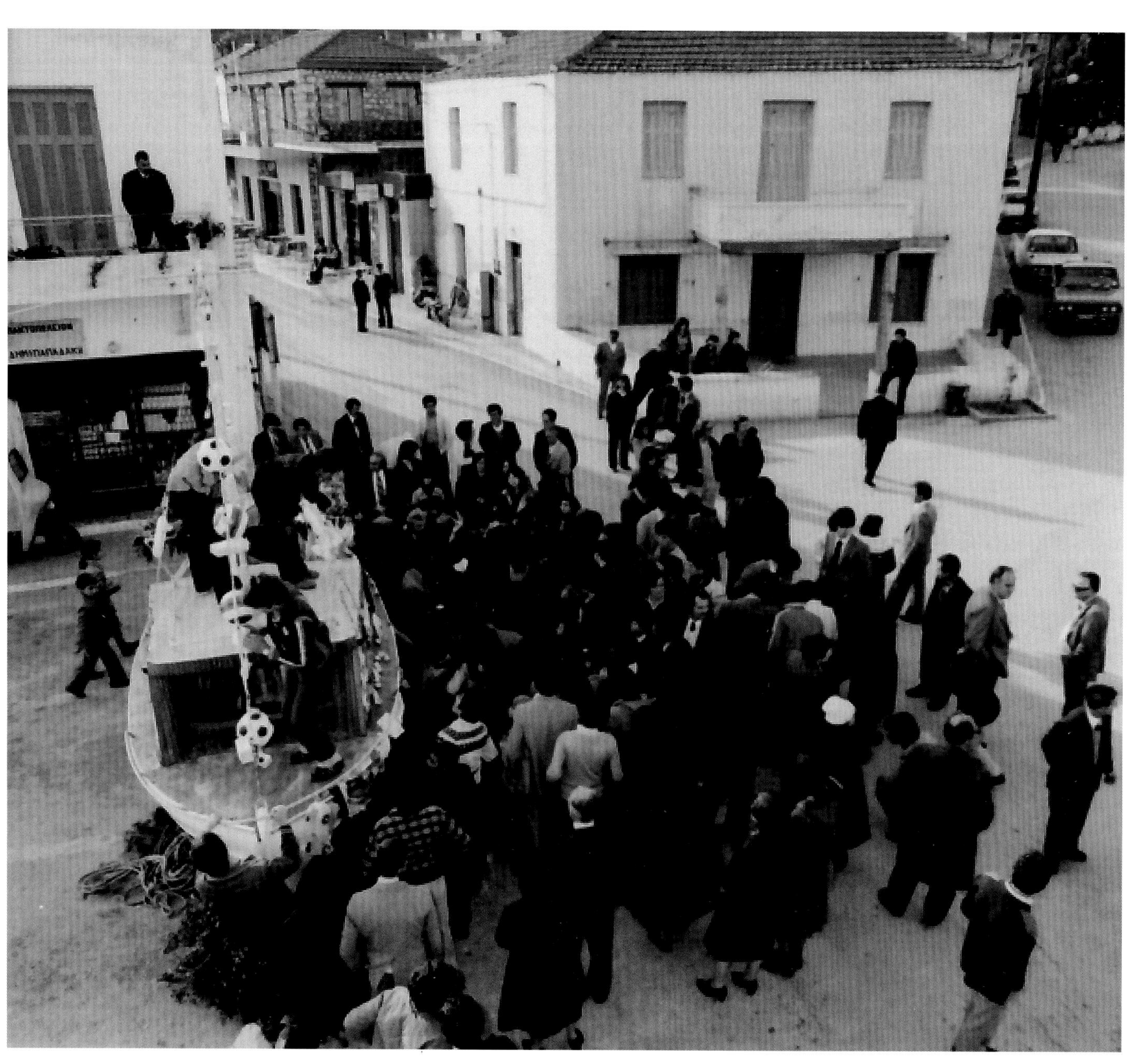

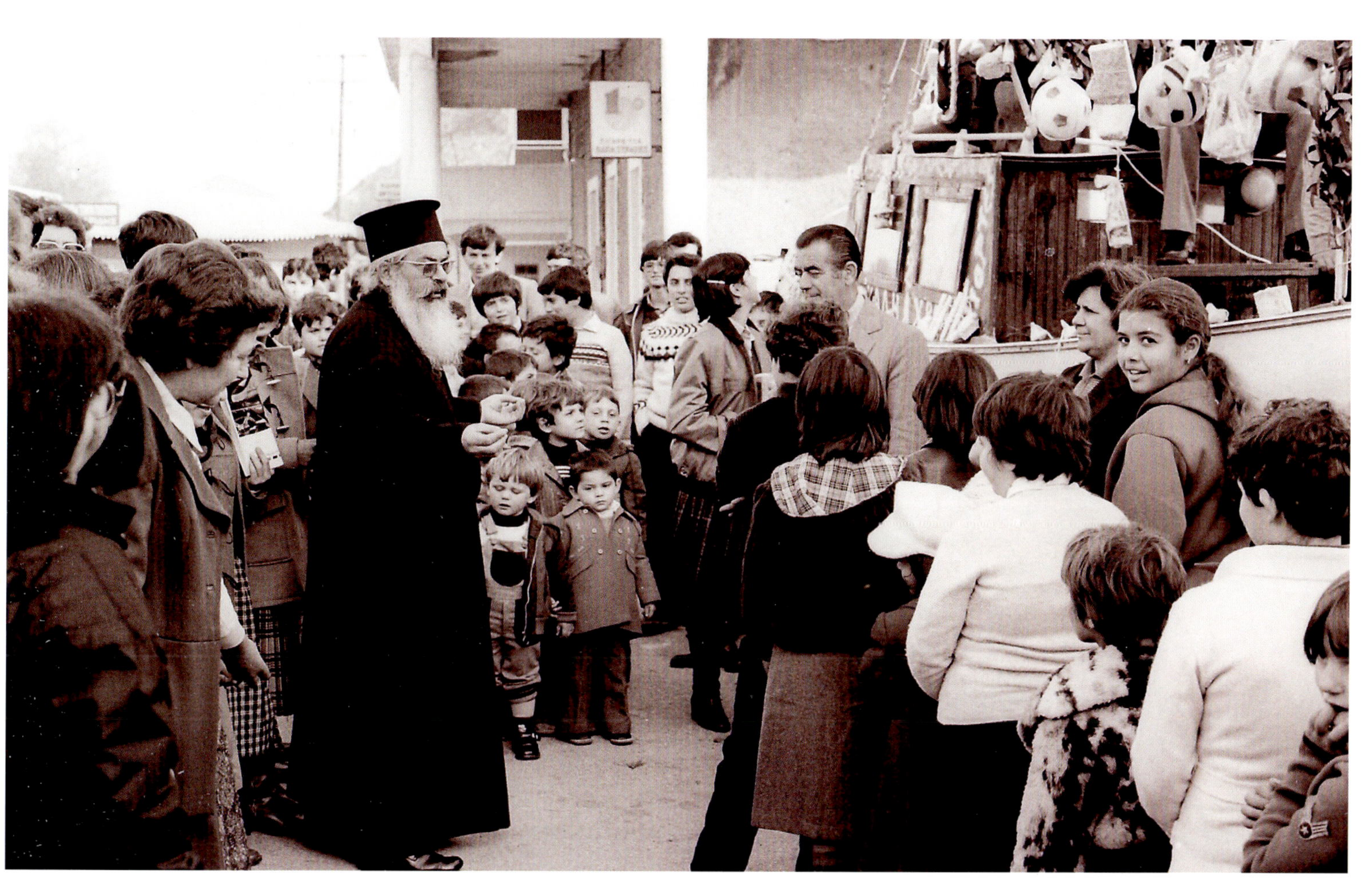

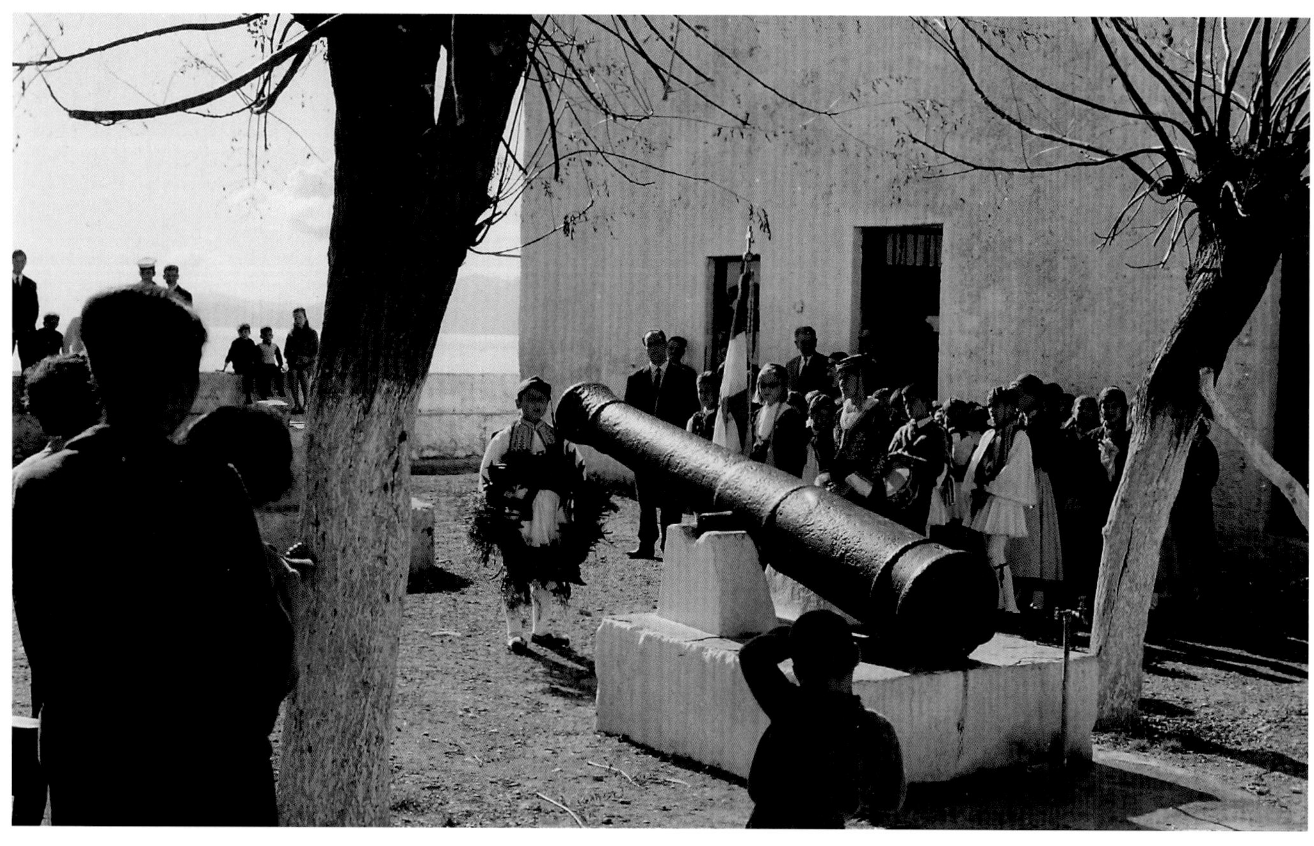

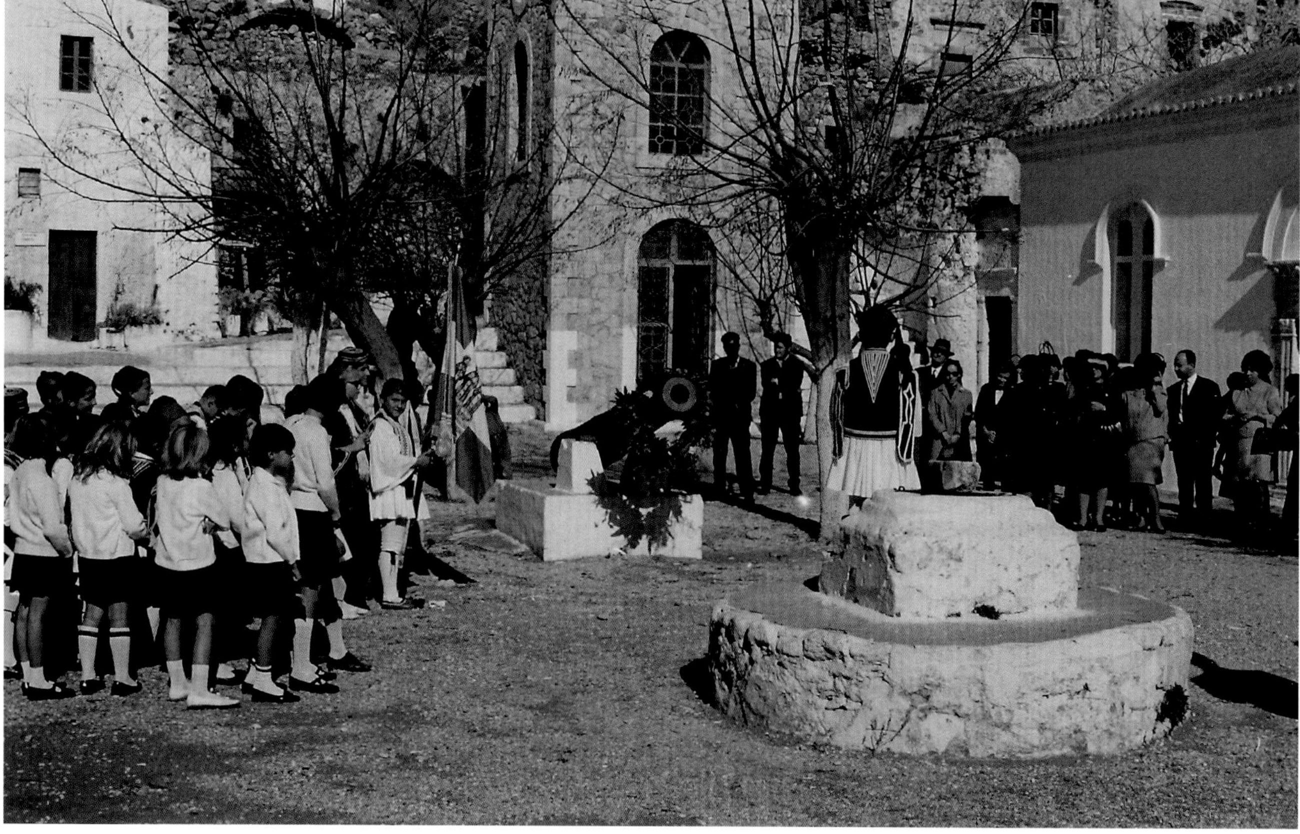

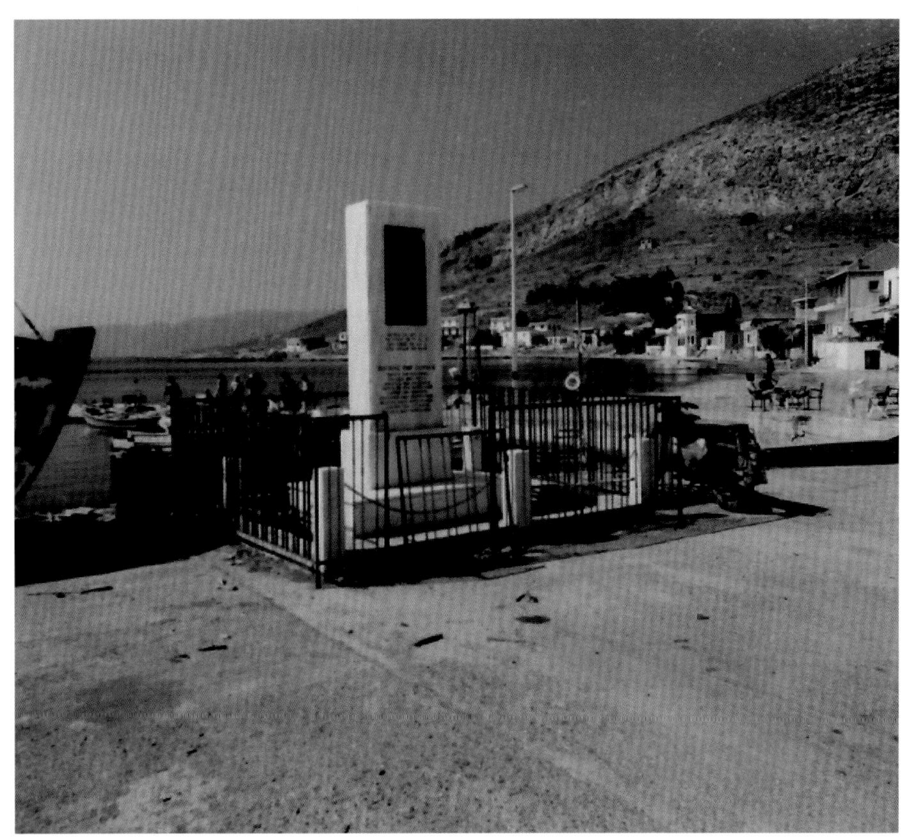

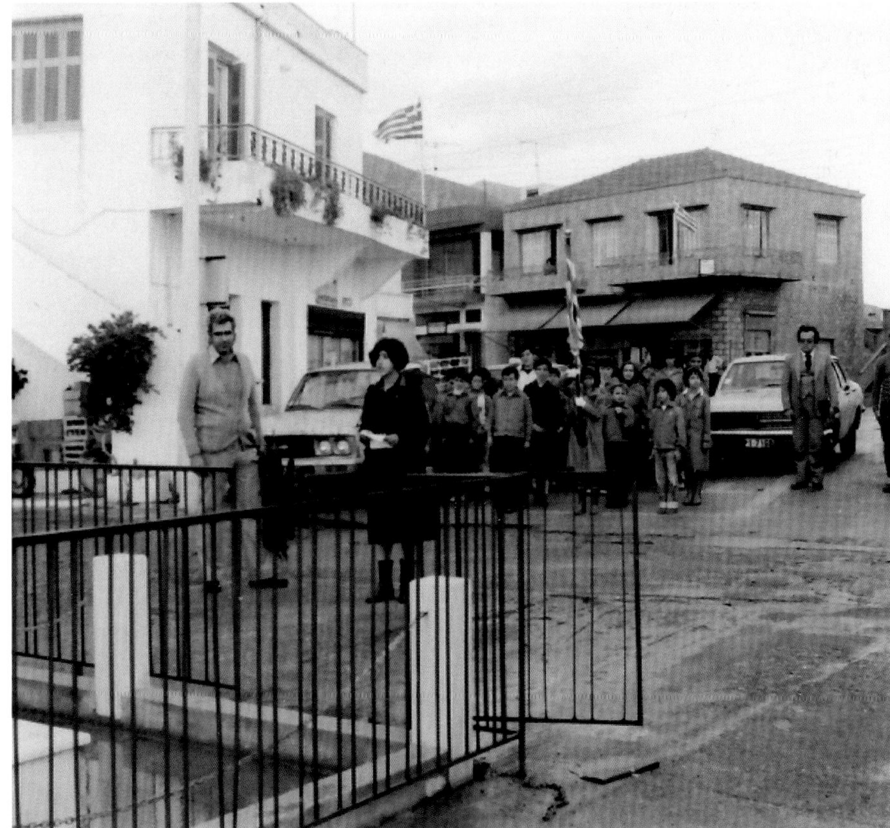

The story of a nation must also be the story of how people have thought about themselves, and the world, and their place in it.

RODERICK BEATON, *GREECE: BIOGRAPHY OF A MODERN NATION*, 2019

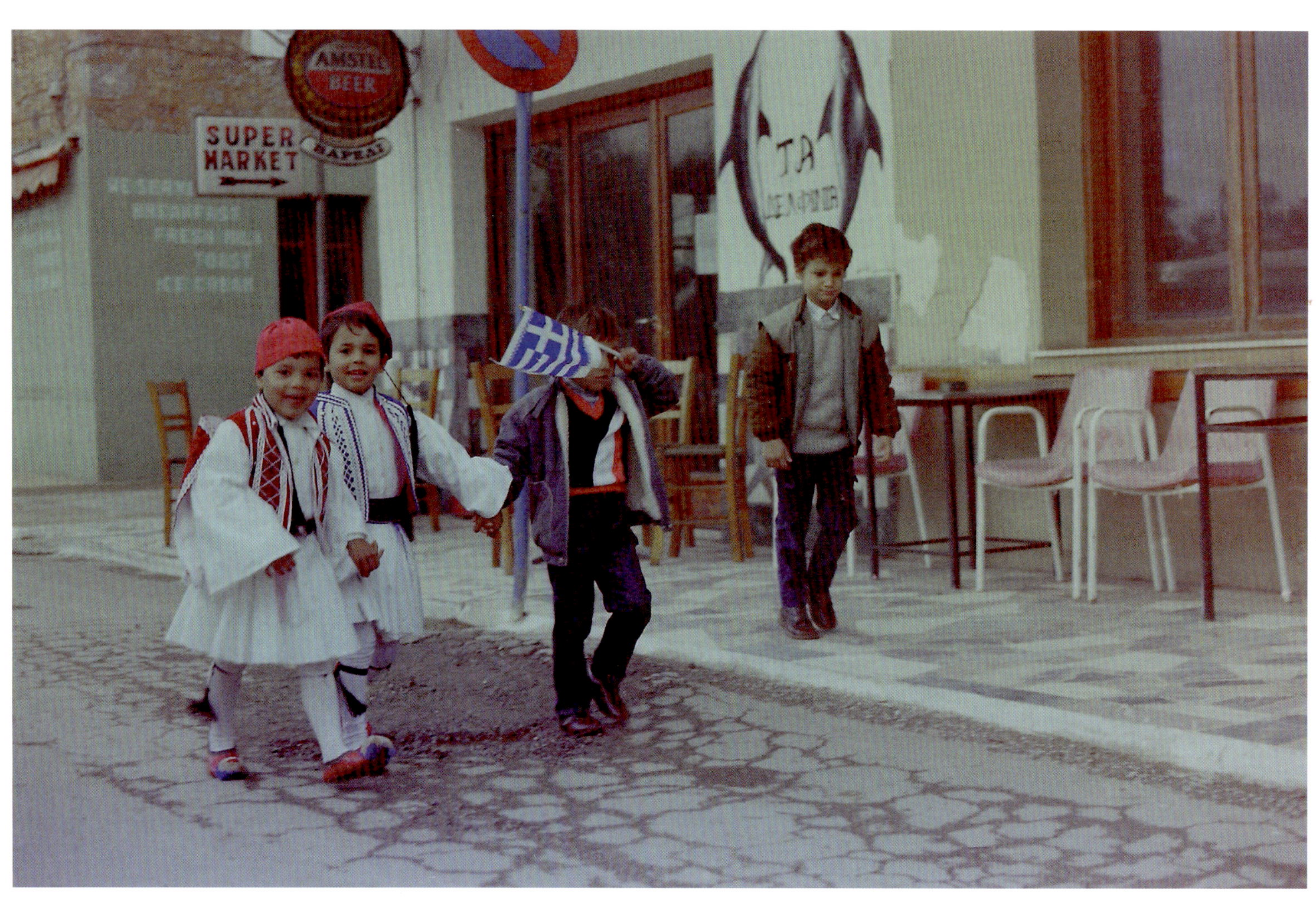
AMSTEL BEER
SUPER MARKET
ΤΑ

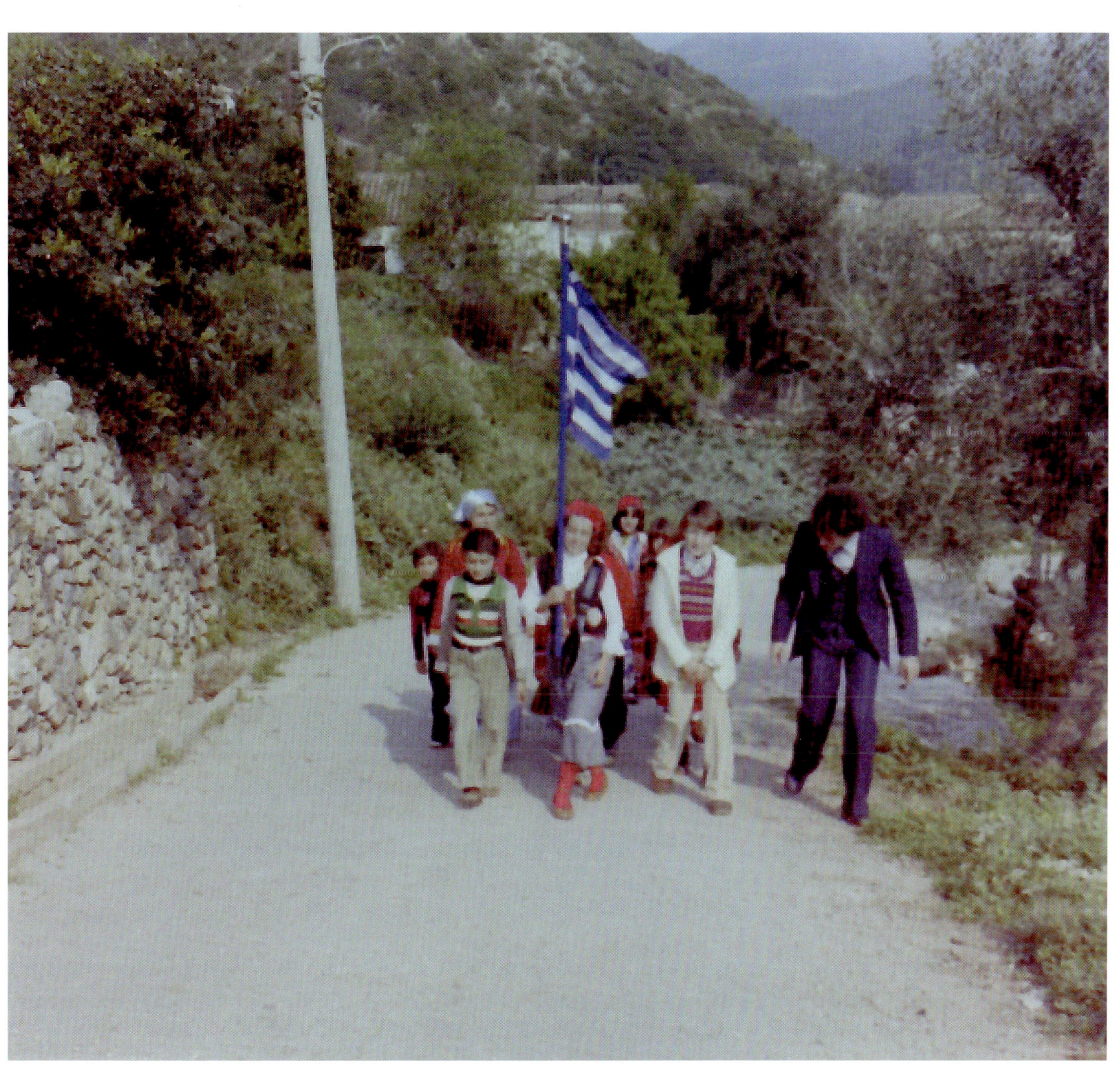

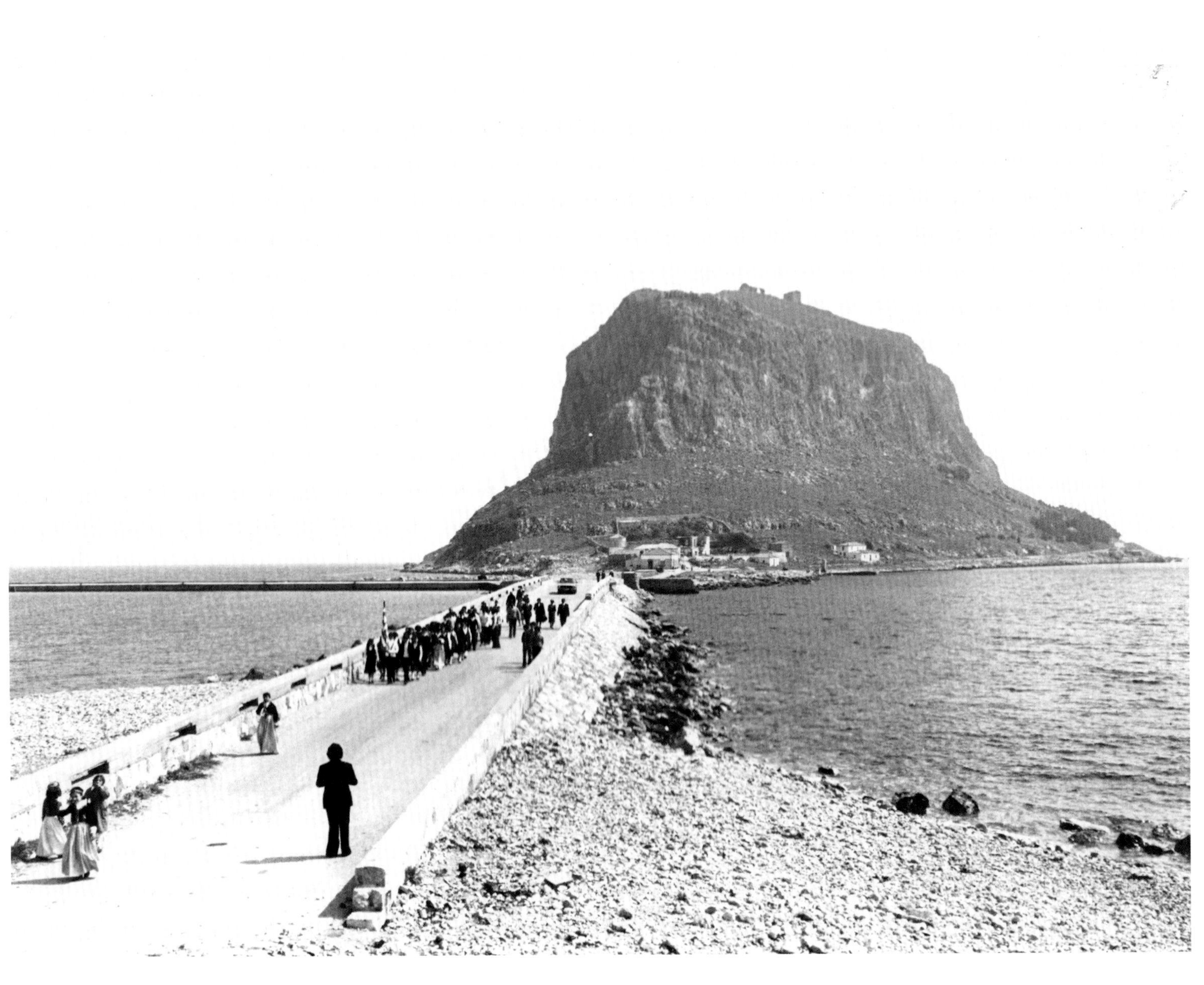

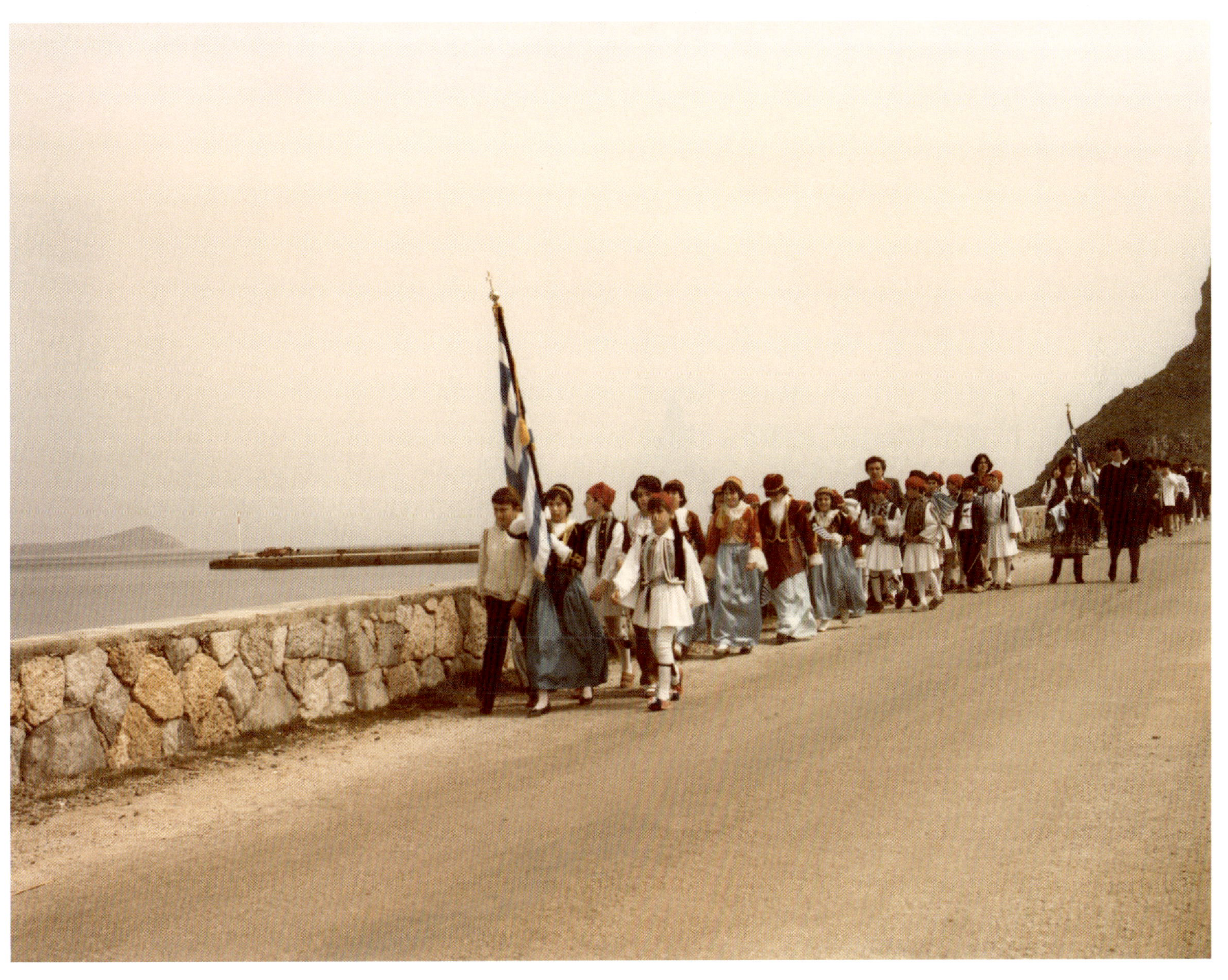

There is little room for improvisation in these rituals, and attending them is part of the socialisation of any Greek child.

BRUCE CLARK, *ATHENS: CITY OF WISDOM*, 2021

Celebrations

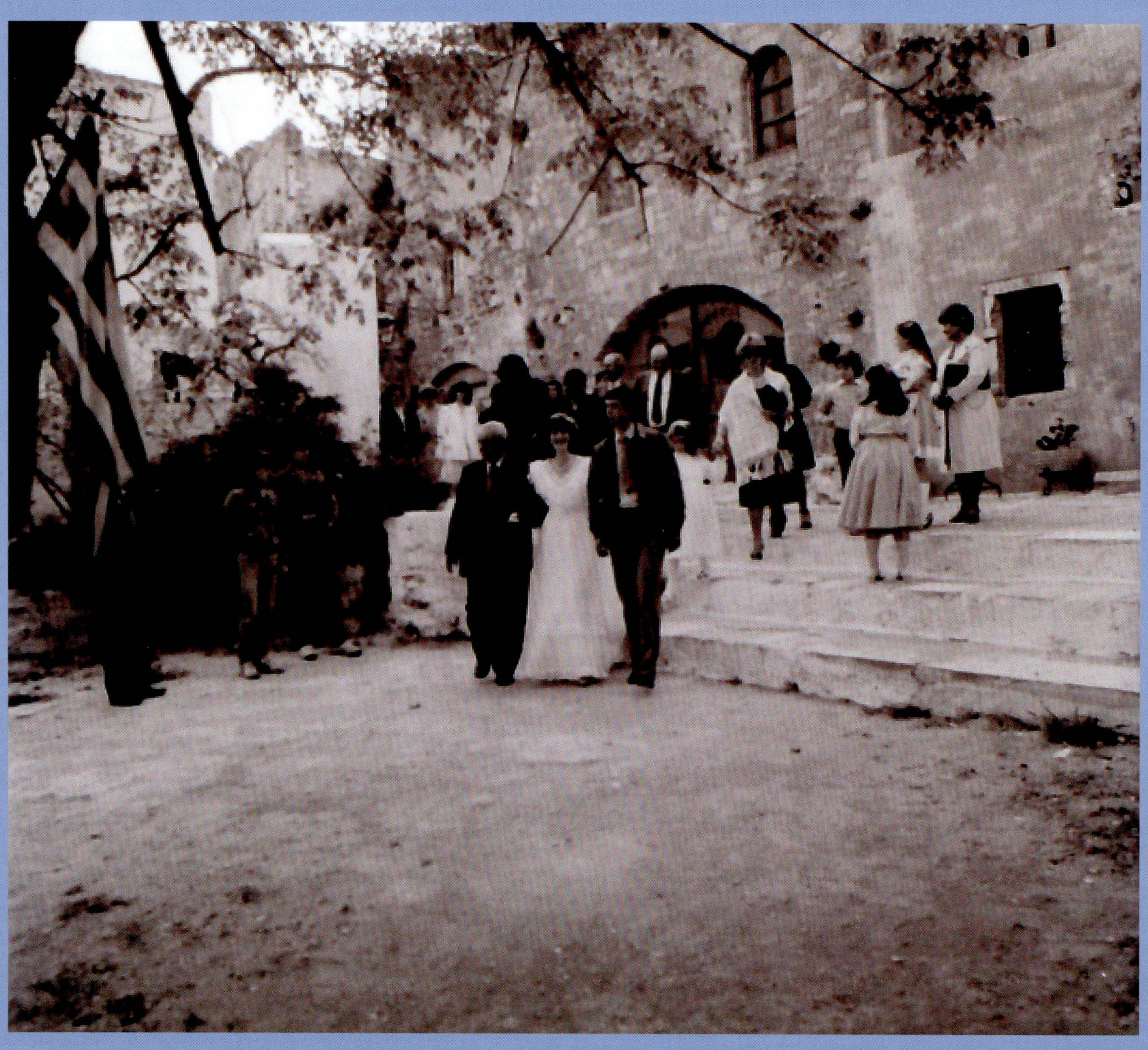

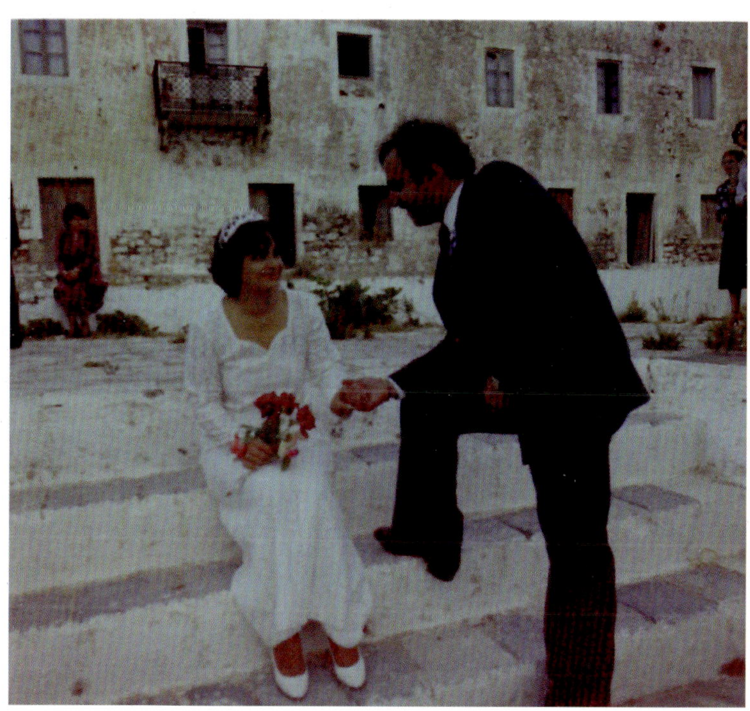

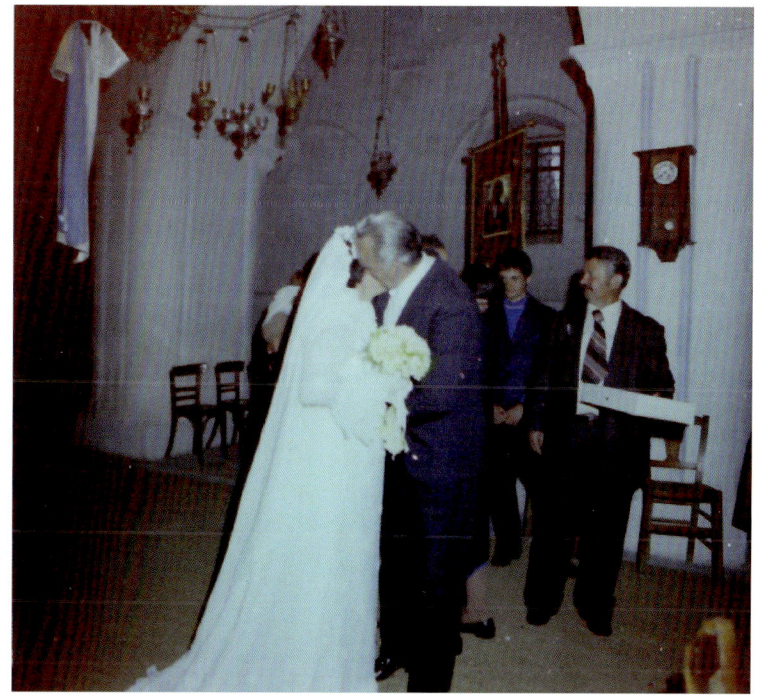

The bride is a child from Monemvasia, the groom from Sparti. The bride will follow the groom – one less inhabitant in this slowly dying village.

GUNDER ADRIAN, *ROCK OF MONEMVASIA*, DOCUMENTARY FILM, 1964

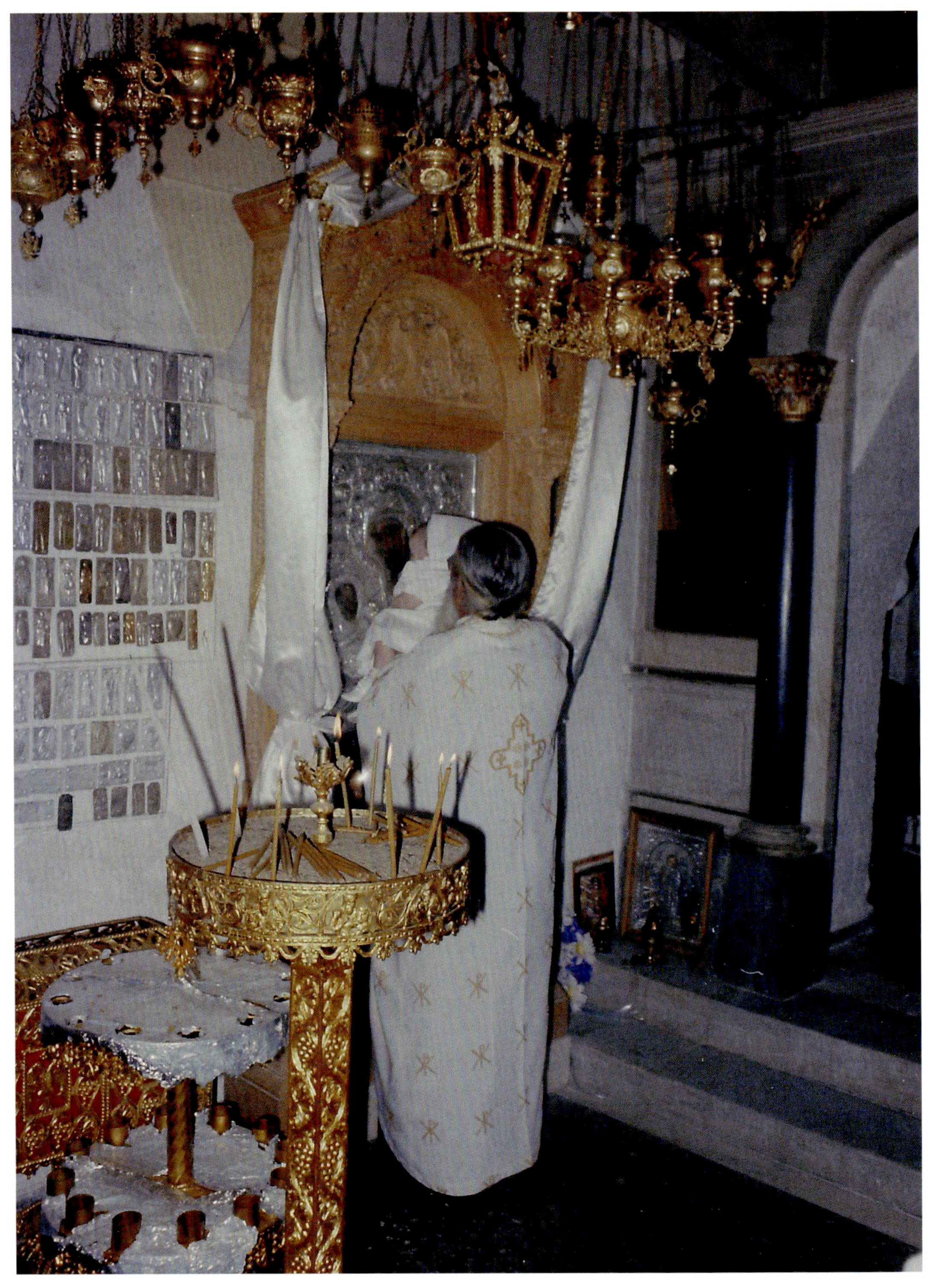

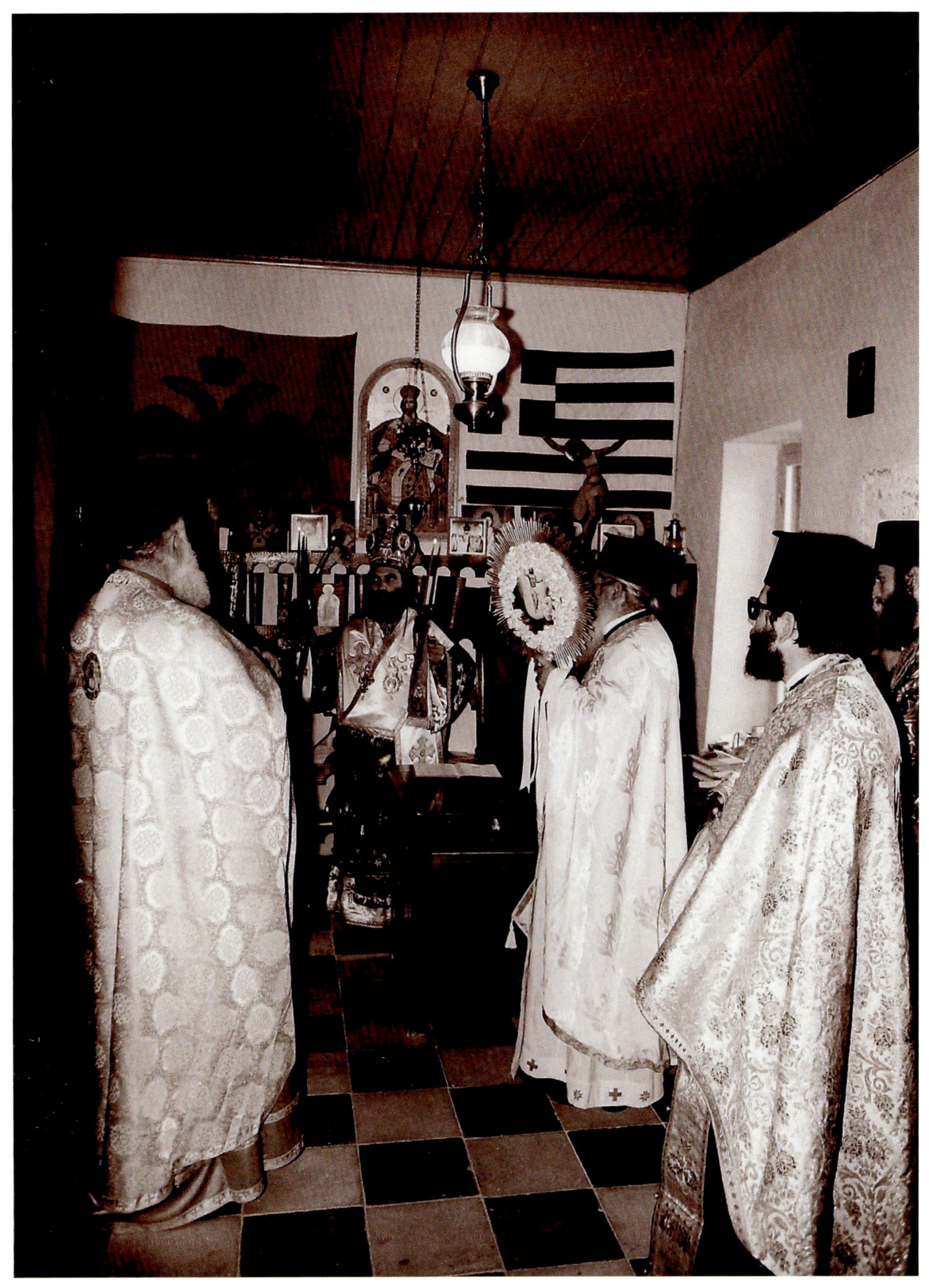

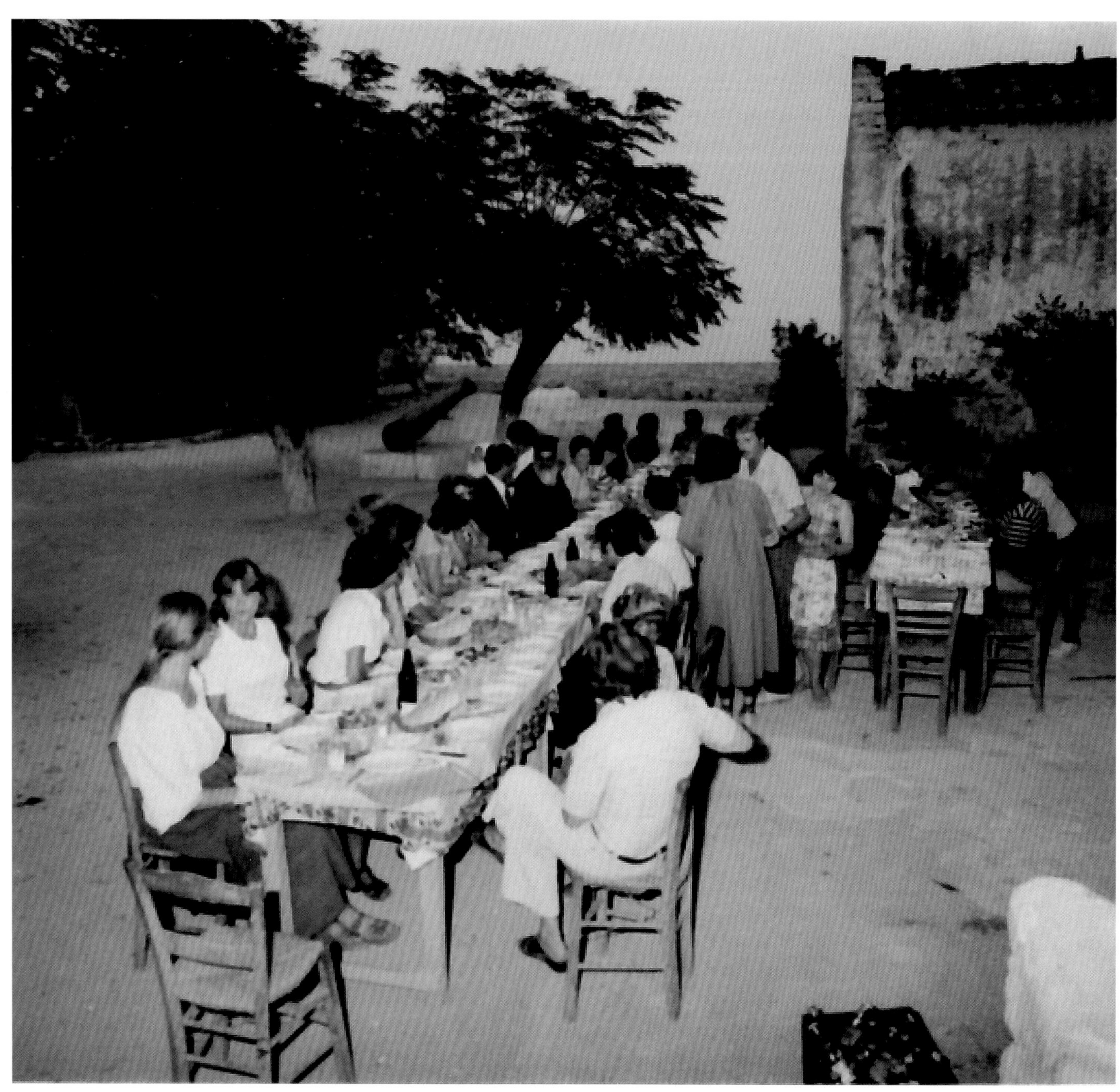

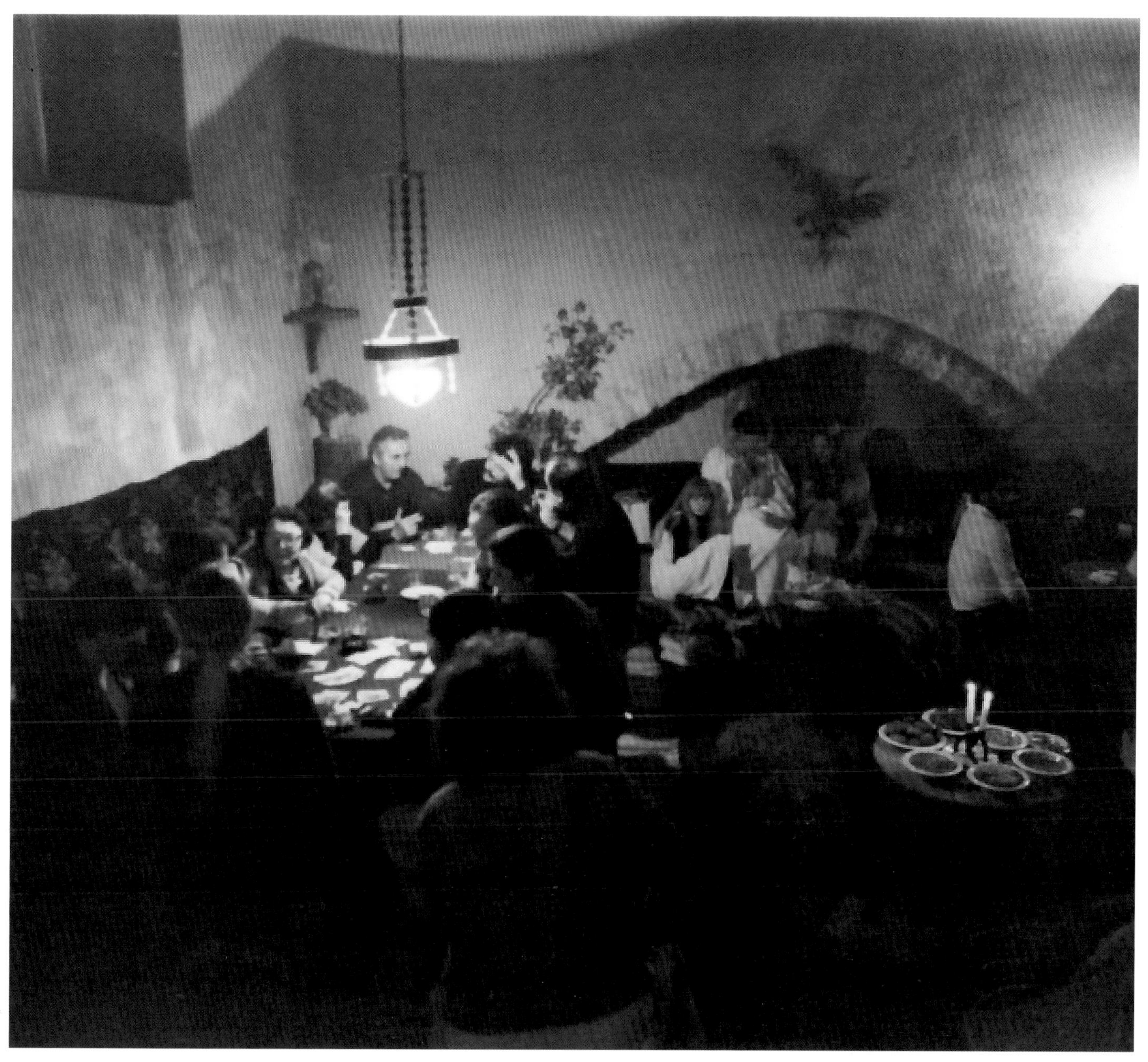

We cannot change Monemvasia, it would ruin everything...
We were not supposed to last here, in isolation and cut into a cliff of rock.
But here we are. Hundreds of years later, here we still are.

MATOULA RITSOS, 93 YEAR OLD RESIDENT AS QUOTED IN THE *NEW YORK TIMES*, 2006

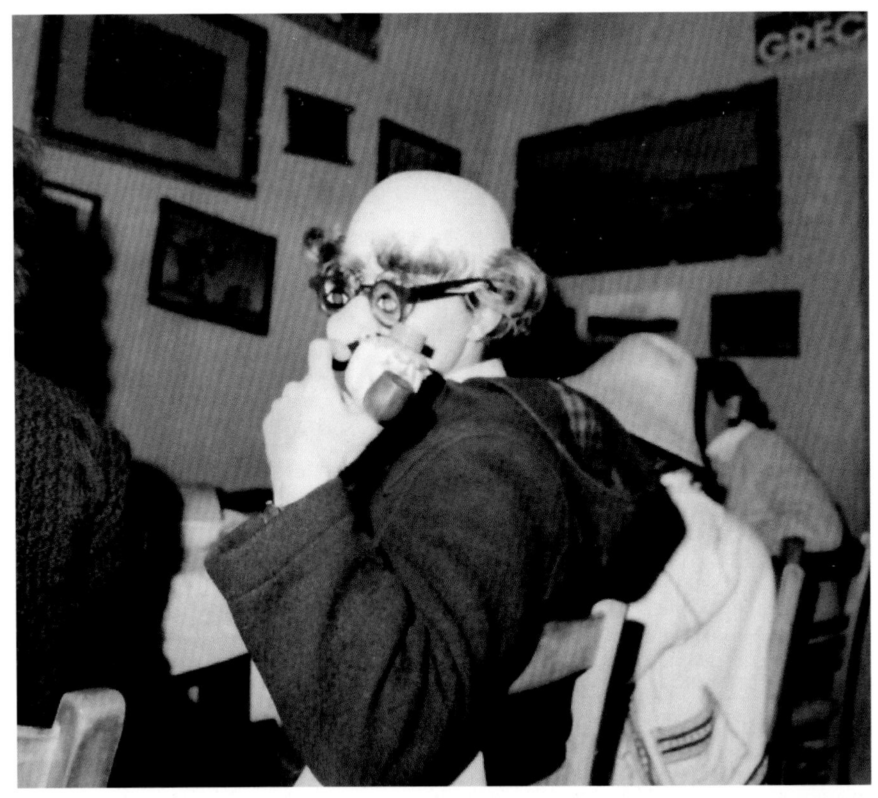

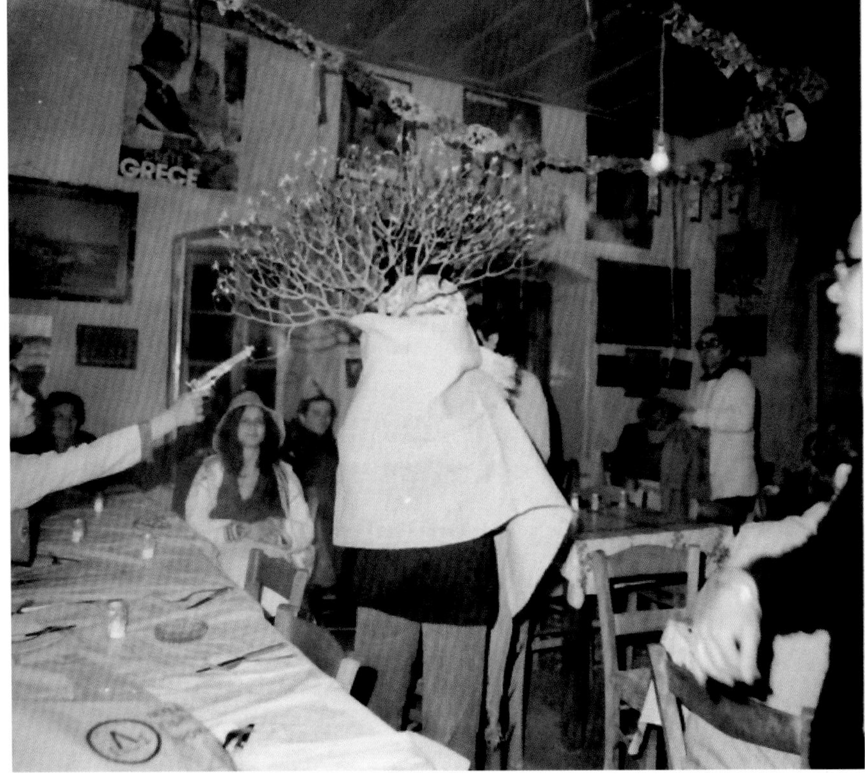

The basic elements of the traditional carnival are ... the masquerade and boisterous merrymaking.

JOHN L. TOMKINSON,
FESTIVE GREECE: A CALENDAR OF TRADITION, 2003

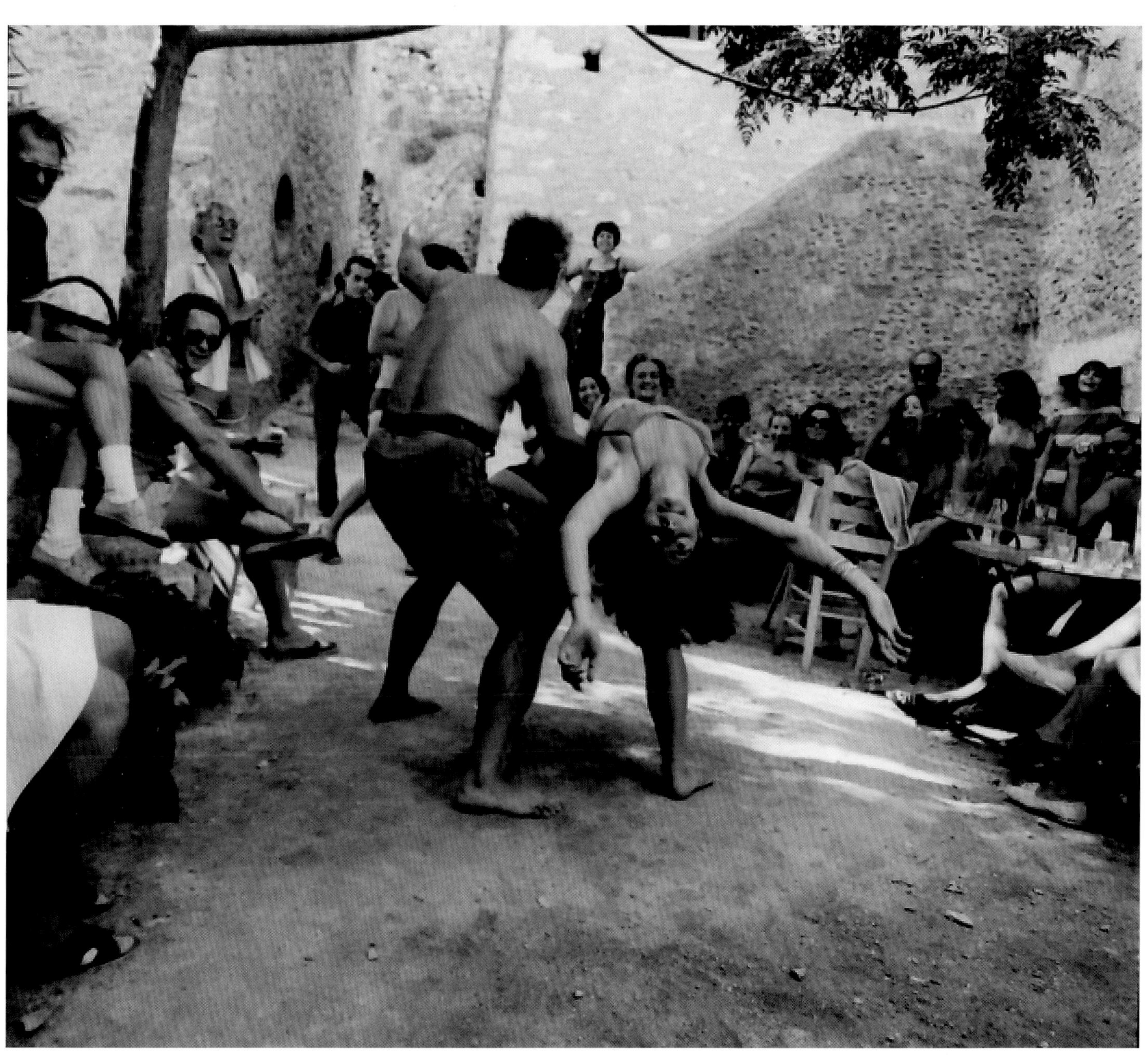

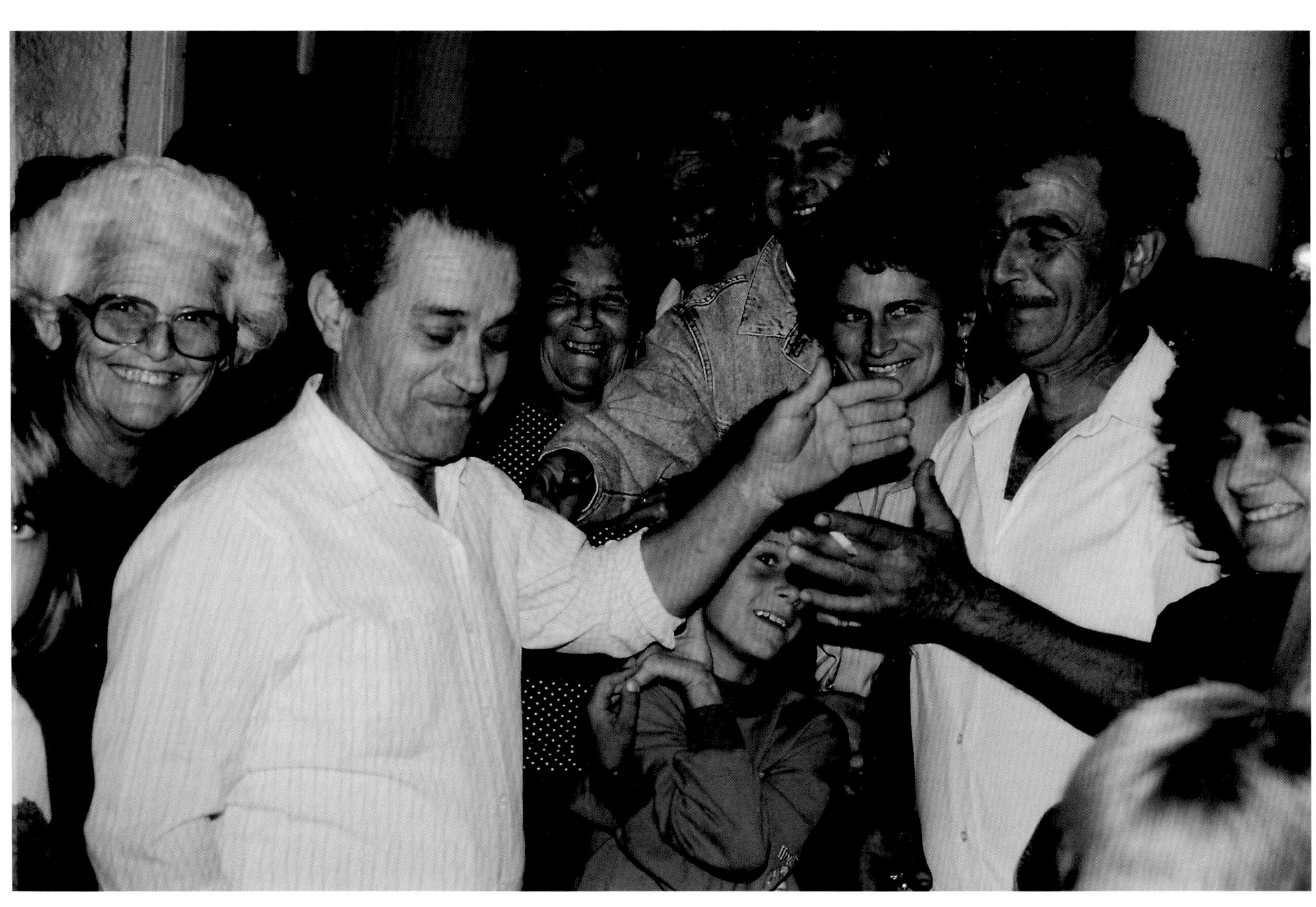

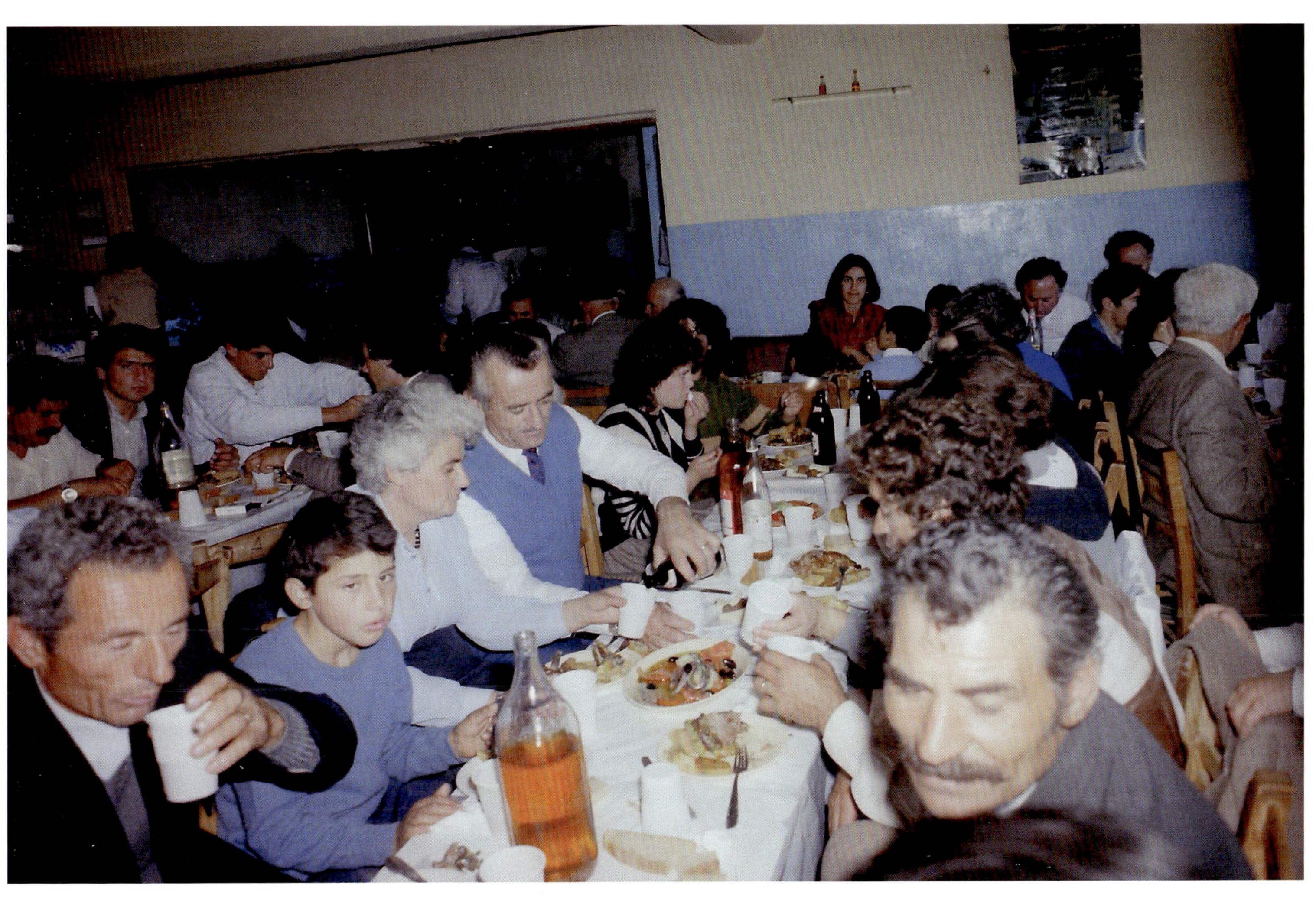

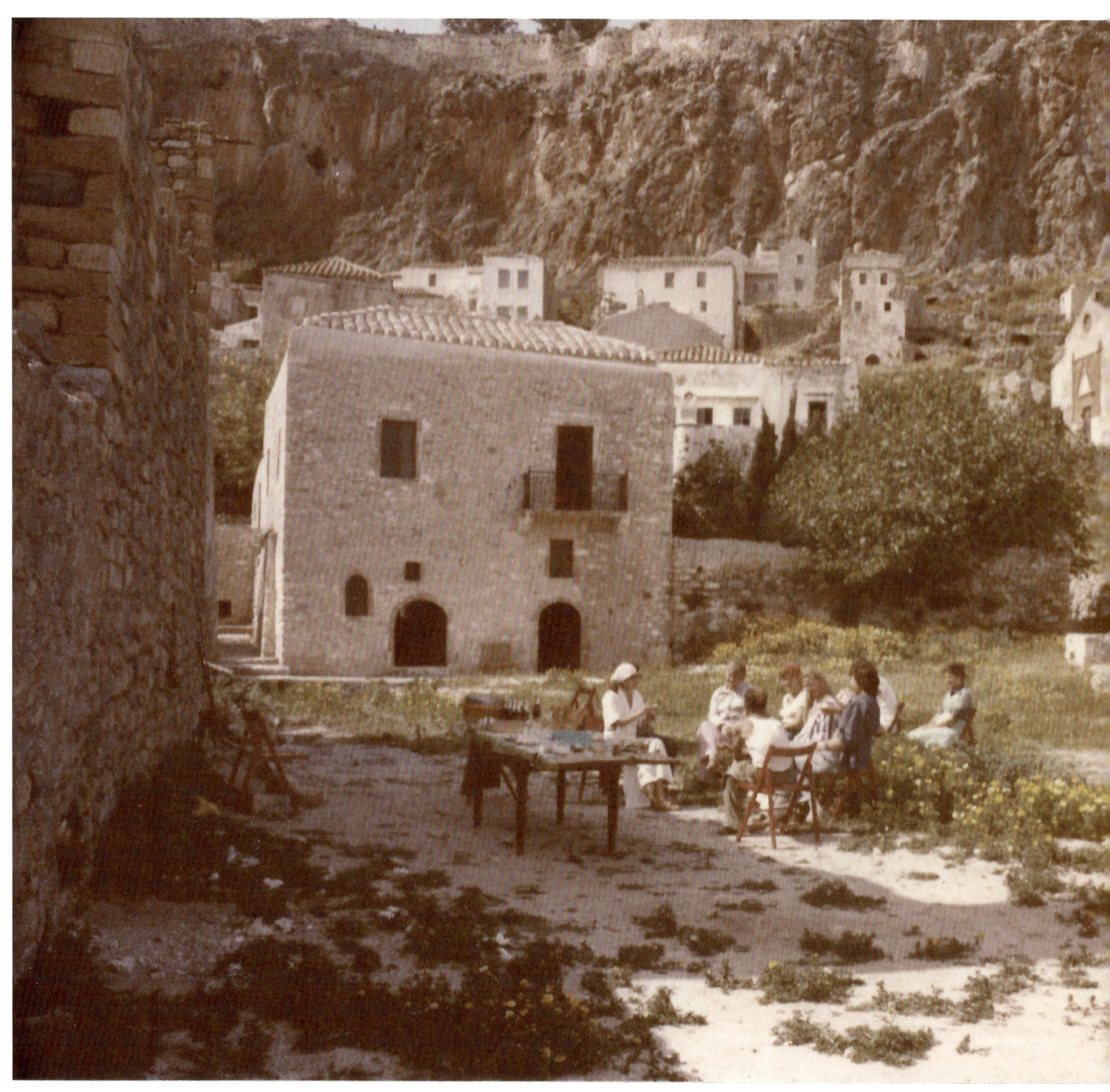

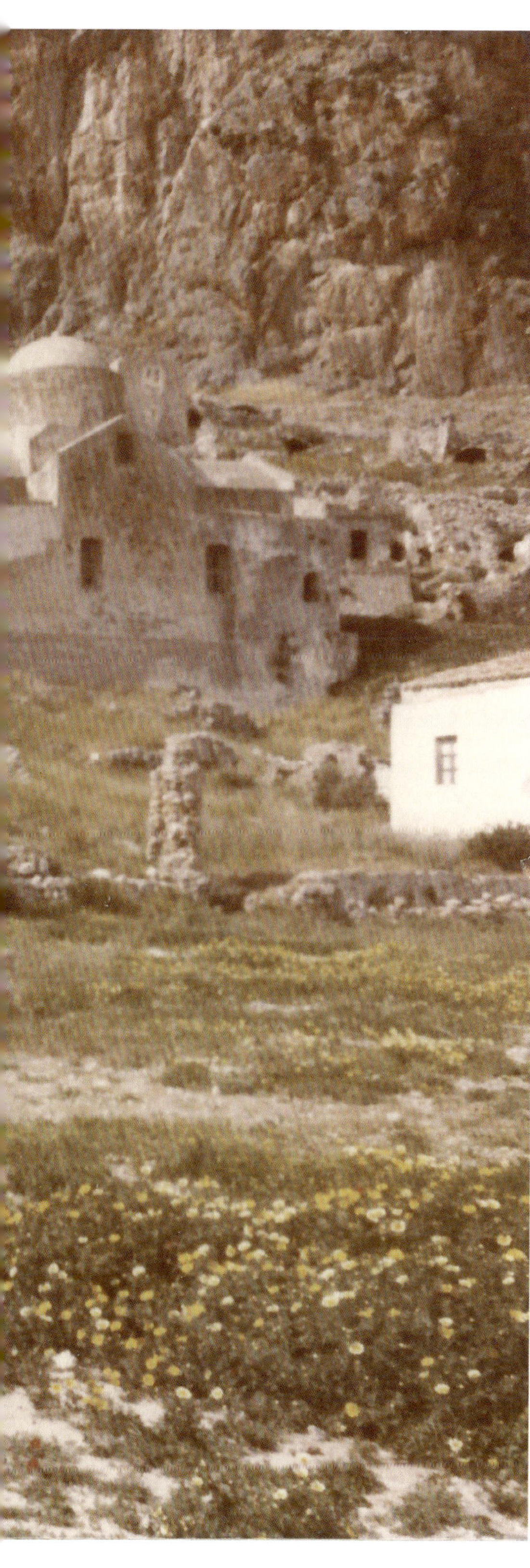

It is interaction, not place, that is the essence of the city and city life.

CHRISTIAN NORBERG-SCHULZ,
EXISTENCE, SPACE & ARCHITECTURE, 1971

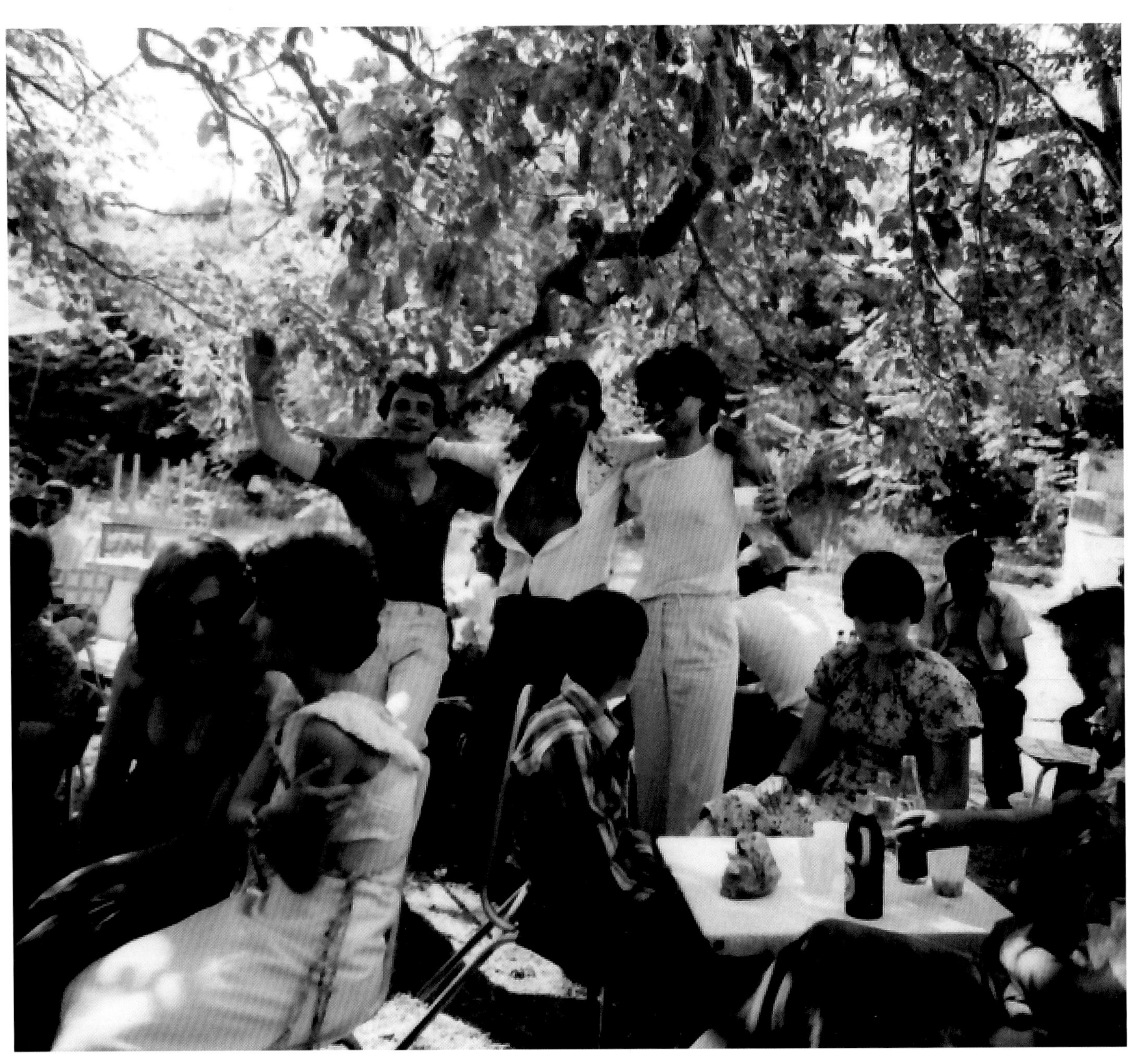

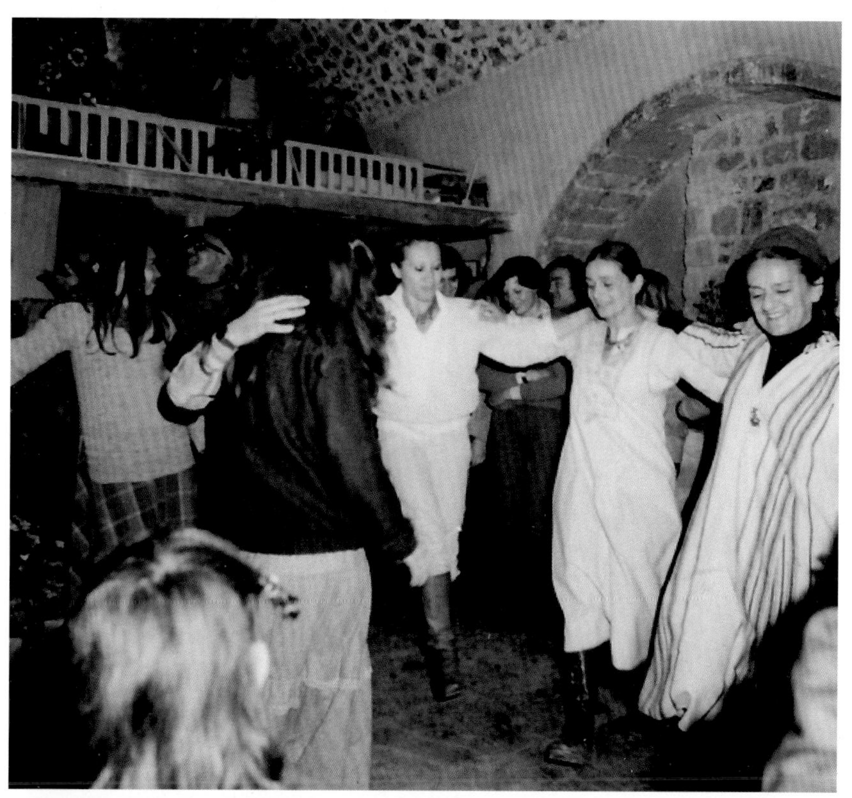

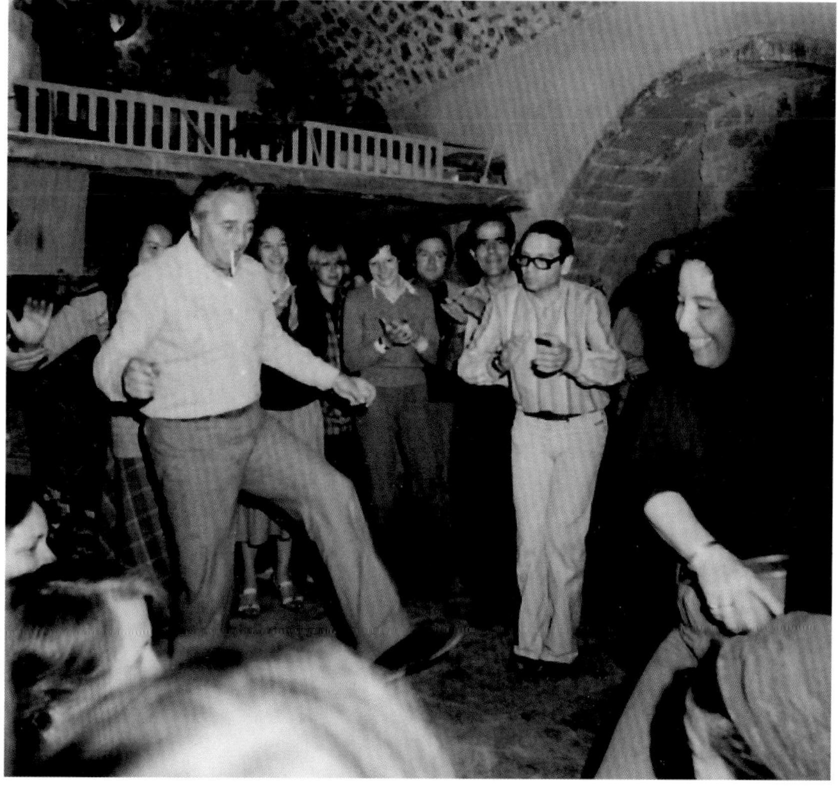

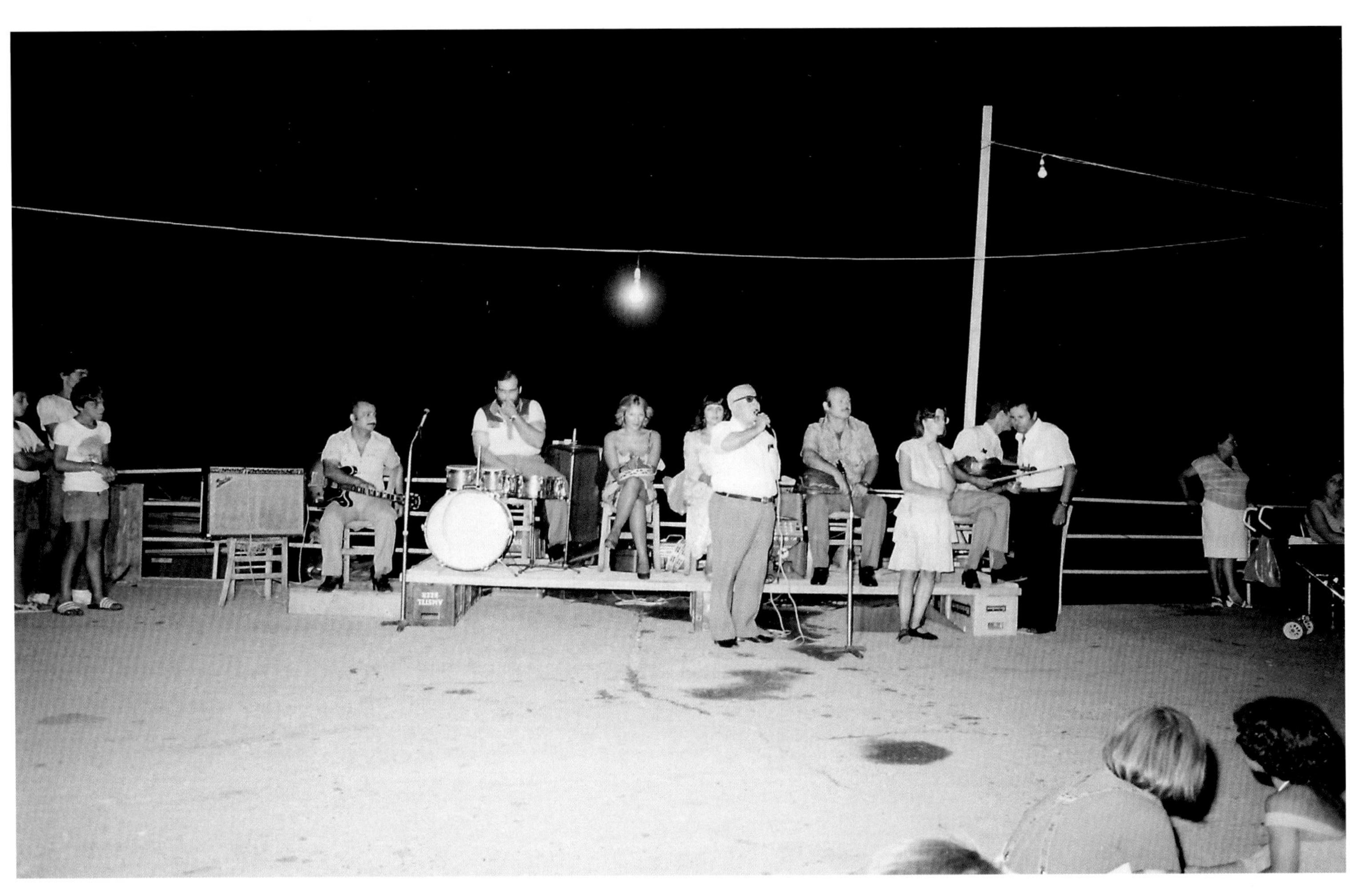

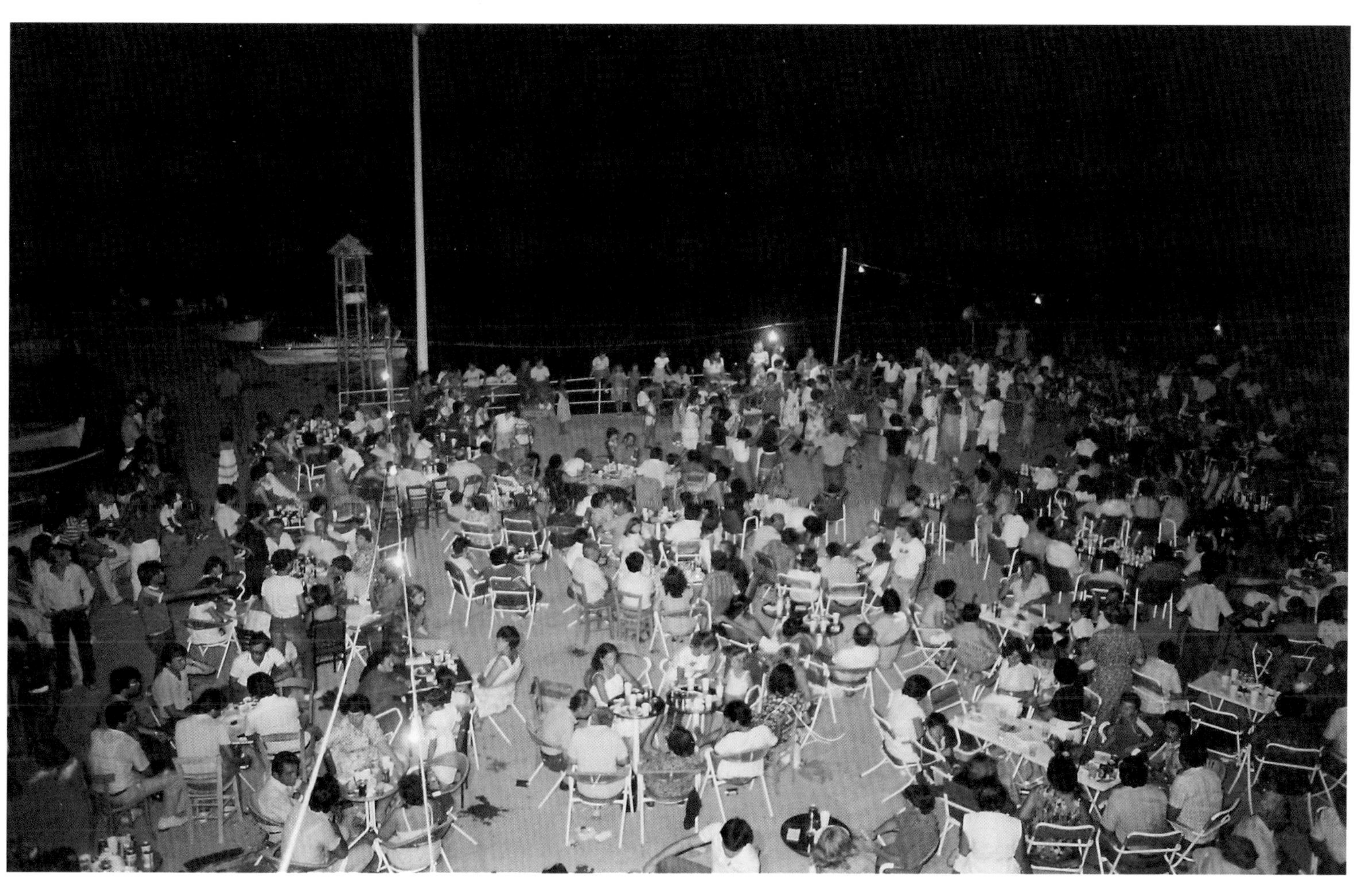

CHAPTER 5 · THE LIFE · Η ΖΩΗ

Cafés and Tavernas

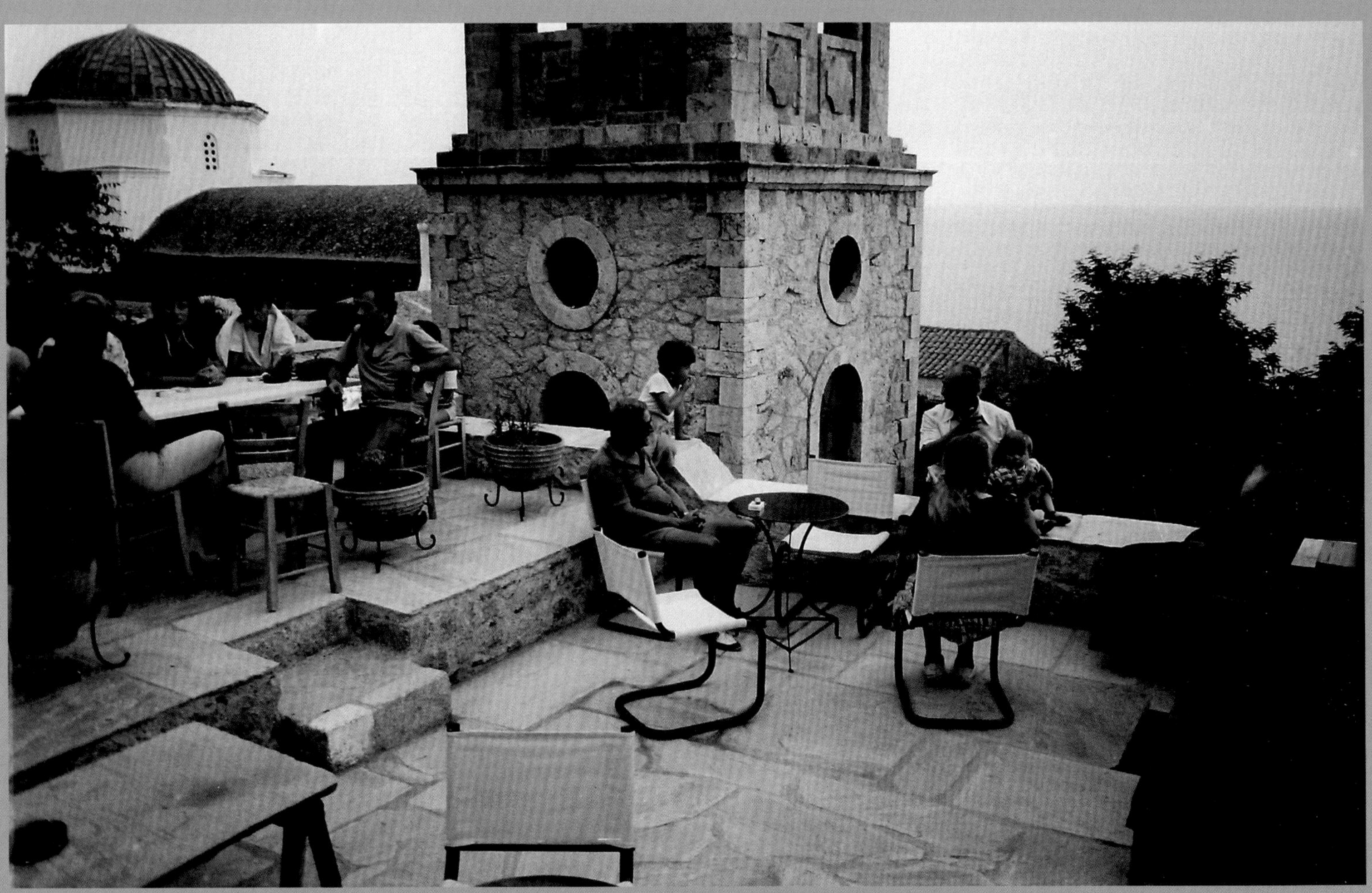

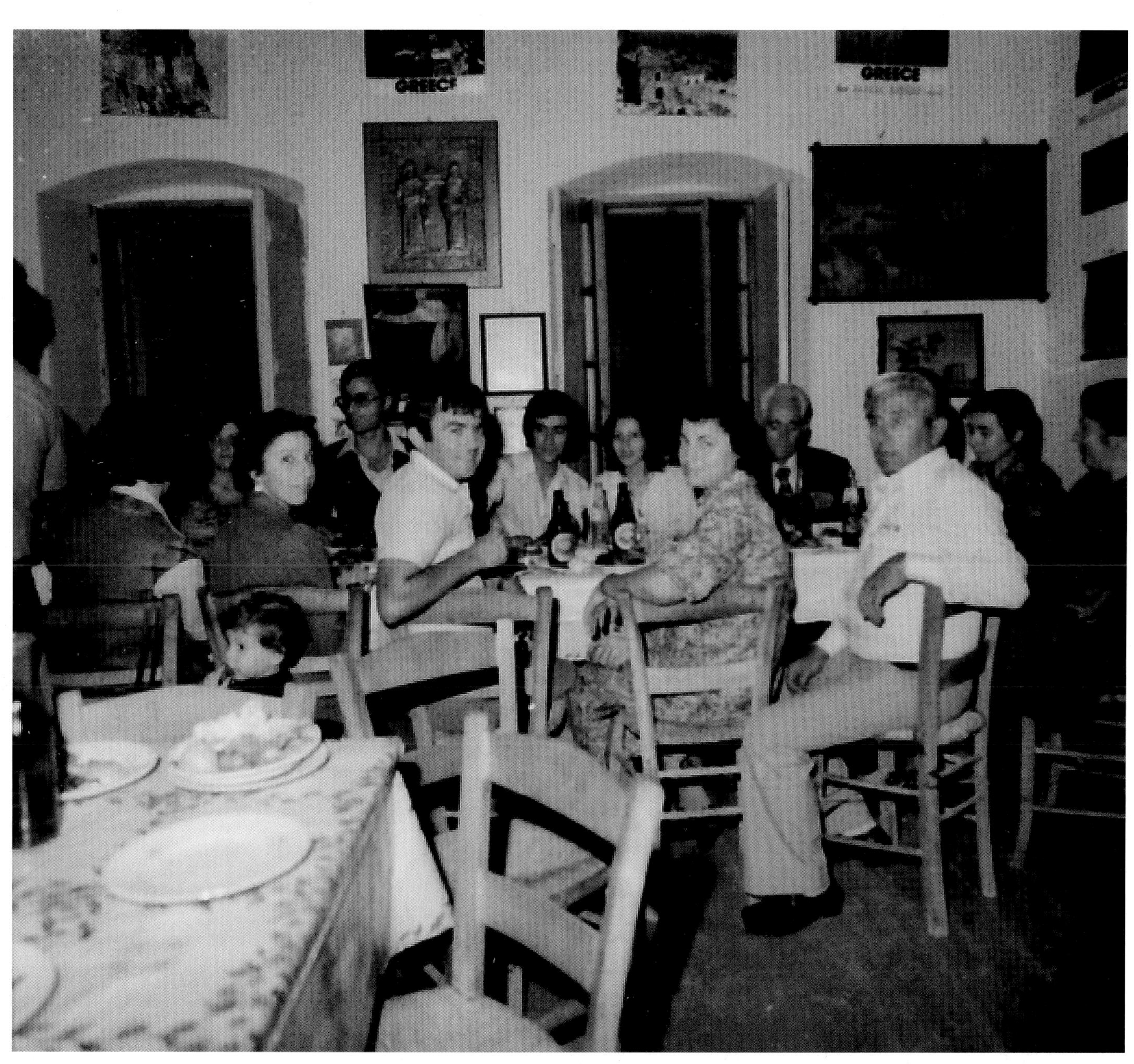
GREECE

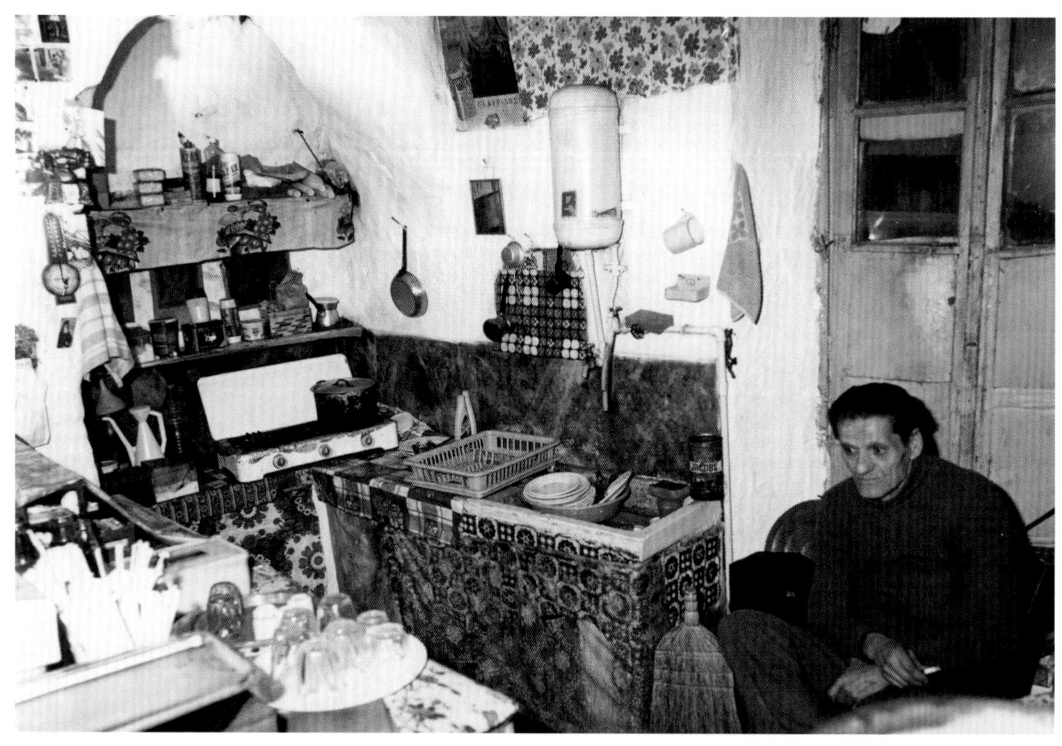

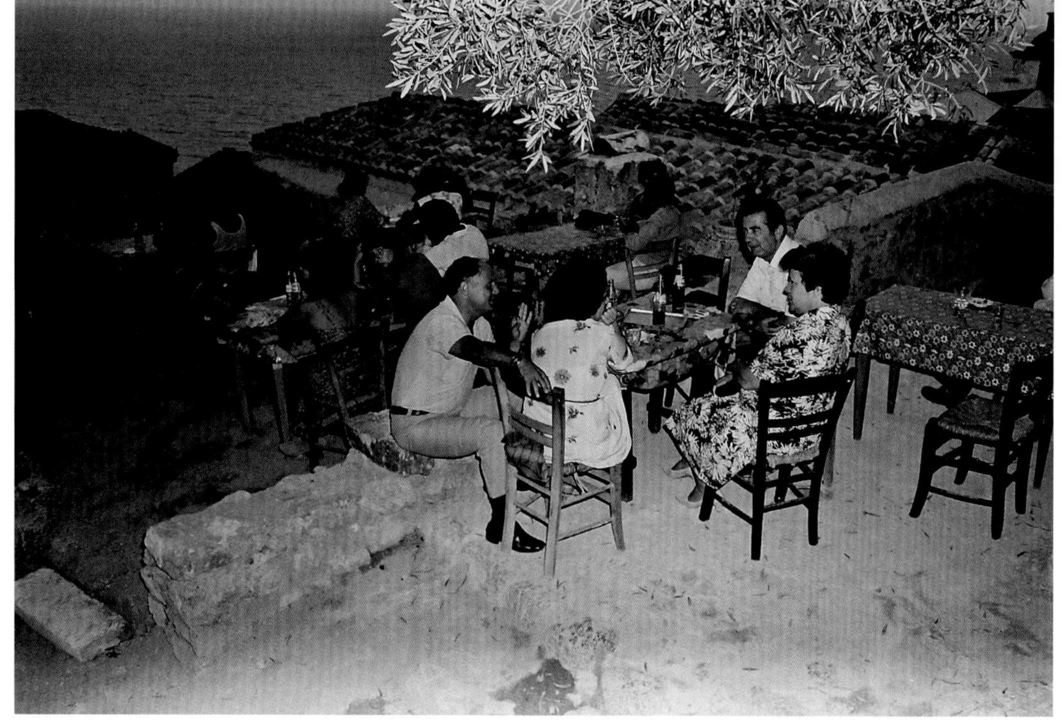

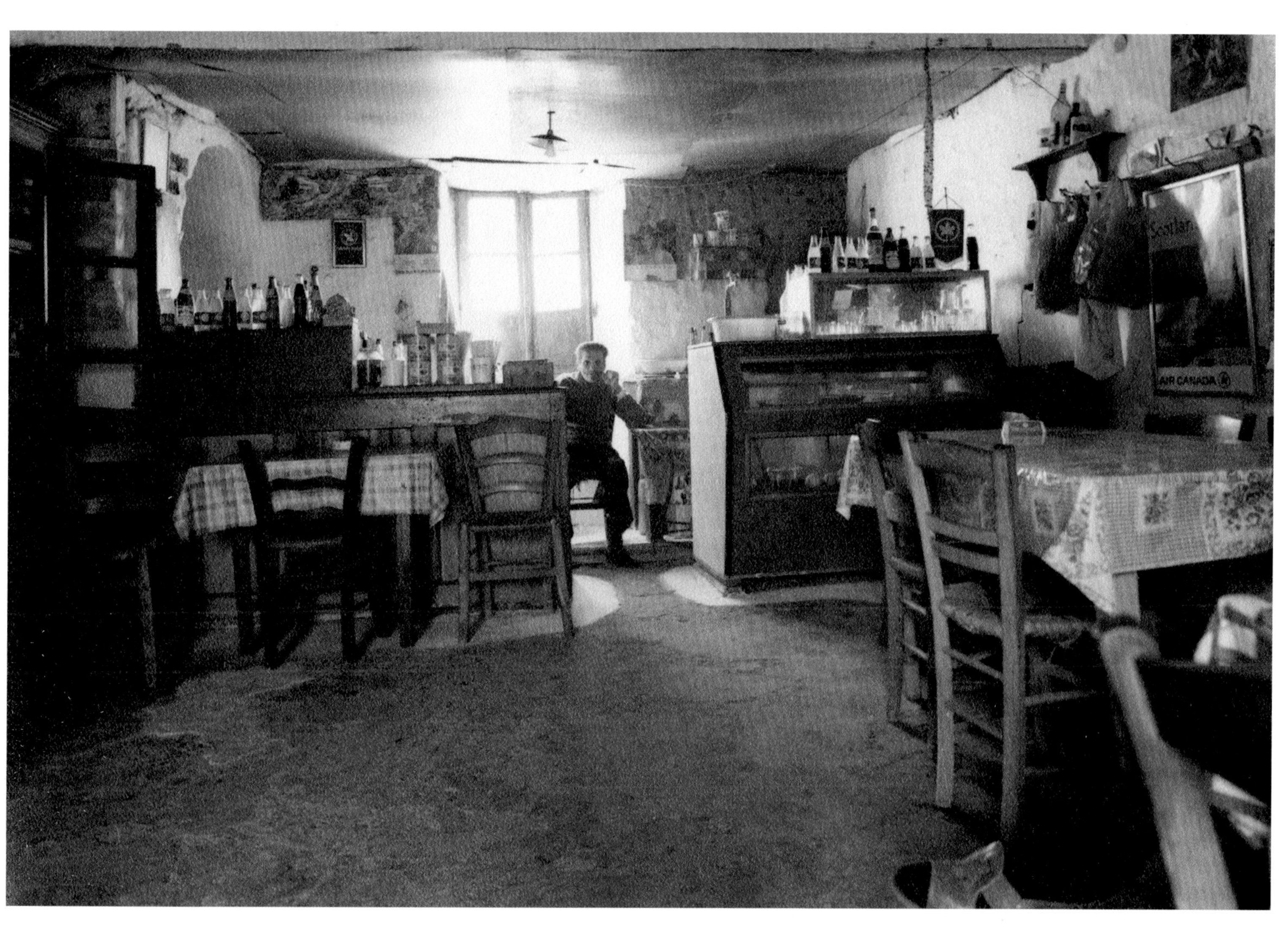
AIR CANADA

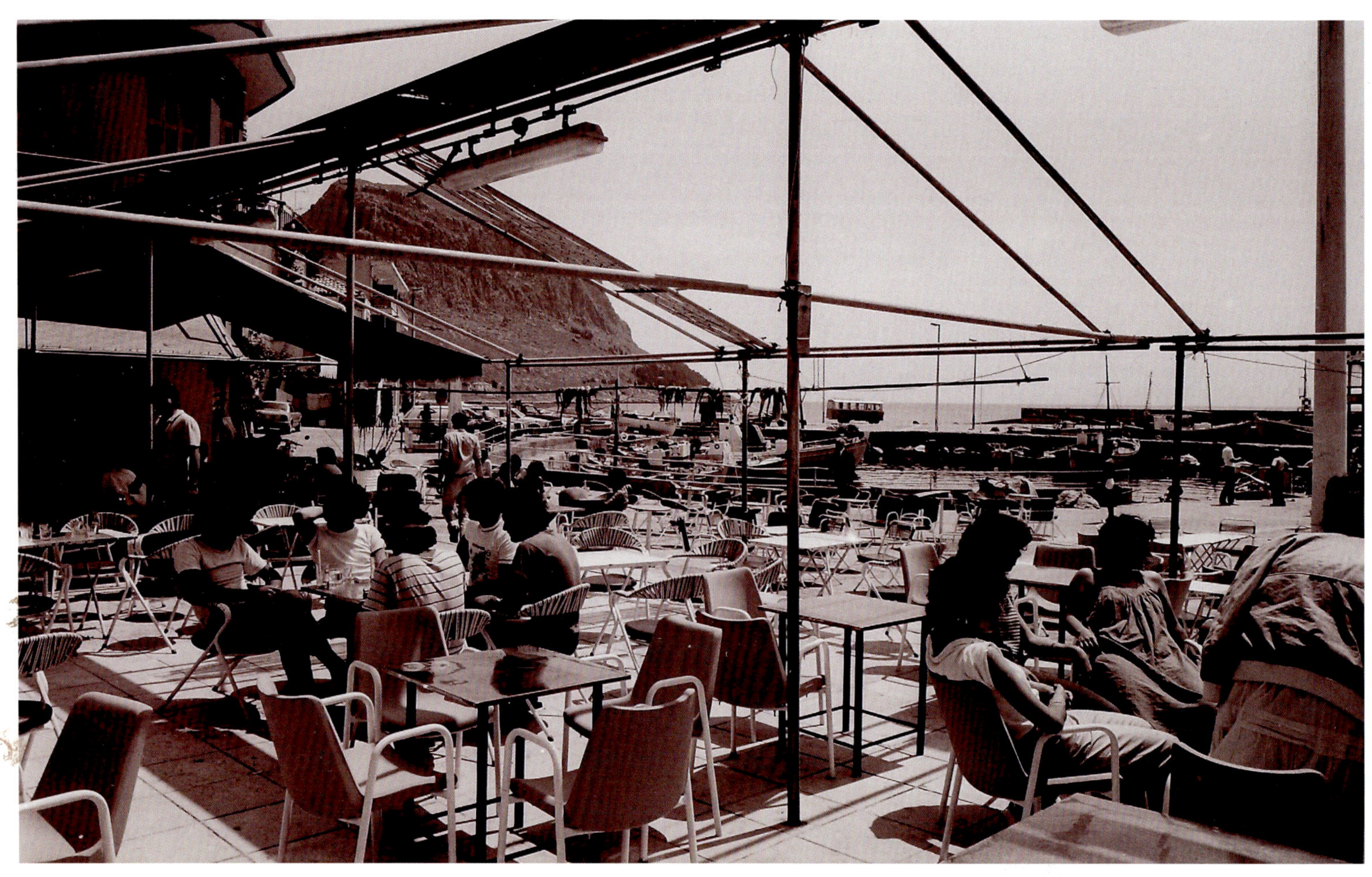

The traditional men only kapheneion began to be displaced by smart bars where young people of both sexes would congregate.

RODERICK BEATON, *GREECE: BIOGRAPHY OF A MODERN NATION*, 2019

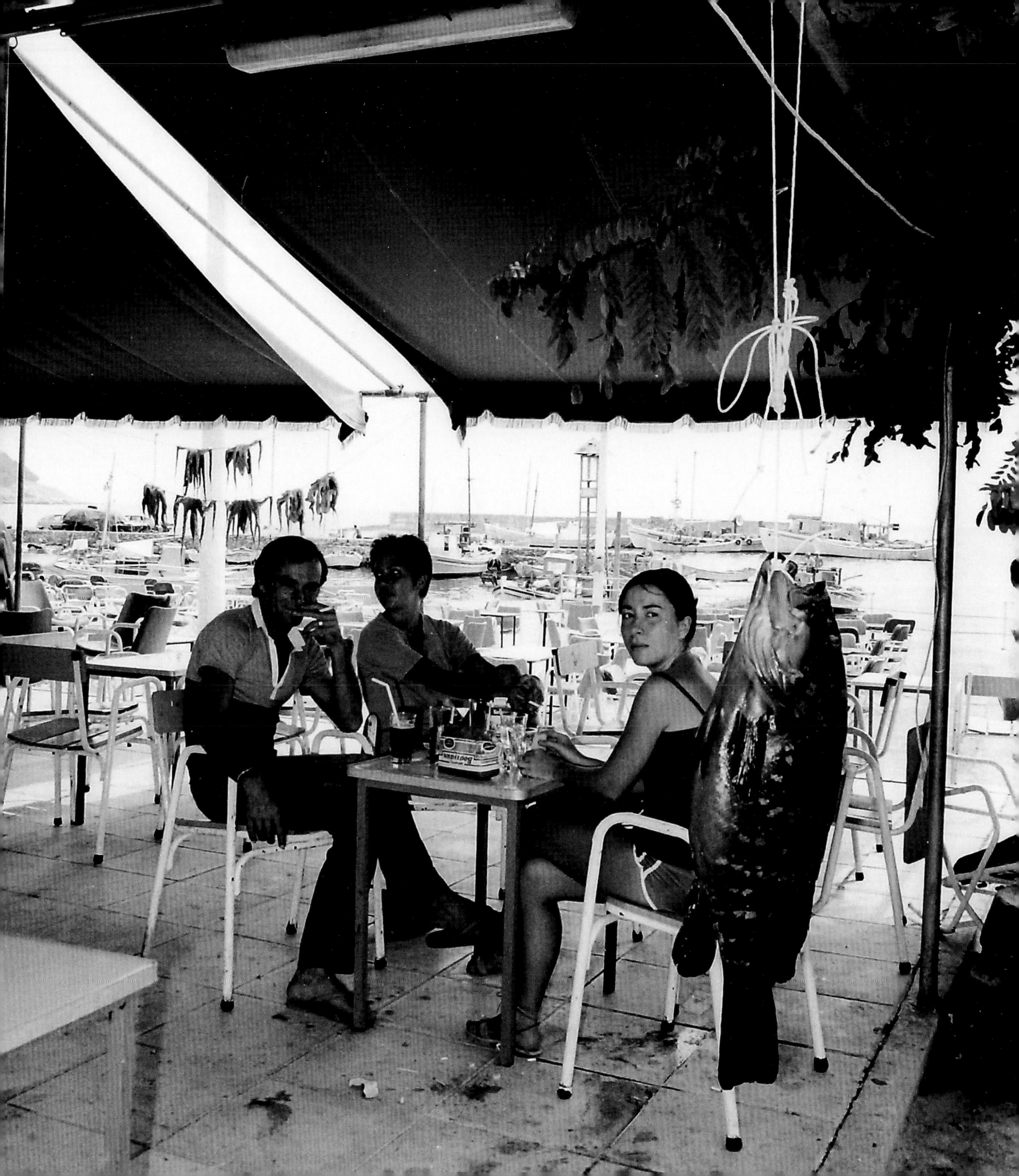

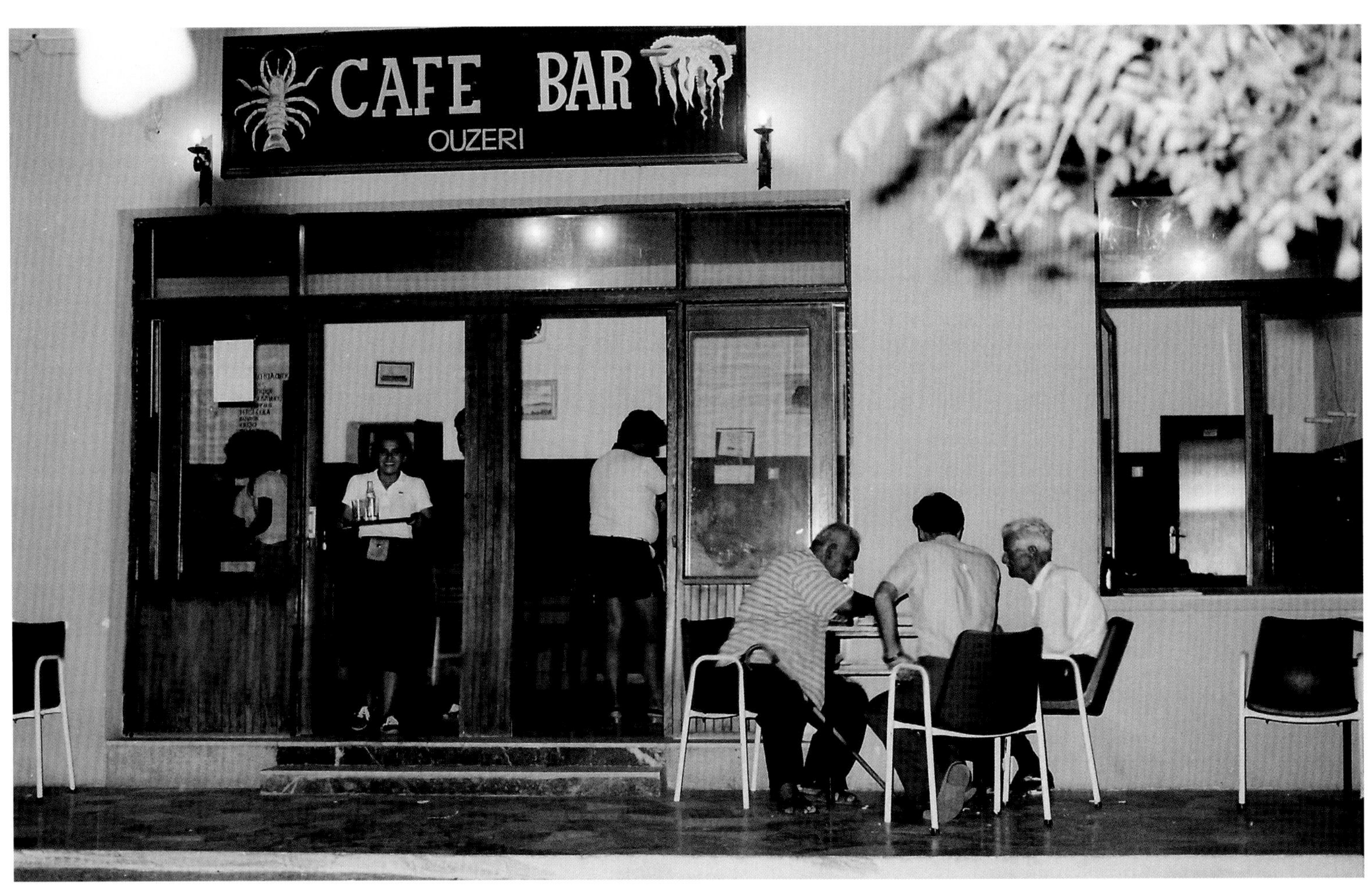
CAFE BAR
OUZERI

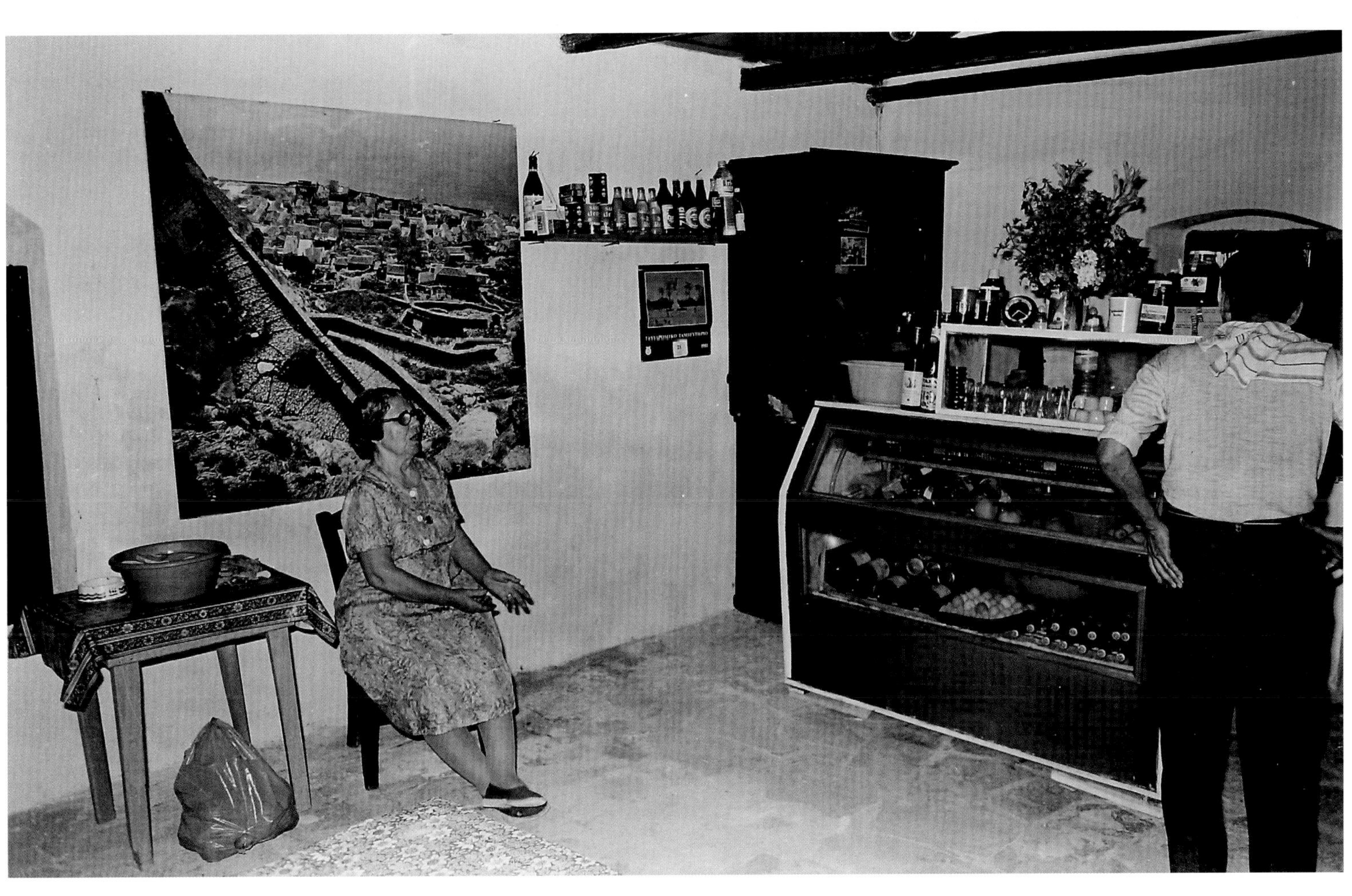

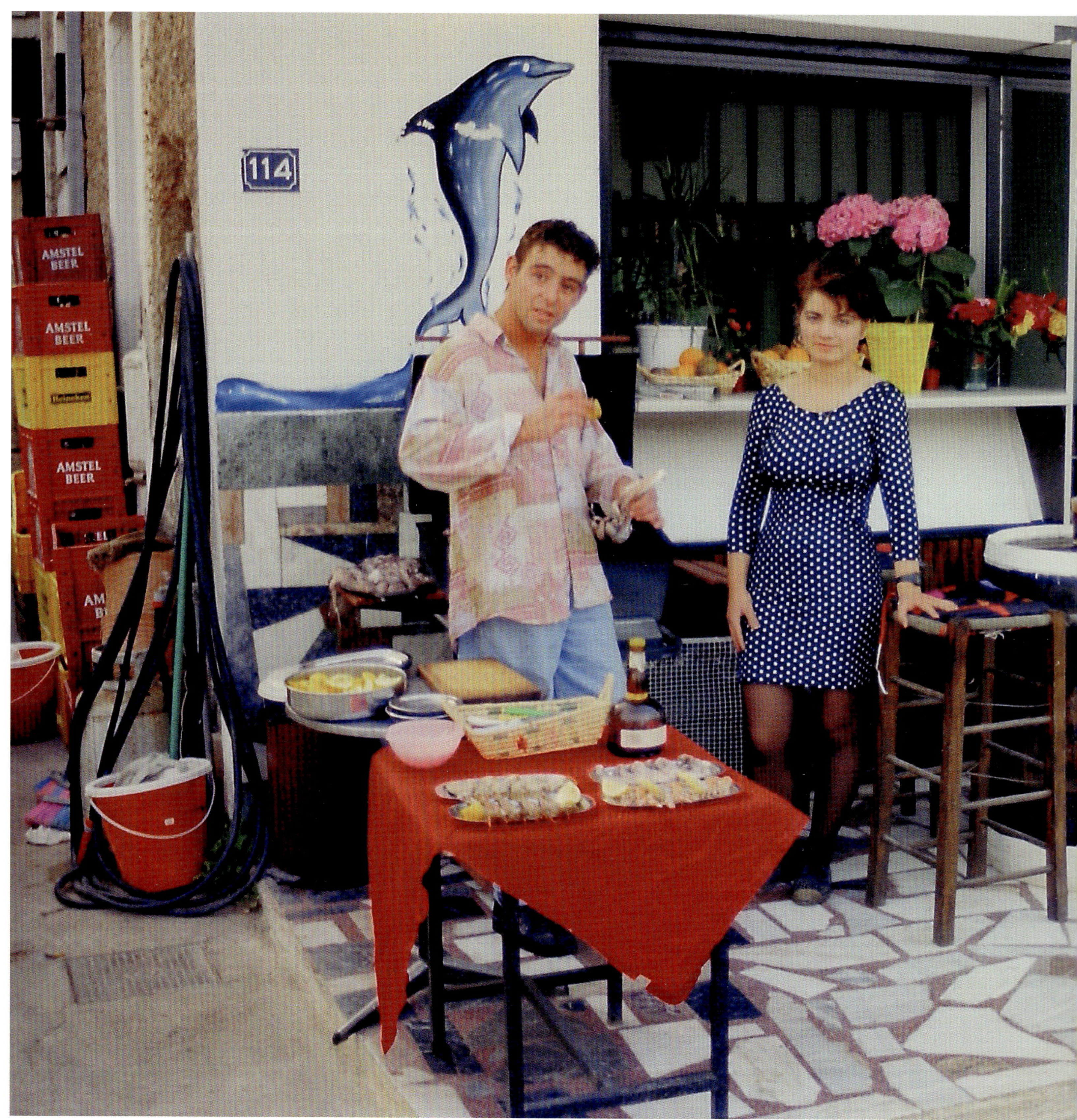
114
AMSTEL BEER
AMSTEL BEER
AMSTEL BEER

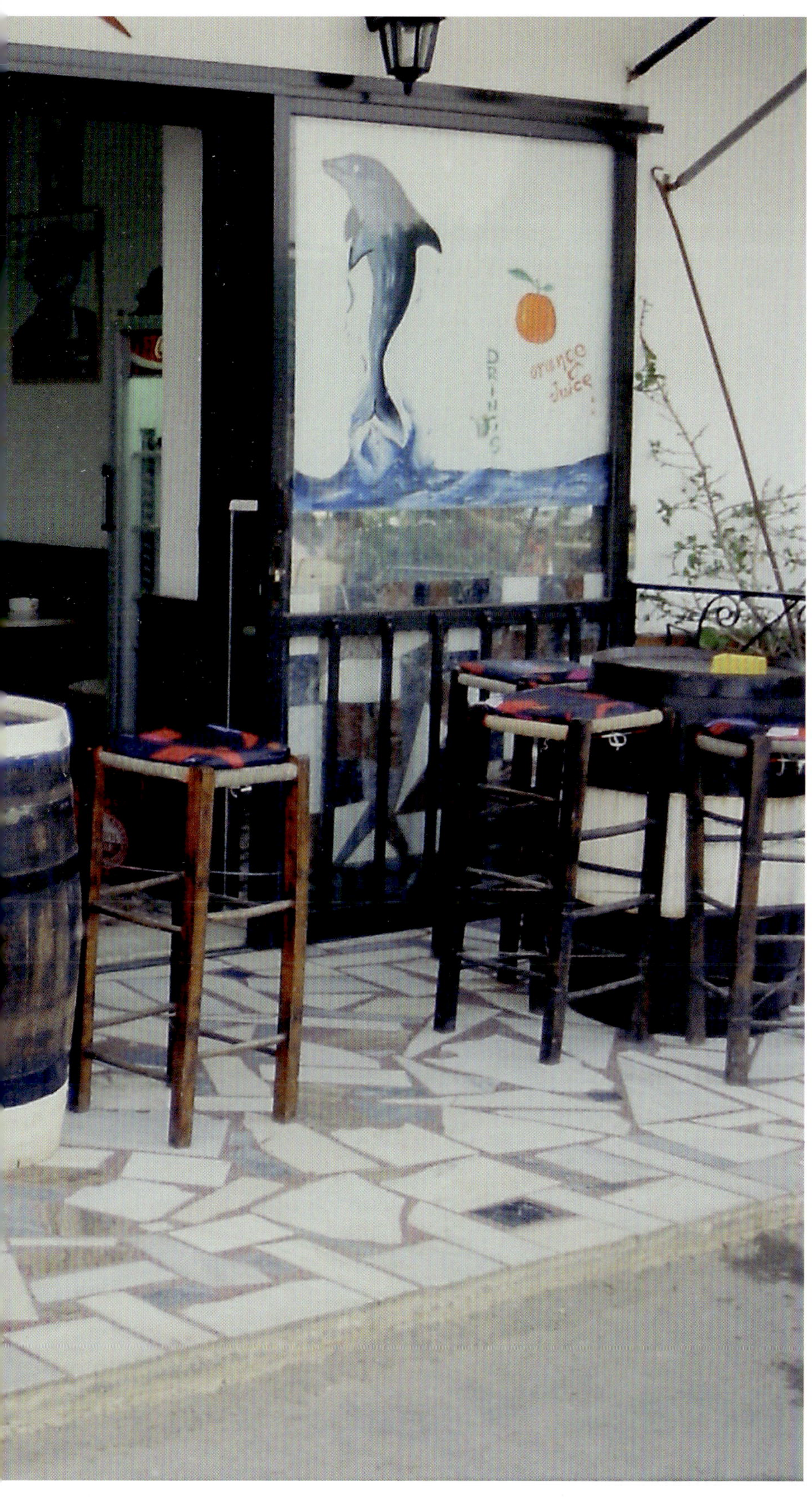
DRINKS

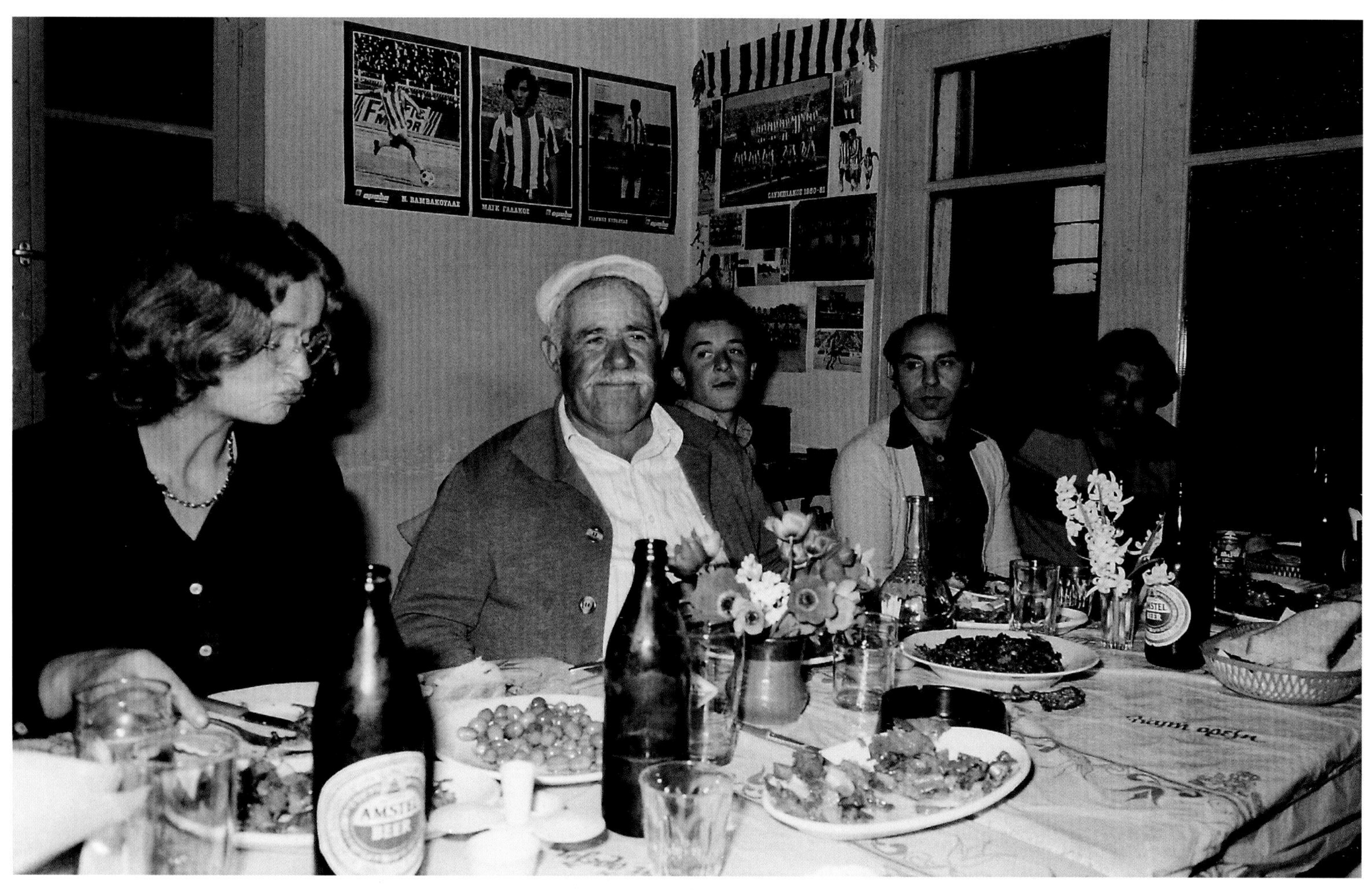

If the pot boils, Friendship lives.

OLD GREEK PROVERB
NICHOLAS GAGE, *HELLAS. A PORTRAIT OF GREECE*, 1993

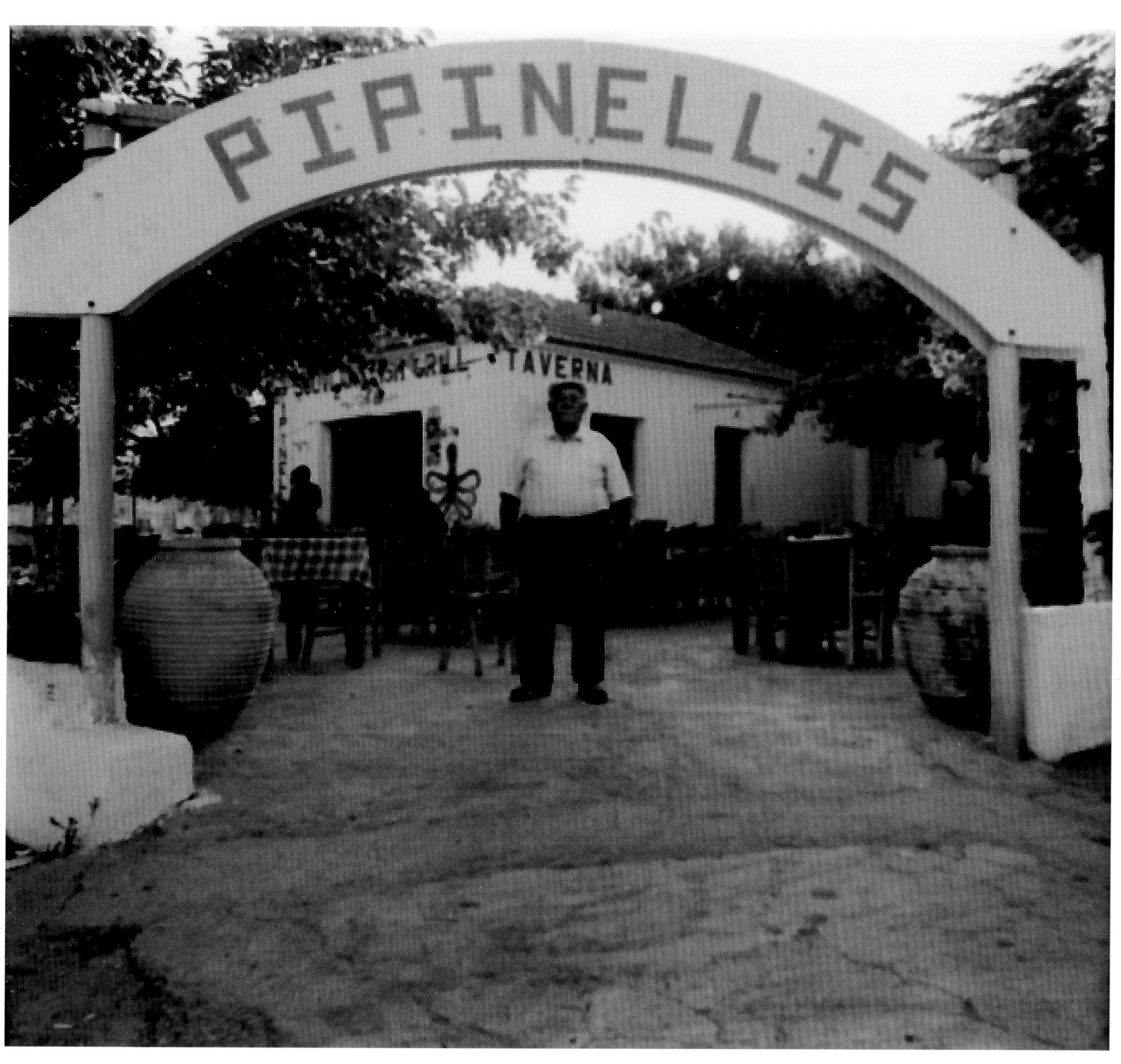
PIPINELLIS
TAVERNA

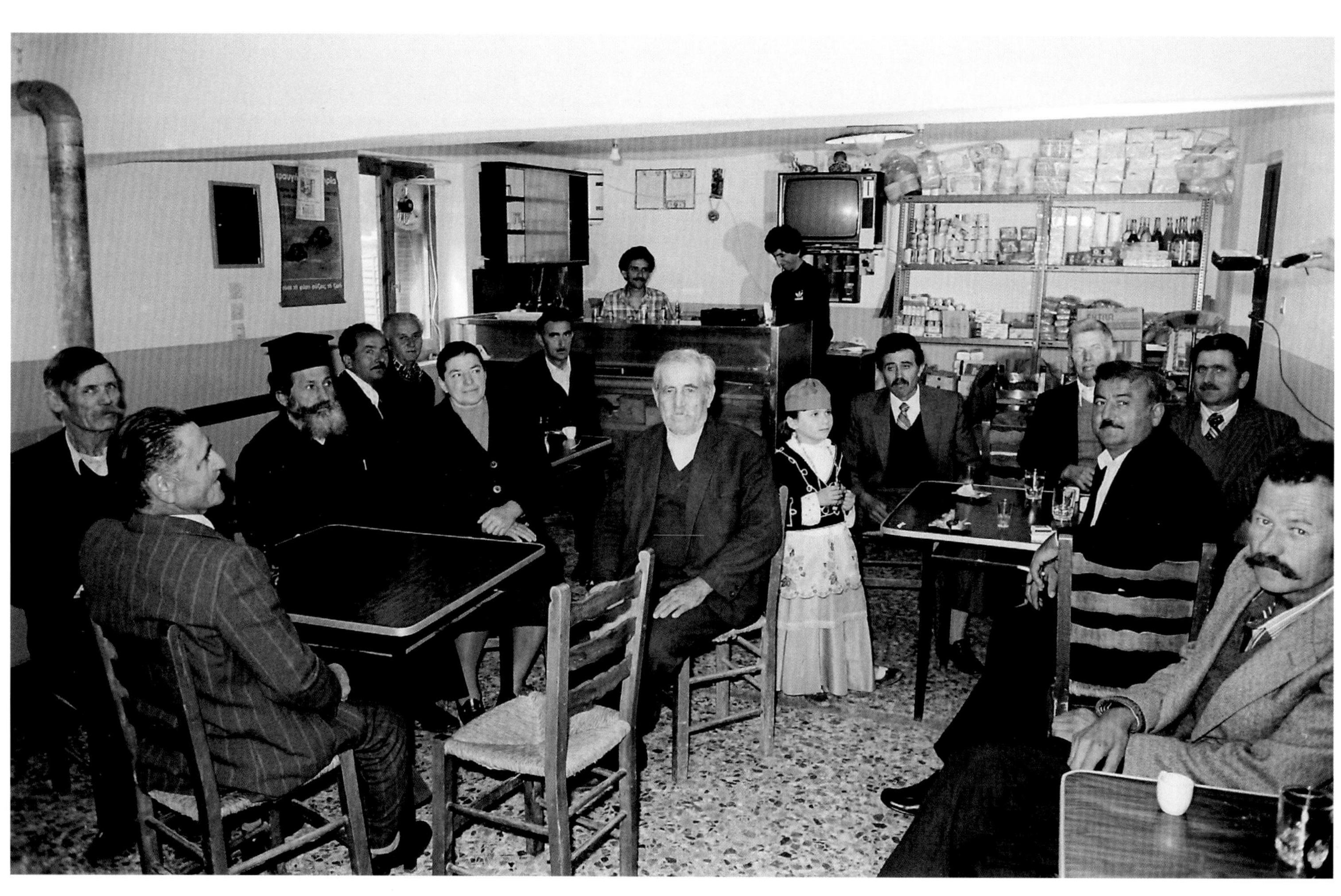

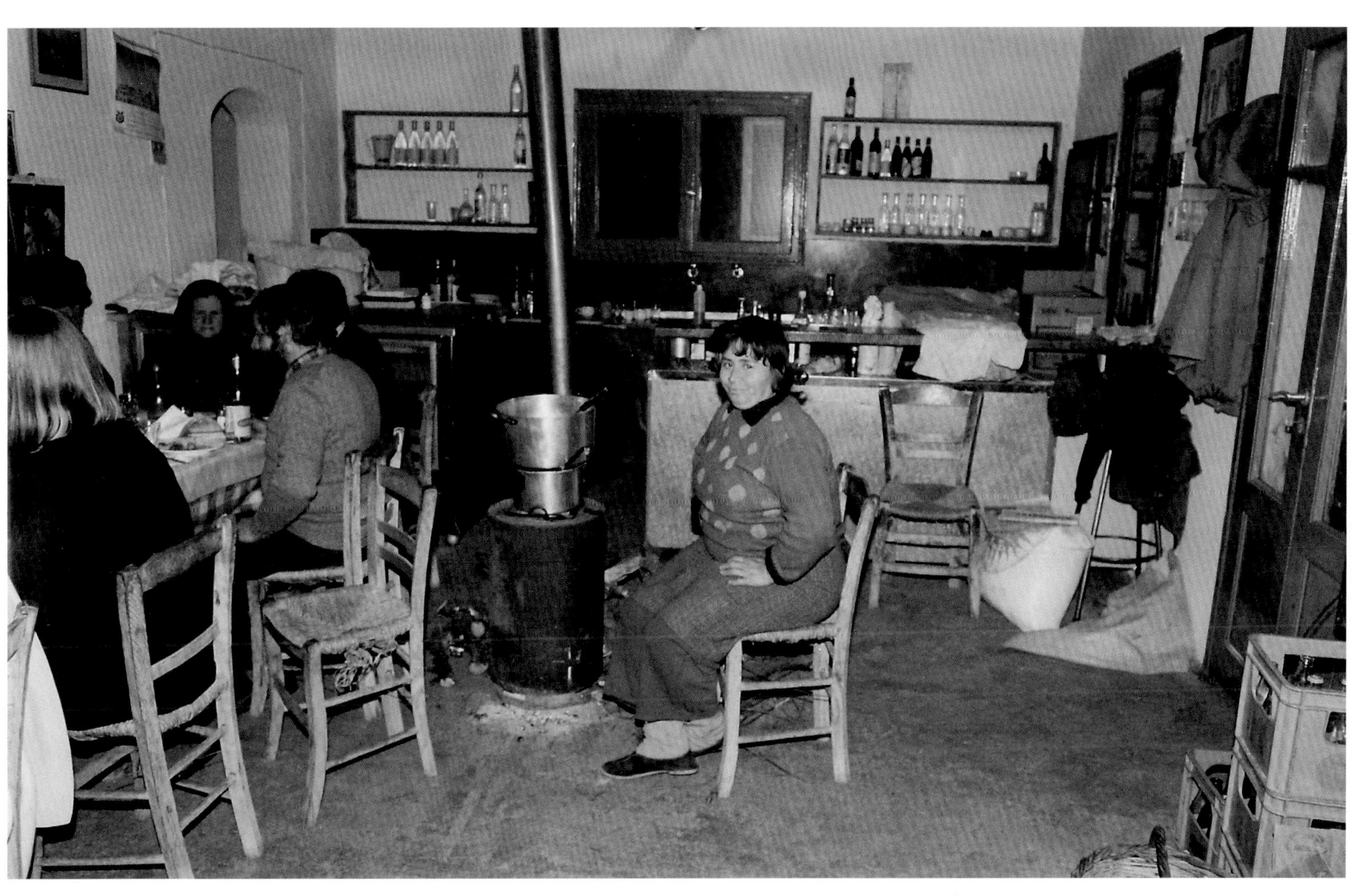

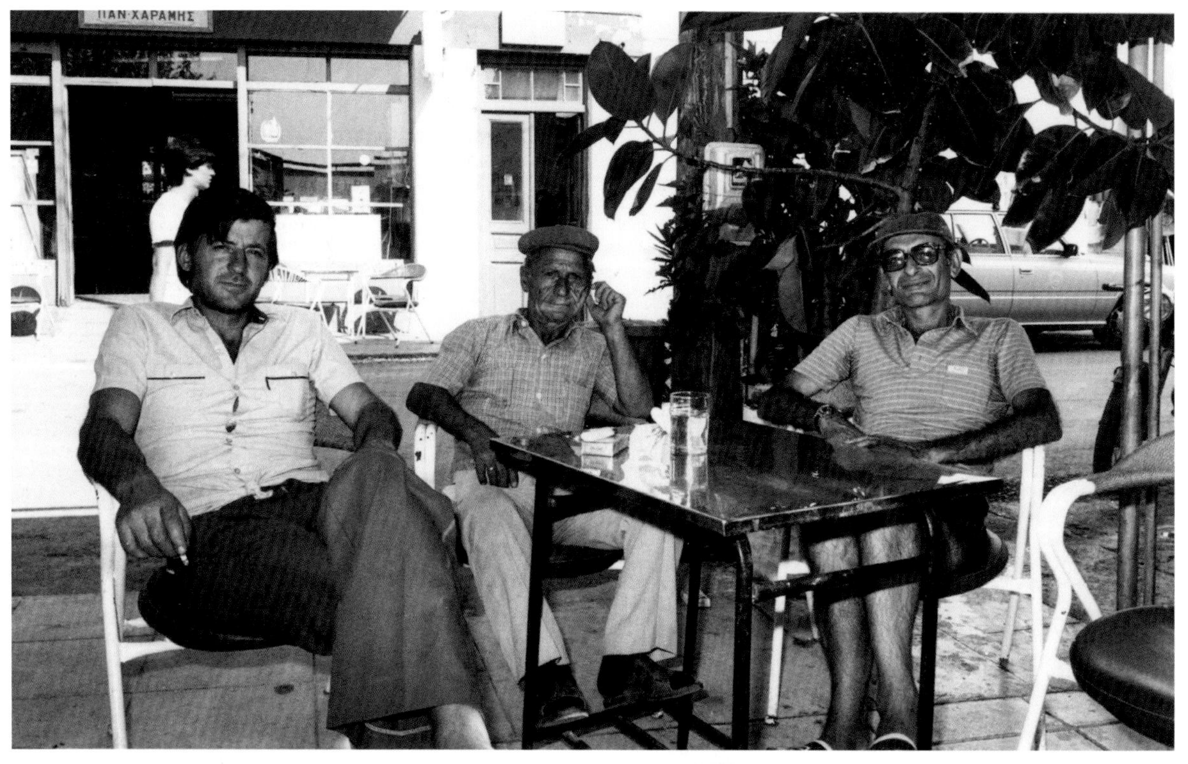
ΠΑΝ·ΧΑΡΑΜΗΣ

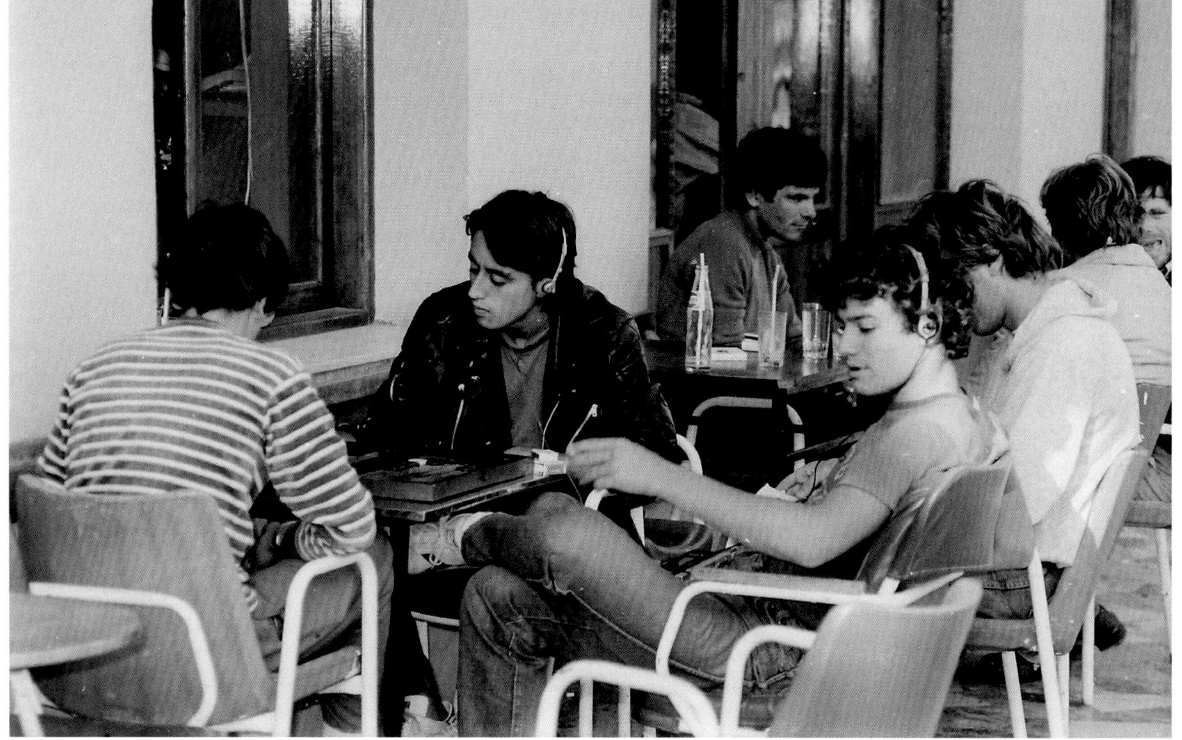

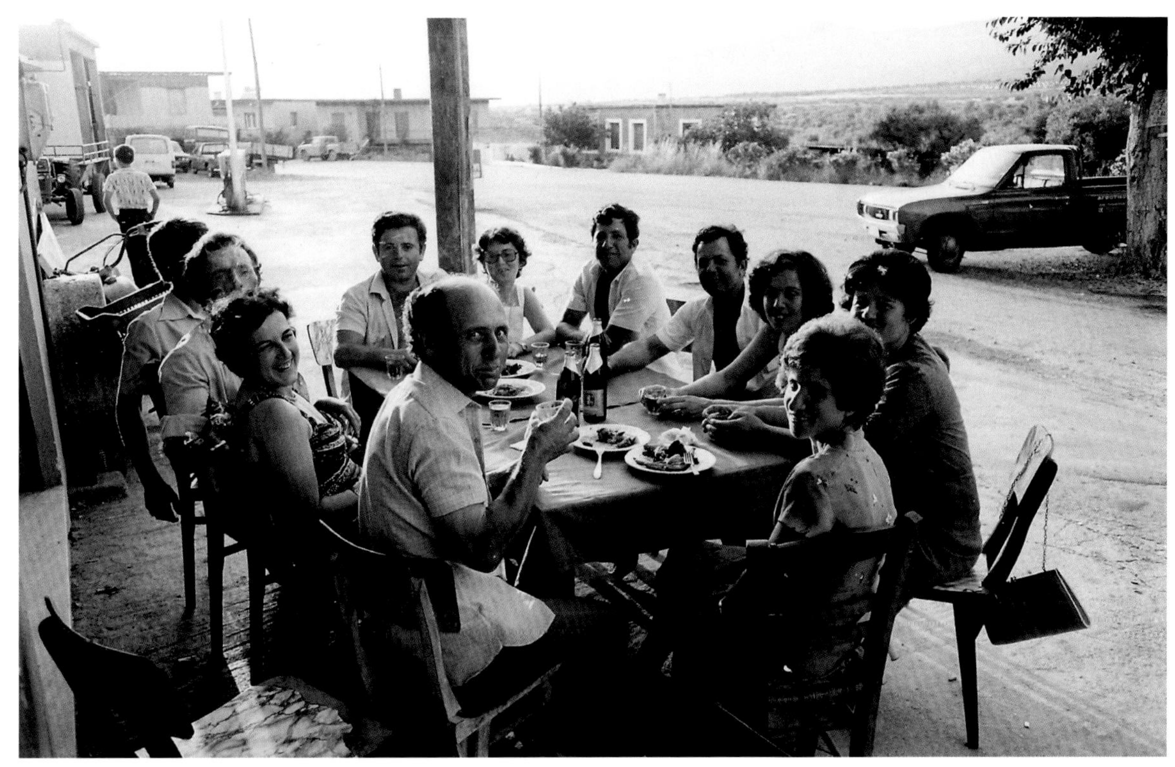

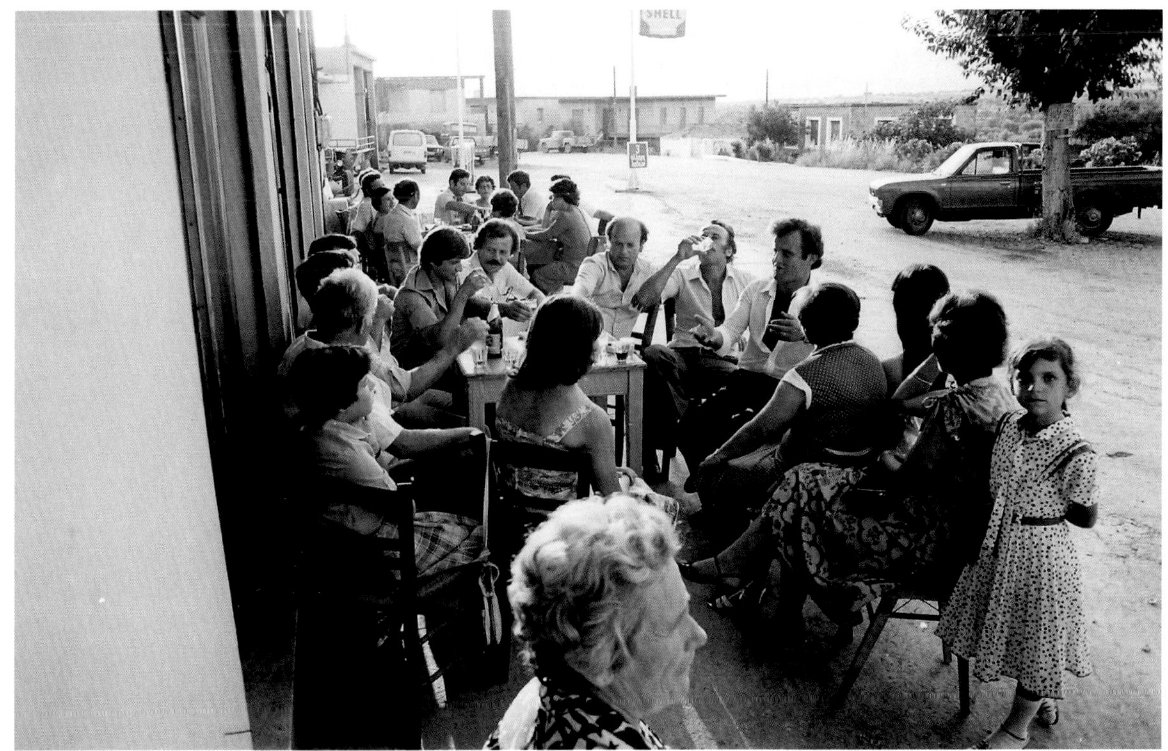
SHELL

Pastimes

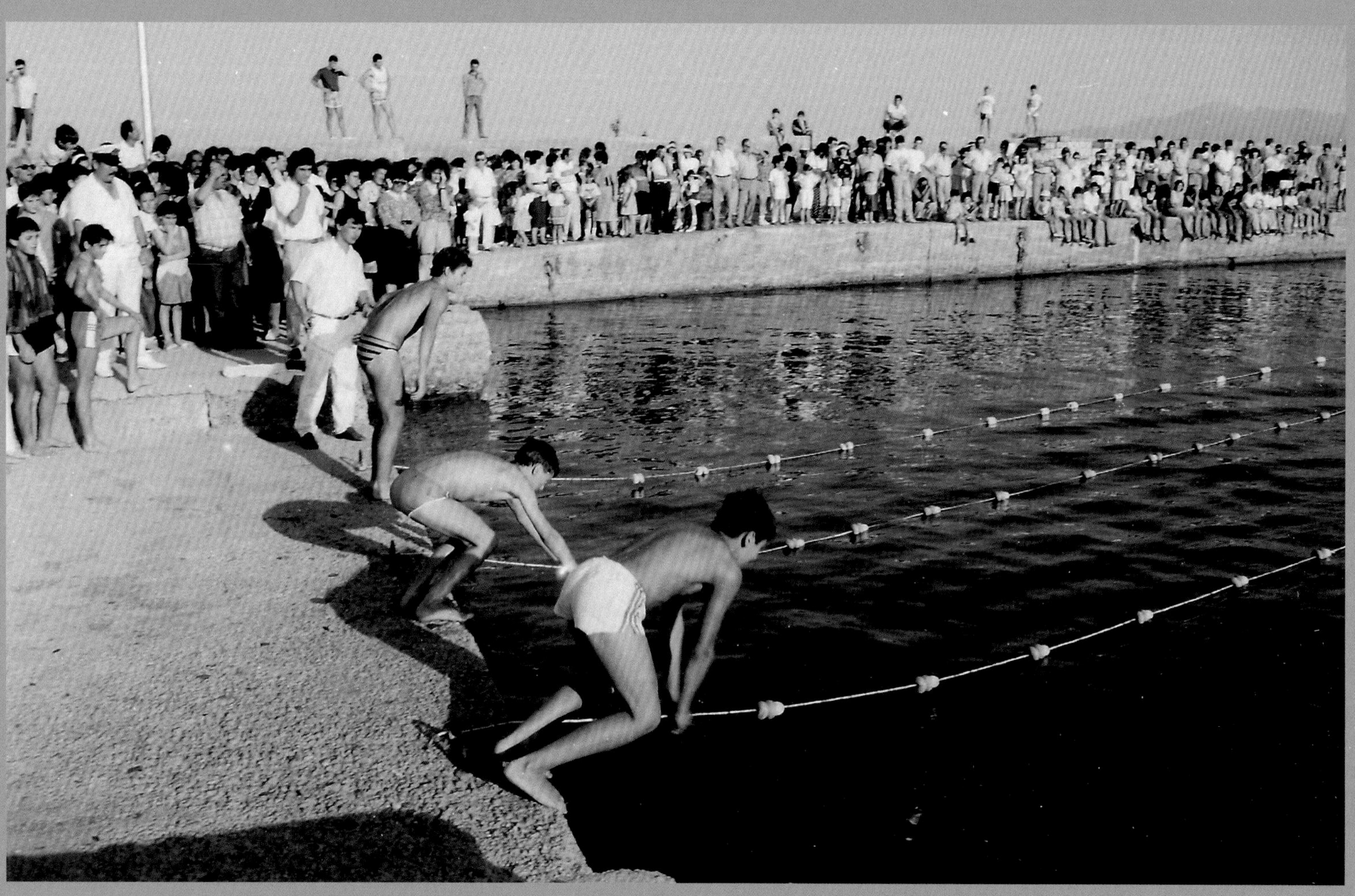

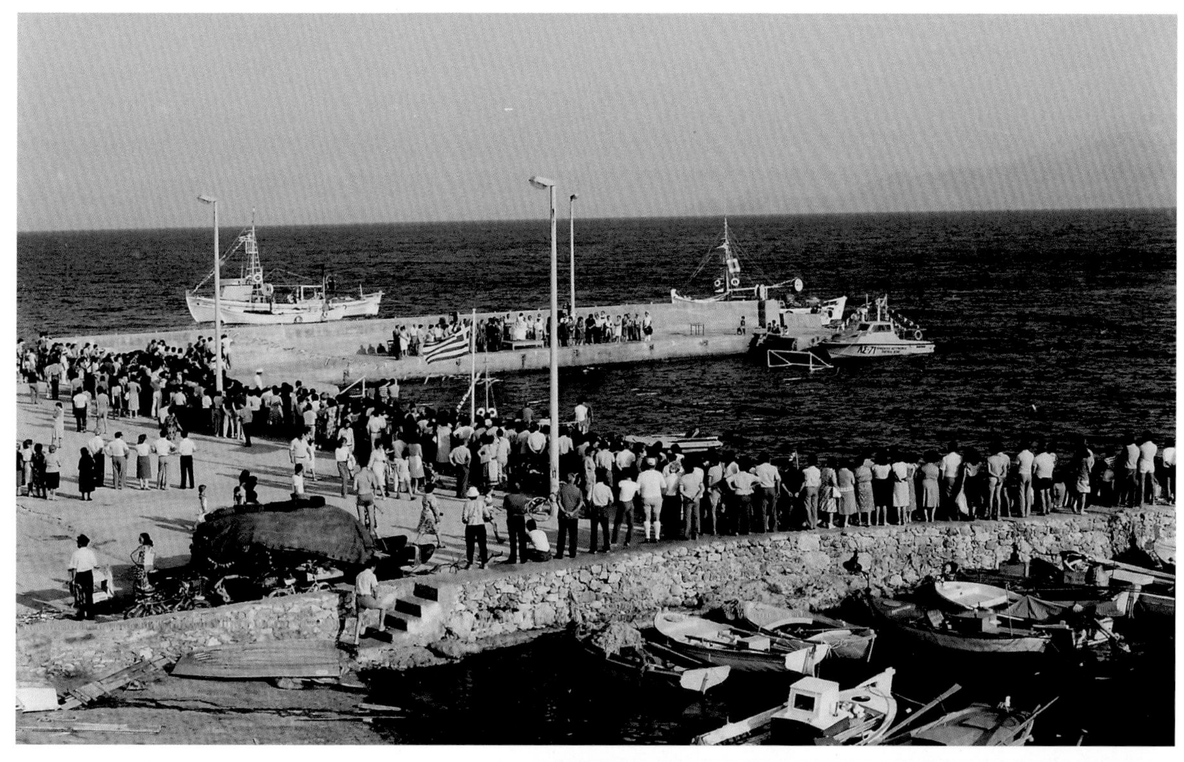

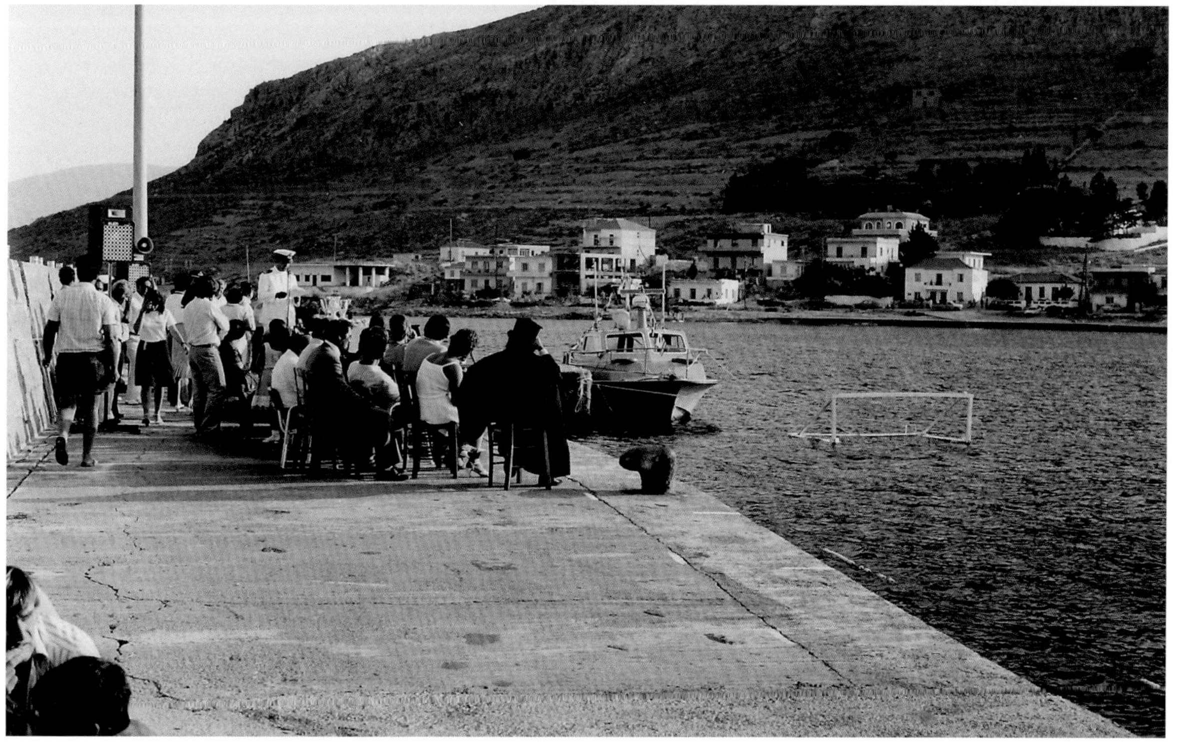

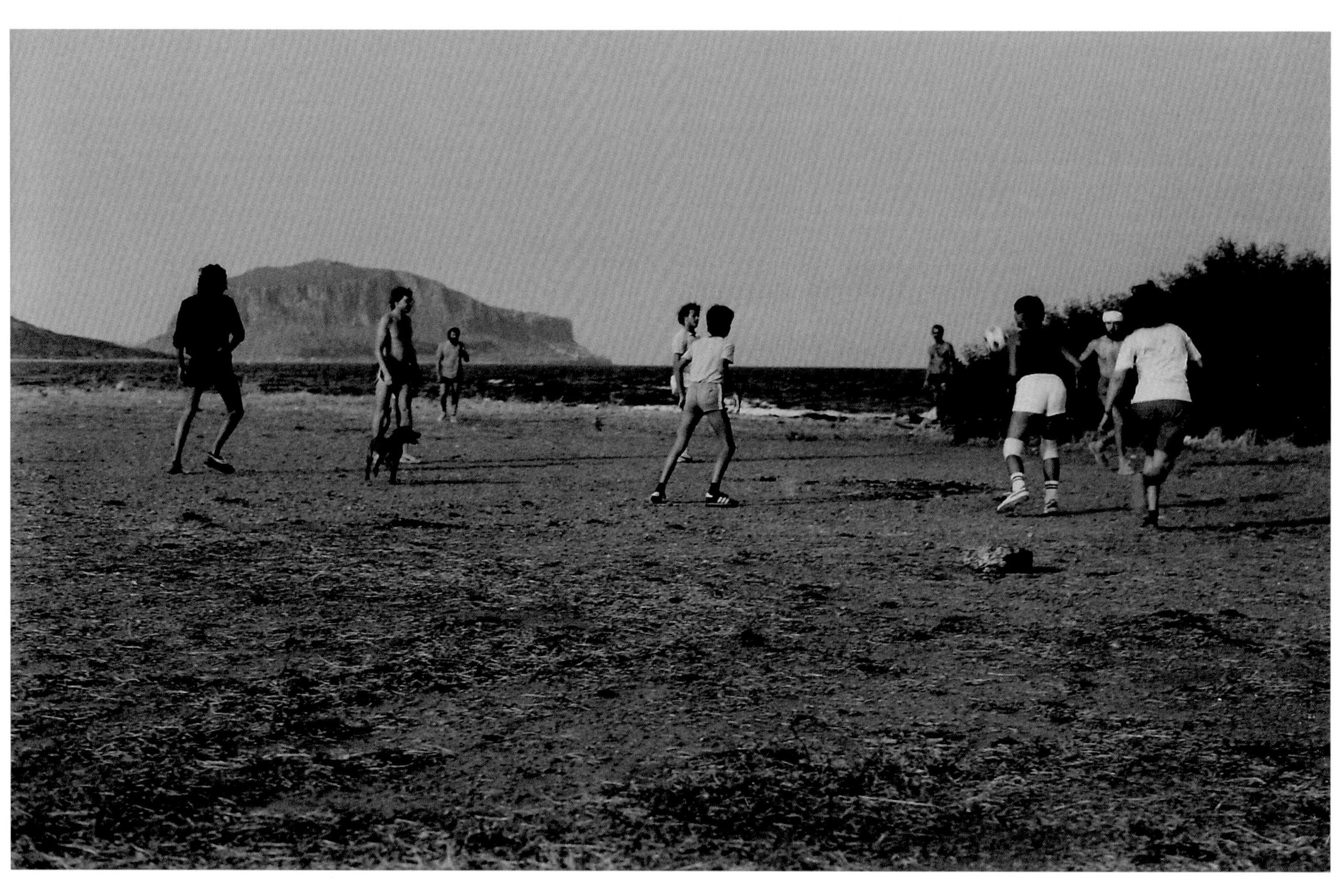

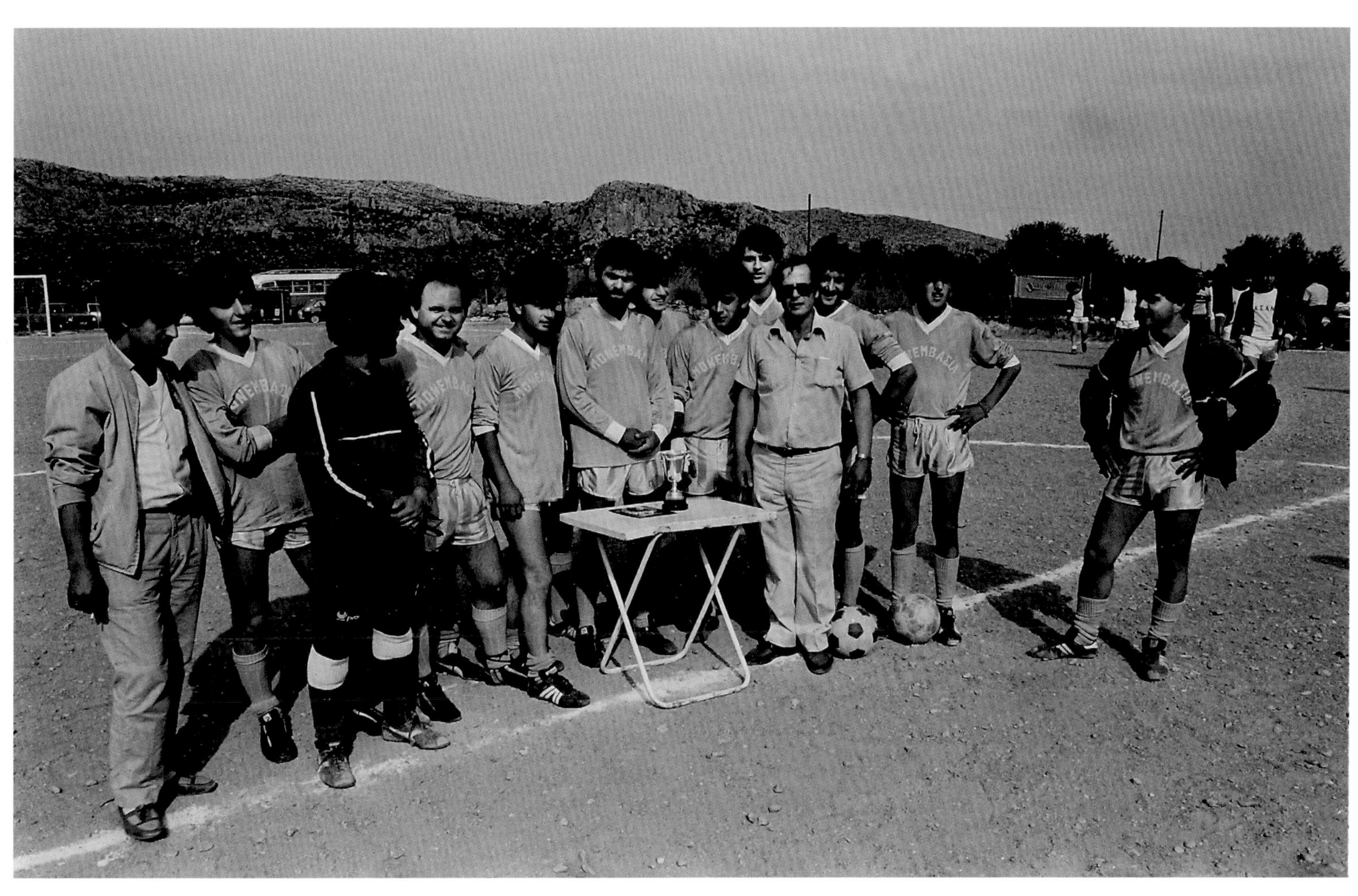

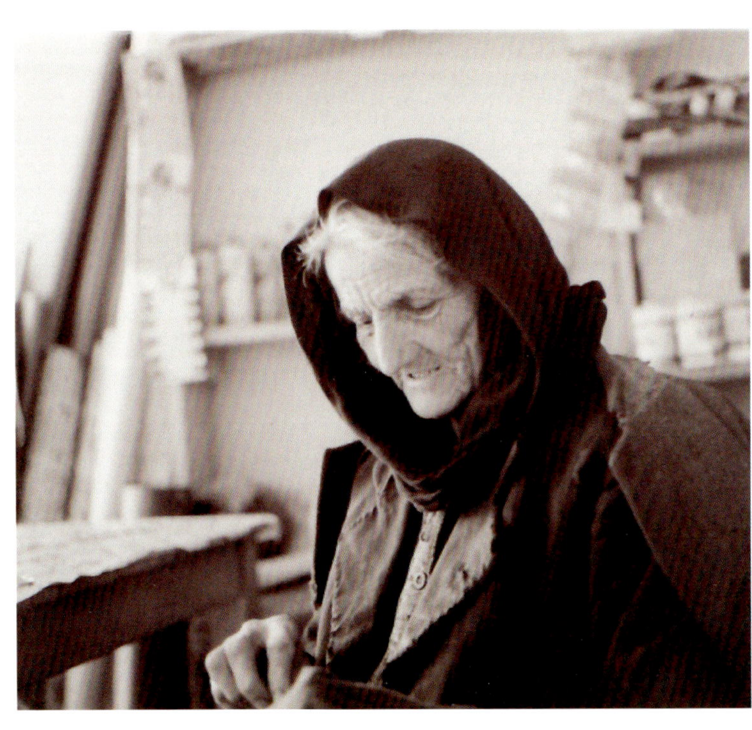

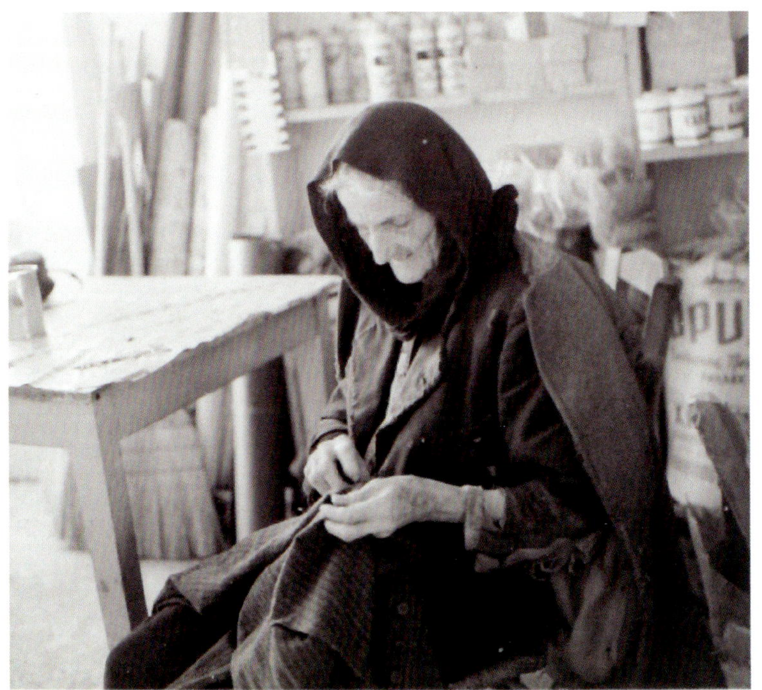

It will be very interesting to follow the pattern of our life as it is spread out like a beautiful tapestry ... in looking back over the years we can discover a red thread goes through the pattern of our life.

MARIA AUGUSTA VON TRAPP,
MARIA: MY OWN STORY, 1972

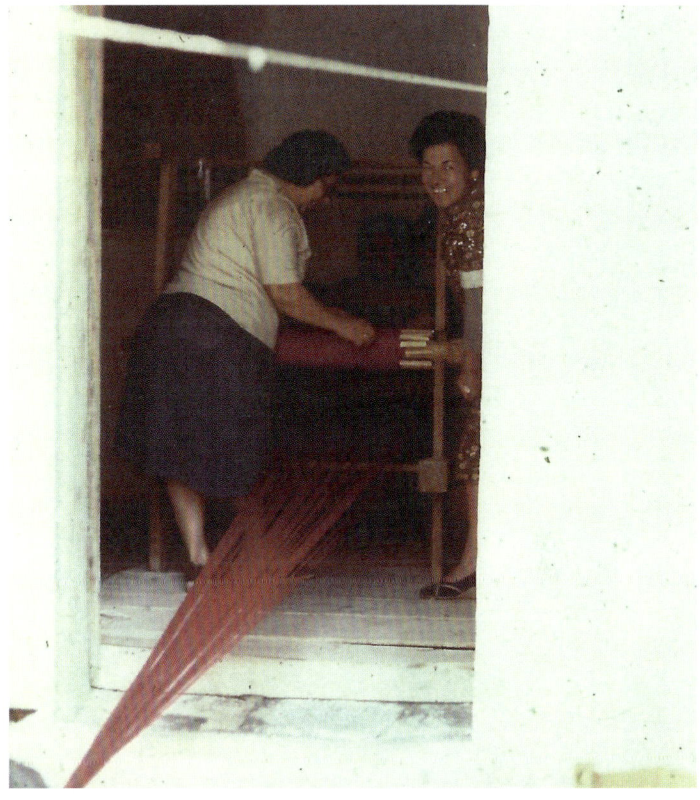

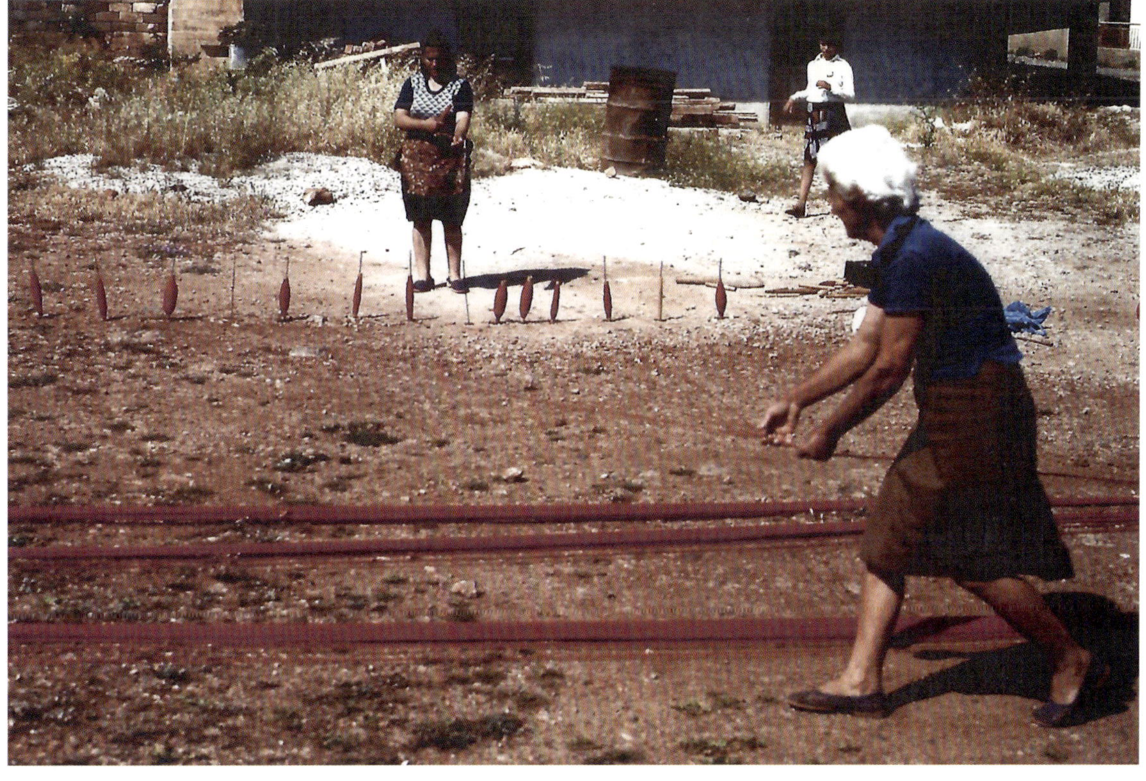

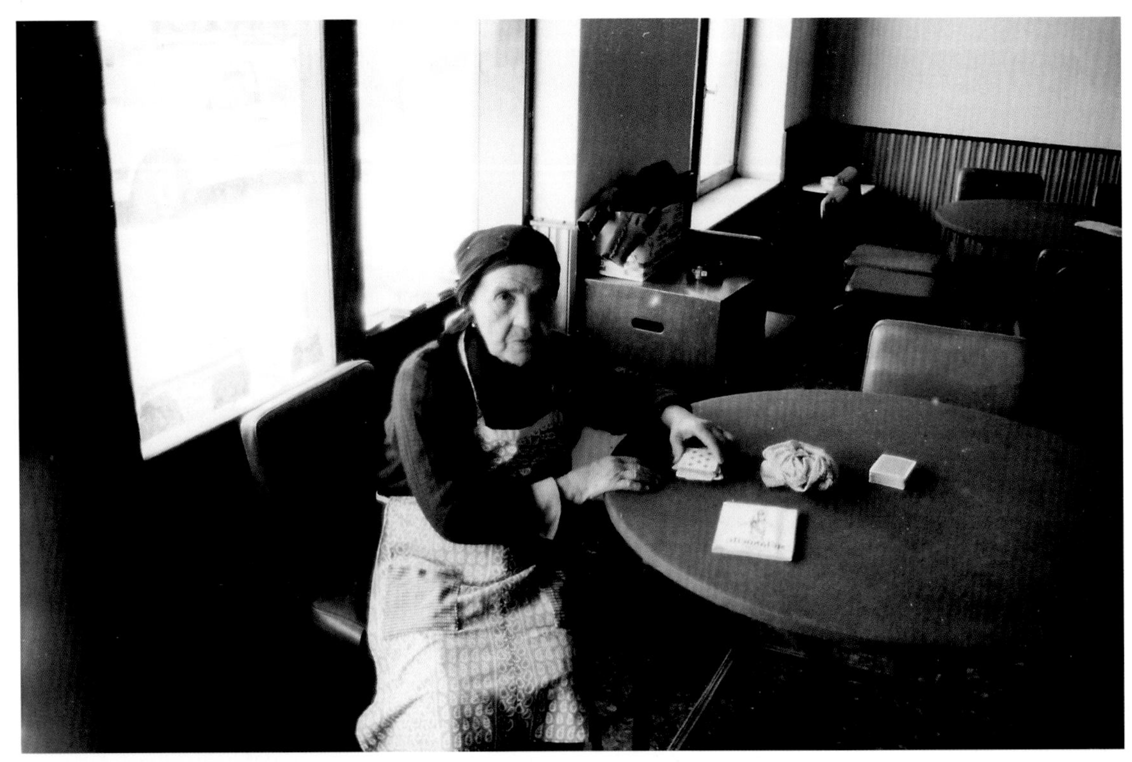

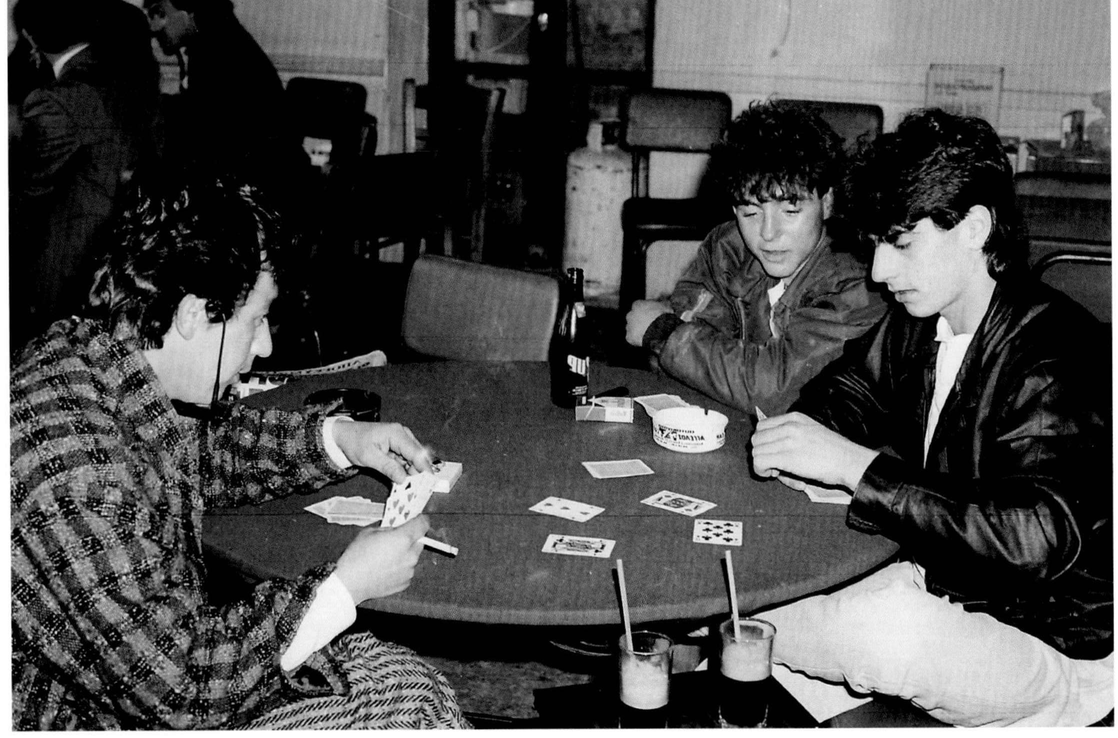

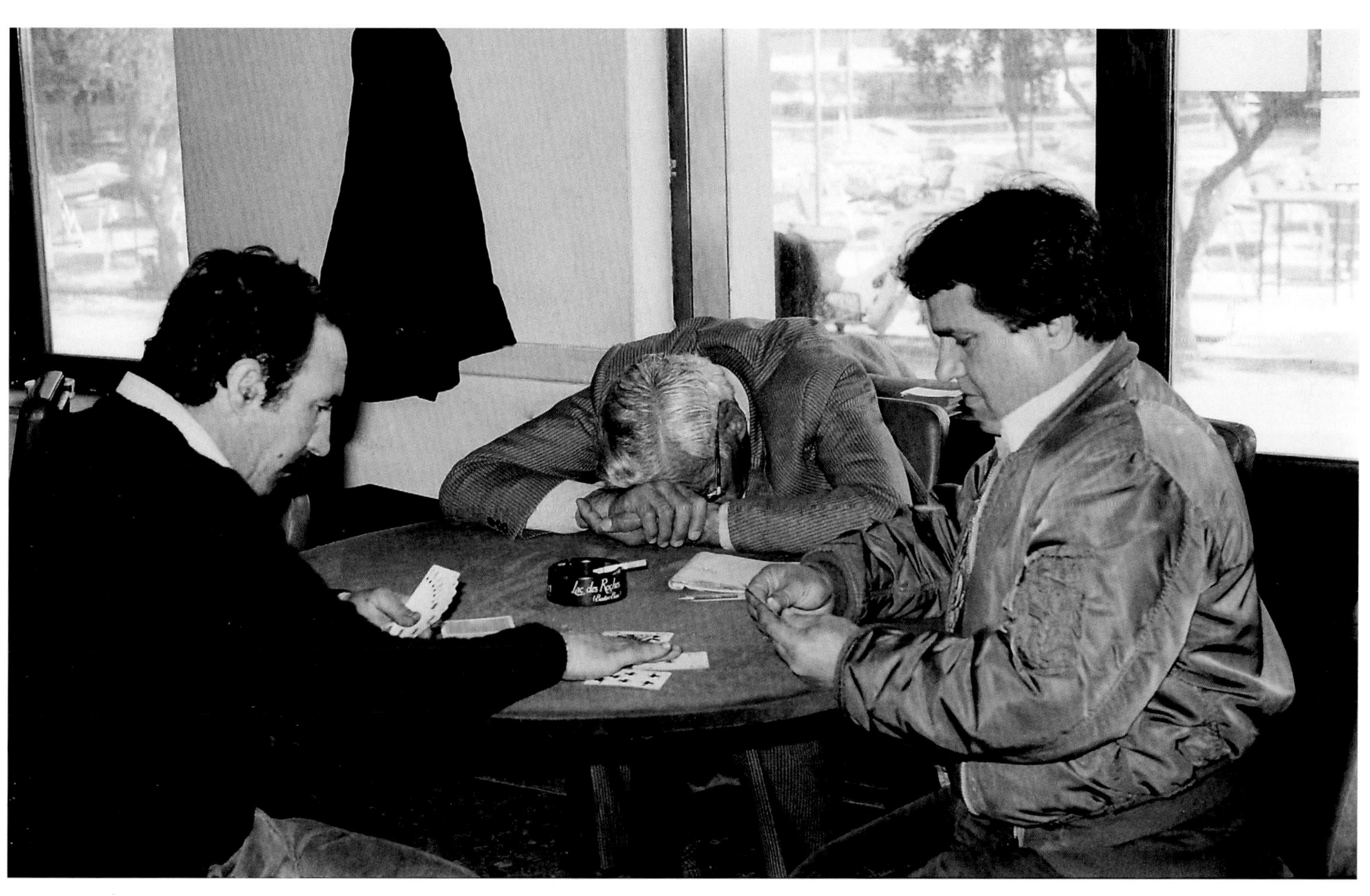
Lac des Roches

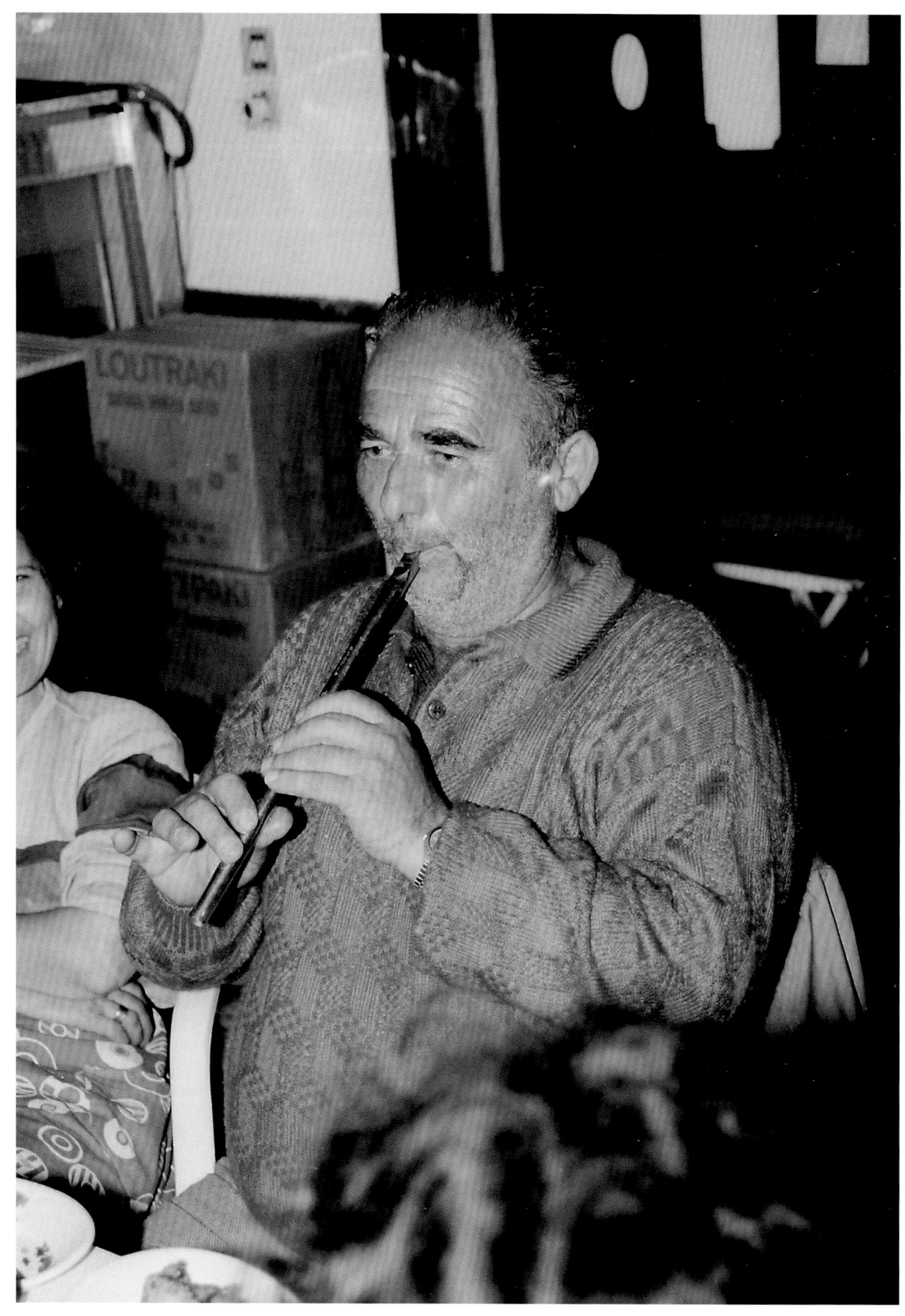
LOUTRAKI

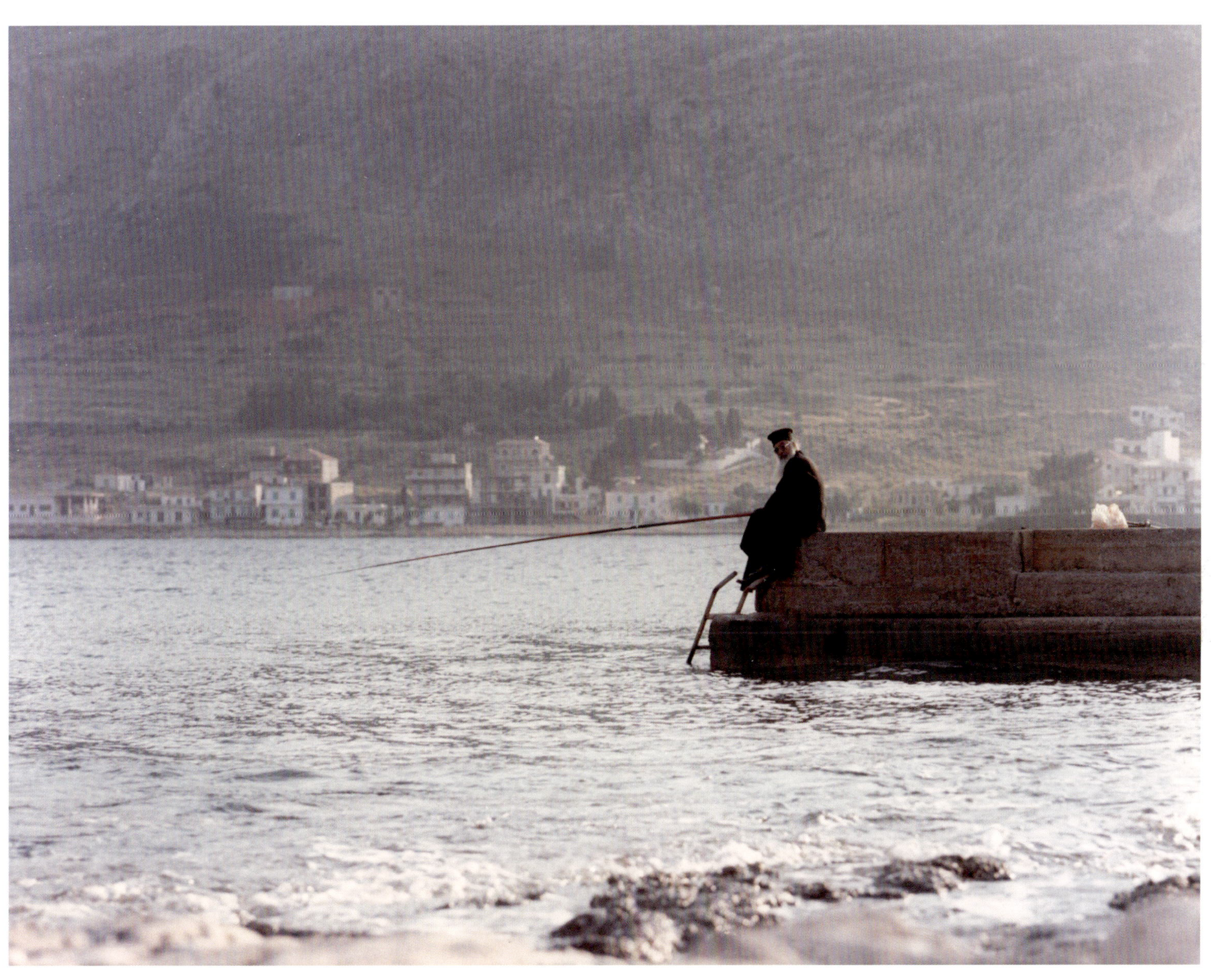

Renaissance

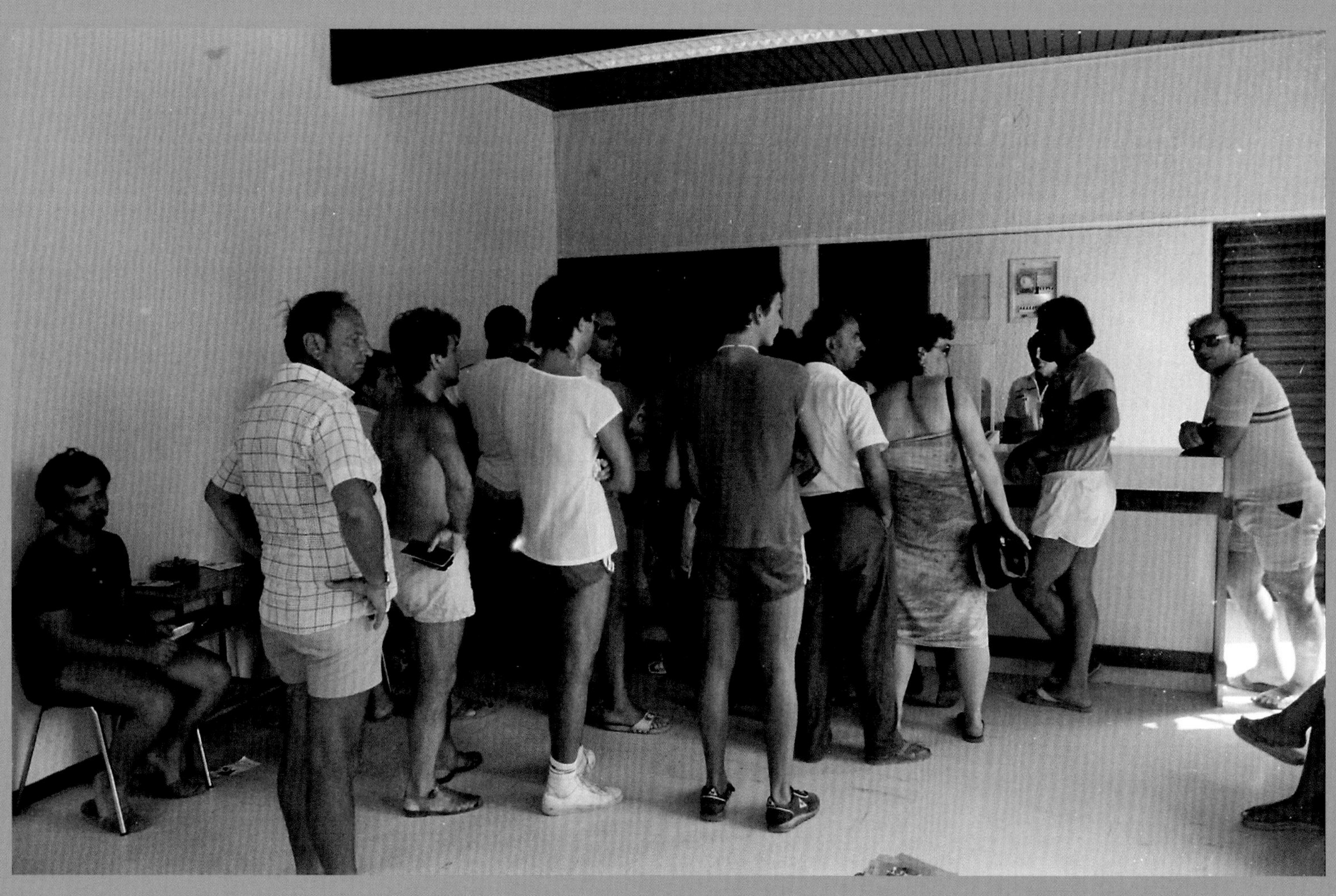

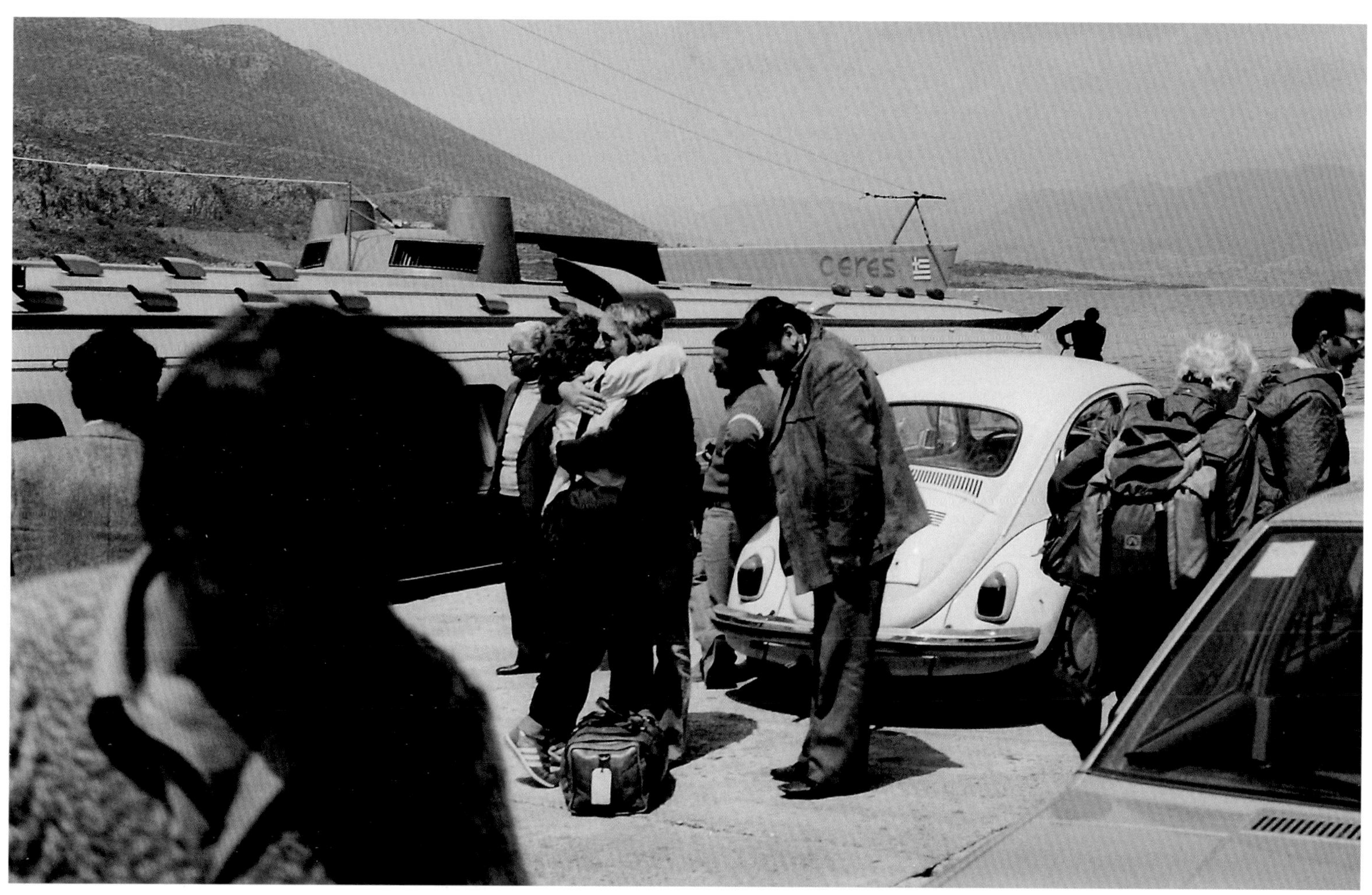

No one passed through because the road ended there, the ordinary steamer only called once a week and only in summer, and there was only one daily bus. All new arrivals were therefore regarded with interest.

NINA BAWDEN, *REBEL ON A ROCK*, 1978

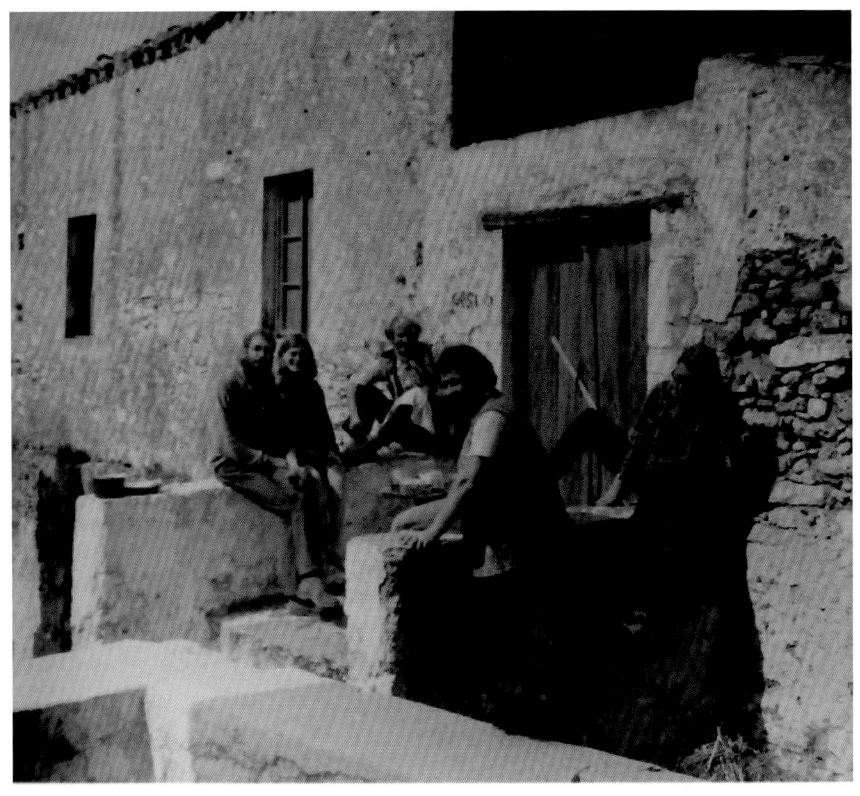

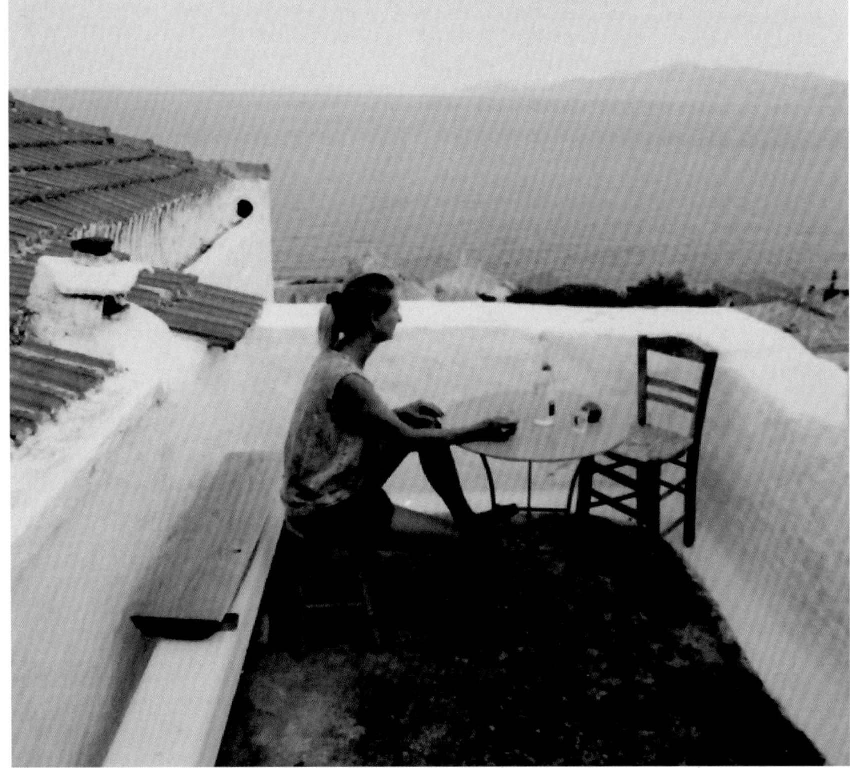

She was the fiancée of a local fisherman who lived in the next bay and she often used to visit to talk about literature.

KEVIN McGRATH, *ON FRIENDSHIP*, 2024

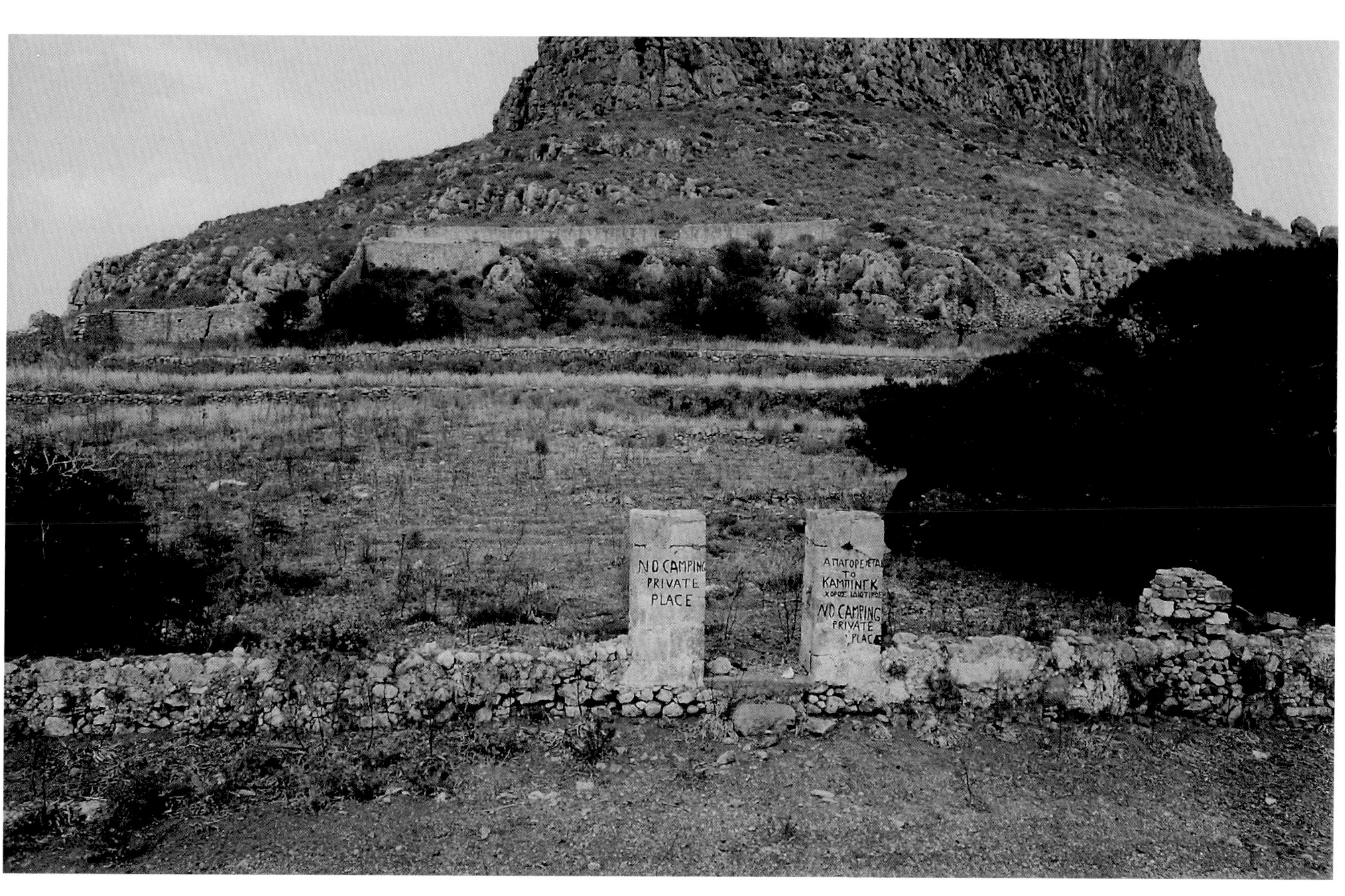
NO CAMPING
PRIVATE
PLACE
ΤΟ
ΚΑΜΠΙΝΓΚ
NO CAMPING
PRIVATE

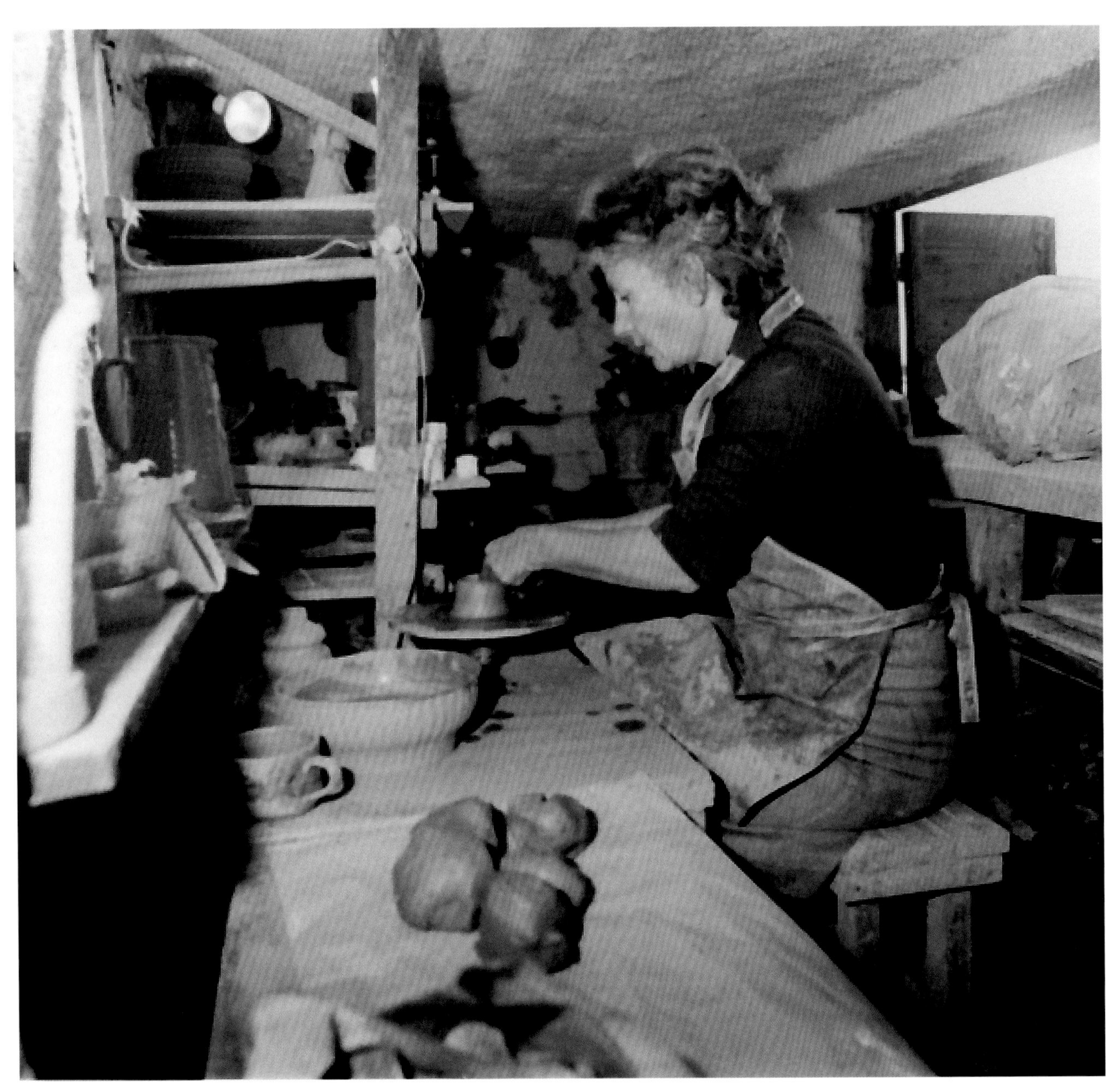

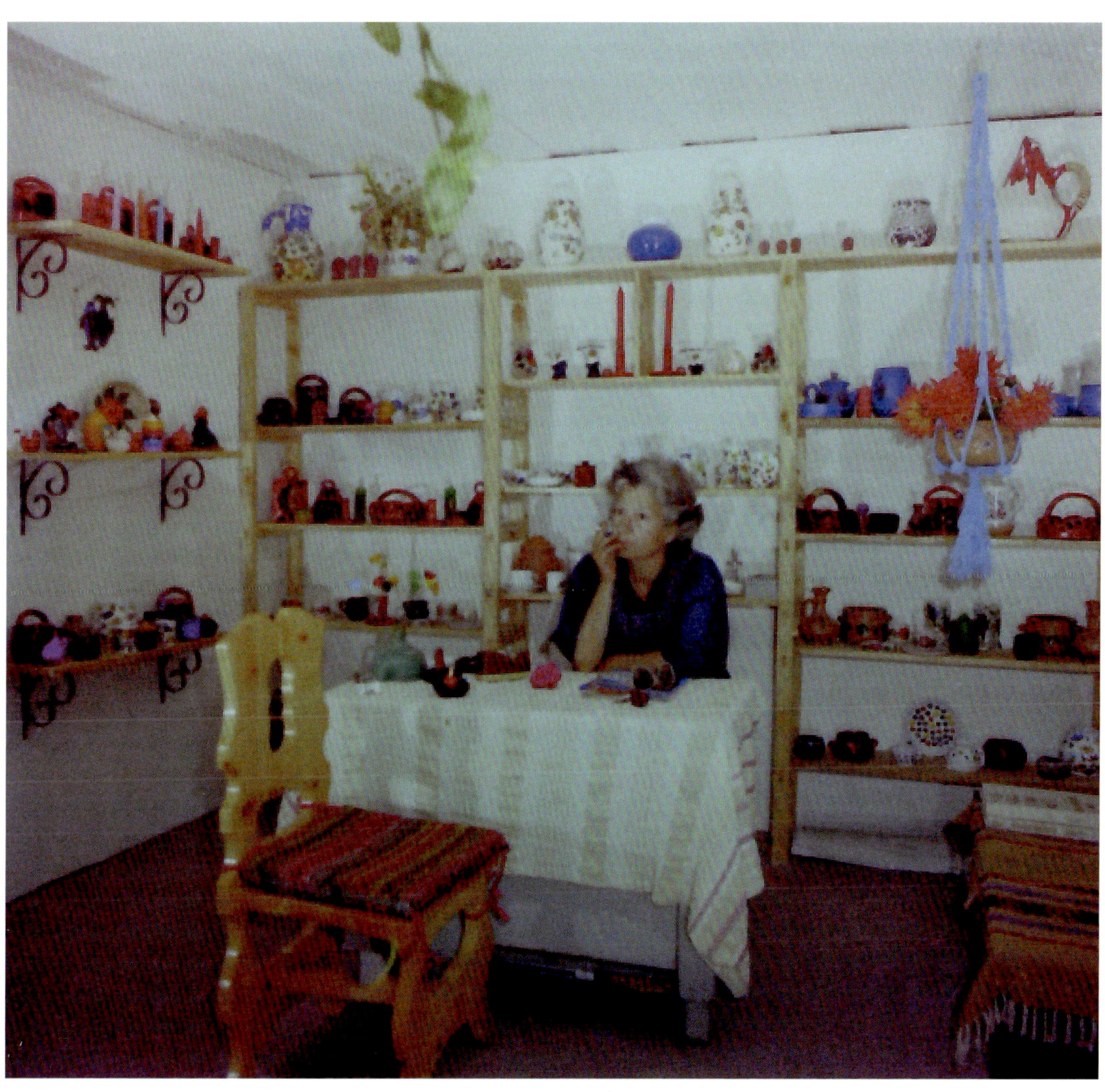

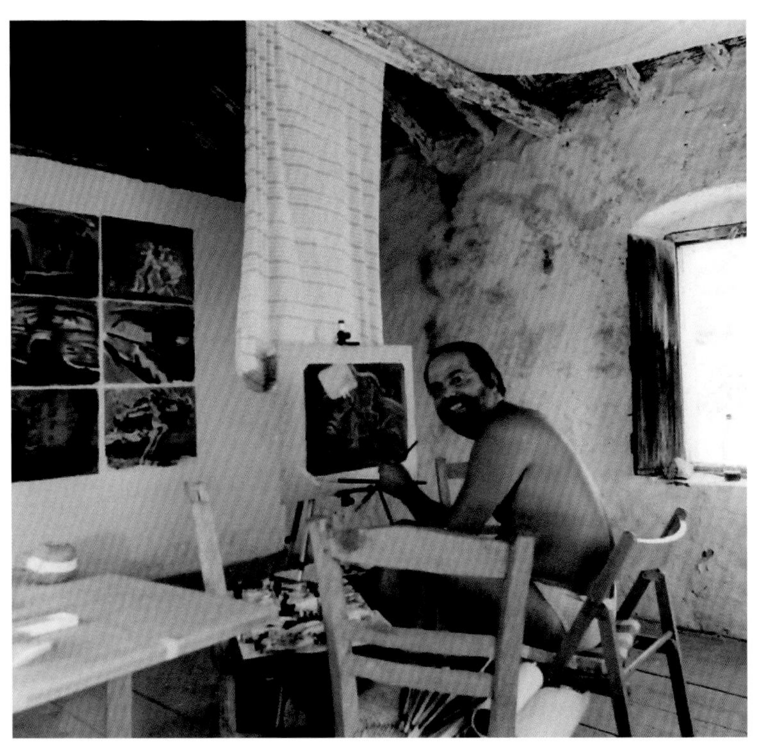

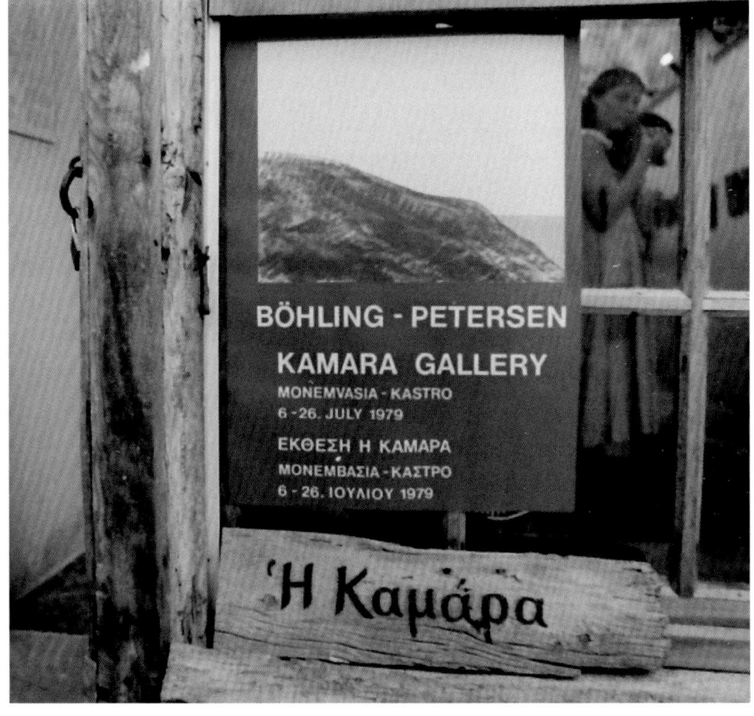
BÖHLING - PETERSEN
KAMARA GALLERY
MONEMVASIA - KASTRO
6 - 26. JULY 1979
ΕΚΘΕΣΗ Η ΚΑΜΑΡΑ
ΜΟΝΕΜΒΑΣΙΑ - ΚΑΣΤΡΟ
6 - 26. ΙΟΥΛΙΟΥ 1979
Ἡ Καμάρα

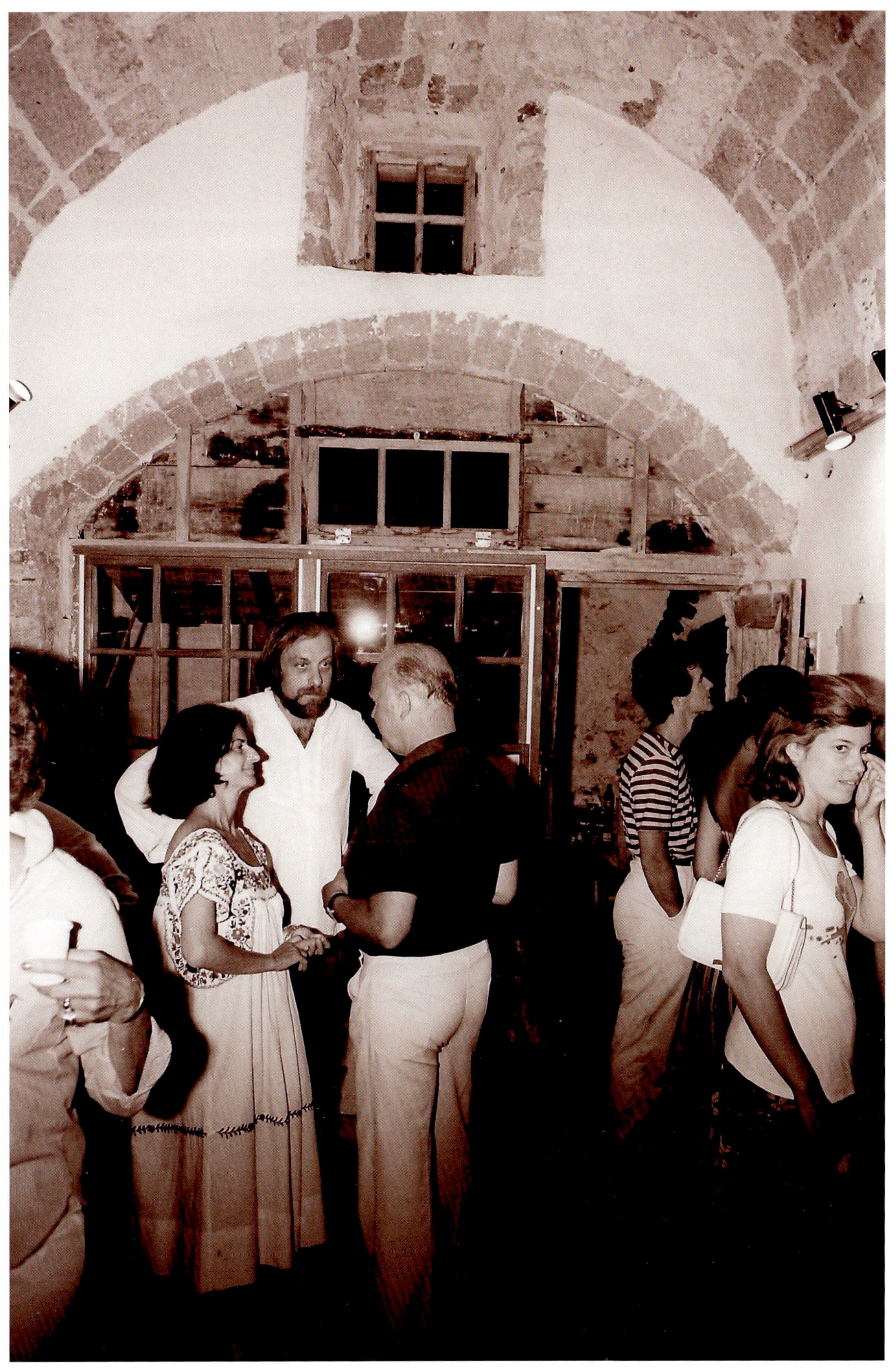

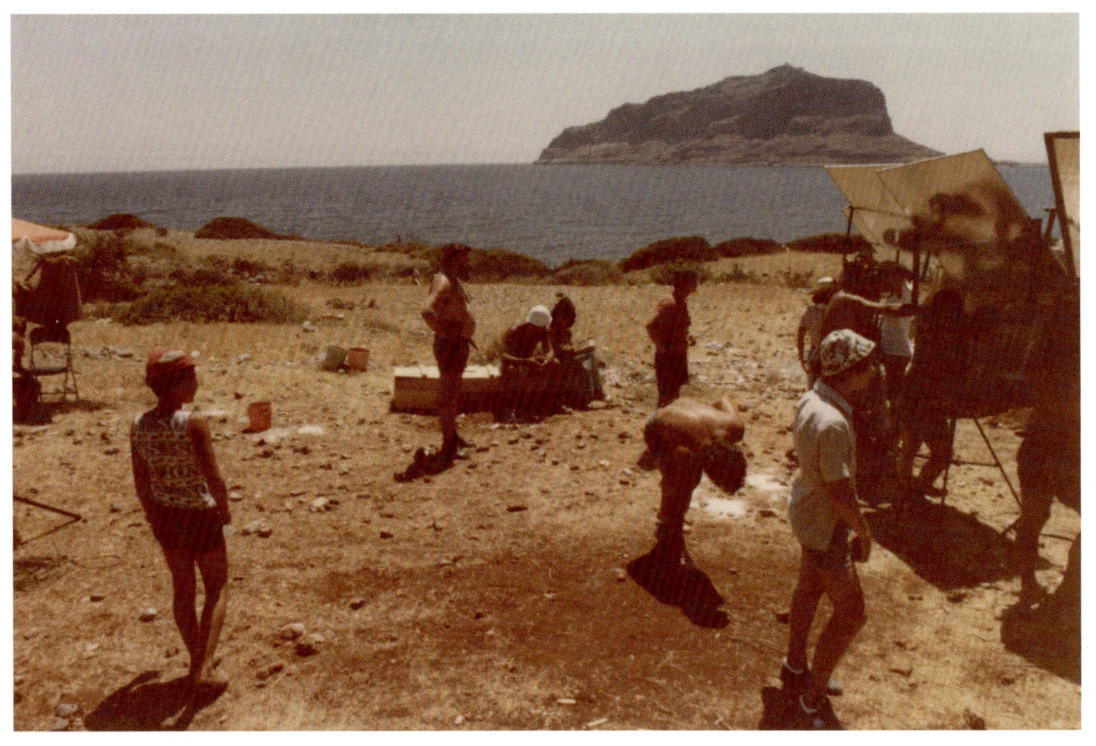

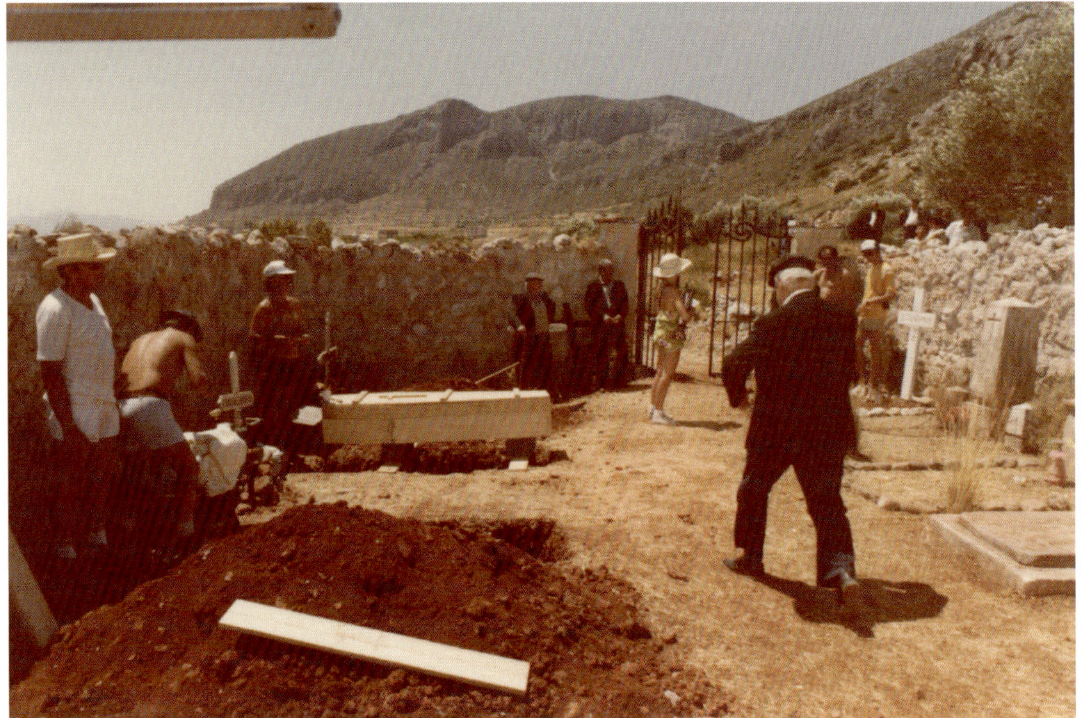

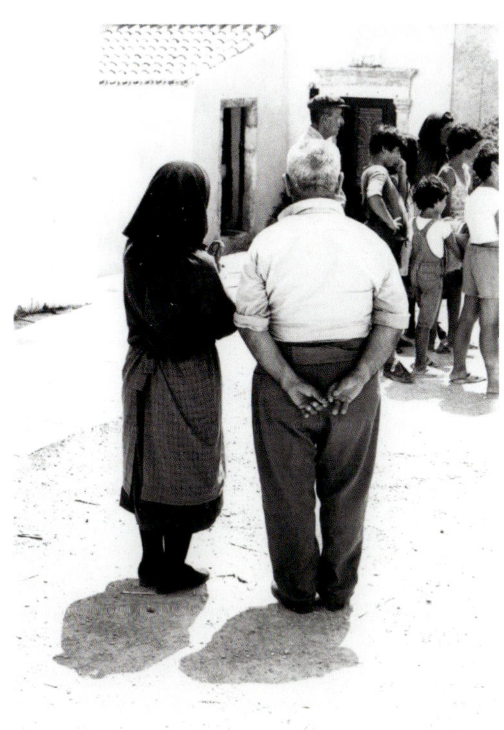

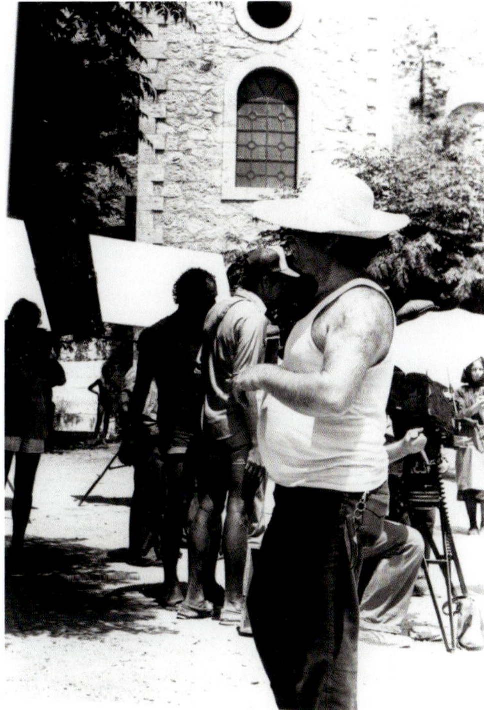

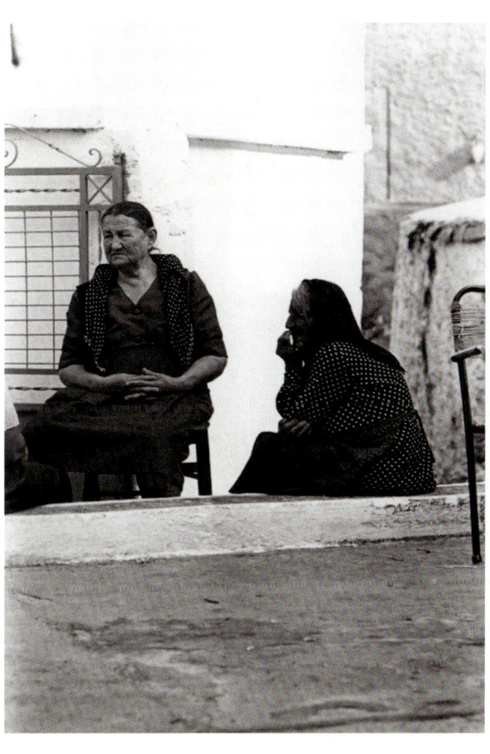

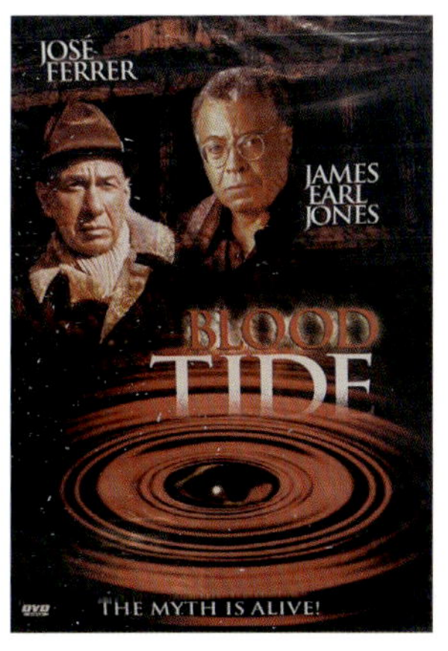

Besides the very good acting, the scenic and breath-taking photography of the Greek Island and the surrounding Aegean Sea kept you awake and observant of what was happening on screen.

SOL-KAY, IMDB REVIEW, 2005

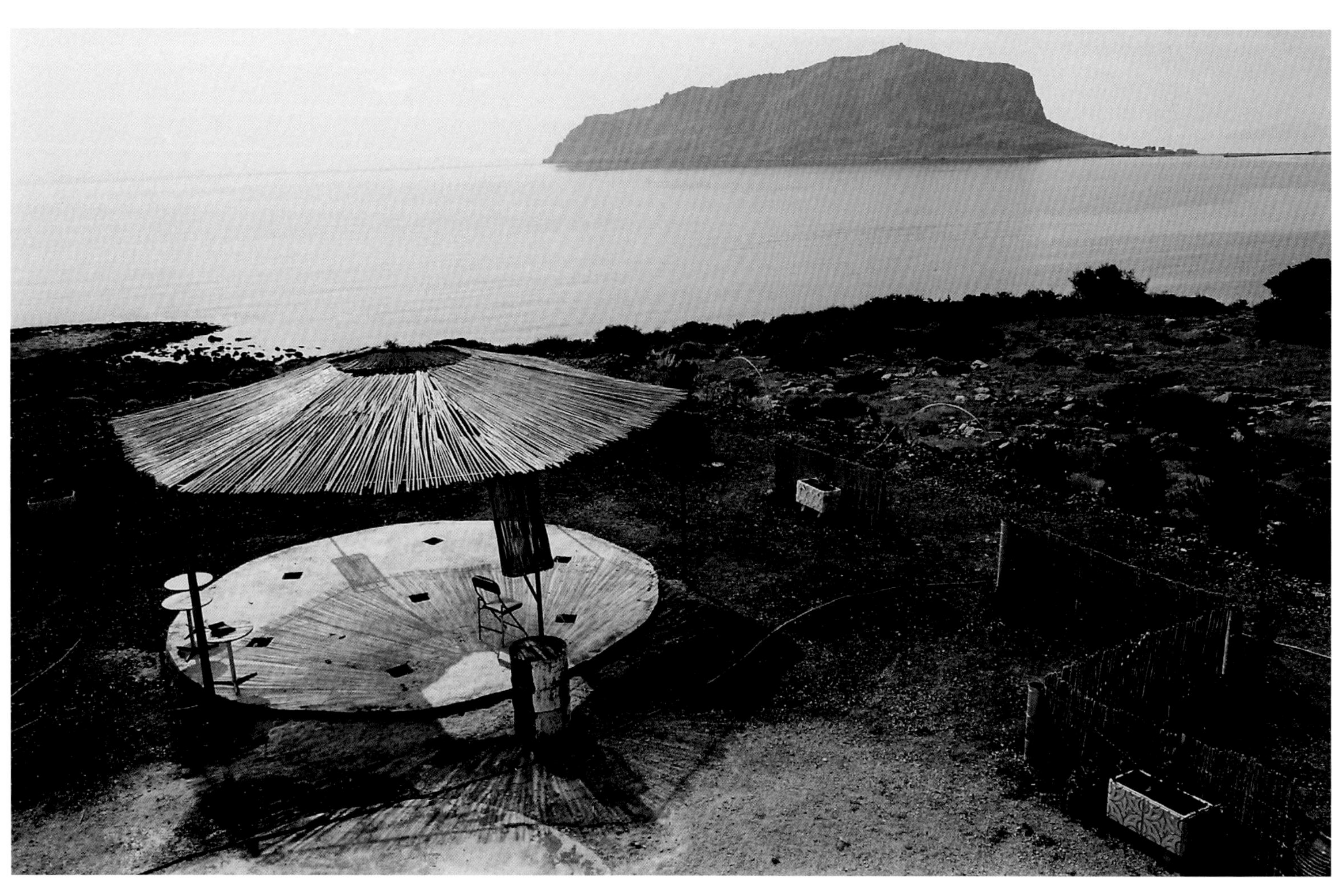

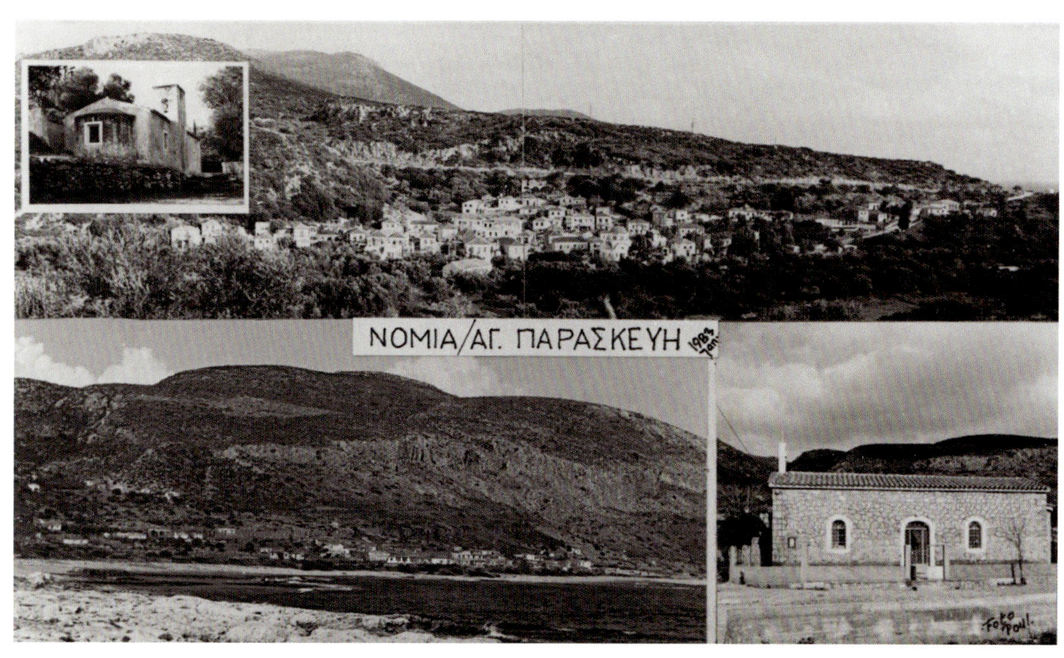
ΝΟΜΙΑ/ΑΓ. ΠΑΡΑΣΚΕΥΗ

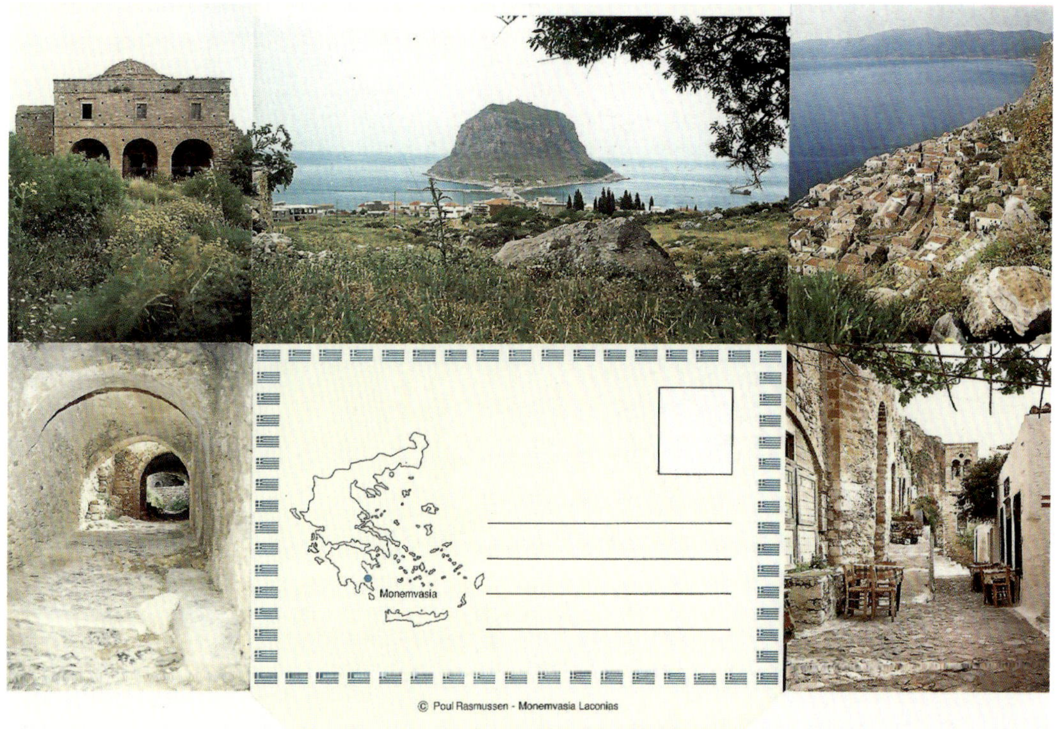
Monemvasia
© Poul Rasmussen - Monemvasia Laconias

Portraits

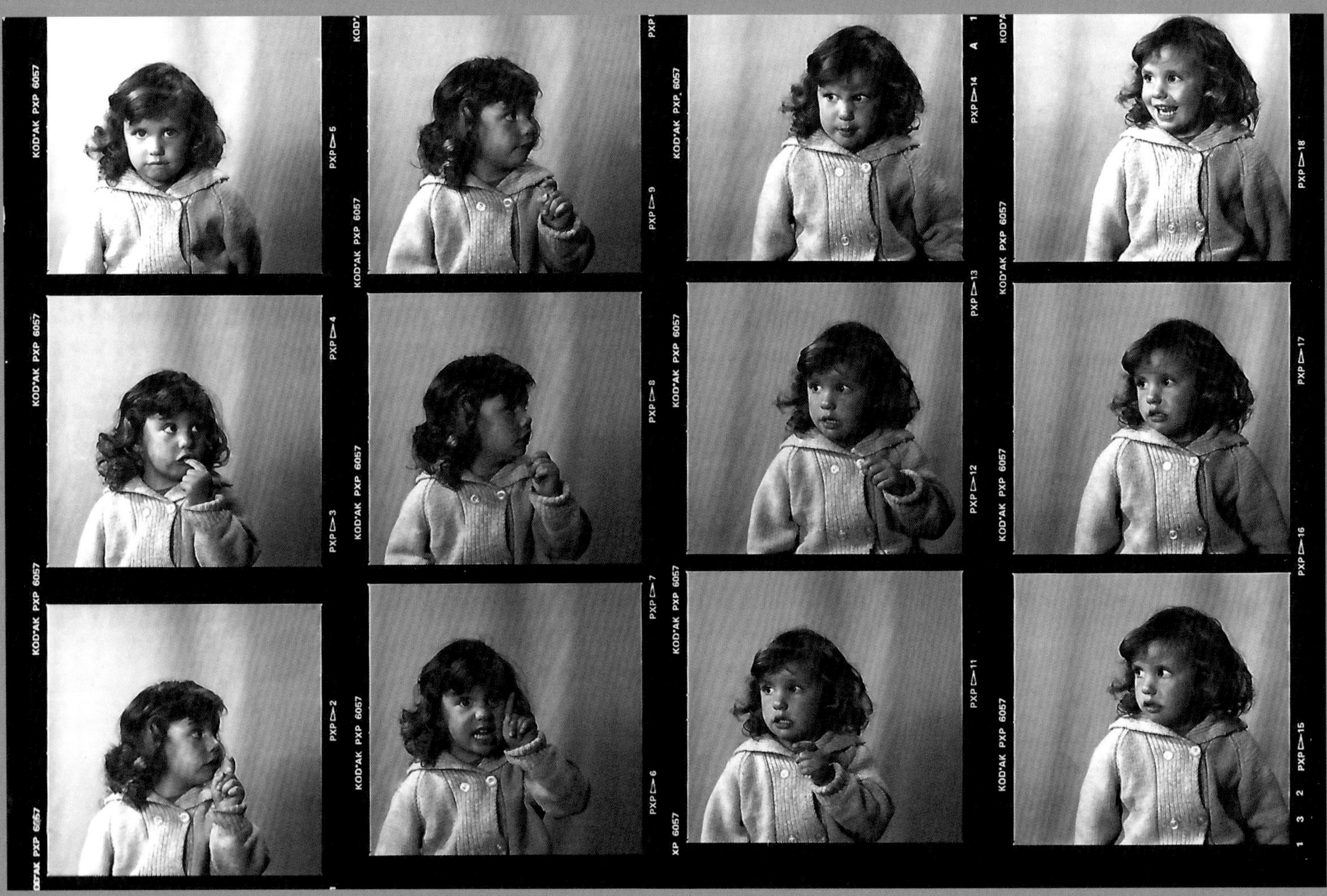

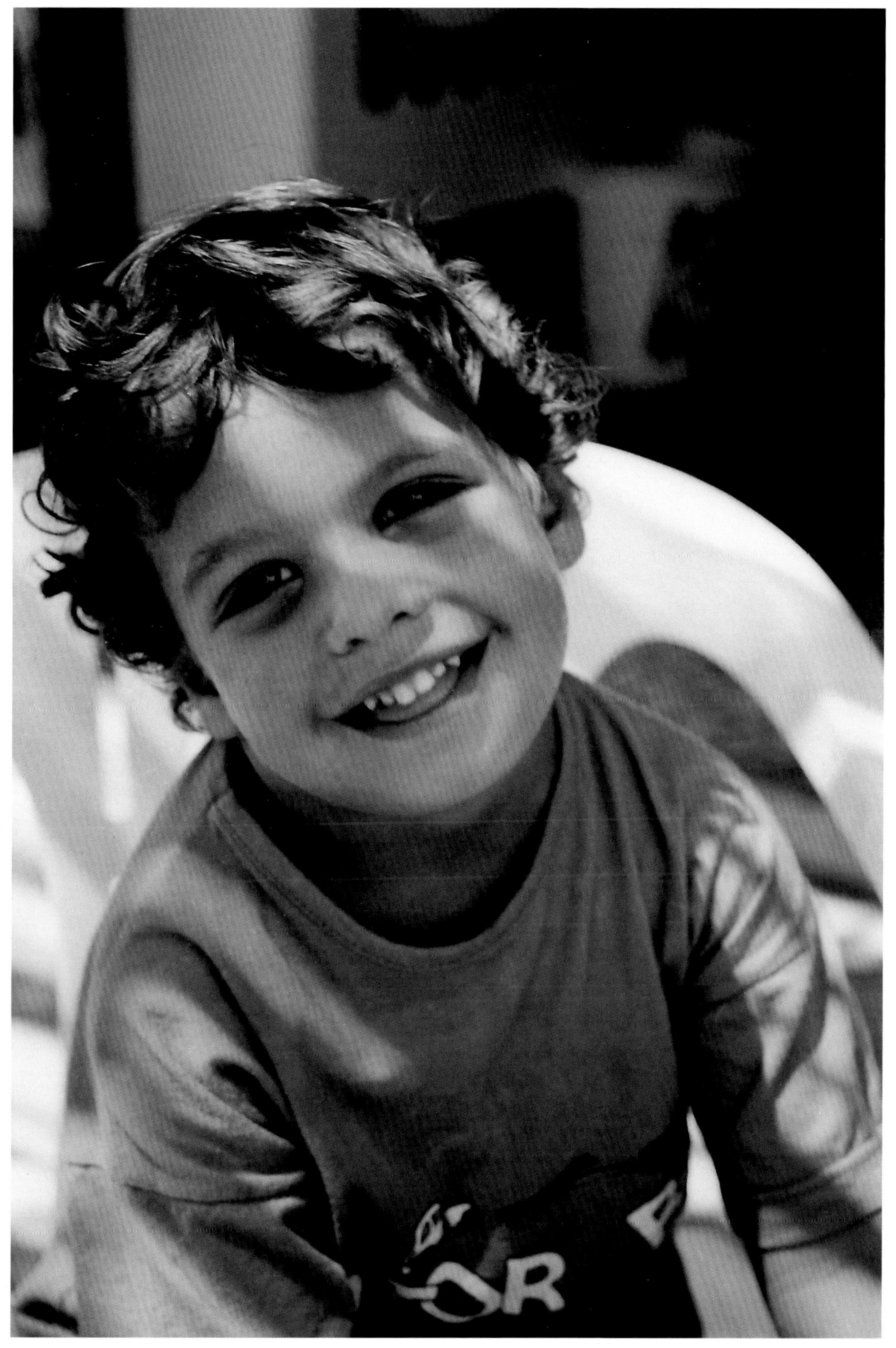

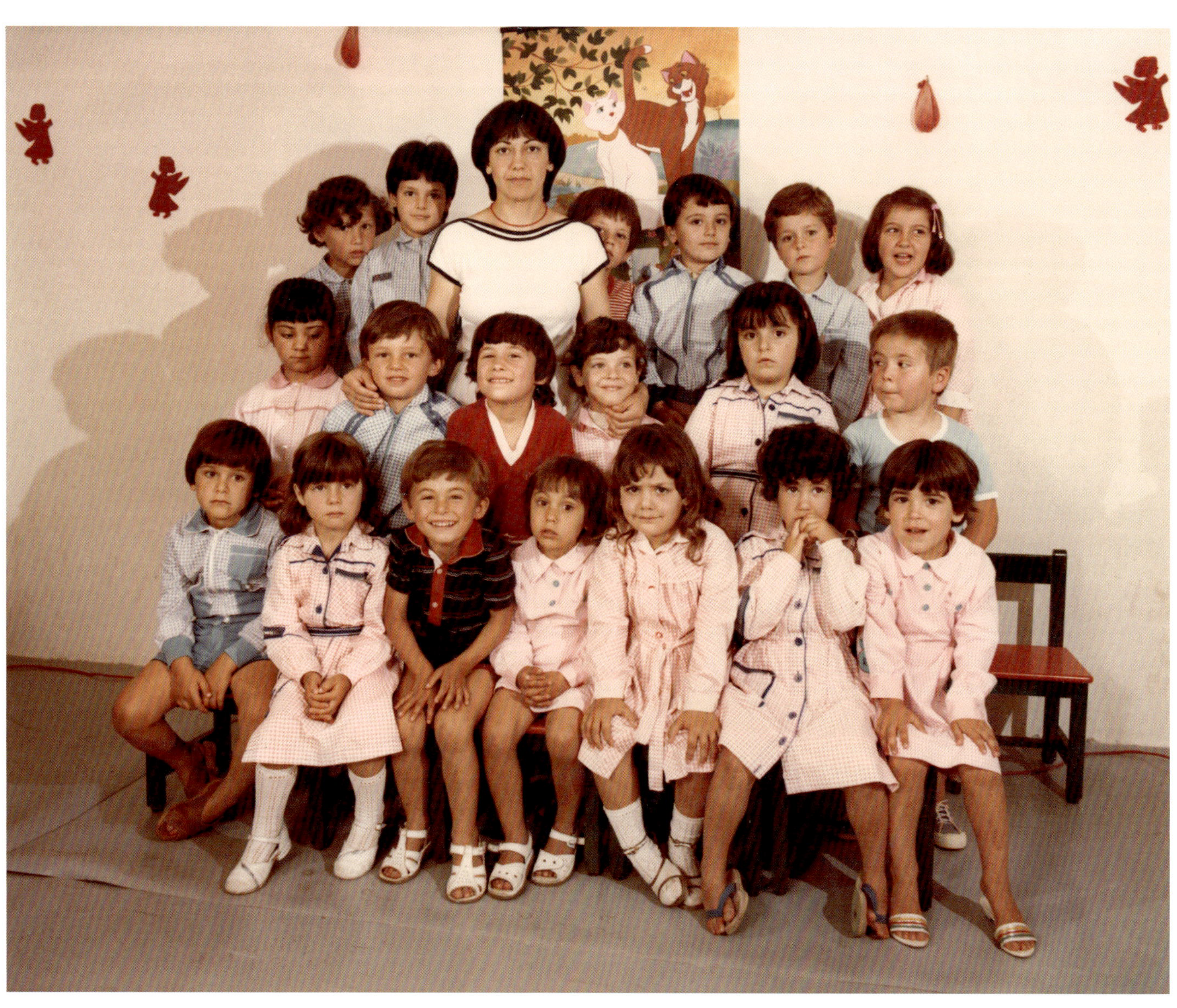

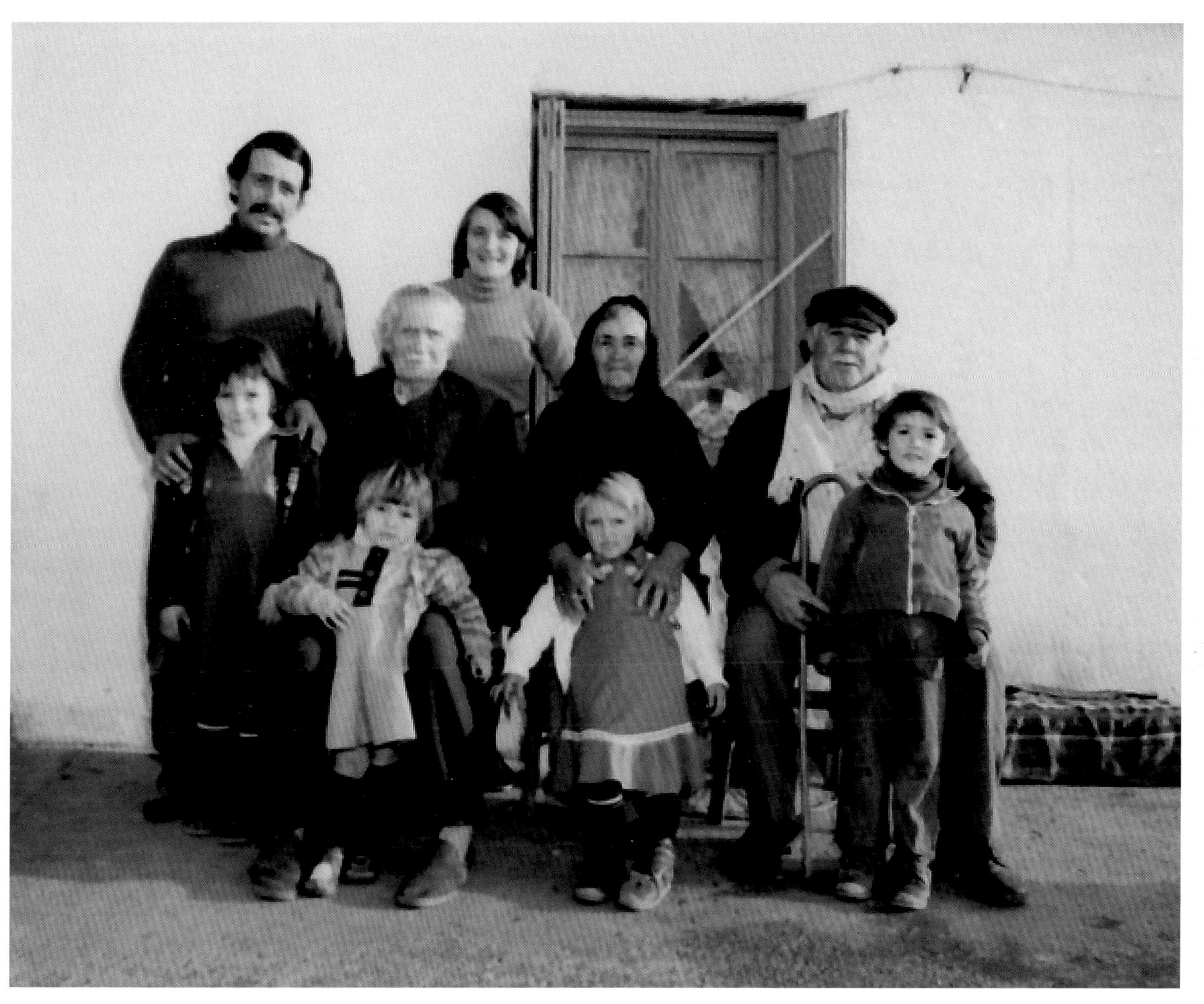

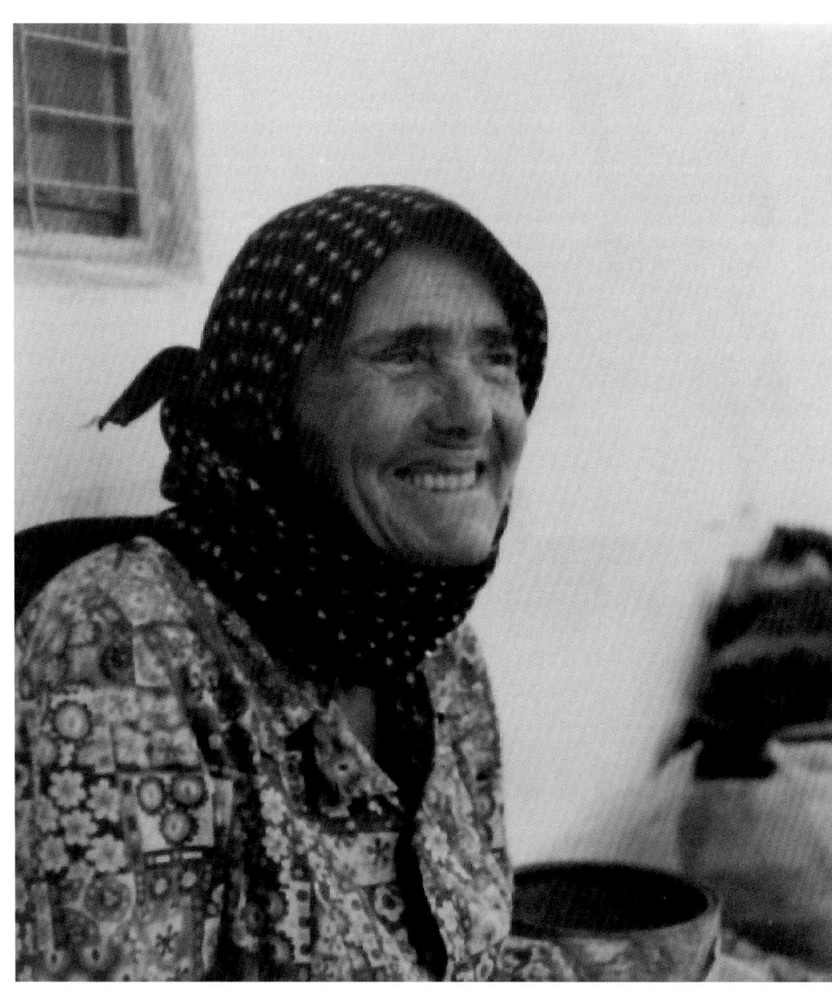
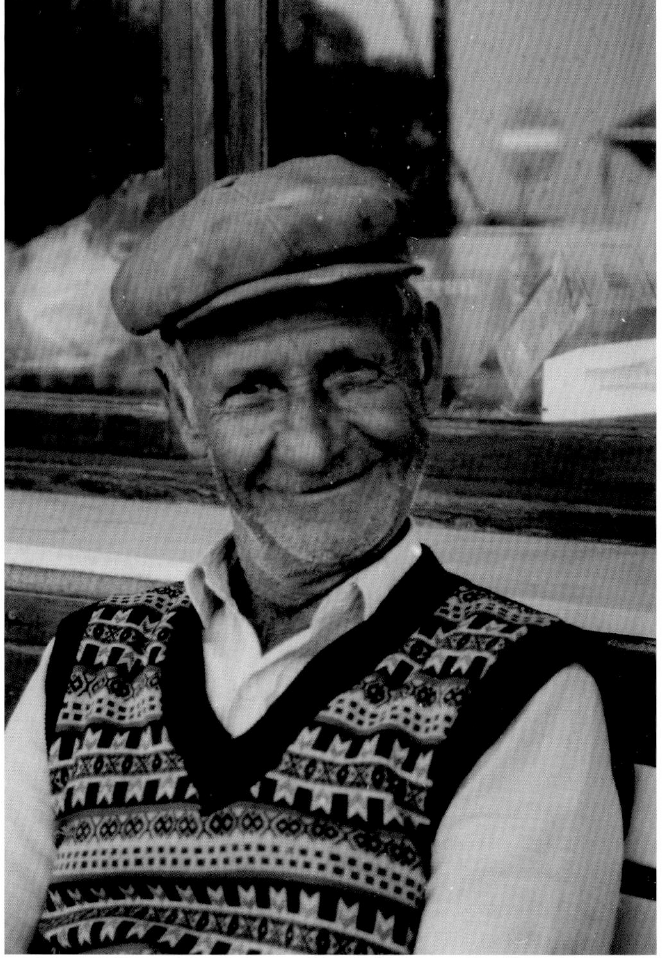

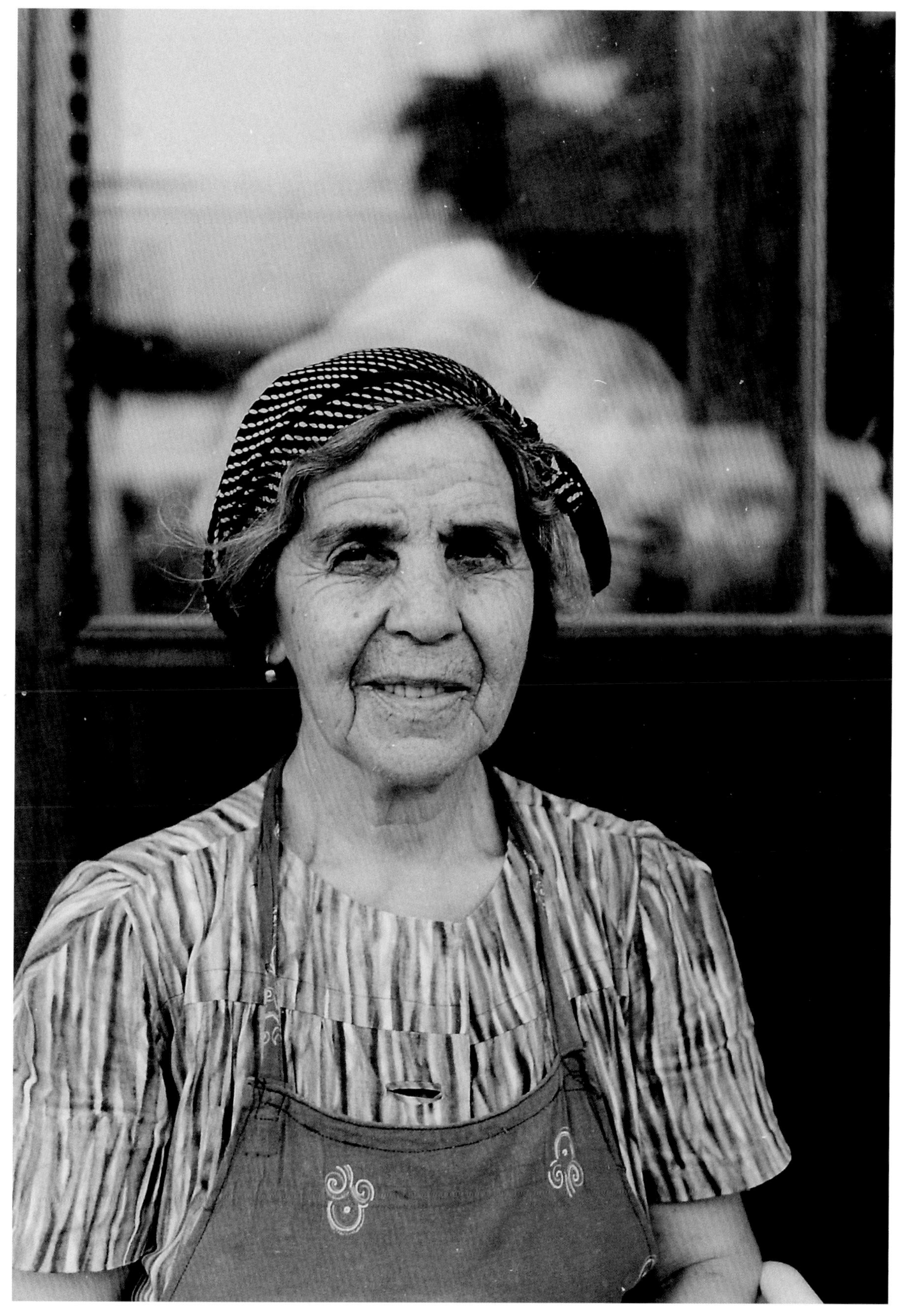

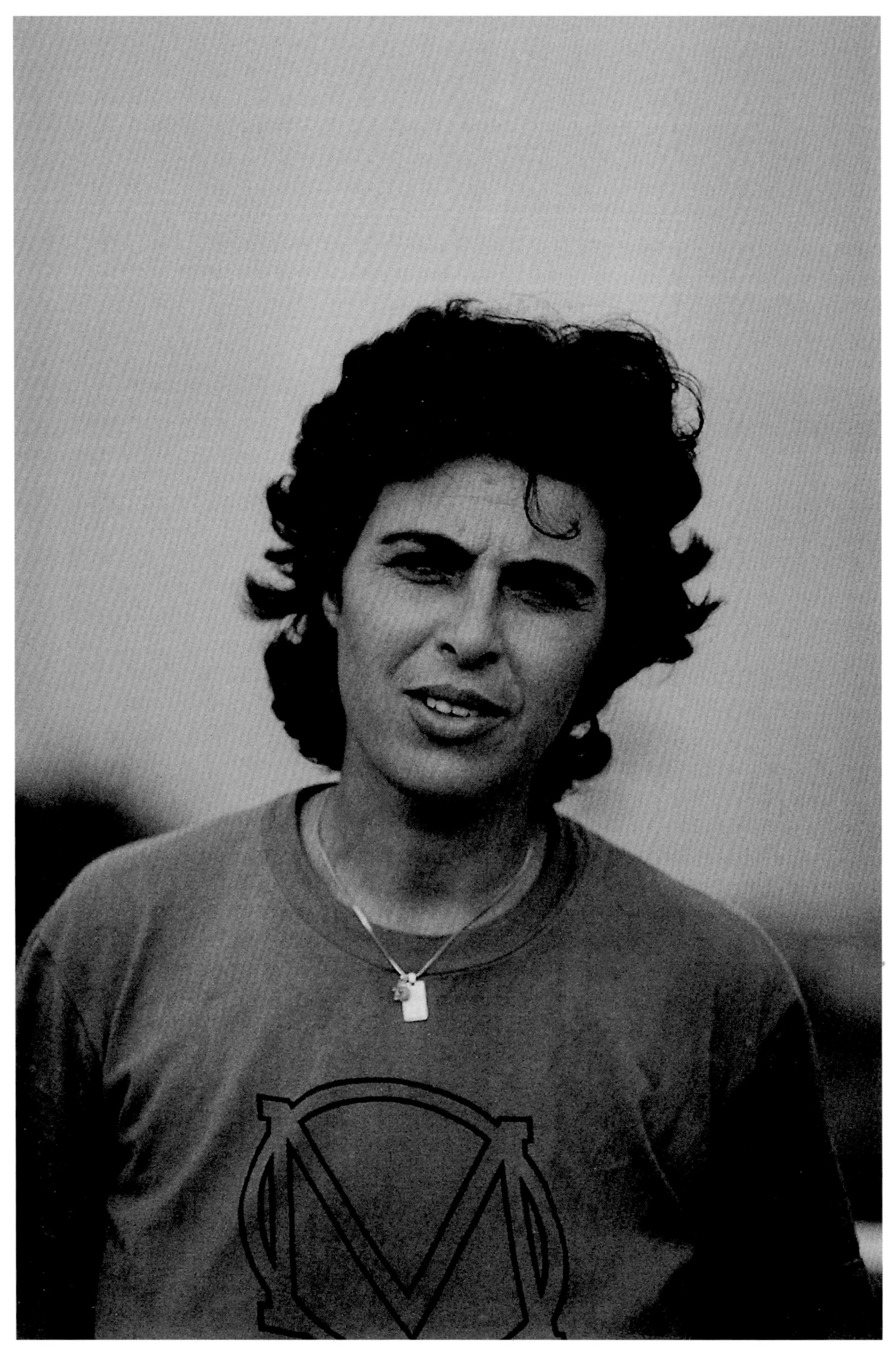

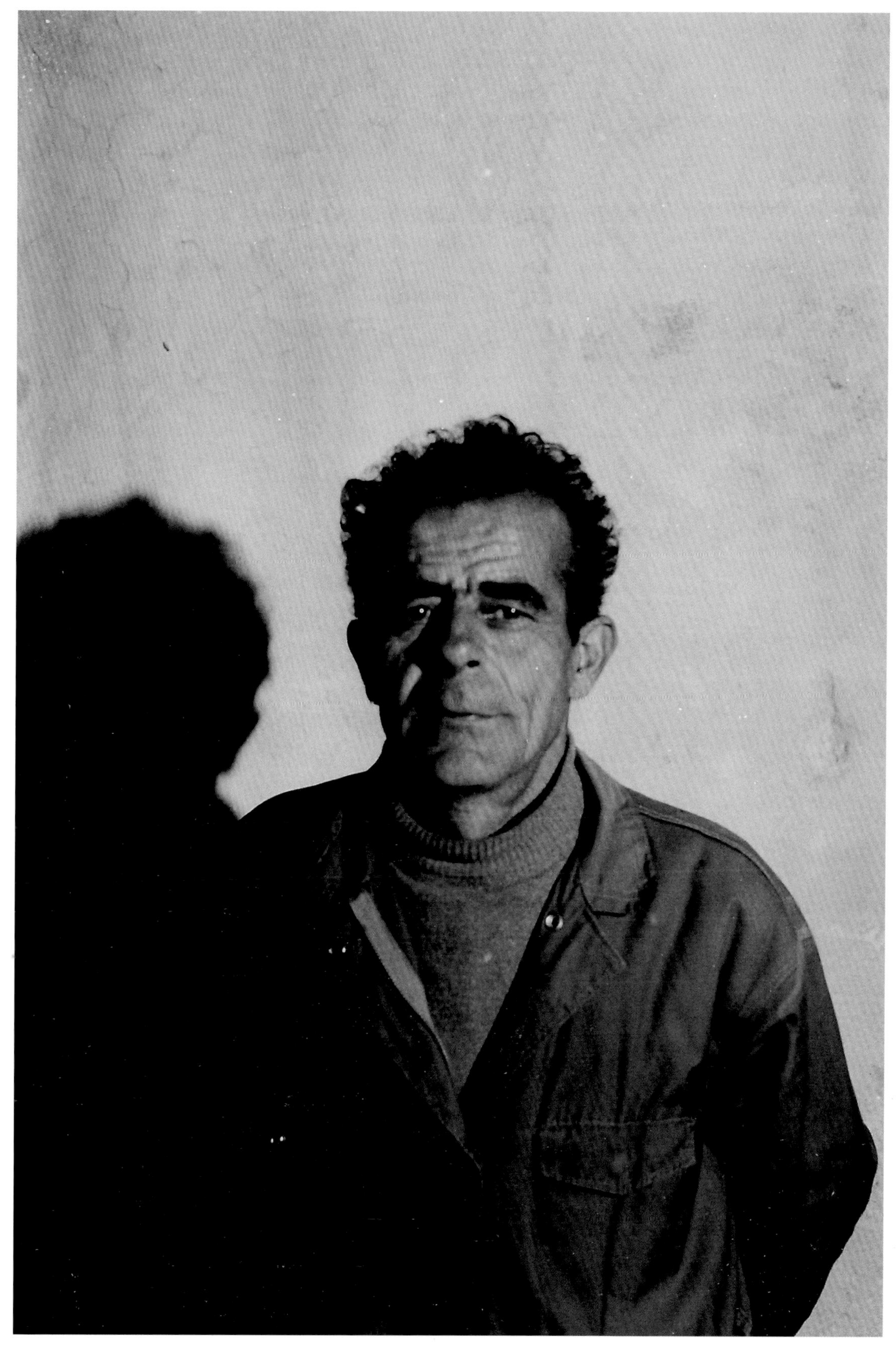

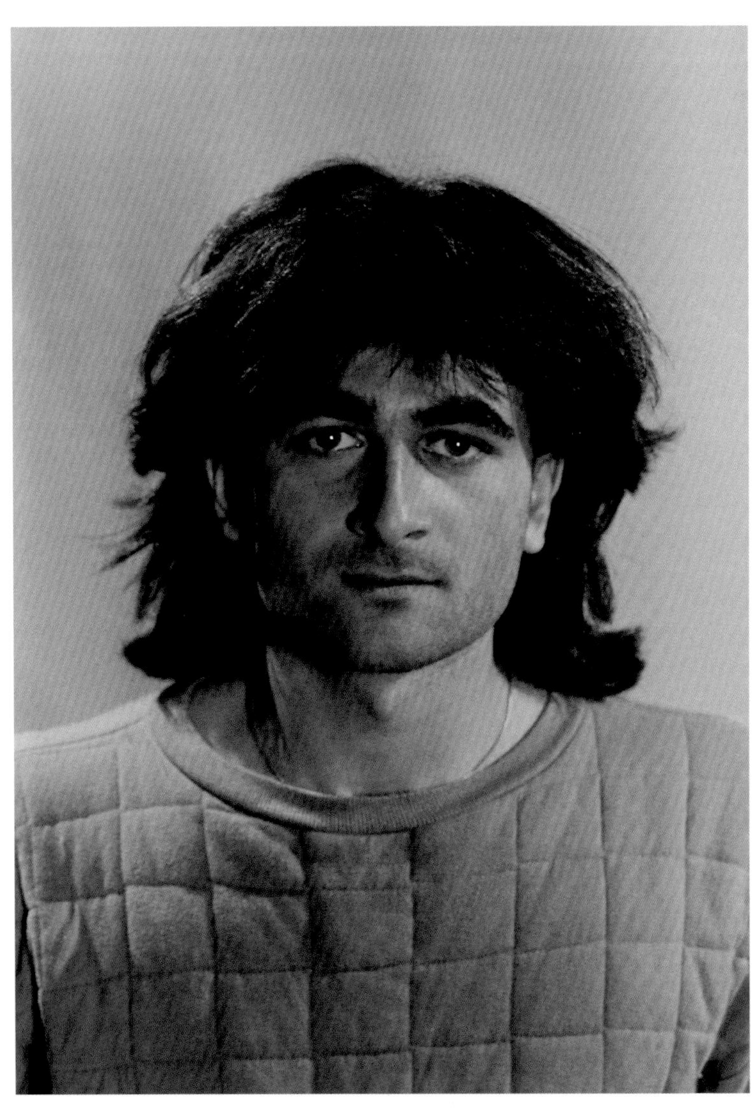

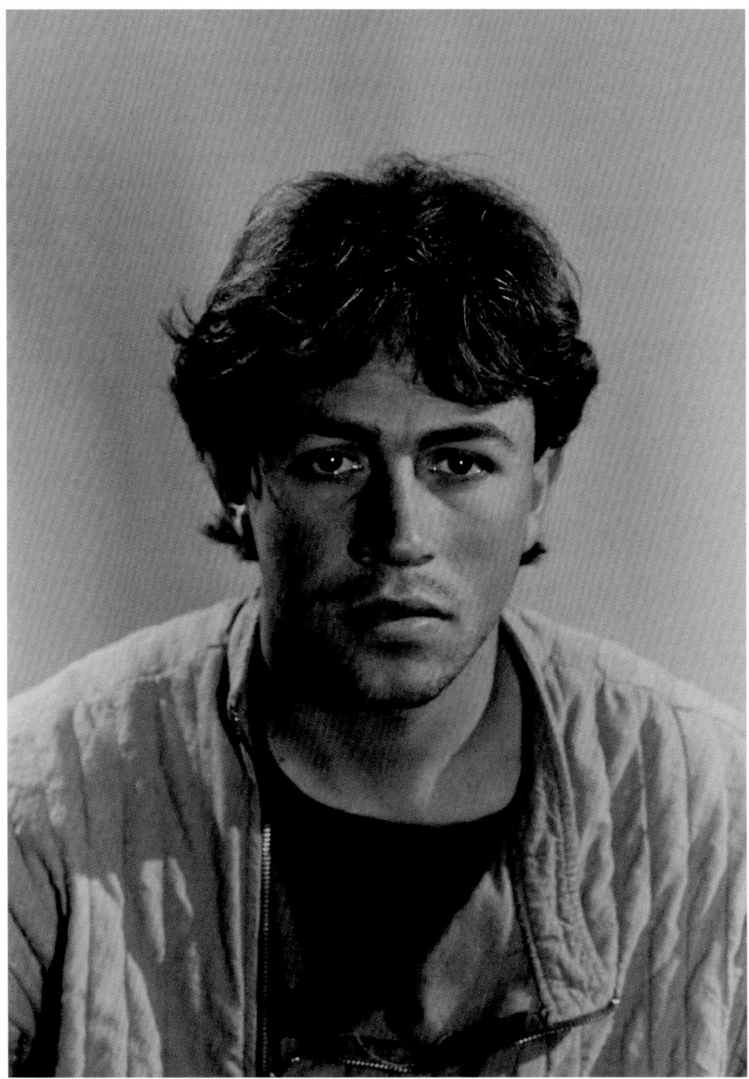

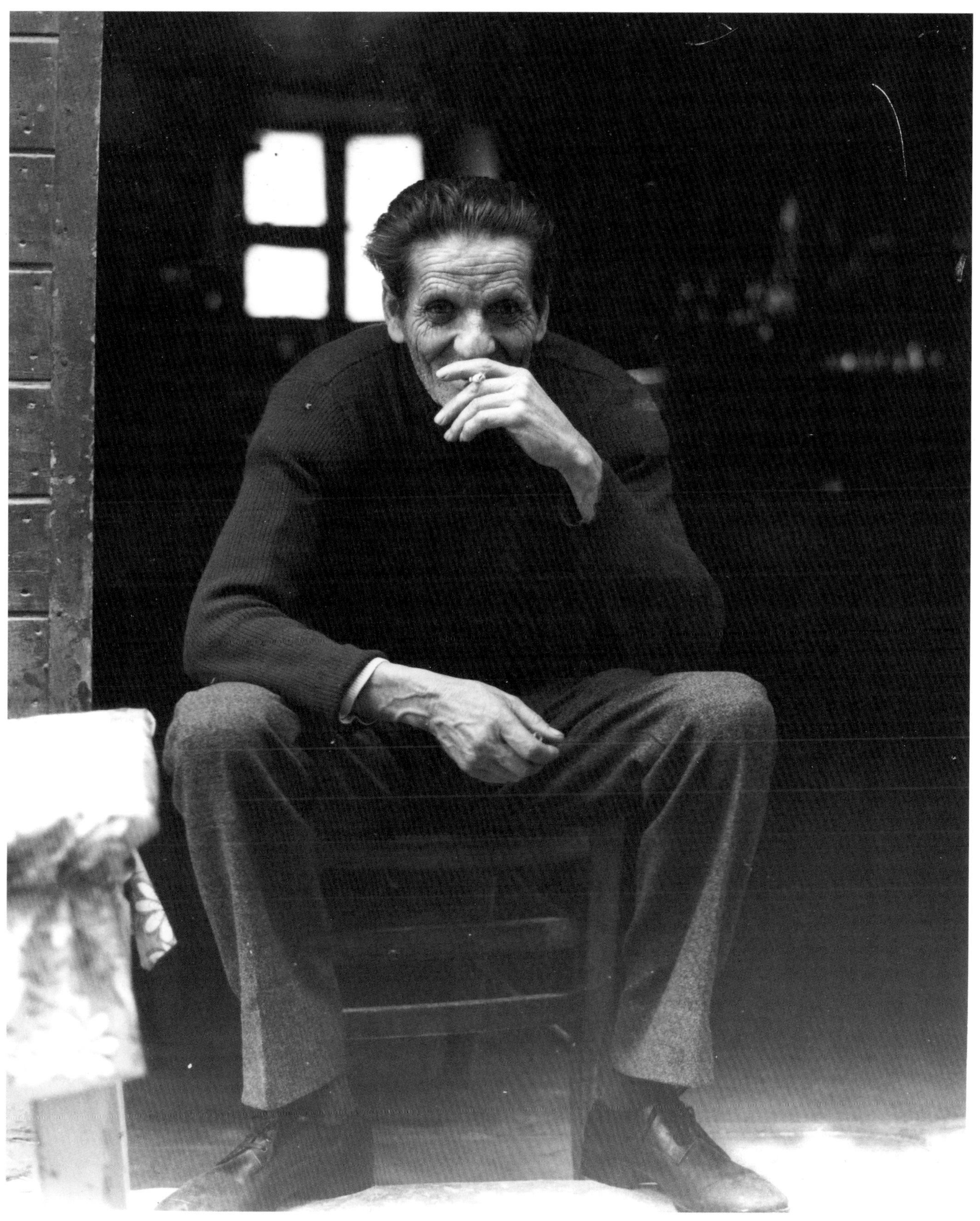

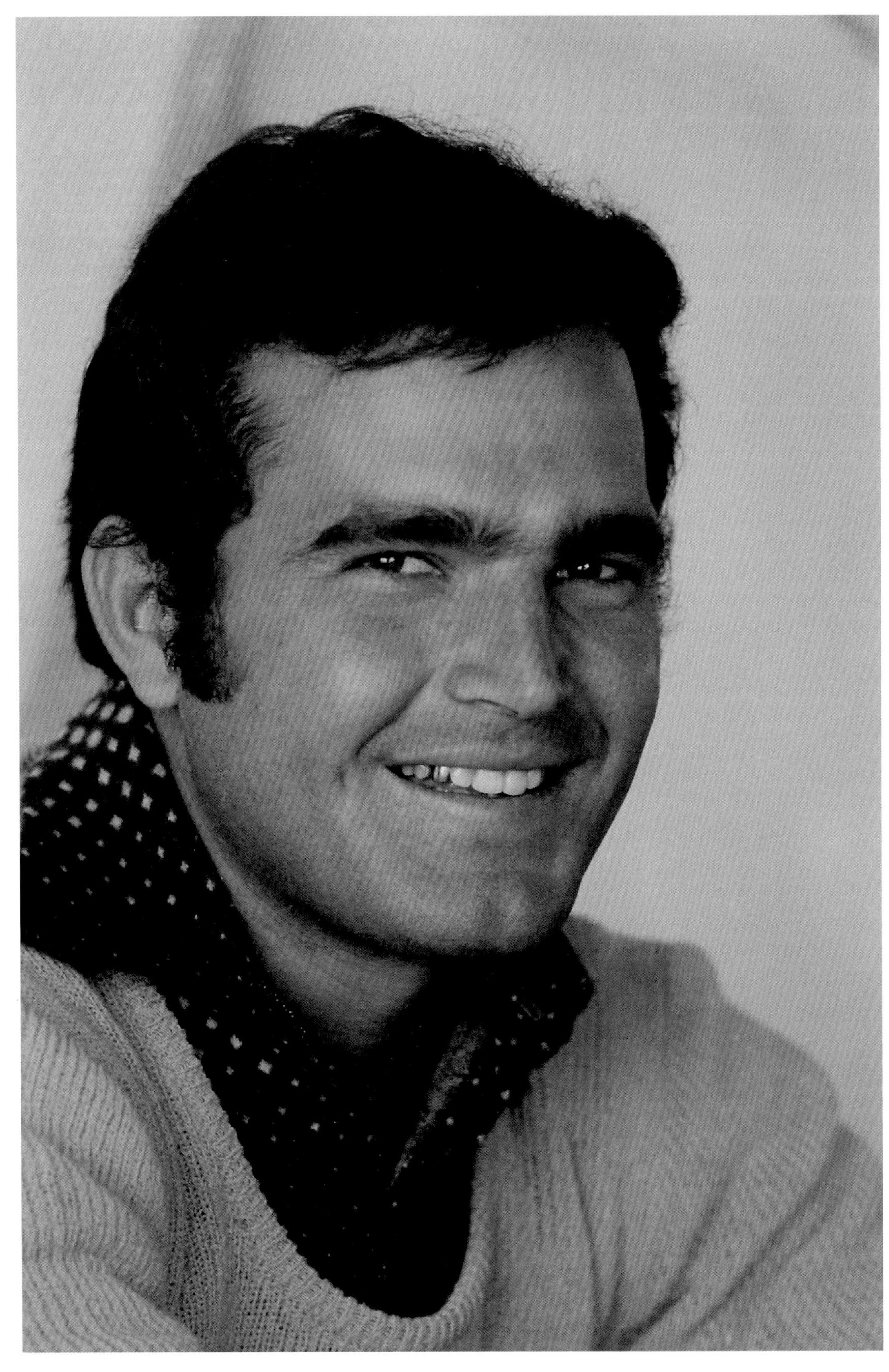

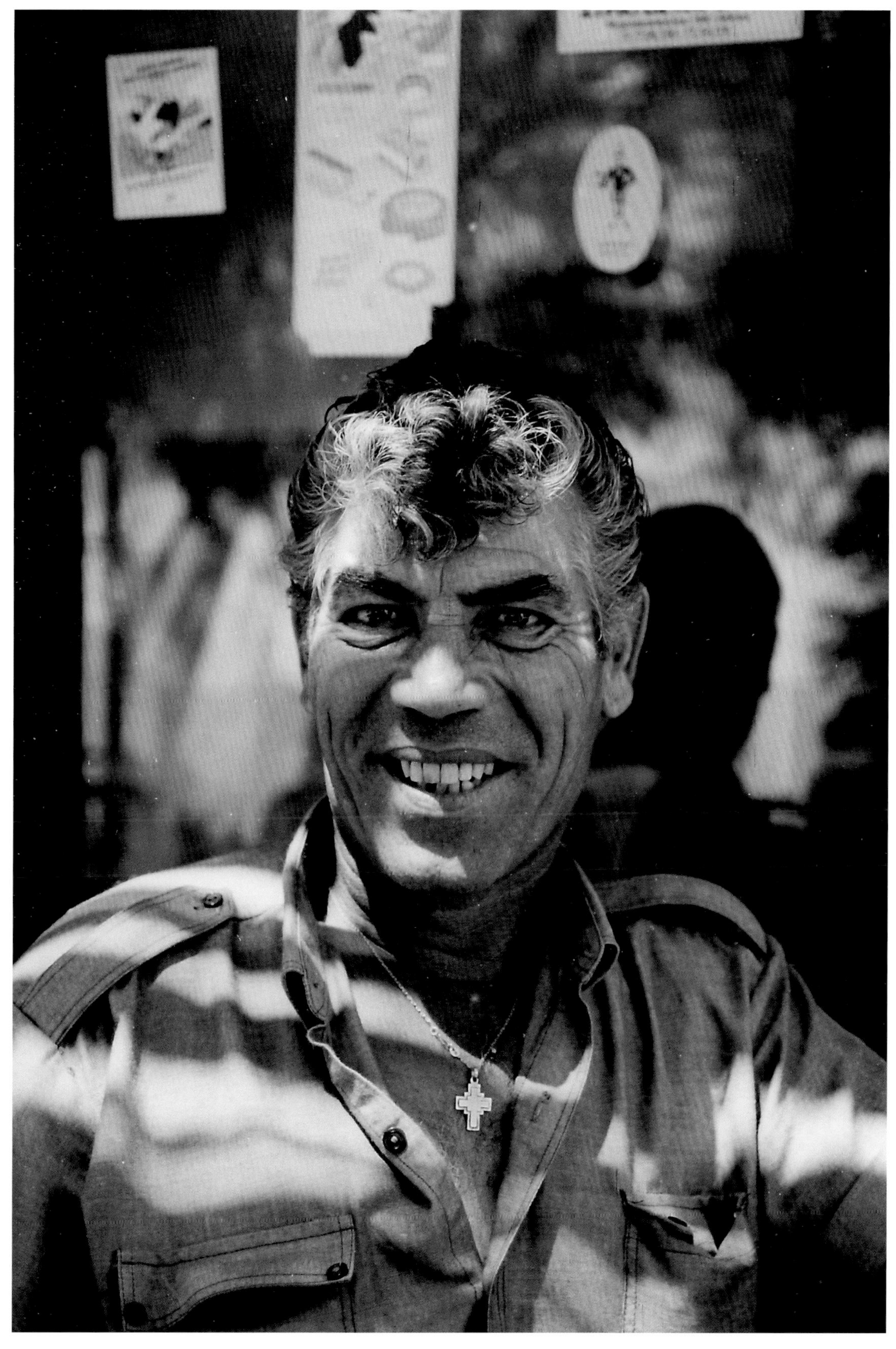

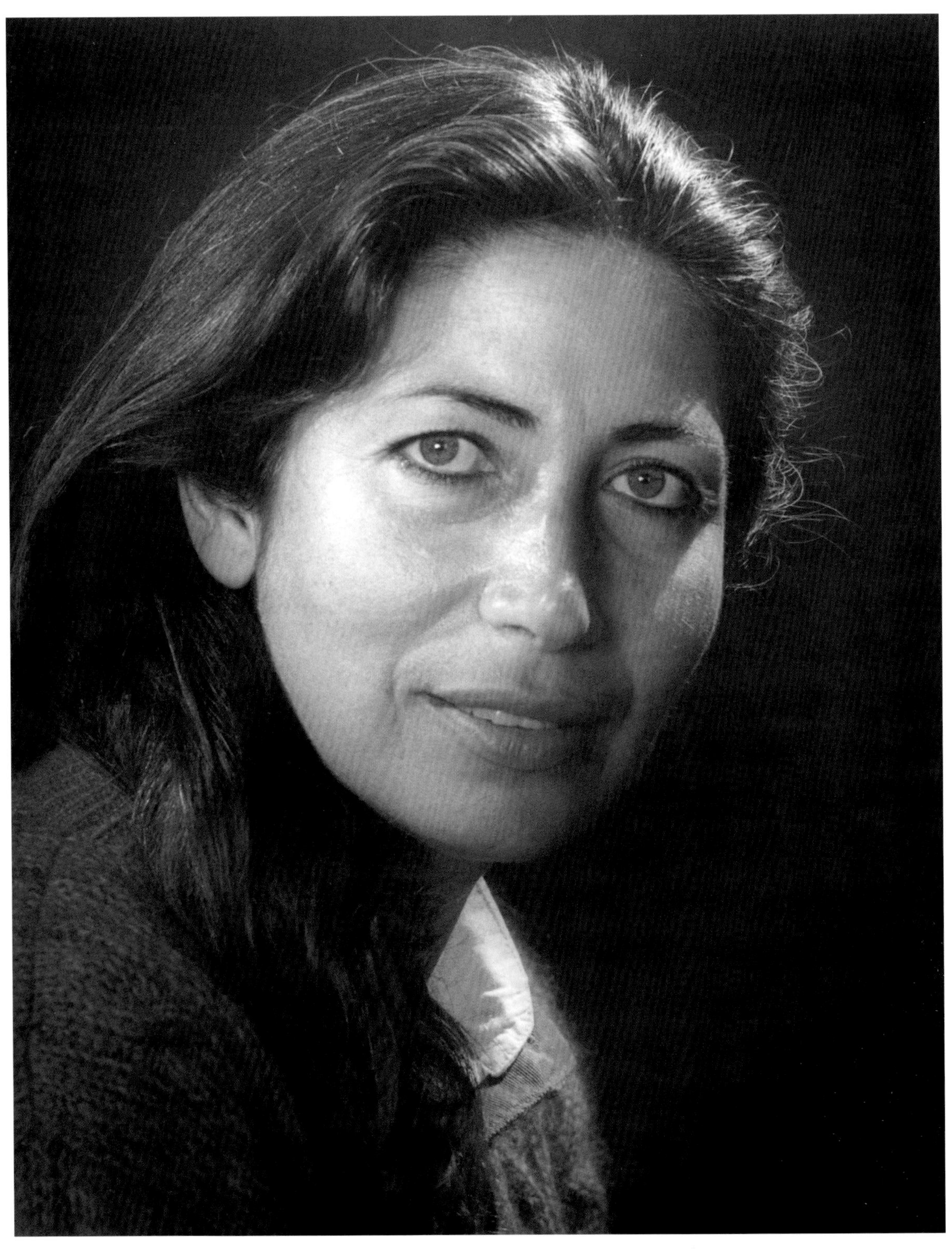

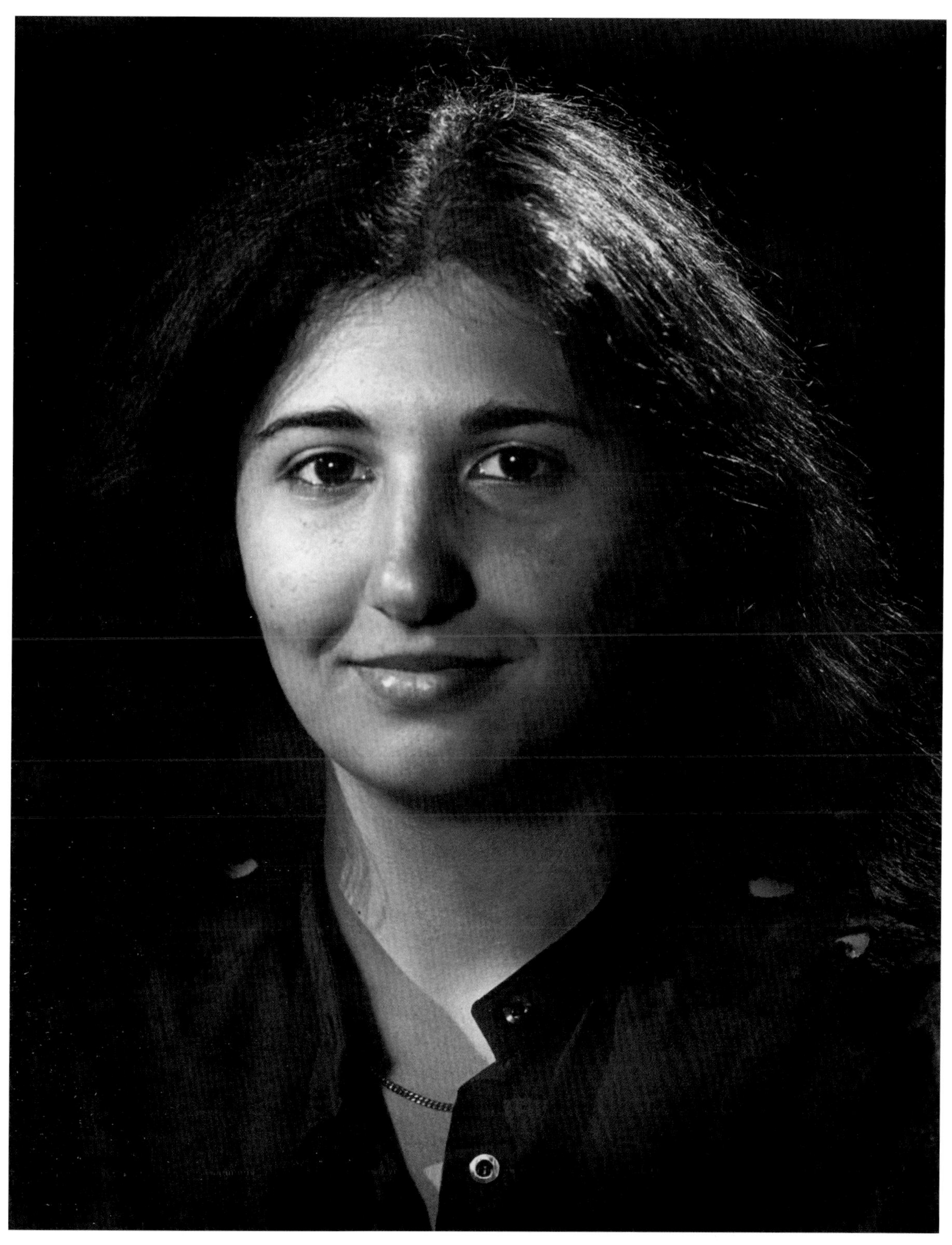

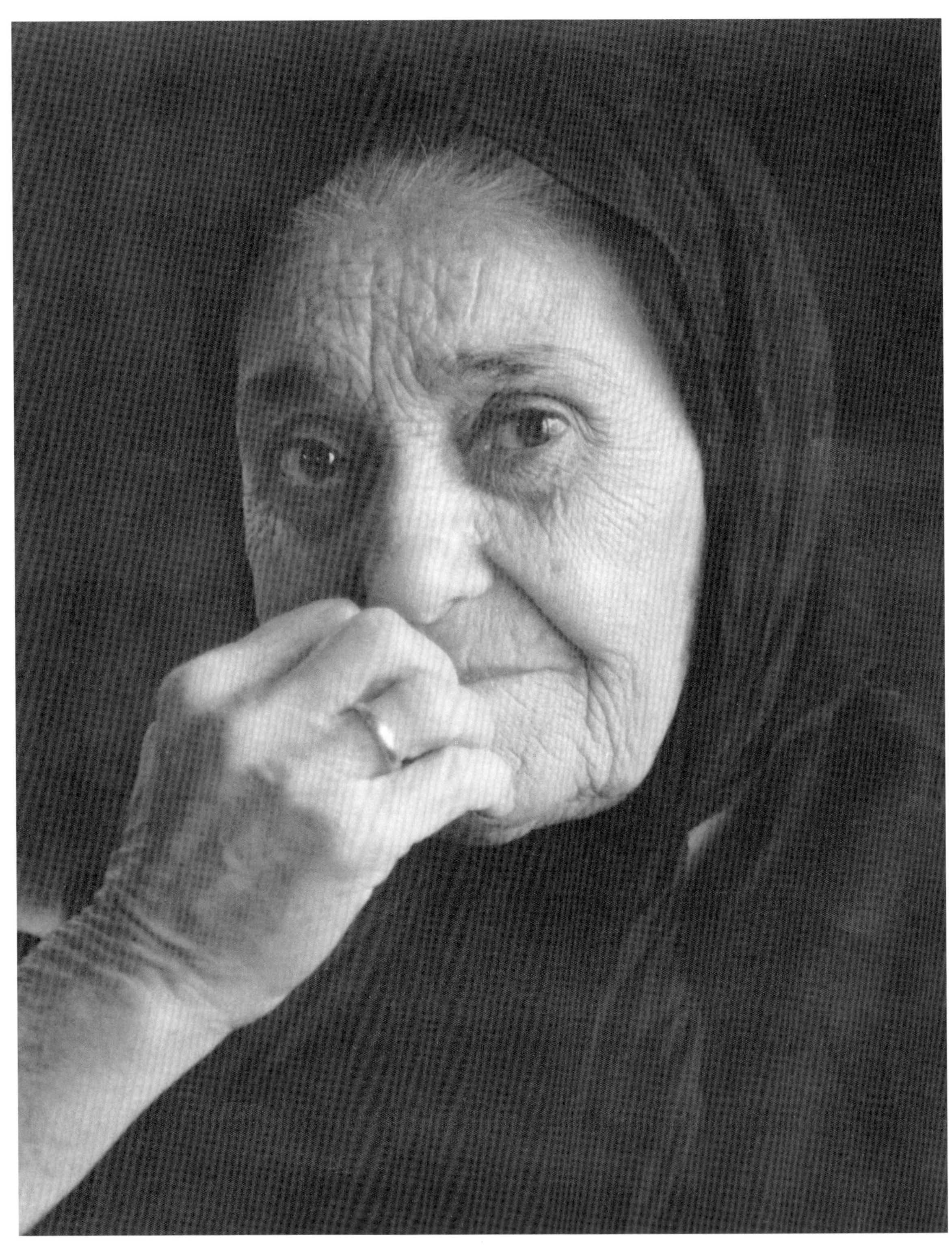

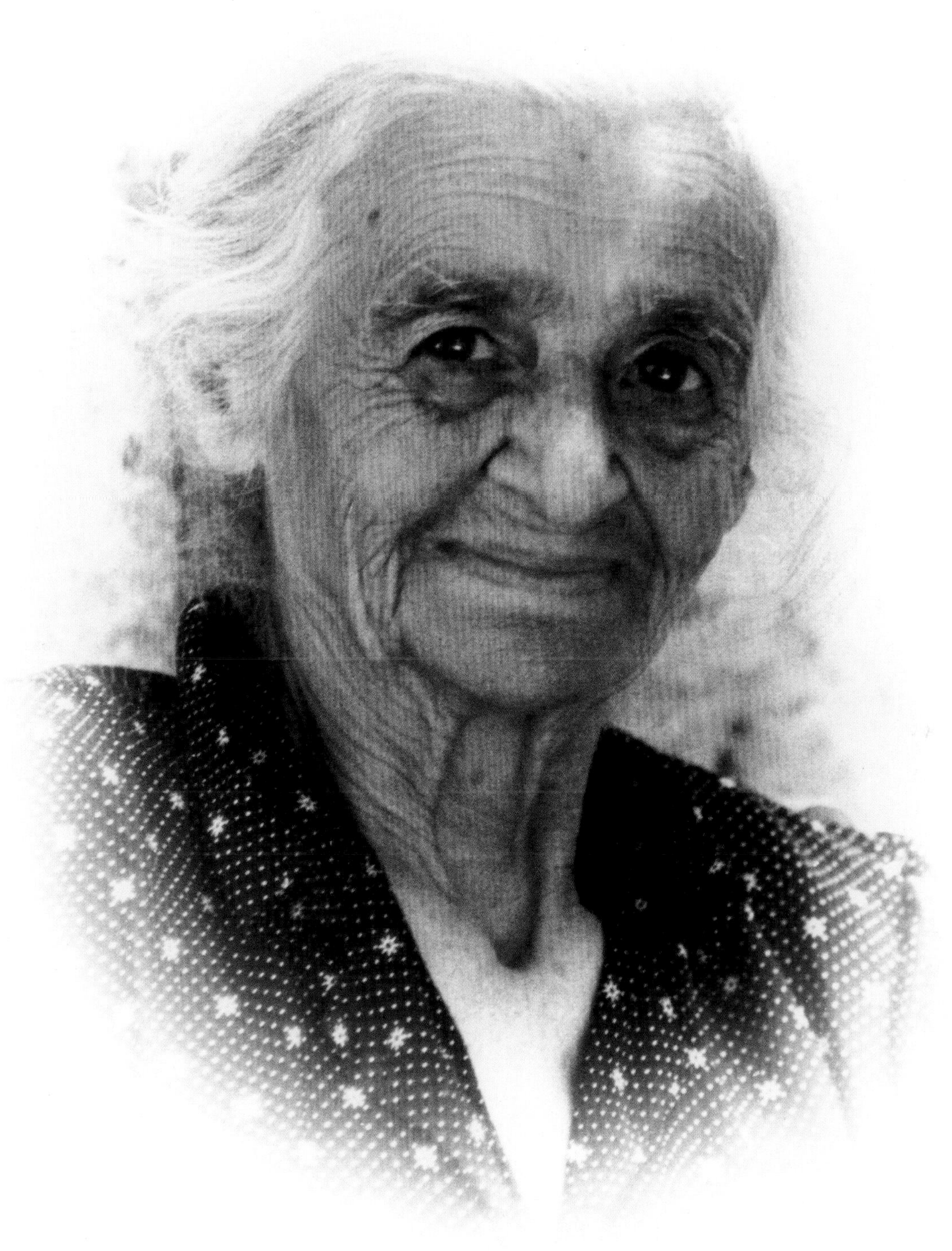

CHAPTER 6 · THE PEOPLE · ΟΙ ΑΝΘΡΩΠΟΙ

Private Lives

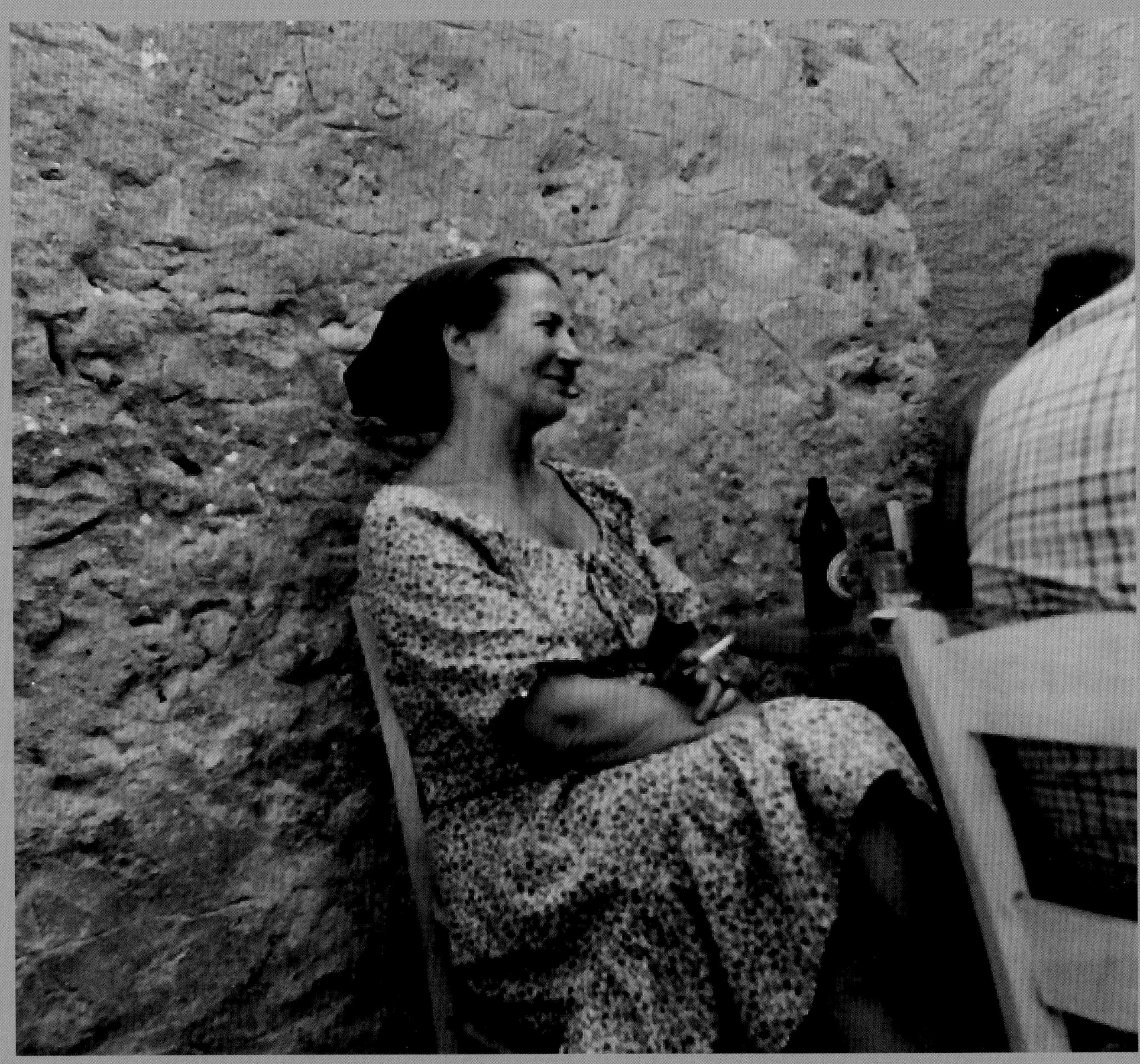

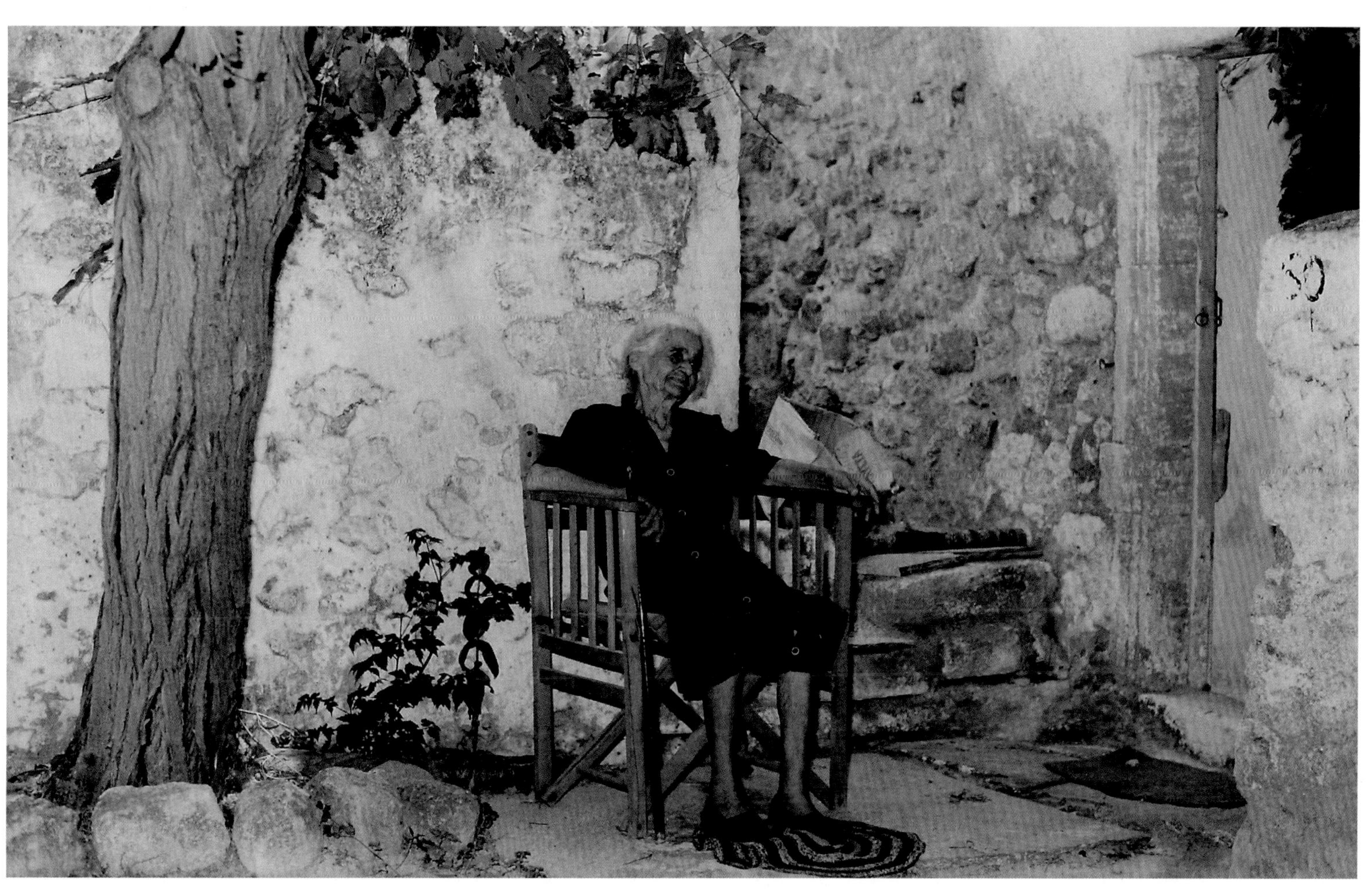

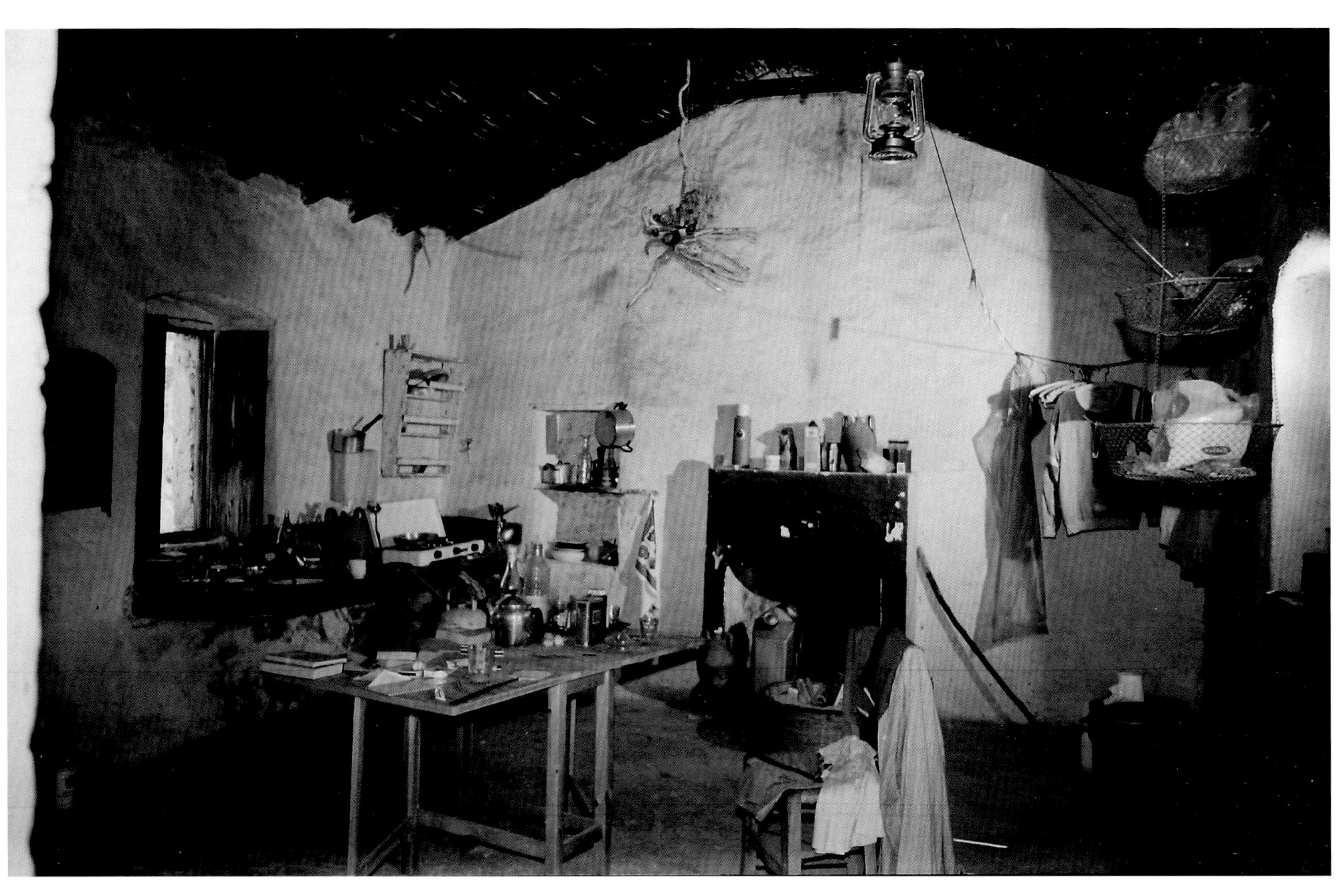

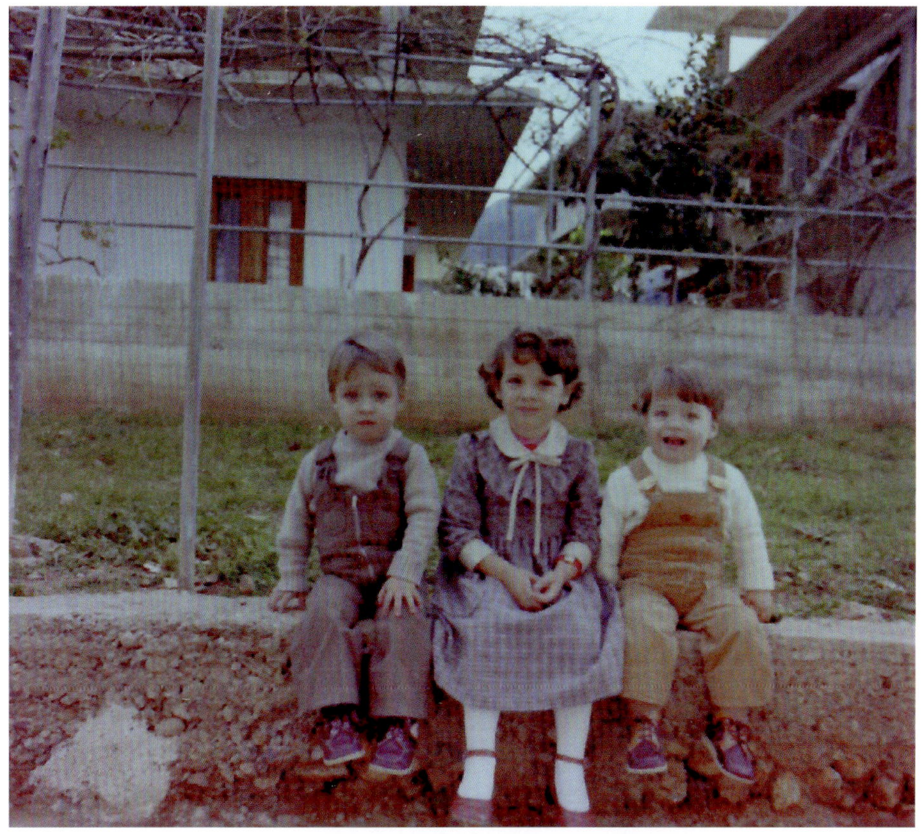

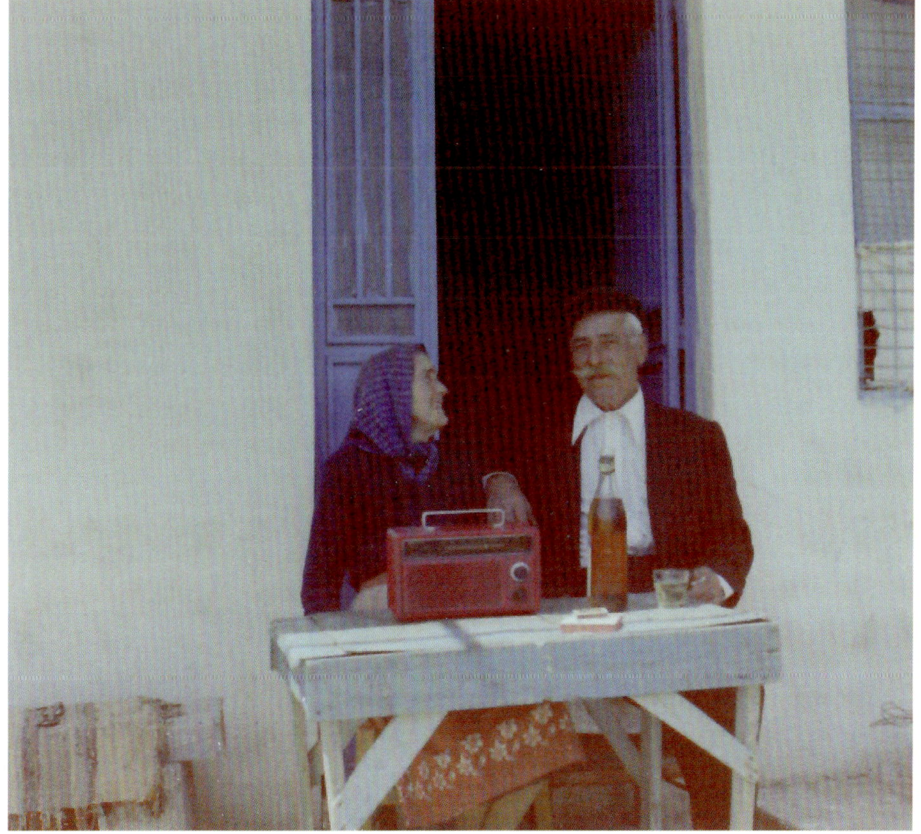

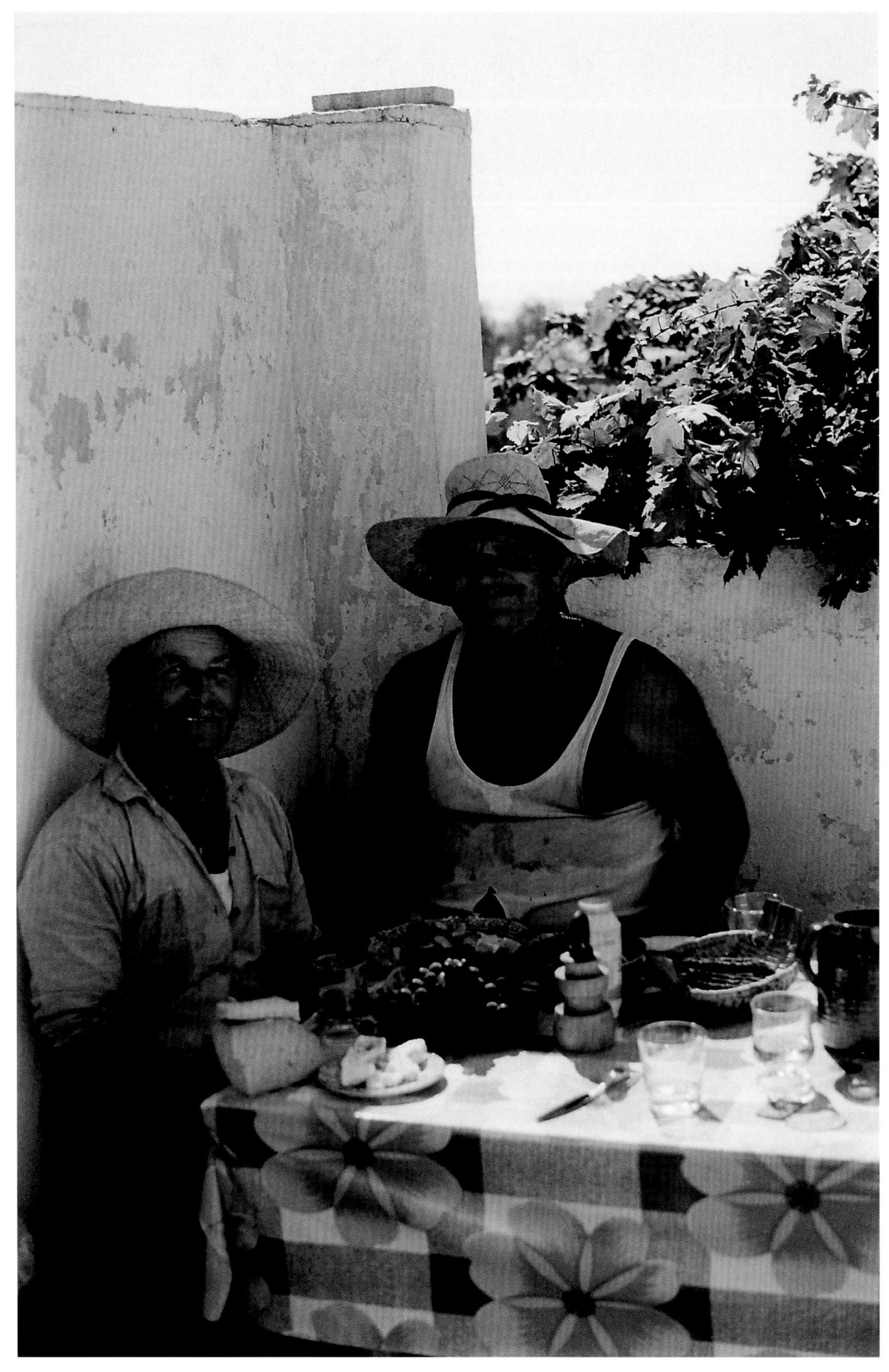

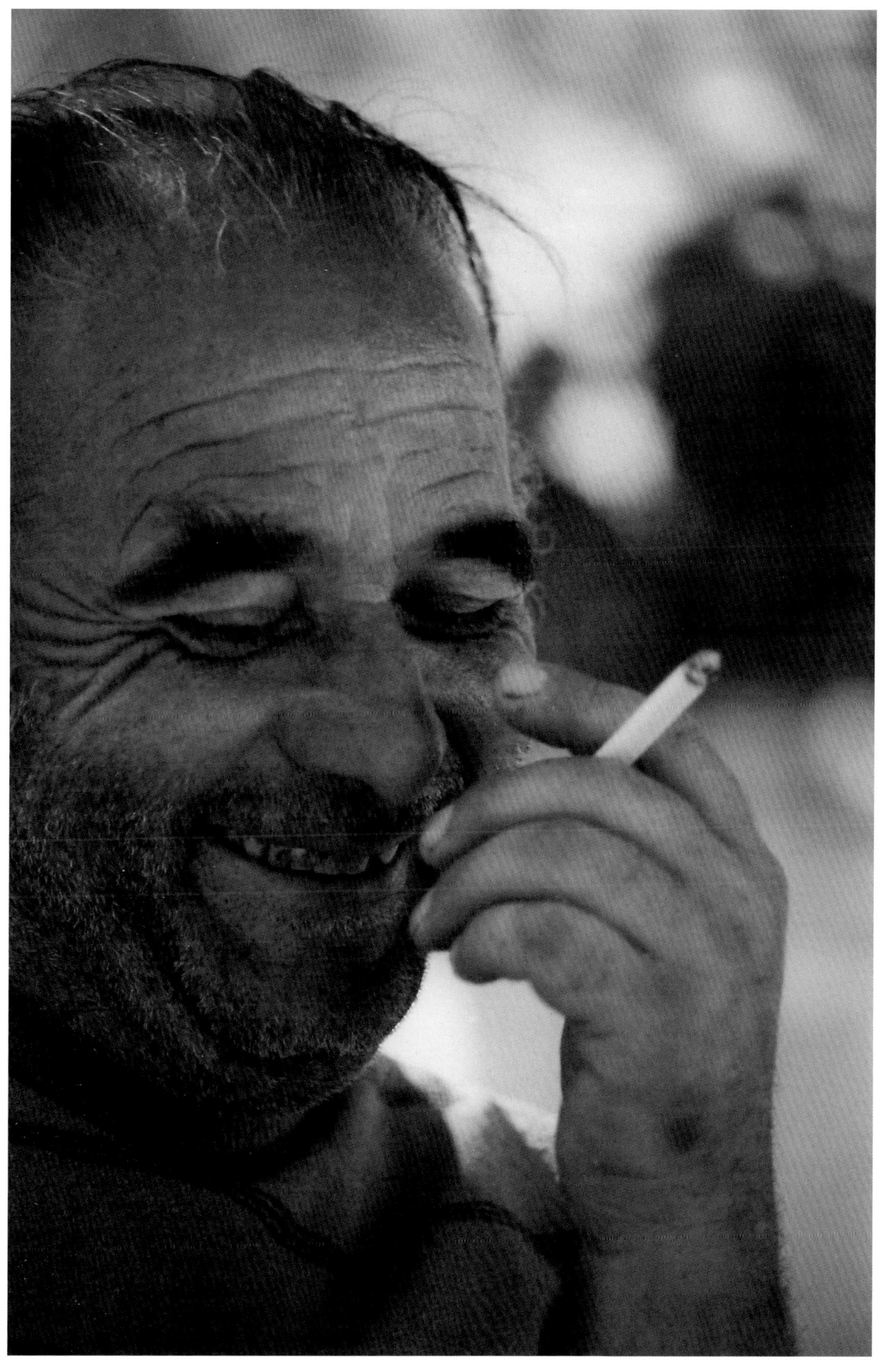

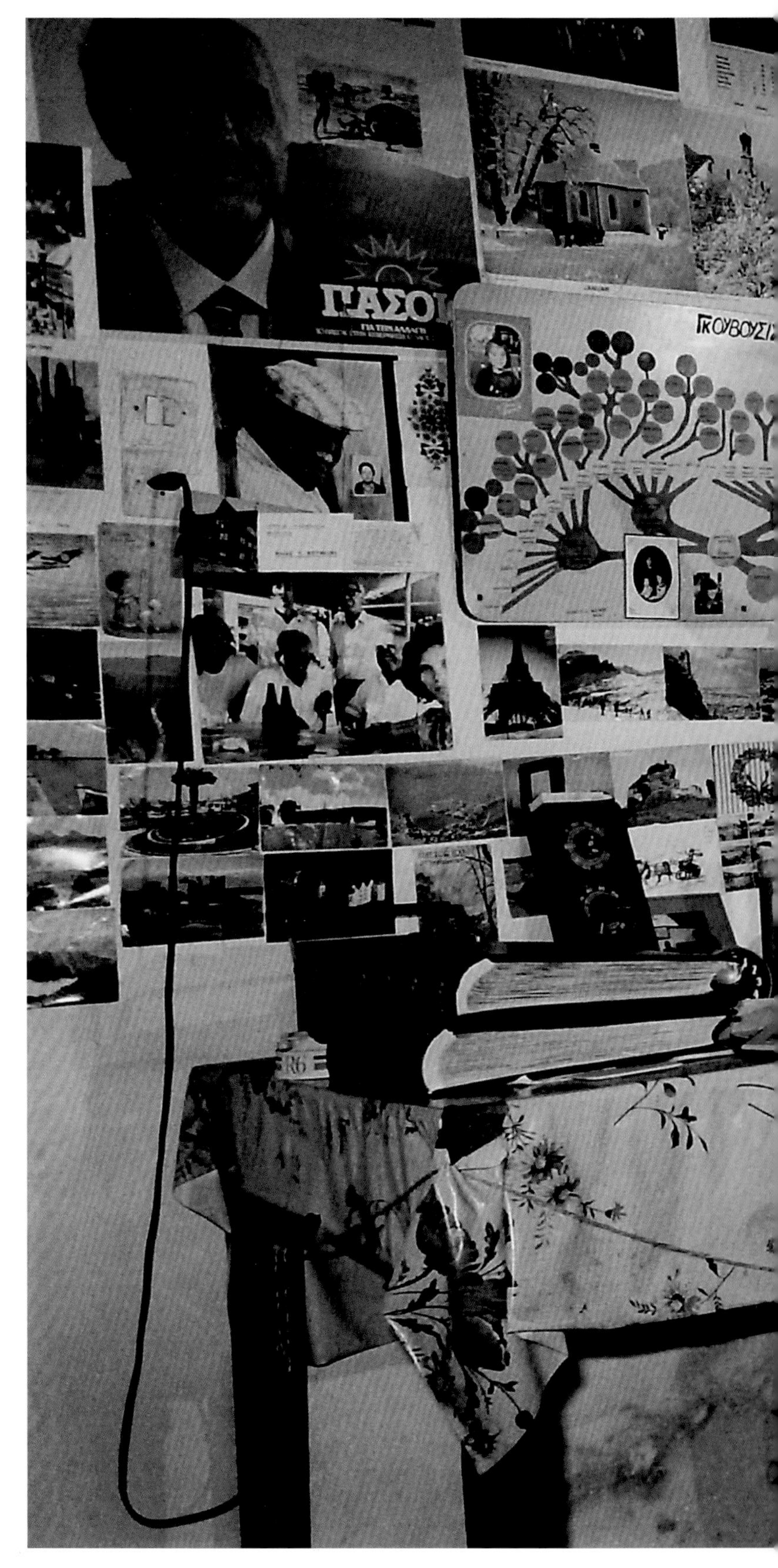

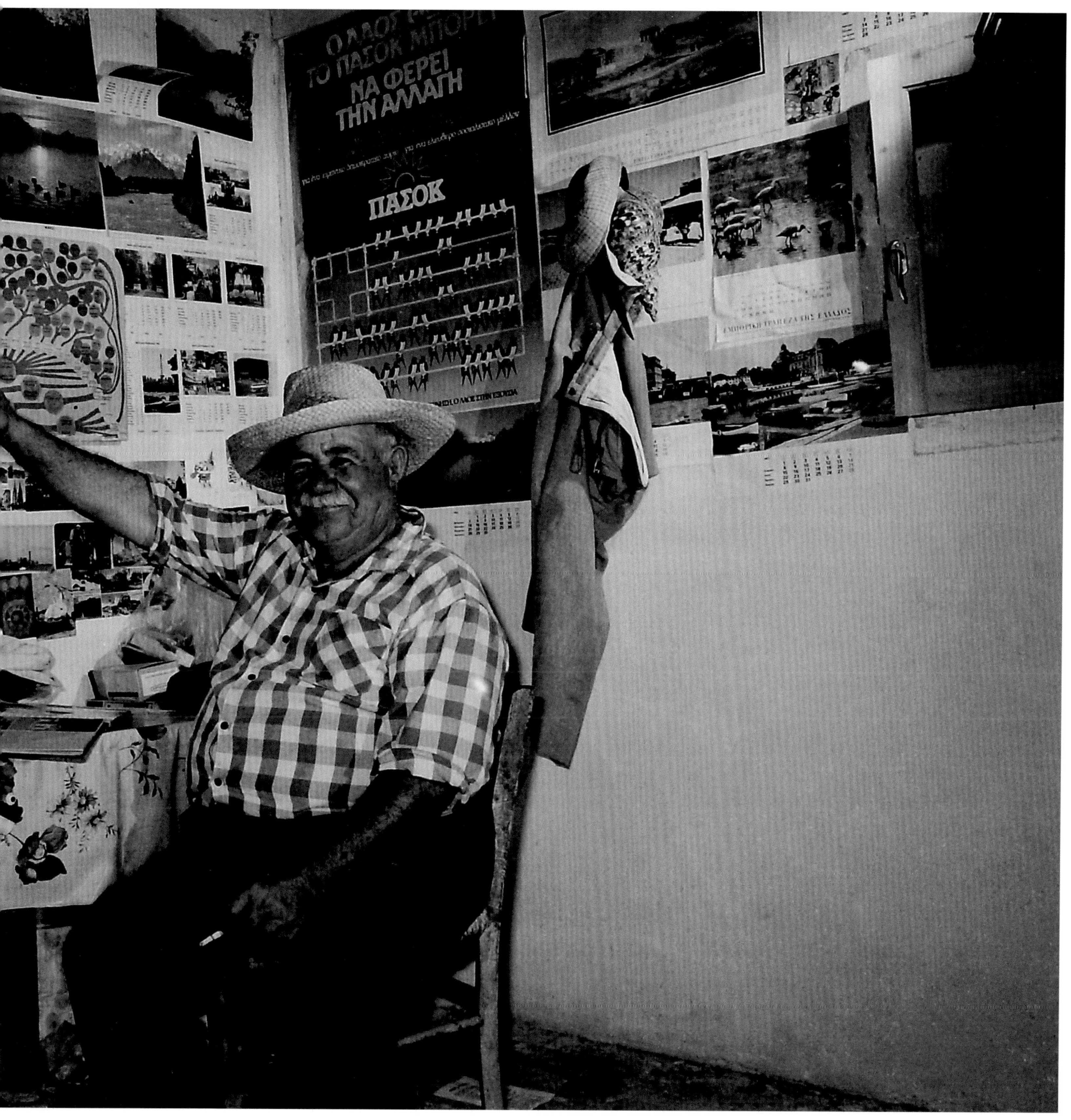
ΤΟ ΠΑΣΟΚ ΜΠΟΡΕΙ
ΝΑ ΦΕΡΕΙ
ΤΗΝ ΑΛΛΑΓΗ
ΠΑΣΟΚ

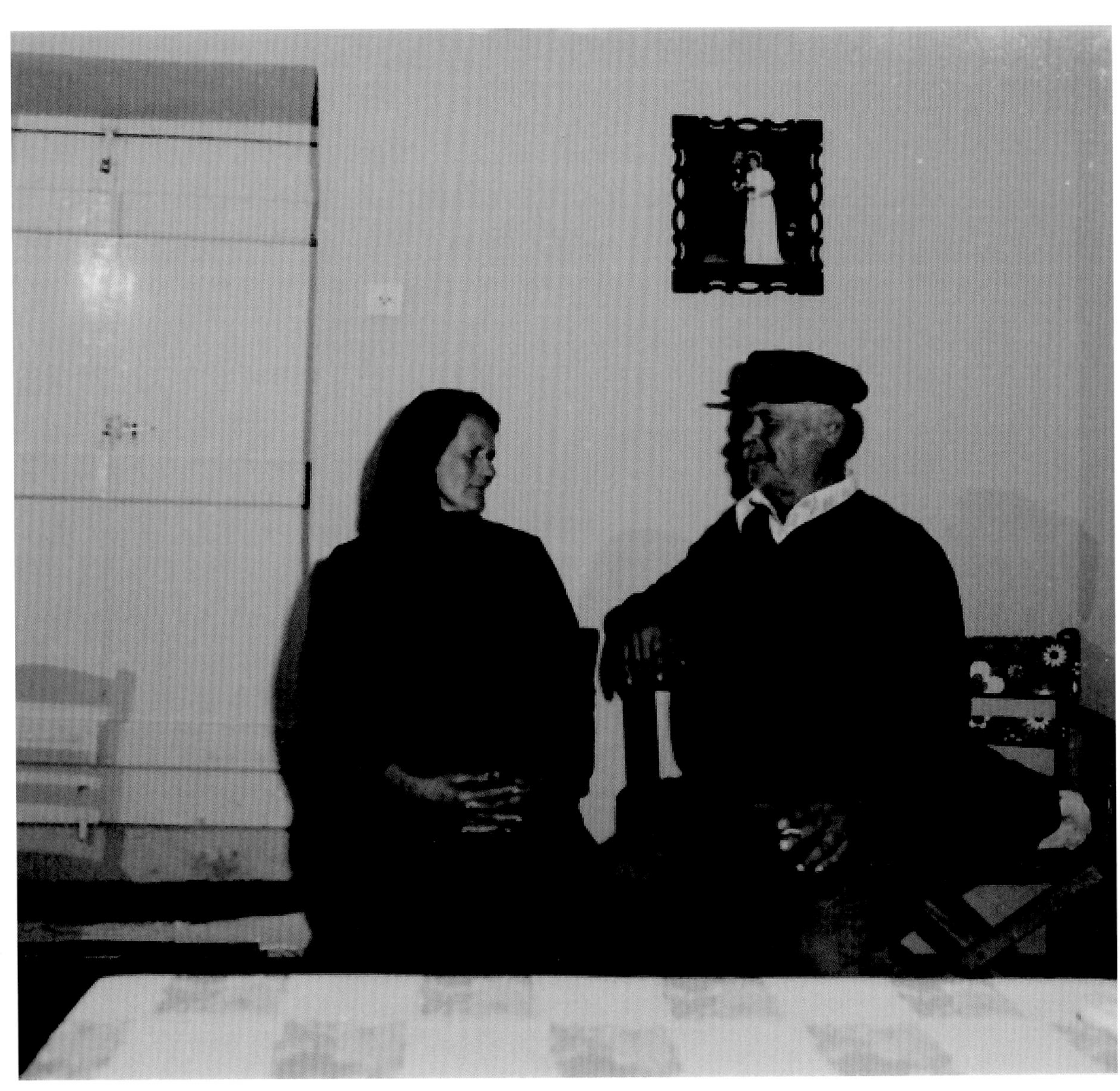

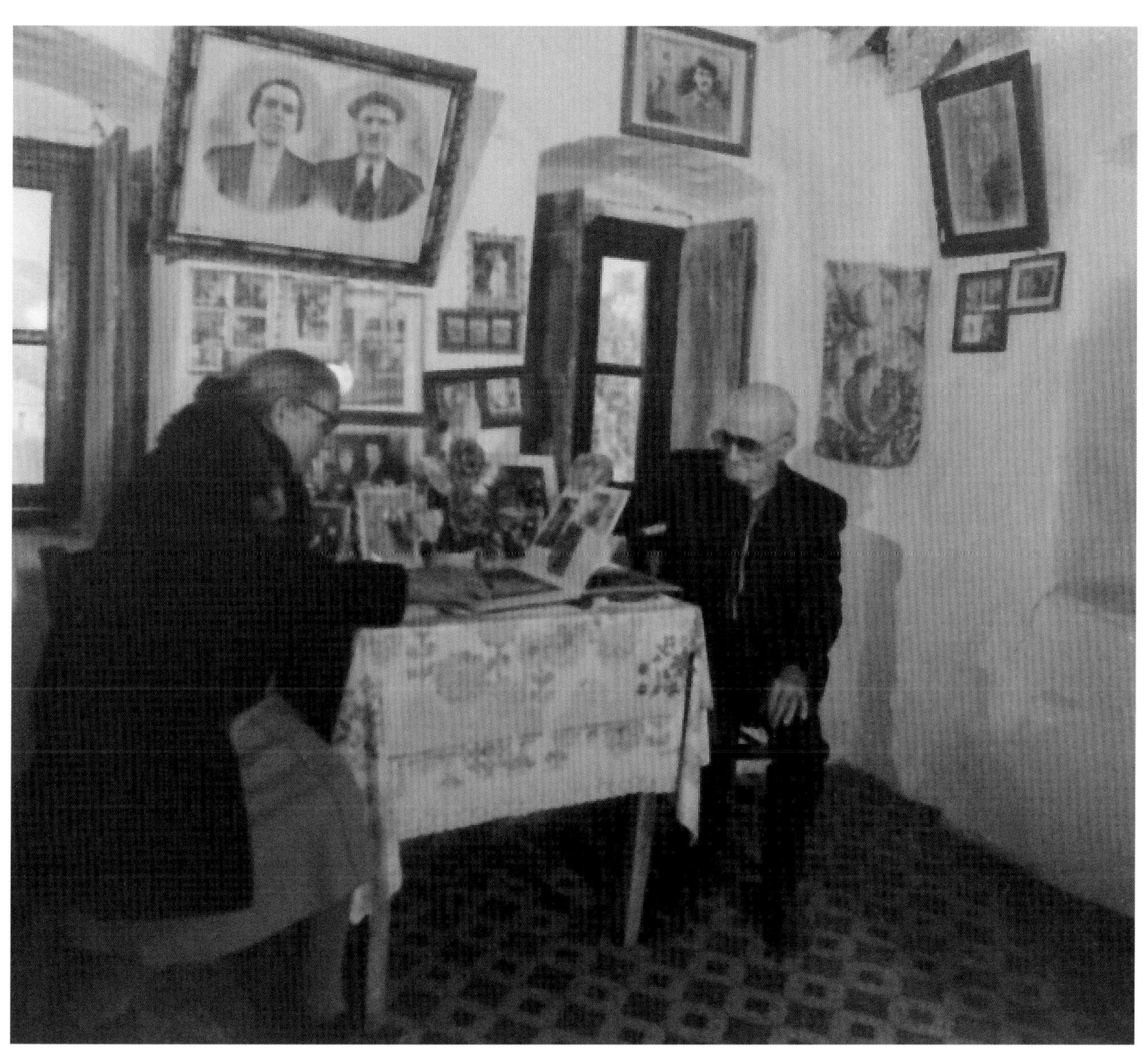

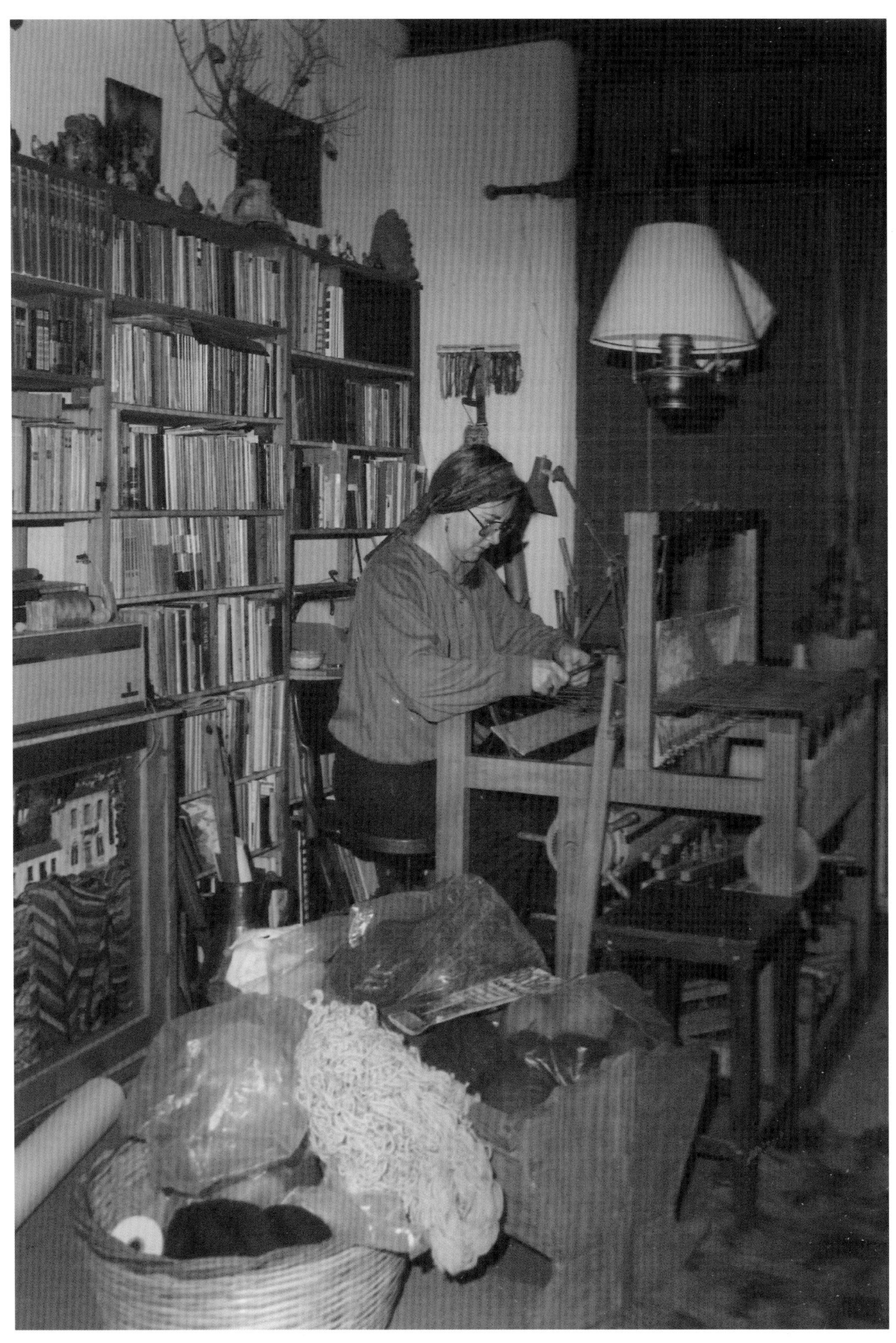

Each living thing is bound to its world by many threads, weaving the intricate design of the fabric of life.

RACHEL CARSON,
THE EDGE OF THE SEA, 1955

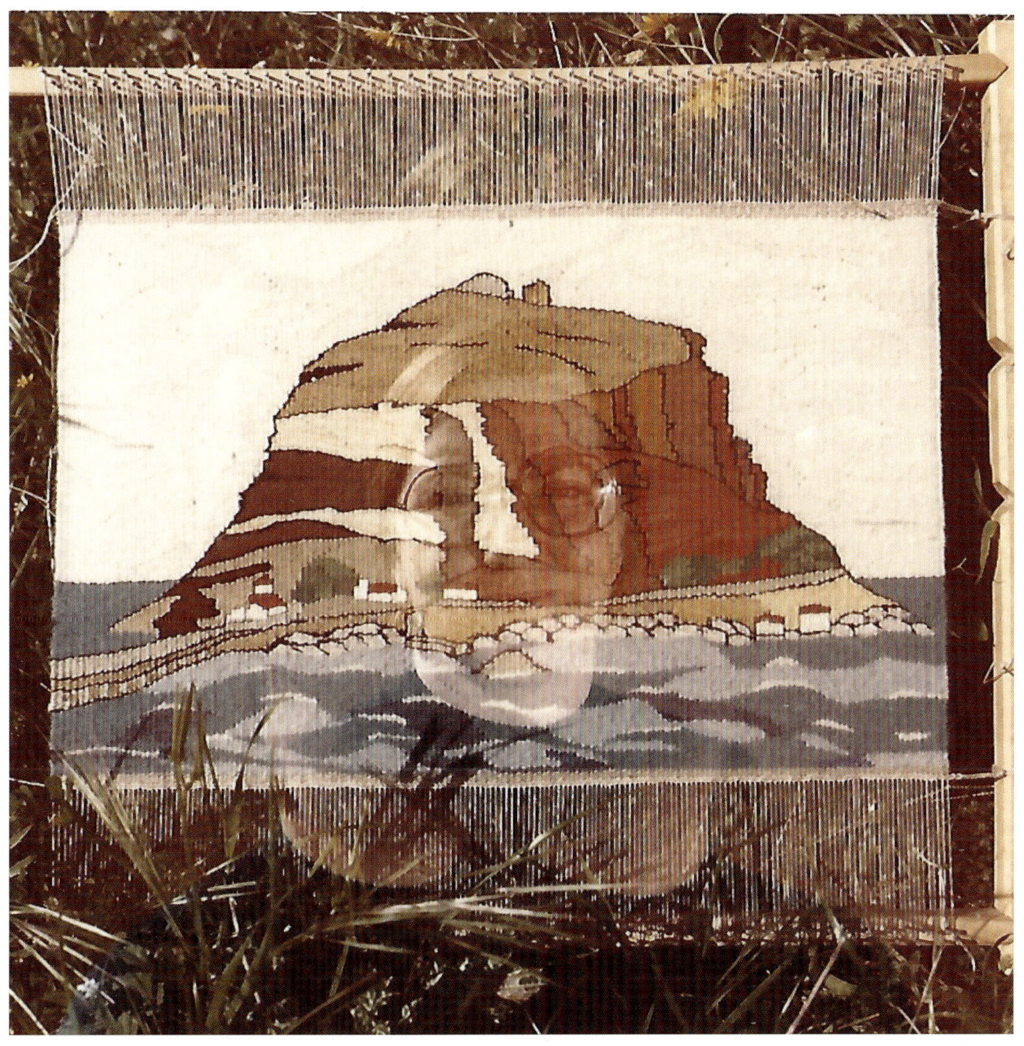

Thump thump goes the shuttle knock – knocking in on golden noons – and how small waves below and the cicadas above replied.

YANNIS RITSOS, 'THE WOMEN OF MONEMVASIA', 1975

List of Photographs

The Monemvasia Society would be delighted if readers were able to provide further information relating to photographs contained in the book. This will contribute to our photographic archive.

p.156-57, Yefira. Navy Week, 01.05.1990.
p.158, Aghia Paraskevi. Football practice. 1984.
p.159, Monemvasia Football Team. Cup winners. 01.07.1987.
p.160, Aghios Stephanos. Maria Patoucha in her shop.
p.161t, Yefira. Women working on the loom.
p.161b, Yefira. Women dying thread.
p.162t, Yefira. Woman with cards. 1990.
p.162b, Yefira. Men playing cards. 1987.
p.163, Yefira. Men playing cards. 1987.
p.164, Man playing flute.
p.165, Yefira. Priest fishing at the jetty.
p.166, Yefira. Tourist Office. 1984.
p.167, Yefira. Flying Dolphin at the jetty. 1984.
p.168t, Castro. Young visitors.
p.168b, Castro.Young woman on terrace. 1990.
p.169, Yefira/Castro. No camping. 1986.
p.170-71, Youli Georgopoulou. Potter and her shop.
p.172l, Local painter. 1985.
p.172r, Castro. Poster for Harald Bohling-Petersen Art Exhibition. Danish resident. 06.07.1979.
p.173, Harald Böhling-Petersen Art Exhibition. 03.07.1982.
p.174, Pori. Filming of *Blood Tide*. 1980.
p.175t, Castro. Filming of *Blood Tide*. 1980.
p.175b, *Blood Tide* film poster. 1982.
p.176, View to Rock from the Discotheque.
p.177t, Postcard of Nomia and Ag. Paraskevi designed by Poul Rasmussen.
p.177b, Postcard envelope designed by Poul Rasmussen.

—

p.178, Portraits. Contact sheet.
p.179, Portrait.
p.180, Monemvasia Infant School. Teacher and class.
p.181, Family portrait, 1983.
p.182l, Portrait.
p.182r, Portrait.
p.183, Kalliopi Sarbani. 1982.
p.184, Magda Alisafou.
p.185, Mitsos Giannoukos. 1981.
p.186l, Kostas Kastanias. 1984–1985.
p.186r, Nektarios Koutsandreas. 1984–1985.
p.187, O Bobos. Georgios Vougiourdis.
p.188, Yannis Traiforos. 1982.
p.189, Portrait.
p.190, Maria Giovannis.
p.191, Tasia Livieratou.
p.192, Vassiliki Chatzioannou. 1982.
p.193, Portrait.
p.194, Fani Antonouli.
p.195, Sitting in the courtyard.
p.196, House interior.
p.197t, Three children. 1982.
p.197b, Vangelis and his wife, Diamanto.
p.198, Portrait of two men. 1984.
p.199, Yorgos Manolakakis.
p.200-201, Family tree. 1982.
p.202, Couple. 1983.
p.203, Couple with photographs. 1983.
p.204, Thea Rasmussen weaving on Poul Rasmussen's handmade loom.
p.205, Thea Rasmussen, woven wall hanging: *The Rock of Monemvasia.*

Quote Sources

p.6, H.A. Kalligas, *Monemvasia: A Byzantine City State,* Routledge, Oxford 2010, p.xii

p.7, R.A. McCabe, *Greece: Images of an Enchanted Land 1954–1965,* Patakis Publishers, 2004. *Moments Gone Never to Return,* Andrew Segedy-Maszak, p.22

p.13, K. McGrath, *On Friendship,* Saint Julian Press Inc, 2024, p.48

p.16, N. Kazantzakis, *Journey to The Morea* trans. by F.A. Read, Simon and Shuster, New York, 1965, p.148

p.18, S. Runciman, *A Traveller's Alphabet, Partial Memoirs,* Thames and Hudson Ltd, London, *1991,* p.92

p.21, W.R. Elliot, *Monemvasia,The Gibraltar of Greece,* Dennis Dobson, London, 1971, p.99

p.22, N. Kazantzakis, *Journey to The Morea* trans. by F.A. Read, Simon and Shuster, New York, 1965, p.154

p.25, Y. Ritsos, *XXI Time, Yiannis Ritsos: Selected Poems 1938–1988,* ed. and trans. by K. Friar and K. Myrsiades, Boa Publications, Rochester, NY, 1989, p.365

p.29, W.R. Elliot, *Monemvasia, The Gibraltar of Greece,* Dennis Dobson, London, 1971, p.18

p.34, K. McGrath, *Consciousness,* Correspondence, 2023

p.43, N. Kazantzakis, *Journey to The Morea,* trans. by F.A.Read, Simon and Shuster, New York, 1965, p.154

p.45, G. Seferis, 'Mythistorima', in *George Seferis: Collected Poems 1924–1955,* ed and trans. by Edmund Keeley and Phillip Sherrard, Jonathan Cape, London, 1969, p.37

p.54, S. Runciman, *A Traveller's Alphabet, Partial Memoirs,* Thames and Hudson Ltd, London, *1991,* p.94

p.57, L. Kain Hart, *Time, Religion and Social Experience In Rural Greece,* 1992, p.4

p.68, Y. Ritsos, 'Peace', in *Yannis Ritsos: Selected Poems 1938–1988,* ed. and trans. by K. Friar and K. Myrsiades, Boa Publications, Rochester, NY, 1989, p.52

p.72, R. Beaton, *Greece: Biography of a Modern Nation,* Allan Lane 2019, Penguin Books, 2020, p.351

p.81, H.A. Kalligas, *Byzantine Monemvasia: The Sources,* Akroneon, Monemvasia, 1990, p.109, refering to S. Binon, *Echos d'Orient,* vol. 37, 1938, p.306

p.83, K. McGrath, *Hellas,* Saint Julian Press Inc, 2023, p.1

p.85, H. Miller, *The Colossus of Maroussi,* Colt Press 1941, Penguin Classics p.76

p.89, Hesiod, *Theogony and Works and Days,* trans. M.L. West, Oxford University Press World Classics paperback 1988, line 303ff, p.46

p.95, *Greece Is* magazine*: Monemvasia A Greek Castle Town for Lovebirds,* 20 November 2016

p.99, Y. Ritsos, 'Peace', in *Yannis Ritsos: Selected Poems 1938–1988,* ed. and trans. by K. Friar and K. Myrsiades, Boa Publications, Rochester, NY, 1989, p.52

p.103, J.S. Koliopoulos and T. Veremis, *Greece: The Modern Sequel: from 1821 to the Present,* C. Hurst & Co Publishers Ltd, 2007, p.272

p.115, Y. Ritsos, 'The Women of Monemvasia', in *Monovasia and the Women of Monemvasia,* Nostos Publications, Minneapolos, MN, 1987, p.52

p.119, R. Beaton, *Greece: Biography of a Modern Nation,* Allan Lane 2019, Penguin Books, 2020, p.xx

p.123, B. Clark, *Athens. City Of Wisdom,* Head of Zeus Ltd, 2021, p.462ff

p.125, G. Adrian, film director and author, *Rock of Monemvasia,* German documentary film, 1964

p.129, J. Kakissis, *New York Times,* 3 September 2006

p.130, J.L. Tomkinson, *Festive Greece: A Calendar of Tradition,* Anagnonis Publications, 2003 p.27

p.134–5, C. Norberg-Schulz, *Existence, Space & Architecture,* Studio Vista Ltd, 1971, p.35 quoting M.M. Webber, *Explorations into Urban Structure,* University of Pennsylvania 1964

p.144, R. Beaton, *Greece: Biography of a Modern Nation,* Allan Lane 2019, Penguin Books, 2020, p350

p.150, N. Gage, *Hellas. A Portrait of Greece,* Efstathiadis Group S.A., 1993, p.115

p.161, M. von Trapp, *Maria My Own Story,* Creation House, 1972

p.167, N. Bawden, *Rebel on a Rock,* Heinemann Educational Books Ltd, 1978, p.61

p.168, K. McGrath, *On Friendship,* Saint Julian Press Inc, 2024, p.47

p.175, Sol-Kay, IMDB Film Review, 2005

p.204, R. Carson, *The Edge of the Sea,* Library of America, 1955, republished Unicorn Press, 2015, p.19

p.206, Y. Ritsos, 'The Women of Monemvasia', in *Monovasia and the Women of Monemvasia,* Nostos Publications, Minneapolos, MN, 1987, p.42

Published in 2024
by Unicorn, an imprint of Unicorn Publishing Group
Charleston Studio, Meadow Business Centre
Lewes BN8 5RW
www.unicornpublishing.org

ISBN 978-1-916846-17-3
10 9 8 7 6 5 4 3 2 1

Designed by Felicity Price-Smith
Printed by Fine Tone Ltd